D0759966

Army of Amateurs

ARMY OF AMATEURS

General Benjamin F. Butler and
the Army of the James, 1863–1865

Edward G. Longacre

STACKPOLE
BOOKS

Published by
STACKPOLE BOOKS
5067 Ritter Road
Mechanicsburg, PA 17055

Printed in the United States of America

10 9 8 7 6 5 4 3 2 1

FIRST EDITION

Library of Congress Cataloging-in-Publication Data

Longacre, Edward G., 1946–
    Army of amateurs : General Benjamin F. Butler and the Army of the James, 1863–1865 / Edward G. Longacre.
        p.   cm.
    Includes bibliographical references and index.
    ISBN 0-8117-0135-2
        1. United States. Army of the James.   2. Butler, Benjamin F. (Benjamin Franklin), 1818–1893.   3. Virginia—History—Civil War 1861–1865.   4. North Carolina—History—Civil War, 1861–1865—Campaigns.   I. Title.
E467.1.B87L66   1997
973.7'092—dc21
    [B]   97-20605
                                                                                CIP

In memory of my great-grandfather,
Sergeant Henry M. Flanagin,
5th Pennsylvania Cavalry,
Army of the James

The movement of the forces under Butler was close to the boundary line between the true art of war and the game of bumblepuppy.

—*General William Farrar Smith*

The ignorant officer is a murderer.

—*Anonymous*

CONTENTS

ACKNOWLEDGMENTS

SINCE BEGINNING RESEARCH ON THE ARMY OF THE JAMES MORE THAN twenty years ago, I have been aided by scores of librarians, archivists, and curators who provided source material critical to the success of my undertaking. The following individuals rendered the greatest assistance:

Laura P. Abbott, librarian, Vermont Historical Society; Gary J. Arnold, manuscripts cataloger, Archives-Manuscripts Division, Ohio Historical Society; John C. Broderick, chief of the Manuscript Division, Library of Congress; Marie Byrne, assistant head, Manuscripts Division, Bancroft Library, University of California at Berkeley; David G. Carroll, historic site assistant, Washington's Headquarters and Museum; Phyllis Cassler, interlibrary loan director, U.S. Army Military History Institute; Roseanne Ewing, Bellevue, Nebraska; Dale E. Floyd, historian, U.S. Park Service; Thompson Horlow, director, Connecticut Historical Society Library; Clifton H. Johnson, executive director, Amistad Research Center, Dillard University; William L. Joyce, curator of manuscripts, American Antiquarian Society; Michele Leiser, manuscripts specialist, Stanford University Libraries; Paul Loane, Merchantville, New Jersey; Linda M. Matthews, reference archivist, Special Collections, Robert W. Woodruff Library, Emory University; Wayne Maxson, interlibrary loan director, Samuel W. Paley Library, Temple University; Will Molineux, Williamsburg, Virginia; Mary-Elizabeth Murdock, director, Sophia Smith Collection, Smith College; Russ Pritchard, curator, War Library, National Commandery, Military Order of the Loyal Legion of the United States; Mary Jo Pugh, reference archivist, Michigan Historical Collections, Bentley Historical

Library, University of Michigan; Judith A. Schiff, chief research archivist, Manuscripts and Archives, Sterling Memorial Library, Yale University; Richard J. Sommers, archivist-historian, U.S. Army Military History Institute; Julia Ward Howe Stickley, Washington, D.C.; Bryce Suderow, Washington, D.C.; Lillian Tonkin, reference librarian, Library Company of Philadelphia; and Ellen Wall, reference librarian, David Leo Lawrence Memorial Library, La Salle University.

I also wish to thank Dr. James I. Robertson, Jr., who directed my manuscript to the attention of Stackpole Books. At Stackpole, Jack Davis, Sylvia Frank, and Michelle Myers were instrumental in bringing the book to fruition. Thanks also to Barry Lauer, who provided pictorial support, and Paul Dangel, who designed the detailed yet uncluttered maps. My heartfelt appreciation goes to Dr. Russell F. Weigley of Temple University, who patiently and caringly guided me through my doctoral career, and to my wife, Ann, without whose love and support I never would have completed this project.

PREFACE

THE ARMY OF THE JAMES HAS BEEN RELEGATED TO A FOOTNOTE IN THE history of our most important war. On the surface, at least, it is not difficult to understand why. It was in existence for less than a year and a half. Its relatively small size (no more than 36,000 officers and men at the height of its strength) and the backwater status of its original base of operations (southeastern Virginia below the line of the James River) resulted in its being overshadowed, in its own time and afterward, by the larger and more highly publicized Army of the Potomac, with which it shared the Virginia theater. Perhaps the easiest explanation for the dearth of historical attention accorded the Army of the James is its combat record: it lost virtually every campaign, battle, and engagement it fought, earning a reputation for futility matched by no other Civil War command and perhaps by no other fighting force in American history.

The Army of the James was, to a large extent, an army of amateurs, especially at the highest level. Only 30 percent of the generals who served, at one time or another, in its ranks had a West Point education or prewar military experience. By comparison, during the 1864 campaign, almost 80 percent of the generals in the Army of the Potomac and more than half the generals in William T. Sherman's Military Division of the Mississippi had a West Point or Old Army background. In many respects, the Army of the James was the preeminent civilian army of its day, with all the good and bad influences that distinction carries.

In place of trained commanders the army had a gaggle of political generals, more than any other command, Union or Confederate. For all but the last three months of the war, it was led by Major General Benjamin Franklin Butler, the only politician in uniform—an active if unannounced presidential aspirant, no less—to lead more than a single army corps. Some of the army's politicians appear to have spent as much time jockeying for influence as they did battling the Confederacy. Politics being the lifeblood of every Civil War army, especially in an election year such as 1864, most of the powerful but untutored men who ran the army remained in place throughout the last, critical year of the war in the eastern theater.

The army's nonprofessional military orientation (and, to a lesser extent, the internal friction generated by the egotism and ambition of those who led it) doubtless contributed to its tactical failures. Largely because of those failures—especially its inability to capture the enemy capital at Richmond despite several promising opportunities—the Army of the James has come down to us as a stigmatized command, something of an embarrassment to the Union War effort, and a subject to be overlooked by the serious historian.

The army does not deserve such neglect. The importance of its primary objective—by 1864, Richmond's seizure might have dealt a blow serious enough to cripple the Confederacy—by itself should justify an inquiry into the army's woes. Even given its apparent ineffectiveness as a fighting force, several characteristics make the army a worthy subject. Its identity as the most highly politicized army in American history raises issues critical to an understanding of mid-nineteenth-century civil-military relations. The army is also noteworthy for its forward-looking approach to warfare. Its innovations ranged from testing machine guns and flame-throwers to deploying mobile surgical hospitals, forerunners of the M*A*S*H units of twentieth-century warfare. Finally, the Army of the James boasted the largest contingent of African-American troops among the Union armies. It was the only fighting force in our history to boast an army corps composed exclusively of black units. Their story on and off the battlefield is certainly worth telling.

CHAPTER ONE

Ben Butler Takes Command

MAJOR GENERAL BENJAMIN FRANKLIN BUTLER CONSIDERED HIMSELF A reasonable man; he also understood power and when to use it. In the first week of May 1862, when the 12,500 Federal troops under his command occupied New Orleans, the Confederacy's largest city, Butler could test the two basic approaches to problem solving, persuasion and coercion.

On the evening of May 1, although only a portion of his expeditionary force had disembarked, the general moved to take formal possession of the Crescent City. Escorted by several hundred infantrymen, he marched unopposed through the streets to the U.S. Customs House and dispatched regiments to quarters he considered in need of conspicuous security. Then, escorted by a single company of infantry raised in his home state of Massachusetts, the balding, portly commander made his way to the St. Charles Hotel, a first-class hostelry where he established his headquarters as military governor of the city.

The following morning, Butler summoned the mayor and several members of the city council. He received them respectfully, even cordially, in a commodious room adjoining a balcony that overlooked the intersection of St. Charles and Common Streets. To his mild surprise, Butler found his visitors in a truculent mood, which he determined to moderate one way or another.

Initially resistant to Butler's intent to impose martial law, the visitors were cordially told the penalties such opposition would merit. Butler stressed his desire to interfere as little as possible with municipal affairs consistent with his duty to secure the city for the Union, protect U.S. prop-

1

erty, and ensure the safety of loyalists. That said, he would not tolerate opposition to his regime from elected officials or the public.

Butler's visitors appeared dubious that he could overawe nearly 170,000 diehard secessionists with fewer than one-tenth as many soldiers. He was endeavoring to persuade them otherwise when—as if to dramatize the point in dispute—"a very clamorous and obstreperous mob" gathered outside the hotel and, as Butler complained, "interrupted our consultation by their noise very considerably."

The initial object of the crowd's displeasure was a prominent local unionist being escorted to safety by a troop of soldiers. Soon, however, the mob, which had swelled to alarming proportions, discerned a new outlet for its ire. Directing its attention to the balcony of Butler's hotel, the throng began to jeer and curse the most notorious representative of Yankee occupation: "Where's old Butler? Let him show himself; let him come out here if he dare!" To demonstrate their defiance of Butler's rule, some in the street set upon members of his staff, jostling and bruising several, and nearing tearing the uniform from Captain Drake De Kay as he entered the hotel. Fearful of being overwhelmed, the few troops on the scene retreated to the entrance of the St. Charles, nervously fingering the triggers of their rifles.

With an air of "I told you so," the mayor and several of the councilmen went out on the balcony to calm the crowd. Instead, their words increased the clamor. At last Butler declared that he had "borne this noise and confusion as long as I choose to." He barked an order to Captain De Kay, whom he sent out of the hotel by a side door. A few minutes later, Butler replaced the city fathers on the balcony. Striding to the railing, he peered down at the mob, summoned up his deepest voice, and cried: "Who calls me?"

Upon his appearance, the crowd was hushed. Before it could regain its voice, what the general called "a wonderful noise" directed everyone's attention to St. Charles Street. Pounding up were seven teams of horses, each hauling a light artillery piece, "every horse driven at the fullest speed and the bugles sounding the charge."

The sight stunned the crowd and thrilled Butler's heart: "No one who has not seen such a charge can imagine the terrible noise and clamor it makes, the cannoneers clinging to their seats, and the wheels of the guns bounding up inches as they thunder over the uneven stones." A minute later, the four six-pounder rifles and three twelve-pounder howitzers of the 1st Maine Battery under Captain Edward W. Thompson reached the edge of the crowd, which scattered in terror and consternation. Butler noted that by the time the guns went into battery astride the intersection, "the scene was as quiet as a children's playground."

The secessionists of New Orleans had been taught a lesson in the use of power, delivered by a master showman. The mob did not reassemble and the city fathers, who suddenly appeared as overawed as their constituents, returned meekly to the conference room. Later Butler observed with more than a hint of satisfaction: "From that hour until the time I left New Orleans, I never saw occasion to move man or horse because of a mob in the streets of the city."[1]

Butler's seven-month stint in the Crescent City was punctuated by numerous acts just as provocative as the opening scene. In fact, well before he was relieved from his military governorship in December 1862, he had become among secessionists everywhere the vilest, most despicable Yankee on the planet. His seemingly outrageous actions in repressing rebellion eventually prompted Confederate officials to declare him a war criminal liable to execution if captured. At the same time, to the people of the North, especially those who desired to restore the Union as quickly as possible by whatever means necessary, he was celebrated as the first field commander to take his gloves off. In fact, throughout his life, Ben Butler had been a scrapper who went all out to gain the advantage.

Born in Deerfield, New Hampshire, in November 1818, he was the son of a sea trader who had fought as a captain of dragoons in the War of 1812. In his youth Butler moved to Massachusetts with his widowed mother. After graduating from Waterville (later Colby) College, he taught school, read law, and was admitted to the bar in Lowell. He gained a reputation as a shrewd practitioner of the law, specializing in defending the working class, especially Irish immigrants, against men of power. Fighting for the underdog became a way of life for him. It earned him a steady if not spectacular income and propelled him into public life. By the late 1840s he was a prominent Jacksonian Democrat. In 1852 he won election to the Massachusetts House of Representatives and six years later to the state senate.

Butler owed his rise to a sharp mind, a will to succeed, and his extraordinary powers of persuasion. These strengths overcame less prepossessing traits, including an appearance many found ludicrous. One observer characterized him as "the strangest sight . . . you ever saw; it is hard to keep your eyes off him." Even before he reached middle age, his rotund body, unnaturally short limbs, bloated face, and droopy eyes gave him the look of a dissipated toad.[2]

Major General Benjamin F. Butler. LIBRARY OF CONGRESS.

Early in his public career, Butler developed military ambitions. His advancement through the ranks of the Massachusetts militia was as swift as his climb up the political ladder: he was a colonel at thirty-five and a brigadier general before he turned forty. Politics, however, remained his consuming interest. In 1860, as a delegate to the Democratic national convention in Charleston, Butler named Jefferson Davis of Mississippi as his presidential candidate on fifty-seven consecutive ballots. When the convention deadlocked, he helped nominate another Southern candidate, John C. Breckinridge. At war's outbreak, however, Butler betrayed no compunction about fighting against his presidential choices, who were now high Confederate officials.

When his militia command was sworn into Federal service in the spring of 1861, Butler became one of the Union's earliest, and least likely, heroes. Late in April his troops relieved Washington, D.C., and the following month occupied secessionist Baltimore, an unauthorized move that helped keep Maryland in the Union. Though his precipitate action won Butler the rank of major general in the volunteer forces, it also relegated him, for a time, to administrative duties at Union-held Fort Monroe, at the tip of the Virginia Peninsula. Even though he was on the sidelines of the conflict, his behavior endeared him to hard-war Unionists and drew the wrath of Confederates. At a time when the army had yet to form a policy on dealing with escaped slaves, Butler unilaterally awarded them the status of contraband—the legitimate spoils of war.

When he took the field for active campaigning, Butler's tactical acumen could not match his skills as politician and administrator. Early in June 1861, an expeditionary force under his remote control blundered into defeat at Big Bethel, Virginia, the first sizable land engagement in the eastern theater of operations. Ten weeks later he recouped prestige by leading an amphibious force against Fort Hatteras and gaining a foothold on the North Carolina coast. The prominence accorded this feat, magnified by Union setbacks in other areas, gained him the command of an expedition to seize the Confederacy's greatest metropolis and its most strategic port. Thanks to the firepower of a fleet under Flag Officer David G. Farragut, Butler's troops occupied New Orleans with minimal effort and he began his stint as conqueror, occupier, and chief administrator.

Butler's seven months in command of the so-called Department of the Gulf was a study in confrontation, controversy, and scandal. By threatening to treat as a prostitute any woman who insulted or harassed his troops, he offended Southern sensibilities and inflamed foreign opinion; he became known throughout the Confederacy as "the Beast of New

Orleans." The hanging of a civilian who defiled the U.S. flag made Butler a candidate for the Confederate gallows.

Butler could be a terror to his superiors as well as to secessionists. His efforts to indict European consuls for aiding the Confederacy, in violation of neutrality laws, prompted President Abraham Lincoln to relieve him. Meanwhile, his commercial dealings in New Orleans as well as those of his brother Andrew, a shady merchant, led to charges of corruption. Butler even was accused of filching a silver setting from the home he used as his headquarters. Hard evidence of criminal conduct never came to light; nevertheless, the taint of scandal (and the nickname "Spoons") clung to him ever after.[3]

Butler did purchase goods cheaply from Southern agents and sold them dearly in the North. Conceivably, he also profited from the sale of confiscated property. Yet he was too sharp to incriminate himself, as his many critics were frustrated to discover. One disgruntled subordinate described Butler as "an astute quick witted unscrupulous audacious man" willing to trample anyone who blocked his ambition. Another officer was similarly expressive: "Butler is sharp, shrewd, able, without conscience or modesty—overbearing. A bad man to have against you in a criminal case."[4]

If Butler was no saint, neither was he beyond redemption. In New Orleans, he improved sanitation, virtually eradicating that city's historic susceptibility to yellow fever. He stabilized the city's currency and gave it a more efficient administration than any civilian rule had. He took special pains for the local poor, especially blacks. After initial reluctance, he recruited former slaves for his Army of the Gulf. Moreover, he saw to it that once in uniform, blacks received treatment equal to that of whites. Though his solicitude toward black troops began as a means of courting abolition-ists, liberals, and hard-war advocates, Butler exceeded political expediency in promoting racial equality.[5]

Despite these efforts, Butler became an embarrassment to the Lincoln administration. His provocative behavior, especially toward foreign offi-cials, led to his relief from command in December 1862. Lincoln exhibited no fear that this action would return to haunt him. As a soldier, Butler had risen no further than mediocrity; his reputation as a strategist and tactician was nil. Many of his contemporaries, in fact, considered him unfit to lead troops in active operations.

Whether the consensus opinion of Butler will prevail is difficult to assess, given his sometimes contradictory responses to the demands of field command and the doubtful motives of his critics, many of whom were ill disposed toward him for one reason or another. To be sure, Butler lacked active military experience; his prewar training, coming as it did in the "unorganized militia" of the period, stood him in poor stead when the shooting started in 1861. In North Carolina and Louisiana, he had rejected opportunities to take personal command of his troops, deferring to officers such as Farragut. When he did issue orders, it was from far in the rear. This perhaps was understandable, since his capture would mean a quick hanging. Still, by remaining so far from the action, Butler could not ensure that his directives were carried out quickly and precisely.

As for his ability as a military administrator, the contemporary consensus is clearly positive. Even those who belittled Butler's military acumen or disliked him personally praised his organizational expertise and the deftness with which he handled his myriad responsibilities. One colonel who considered him unscrupulous, devious, and capable of "extreme vindictiveness" conceded that "nothing was too insignificant for Butler's attention" if he believed it affected the welfare or efficiency of his command. A Massachusetts officer, once skeptical of Butler's ability to command, came to see that the general "possessed talents for organization and administration of the first order." Another subordinate, who distrusted political generals as a class, praised the man from Massachusetts not only for his executive talent but also for his ability to outline a plan of operations so clearly and concisely that even the densest officer could appreciate his role in it.[6]

Contemporary opinions on Butler's administrative success were many and varied. One of his company officers cited the general's "love of work and a capacity for it that was almost without limit." Brigadier General Joseph B. Carr, who served under Butler at Fort Monroe early in the war, recalled that his superior "showed courage and determination in any project in which he was interested." Other evaluators attributed Butler's abilities to physical and mental toughness. An aide to another army commander praised Butler as "a man of untiring industry," and a regimental officer marveled at "that promptness and energy so characteristic of Gen. Butler." Butler's wartime biographer, James Parton, believed he knew the reason for Butler's success as an administrator: "Brains are the great secret. He is endowed with a large, healthy, active, instructed, experienced brain."[7]

Of all those who probed Butler's success in command of expeditionary forces and military departments, Brigadier General Joseph Roswell Hawley of Connecticut probably struck closest to the mark. Despite his bitter animosity toward Butler, Hawley attributed to him several gifts, including force of character, native shrewdness, and intimate acquaintance with the complexities of human nature. Hawley added, "I regret that he has not as much capacity for handling troops judiciously in the field as he has for 'managing' his superiors and kicking out his subordinates. . . . Yet I wish that some of our accomplished soldiers had some of his peculiar traits, & his knowledge of men & things generally crowded into their somewhat narrow professional minds."[8]

Although Butler's removal from the field dealt no crippling blow to the war effort, his political clout was such that he remained idle for less than a year. At the time of his relief from New Orleans, the general had come to embrace many of those principles dear to the hearts of Republicans, even while maintaining an identity as a War Democrat. He spent much of his inactive service addressing war rallies and lecturing audiences in New England and the mid-Atlantic. A hectic schedule of public appearances throughout 1863 honed his image as an implacable foe of treason. Long before the year's close, prominent civilians were demanding his return to the field; more than a few touted him as a presidential contender.

Butler's timing was judicious. In the third year of the war a growing number of politicians, editors, and private individuals had become disenchanted with Lincoln's moderate policies. These people viewed the Beast of New Orleans as uniquely qualified to quash the fire-eaters in the South and the Copperheads in the North.[9]

Lincoln, who rarely misjudged the public mood, took note of Butler's support. The president perceived himself to be in a dilemma: he regarded the Massachusetts general as a political rival capable of siphoning off the votes of War Democrats and splitting the Republican Party. But Lincoln also coveted the power that Butler could provide to any candidate he supported.

In October 1863, after long deliberation, the president took a chance. He decided to return Butler to Fort Monroe as commander of an organization whose field force would come to be known as the Army of the James.

That organization, the Department of Virginia and North Carolina, encompassed garrisons along the Peninsula, the strategic corridor between the James and York Rivers, as well as several posts across Hampton Roads including Norfolk, Suffolk, and Portsmouth. The command dated to May 1861, when the Department of Virginia was organized under Major General John Ellis Wool. By July 1862 the department contained the thousand-man VII Corps, under Wool's successor, Major General John Adams Dix. The command expanded later that year with the addition of the twenty-five-thousand-man IV Corps, which had been part of Major General George B. McClellan's Army of the Potomac during the Peninsula Campaign. When that offensive against Richmond failed, most of McClellan's command was moved to more promising venues, but the IV Corps remained to garrison posts and depots believed to be valuable.[10]

Dix's command did little until the spring of 1863, when it helped lift the siege of Suffolk by Lieutenant General James Longstreet, commanding a detachment of General Robert E. Lee's Army of Northern Virginia. Two months later elements of the IV and VII Corps attempted to break Lee's lines of communications during his invasion of Pennsylvania. One of the objectives assigned to Dix by Major General Henry W. Halleck, the general-in-chief, was the capture or investment of lightly defended Richmond. The aged and timid Dix, however, failed to launch a strong offensive and instead permitted his less-than-formidable enemy to thrust him back to Fort Monroe.

Dix's faintheartedness had dire repercussions: in mid-July, the War Department removed him from the field and two weeks later dissolved his command. His troops became part of the XVIII Corps, the field force of Major General John G. Foster's Department of North Carolina, which had been established in January 1862 to gain and exploit footholds along that state's lower coast. Upon its expansion, Foster's command—which encompassed coastal operations from the York to the Albemarle River—became known as the Department of Virginia and North Carolina.[11]

The War Department expected greater things of Foster, who had won a fighting reputation in a series of coastal engagements. In the end, however, he was as disappointing as Dix. Guerrillas infiltrated his lines and raided his outposts regularly. He failed to expand Dix's fortifications above Williamsburg or Butler's footholds near Fort Hatteras. He could not win the confidence and enthusiasm of his troops or the fear and respect of his enemy. Late in 1863, when the government projected a more active role for the coastal army, it looked elsewhere for leadership. Northern newspapers were disappointed; early in November a New York journalist stationed at Fort Monroe observed, "What has been accomplished in this command during General Foster's administration, in a military view, is not of much importance."[12]

By its third autumn the Union war effort was facing a major reorientation. Already Lincoln and his secretary of war, Edwin McMasters Stanton, had set in motion events that would elevate Ulysses S. Grant, the Union's most successful field commander, to general-in-chief. In March 1864 Grant would come east from Tennessee to accept the revived grade of lieutenant general, to confer with Lincoln and other government officials, and to establish a working relationship with the Army of the Potomac—now under Major General George Gordon Meade—whose operations would make a critical contribution to Union victory. As chief of staff, Halleck would help Grant fashion a grand strategy in which Meade's command and other armies would exert simultaneous pressure on virtually every part of the Confederacy.

Even before Grant left the western theater, Lincoln, Stanton, and Halleck targeted Richmond for one of these concerted offensives. It was the seat of government, a symbol of the Confederacy's political integrity, and a link between Lee's army and its supply sources in the Deep South. To oversee this effort the War Department required a leader talented in both army administration and field command, preferably a hard-war man who would commit himself to a vigorous campaign no matter how rough the going.

Benjamin Butler was not the logical choice of military men like Halleck, who thought it folly to entrust citizen-soldiers with field command. Lincoln and Stanton, practical politicians of the first order, made the decision in Butler's favor. Lincoln displayed the psyche of a gambler. After all, if Butler should make a triumph of his appointment, he might vie with Lincoln for the presidency in 1864. But at least in the short term, Butler's return to the field would silence the minority who had been agitating on his behalf for the previous ten months and presumably secure the general's good will. Lincoln may have reasoned that Butler's new command was not large enough to ensure him a triumph of epic proportions, nor would it campaign in the mainstream of the Virginia theater. Meade's army would maintain its hold on the North's attention by virtue of its size, its long-term opposition to Lee, and its well-established role as the defender of Washington.

Stanton called Butler to his office in October 1863 and offered him Foster's job. Butler immediately agreed, although he may have cocked his "lop eye" to discern hidden meanings in the secretary's offer.[13]

Butler must have realized that military success promised the most direct route to the fulfillment of political ambitions he had never bothered to disguise. Although active campaigning was done for the year, the next spring would see a massive effort against the South before the 1864 elections. Given their department's position astride the southern approach to Richmond, Butler's troops would play a part in that effort. The timing was such that successes Butler won in the field would enhance his ability to exploit any of Lincoln's political weaknesses. To be sure, the Department of Virginia and North Carolina, which then had fewer than thirty thousand troops, failed to overshadow Meade's army or Grant's Military Division of the Mississippi. Still, it was probably the best a general lacking a professional military background could have hoped for. These considerations, among others, helped secure Butler's acceptance, and on October 28 Lincoln publicly announced his appointment.[14]

The news generated predictable responses. New England rejoiced; the Confederacy fumed. On November 3 Horace Greeley's *New York Tribune,* a left-of-center journal that had appointed itself confidant and adviser to the government, declared that "this change is believed to indicate a disposition to prosecute the war with renewed vigor in that especial section." The *New York Herald* of James Gordon Bennett, a more centrist paper, addressed Butler only indirectly, suggesting that any change at Fort Monroe was for the better. Antiadministration papers portrayed Butler's return to duty as further evidence of Lincoln's bankrupt military policy.[15]

Soon after the story broke, the Rebel press weighed in. One of the more bellicose prints, John Daniel's *Richmond Examiner,* set the tone for the region. Playing down the importance of Butler's assignment, Daniel asked whether it was "proof of patriotism on his part that he descends to so insignificant a sphere, or . . . a compliment to his ability that he is expected to glean additional treasures from a region that seems utterly exhausted to less skillful robbers?" The *Examiner* envisioned a happy prospect:

> He will, no doubt, use all those wise precautions for his personal safety which he has been accustomed to take; yet it is not impossible that his vigilance may be found at fault on some occasion, and it would make a pleasing and appropriate termination to his career if the soil of Virginia, which witnessed his disgraceful defeat in his first essay of arms, should provide the scaffold in which he should meet the merited retribution of his crimes.[16]

Unmoved by Northern hostility or Southern threats, Butler left Washington for his home in Lowell. There he packed for the trip he would make with his wife, Sarah—a resourceful and determined supporter of her husband's career, a spouse any soldier would have cherished—and their daughter, Blanche. The family arrived on November 10 at Fort Monroe, a garrison the general had last seen almost two years earlier when embarking on his Fort Hatteras expedition. At the historic post, Butler was briefed by Foster, met with a few of his subordinates, organized his staff, and began to familiarize himself with his new realm.[17]

Poring over regimental and brigade returns, he discovered that he had 1,231 officers and 27,640 enlisted men present for duty as well as 197 heavy cannon, 191 pieces of field artillery, thousands of horses and mules, and immense stores of arms, ammunition, and supplies. The troops were scattered among a dozen posts in two states. More than 12,000 served in Major General John J. Peck's far-off District of North Carolina, divided among the defenses of New Bern and the subdistricts of Beaufort, the Albemarle, and the Pamlico. Only a few of Peck's troops would be transferred to field service in Virginia in time for the 1864 campaign.

The sally port of Fort Monroe, Virginia. U.S. ARMY MILITARY HISTORY INSTITUTE.

Fort Monroe was garrisoned by a heavy artillery regiment, an outfit of U.S. Colored Cavalry, some Veteran Reserve and Signal Corps personnel, and miscellaneous units that Butler soon placed aboard gunboats in the James River. This last organization, which became known as the "Naval Brigade," was assigned to Brigadier General Charles K. Graham, a veteran of naval service in the Mexican War and more recently an infantry commander wounded at Gettysburg.[18]

Many more troops were on the south side of Hampton Roads. More than a half dozen brigades, comprising units of all arms, were stationed in Norfolk and Portsmouth. Four of them, composed of white and black infantry, were commanded by West Point–trained veterans of the Army of the Potomac, Brigadier Generals James Barnes and George W. Getty; the fifth brigade, composed of three understrength cavalry regiments, was led by an old regular, Colonel Samuel P. Spear. Getty and Barnes, both highly competent commanders, did not remain long enough to be of much assistance to Butler before returning to Meade's command. Spear, who did remain, was much more volatile; though admired by most of his men, "Old Spuds" suffered from erratic judgment and a volcanic temper that had led him to shoot at least one of his men for disobedience.[19]

Spear was not the only question mark among Butler's inherited subordinates. One of Getty's brigades, composed of African-Americans, was led by a Harvard-educated physician, Brigadier General Edward A. Wild. An early and fervid patron of blacks in uniform, Wild was a contentious paranoid who distrusted his superiors and hated the enemy with a blind fury. Artillery fire had cost him his left arm and had maimed his right hand, but he continued to fight Rebels, negrophobes, and reactionary superiors with the zeal of a social crusader.

There were other sources of potential trouble among the department's hierarchy. The few troops stationed near the armed camp at Newport News were commanded by another civilian appointee, Brigadier General Charles Heckman of New Jersey, as was Heckman's cavalry (Colonel Simon H. Mix of New York) and the garrison at Yorktown (Brigadier General Isaac J. Wistar of Pennsylvania). Each lacked a military education and had other deficiencies more or less severe. Heckman was prone to lose his head in times of crisis, lapsing into broken German that confused his troops. Depressed by a deteriorating marriage, Mix displayed mood swings and struck some of his officers as suicidal. More of a paper shuffler than a combat commander, Wistar was an inveterate politician with a deep-seated prejudice against the black troops that predominated in his command, whom he considered "a Government pet and plaything . . . not good to tie to in battle."[20]

If Butler was concerned at the many citizen-soldiers among his lieutenants, he gave no indication of it. Soon after arriving at Fort Monroe, he found his authority enlarged with the addition of the District of Currituck, embracing

Brigadier General Edward A. Wild.
U.S. ARMY MILITARY HISTORY INSTITUTE.

Brigadier General Charles A. Heckman.
U.S. ARMY MILITARY HISTORY INSTITUTE.

portions of both southeastern Virginia and northeastern North Carolina, and the District of Saint Mary's, covering the Maryland county of that name (including the notorious prisoner of war camp at Point Lookout) and the counties of Northampton and Accomack on Virginia's Eastern Shore. To man the new districts, Butler chose nonprofessional soldiers, Brigadier Generals James H. Ledlie of New York and Gilman Marston of New Hampshire. In his initial command assignments, Butler displayed an uneven touch: in the months ahead, Marston would embellish a distinguished record extending from Bull Run to Fredericksburg; Ledlie, who would transfer to the Army of the Potomac the following spring, would prove to be not only a fumbler but also one of the most notorious cowards in the Union ranks.[21]

Butler remained at Fort Monroe for one week. On November 18, as his boss, President Lincoln, left Washington for a speaking engagement at Gettysburg, the new departmental commander departed on a tour of his domain. He went first to New Bern, where he conferred with Peck and inspected the local garrison. Accompanied by Rear Admiral S. Phillips Lee, whose North Atlantic Blockading Squadron had been directed to cooperate with Butler's troops, the general visited Morehead City, Fort Macon, Newport Barracks, Little Washington, Plymouth, Roanoke Island, and his old field of glory, Hatteras Inlet. On November 24, with his inspection of the most far-flung points in his department complete, he returned to Hampton Roads. Following a brief interval at headquarters, he moved up the peninsula. By November 26 he was at Yorktown, where he was greeted by Wistar.

After touring the defenses that McClellan's army had erected the previous year atop the old Revolutionary War battlements, Butler and his subordinate discussed a lengthy list of topics. Sounding out Wistar on the subject of black troops, Butler discerned the brigadier's prejudice. Butler praised their dedication and soldierly behavior and strongly hinted that Wistar should employ them more actively. Butler also urged his host to improve living conditions in the camps of black soldiers' dependents, which had been found to be cold, damp, and cramped. A civilian who had recently visited Wistar's post described them as "reeking with squalor."[22]

Not certain that he had made the desired impression on his subordinate, Butler acted on his own initiative. Within days of returning to Fort Monroe, he dispatched staff officers not only to Yorktown but also to Hampton, Williamsburg, and other outposts where black refugees had gathered. These representatives of the department's new Office of Negro Affairs supervised efforts to eradicate the garrison ghettos. Work parties razed the worst hovels, refurbished salvageable quarters, and built sturdy cabins. Homeless blacks were resettled on property confiscated from secessionists. Within weeks a civilian relief worker, till then a bitter critic of the army's treatment of blacks, would marvel at the "absolute neatness" surrounding the cabins, which she found "well-built, of uniform size, not crowded . . . [with] nothing unclean to be seen either in front, or in the rear."[23]

Butler also broached a number of operational issues with Wistar, one of the most important being a suggestion recently submitted by Colonel Robert M. West, Wistar's subordinate at Williamsburg. West considered it "an auspicious time to strike for the relief of our suffering soldiers in the Richmond prisons." According to local intelligence, no more than fifty defenders stood between West and the Chickahominy River, the principal natural barrier to the Confederate capital. West was convinced that a stealthy force could cross the river at Bottom's Bridge ten miles southeast of Richmond and hit the city before it learned of the danger. Once the raiding column secured the road from the bridge, "the remainder of the work would be easy." The Federals could slip inside the capital at night and throw open Libby and Belle Isle Prisons before sunrise. If time permitted, the raiders could destroy factories, foundries, supply depots, and ordnance caches. West added that "there has not been a time since the war began when the auxiliary force around Richmond was so small as at this time." Nor could Lee's army, wintering well north of the capital, reinforce the local defense battalion on short notice.[24]

The plan had great appeal to Wistar, who, as West's immediate superior, would likely carry it out. Butler, who, as departmental commander, stood to profit most from its success, also considered its merits. Any man who took Richmond—even if he held it for only a few hours—would reap military and political rewards. As one of Butler's more hopeful supporters in Washington wrote him at the time, the presidency was within his grasp could he make "some *coup d'état* before Richmond" in time to influence the election. Here was such an opportunity.[25]

After giving preliminary approval to a raid on Richmond, Butler headed back to Fort Monroe to grapple with administrative and operational challenges. He strove to increase the number of loyalists within his lines by threatening to banish any locals who refused to swear unconditional allegiance to the Union. At the same time, he sought to curtail the illicit traffic in tobacco and naval stores that had long flourished between army officers and Northern speculators. He also labored to repair communication lines damaged by guerrillas, one of the most strategic being the Great Dismal Swamp Canal astride the Virginia–North Carolina line.

At this formative stage of his regime, Butler's most vexing opponents were irregulars who staged hit-and-run strikes against outposts and supply trains as well as canals, railroads, and telegraph lines. From the first he made vigorous if not uniformly successful efforts to destroy the guerrillas' camps and hunt down their leaders. During his inspection tours of North Carolina and the peninsula, infantry detachments were combing guerrilla-infested areas of Mathews County, Virginia. Although the results of this sweep were meager—a dozen partisans and a couple of artillery pieces captured—a later raid by black troops under Colonel Alonzo G. Draper destroyed several guerrilla compounds along the Atlantic sounds.[26]

Then came a larger and more controversial search-and-destroy mission, the brainchild of Draper's superior, Edward Wild. Soon after Butler returned to Fort Monroe in December, Wild led 1,700 black troops into Pasquotank County, North Carolina. They liberated more than 2,500 slaves, most of whom joined the Union ranks, while demolishing four guerrilla camps and burning the property of people suspected of having aided the irregulars.

Wild permitted his troops to forage liberally, "judiciously discriminating in favor of the worst rebels." At some point, things got out of hand. The loyalist governor of Virginia later complained to Washington that "Union men and widows shared the same fate" as Wild's professed targets: "All they had was taken or destroyed." A resident added that an observer could "trace the track of the raid for ten miles by the turkey buzzards, feeding on the carrion made by the destruction of animal life."[27]

Wild was not through; he capped his expedition by making an example of Daniel Bright, a Confederate deserter captured outside Elizabeth City. In Wild's view, a deserter from either side merited the ultimate penalty. To discourage the sort of partisan warfare in which he believed Bright to be engaged, the one-armed general tried his captive by drumhead court, pronounced him guilty, and strung him up. From around his neck swung a placard: "This guerrilla hanged by order of Brigadier-General Wild."

Wild's notions of justice provoked an outcry from the Confederate press and public. Zebulon Vance, governor of North Carolina, and the Confederate Congress branded him an atrocity monger and again indicted Butler, whom they suspected of encouraging Wild as a war criminal. Although embarrassed by Wild's excesses, Butler for a time attempted to defend him, at least in public. But then the controversy took an especially ugly turn. A few weeks after Wild's raid, Major General George E. Pickett, commander of the Confederate Department of North Carolina, hanged one of Wild's soldiers, captured during the raid. Pickett announced that he had acted in retaliation for Bright's execution."[28]

Butler was angered but willing to let the matter rest. Wild was not. Without seeking department permission, he searched southeastern Virginia for prominent Confederates to hold as hostages against the prospect of further enemy retaliation. Instead of arresting soldiers or political officials, Wild took into custody the wives of two prominent private individuals, razed their homes, and imprisoned them at Norfolk.

Predictably, the Confederacy unleashed a torrent of censure upon Butler and his subordinate. Incensed by this outrage against Southern womanhood, Governor Vance called the perpetrators "a disgrace to the manhood of the age; not being able to capture soldiers, they war upon defenseless women. Great God! what an outrage!"[29]

This was too much for Butler. With War Department approval—and over Wild's vehement protest—he mediated an exchange of prisoners, with the women's husbands serving as hostages against reprisals. Eventually both men were released and the controversy cooled. Then, with no warning, Wild captured a Confederate officer and declared him, too, a hostage; North Carolina partisans were threatening to hang another black soldier. Wild worsened the situation by writing to the Confederate

Major General George E. Pickett.
LIBRARY OF CONGRESS.

authorities about his most recent captive: "I shall treat him exactly as your people treat that soldier . . . and you know by this time that I keep my word."[30]

Again Butler absorbed much of the blame for Wild's actions. Again he worked diligently to calm passions; through his intercession, the Confederate officer was released. Although the man later died from the effects of his captivity, the black soldier was also freed. To avoid any such future trouble, Butler put Wild on administrative duties at Norfolk and Portsmouth, where the radical idealist served, more or less quietly, for several months.

Wild's intemperate conduct did not lessen Butler's determination to stamp out guerrilla activity. From November 1863 to March 1864 he launched several efforts, on both sides of the North Carolina line, to eradicate partisan enclaves. Some civilians suspected of guerrilla or terrorist activities were captured; other expeditions destroyed facilities of value to Confederate regulars as well as to partisans. One raid into upper North Carolina, led by Colonel James Jourdan, resulted in the destruction of saltworks that produced a commodity in great demand and short supply throughout the South. Another strike at saltworks and tanneries, conducted by General Marston, wrecked thousands of dollars' worth of facilities and created what one regimental historian called "quite a commotion" in Tidewater Virginia. Throughout the winter, Graham's Naval Brigade steamed up and down the coast and along inland waters, landing troops at strategic points to demolish signal stations, sawmills, and storehouses.

Not every mission was successful. A February incursion toward South Mills, North Carolina, by infantry under General Heckman and horsemen under Colonel Spear ended in disaster. Meeting unexpected opposition, a detachment of the 5th Pennsylvania Cavalry, one of many units in Butler's department to be commanded by a nonprofessional soldier, tumbled into the Dismal Swamp Canal, where some men and several horses drowned.[31]

The largest, most ambitious winter expedition was that aimed at Richmond. Early in February 1864 Butler gave Wistar the go-ahead on Colonel West's plan. With the grudging cooperation of the Army of the Potomac, which conducted diversionary movements within view of Lee's army, Wistar left Yorktown after dark on February 5, halted at Williamsburg to gather his forward detachments, and by 9 A.M. the following day was on his way to Bottom's Bridge. His force of about 4,000, included three regiments of white infantry under West, three black outfits led by Colonel Samuel A. Duncan, 2,500 troopers under Spear, and two batteries of artillery.

The movement out of Williamsburg, conducted in daylight, probably cost the raiders the element of surprise. But even absolute stealthiness would have been useless because Richmond authorities were expecting Wistar. As early as mid-January Lee had reported to Jefferson Davis that Butler was recruiting volunteers to help liberate Libby and Belle Isle Prisons. Thus forewarned, Richmond defense forces had taken steps to halt the Yankees.

Spear's cavalry, leading the column, reached Bottom's Bridge early on February 7, only to find, as Wistar noted glumly, "the enemy there in strong force, with infantry, cavalry, and artillery. . . . The Bridge planks had been taken up, the fords both above and below effectually obstructed, extensive earth-works and rifle-pits constructed, and a strong force of troops brought down by the [Richmond and] York River Railroad, by which large accessions were still arriving."[32]

Suspecting the game was up, Wistar made a halfhearted attempt to force his way across. Hampered by a narrow, marshy approach and finding nowhere else to cross the river, he decided on a frontal assault against the bridge. Betraying his lack of field experience, he sent Spear in a mounted attack against fixed positions, with predictable results. After the troopers came galloping back, minus nine men and ten mounts from artillery and rifle fire, Wistar headed back to Williamsburg. Butler's first attempt to capture Richmond had failed before fairly under way.[33]

Although disappointed, Butler refused to accept blame for Wistar's failure. Nor did he indict the raiding leader, whom he nevertheless suspected of incompetence or faintheartedness, or both. Instead, Butler argued in a masterful lawyer's brief that Lincoln was responsible for the lost opportunity. In a letter to the president, Butler claimed that Wistar's repulse was the handiwork of Private William Boyle of the 1st New York Mounted Rifles, one of Spear's troopers. A few days before the expedition, Boyle had escaped from prison at Fort Monroe through the complicity of a jailer. The fugitive had made his way inside enemy lines and was escorted to Richmond, where he provided the local commander, Major General Arnold Elzey, with details of the upcoming raid. As Butler informed Lincoln, Boyle had been awaiting execution for murdering an officer; he would have been dead long ago had Lincoln not suspended the death penalty within the Department of Virginia and North Carolina. Butler hoped the president "may see how your clemency has been misplaced."[34]

The letter may have had an intended effect, for in early March Lincoln reinstated capital punishment in Butler's realm. For abetting Boyle's escape, his jailer was promptly shot. Afterward Butler wrote Elzey, offering to exchange any number of Confederates in his hands for Private Boyle, but Elzey refused. The incident only whetted the Union leader's appetite to avenge his failure to take the city whose capture might put him in the White House.[35]

CHAPTER TWO

From Desk General to Field Leader

FROM HIS EARLIEST DAYS AT FORT MONROE, BUTLER IMMERSED HIMSELF IN administrative duties. They were many and burdensome, the result of the vastness of his domain, but he embraced them with characteristic energy and determination. Within weeks of his arrival on the peninsula, Butler had overhauled numerous offices and agencies that had functioned less than smoothly under his predecessors, while adding a multitude of new ones. He streamlined the military justice system by convening courts-martial that rapidly reduced a backlog of cases. The president of one tribunal observed that Butler's courts "gained a reputation for prompt work, absolute justice and unusually severe penalties." Once Lincoln rescinded his suspension of capital punishment, the Department of Virginia and North Carolina became notable for the number of murderers, rapists, and deserters shot or hanged at Butler's order. The general's penchant for swift justice produced a dramatic decline in the crime rate.

At times Butler's courts dispensed a brand of justice peculiarly his own, brimming with ingenuity and irony. On one occasion, he tried several officers in a New York regiment who had resigned their commissions en masse, based on grievances the department commander considered without merit. Butler granted their release from the army, then charged them with being civilians loitering in a combat zone. Pronouncing them guilty, he sentenced the ex-officers to don prison garb and set to work on military excavation projects within reach of Confederate artillery. Only when Grant intervened did Butler suspend their sentences.

At another time, Butler tried a chaplain who had written a newspaper article critical of the general. Suspecting that a superior officer was behind the attack, Butler was incensed to find the clergyman unwilling to reveal his sources. To loosen his tongue, Butler tied him to a chair inside a tent filled with boxes of ammunition. Unaware that the containers were empty, the chaplain agreed to talk once staff officers entered his place of confinement, waving torches about.[1]

Butler also adjudicated cases involving civilians, many of whom he jailed in Norfolk for offenses ranging from refusal to take the oath of allegiance to helping the enemy, however slightly. He was especially avid in confiscating the property of secessionists charged with treasonous behavior. Butler's growing involvement in civil law also led him to regulate church services in Norfolk, Portsmouth, and other cities where pulpits became anti-Union forums. Finding Southside communities increasingly discontented, he placed Norfolk under martial law in June 1864, which relieved Butler from observing the legal niceties that would have hampered his administration.

Butler's relations with civilians were not uniformly hostile. As when in command at New Orleans, he adopted a quasi-paternalistic attitude toward local social, commercial, and financial institutions. Like southern Louisiana, Tidewater Virginia was susceptible to seasonal outbreaks of disease, chiefly yellow fever. Butler lectured local officials on improving sanitation and supervised the cleaning of streets, sewers, and food storage facilities. The general reported that military laborers were soon carting "a thousand tons of filth per week from Norfolk, and by this means the yellow fever was kept out." Under another civilian improvement program, military and civilian prisoners cleaned, paved, and maintained outlying areas of Norfolk and Hampton without cost to local government.[2]

Butler's administration assumed some of the trappings of civil authority long before martial law descended on Norfolk. When Portsmouth's leading bank was found to be in such chaos that the savings of thousands of investors were threatened, Butler hired a Massachusetts expert to untangle its affairs. When the managers of the Norfolk gas works, in an apparent attempt to thwart Butler's rule, refused to provide the city with sufficient lighting, army officers took over the utility. Butler also placed subordinates in charge of police and fire departments gutted by manpower losses.

From departmental funds Butler contributed substantially to the few existing social services such as poorhouses and orphanages, while establishing his own commission for the poor. This agency monitored the welfare of thousands of civilians, many of whom were Confederate sympathizers. Administered by the same financial expert who overhauled the Bank of Portsmouth, the Poor Board furnished food and clothing to an average of

500 families per month throughout Butler's tenure. In a typical month it provided from the departmental commissary 11,725 pounds of salt beef, 492 pounds of flour, 23,628 pounds of meal and hominy, 164 pounds of rice, and other food.[3]

Butler's civil involvement did not always spring from altruism. His position between occupied and unoccupied territory spawned a vast, illegal trade that continued until war's end. Only a man of rock-ribbed integrity could have resisted the temptation to turn the situation to his advantage. Through an extensive intelligence and police system, he pursued and brought to justice dozens of merchants—Northerners and Southerners alike—who attempted to smuggle cotton, tobacco, leather goods, naval stores, and other profitable goods through his lines. He reserved his harshest punishment for army officers who colluded with these criminals. Nevertheless, Butler and several of his closest subordinates, including his chief of staff, Colonel J. Wilson Shaffer, and Brigadier General George F. Shepley, the commander at Norfolk, appear to have profited from illicit dealings.[4]

Accusations of corruption had dogged Butler since his stint in command in New England in 1861; they flew fast and furious throughout his New Orleans regime. None of the accusations drew blood, nor was Butler convicted of fraudulent acts at Fort Monroe. Still, much circumstantial evidence places him at the center of numerous efforts to convert the "exigencies of war" into personal gain.

Some of his machinations were simplicity itself. Through the provost marshals he handpicked to police the local population, he sold trade permits to any civilian who wished to do business within his department. Though a portion of these payments went to municipal relief, most seem to have lined the pockets of Butler; his friends and subordinates; relatives, including his brother-in-law; and business partners suspected of crimes against the U.S. Treasury Department.

Through the taxing of imports Butler devised a scheme to receive kickbacks from Northern traders wishing to sell farm implements and other goods to Southern agents willing to pay in cotton. Treasury agents suspected that the general also profited when the cotton was sold in New York or Boston. Butler appears to have used army transports and stevedores to ship Northern cargo to Virginia and North Carolina and to escort return shipments of cotton and tobacco. He may also have profited from the business conducted at government-regulated trading posts along the border of enemy territory, run by cronies of General Shepley.[5]

Government officials were not deaf to rumors of Butler's profiteering. Navy Secretary Gideon Welles considered the general's role in dispensing trade permits a "little, dirty, speculating intrigue." The Unionist governor of Virginia, Francis H. Peirpoint, launched a one-man crusade to link Butler with a variety of corrupt schemes, though Butler effectively used his powers as military governor to limit the damage. In mid-1864 Secretary of War Stanton, in an apparent search for evidence against the general, sent a War Department agent to spy on him. This man obtained a clerical position, on Stanton's recommendation, at department headquarters. When Butler was gone from his office, the spy rifled desks and safes, but before he could complete his mission, Butler unmasked and imprisoned him.

After Butler was ousted from command in January 1865, a commission led by an erstwhile subordinate, Brigadier General George H. Gordon, delved into accusations of departmental corruption. Following months of interviewing witnesses and gathering evidence, Gordon submitted a report that portrayed Butler as standing hip-deep in corruption but settled nothing. Hard proof of criminal activity was elusive, so the government refused to take action.[6]

The military side of Butler's administration presents a happier story than his involvement in civil affairs, for most of what he accomplished at Fort Monroe and later in the field directly benefited his command. Early in his reign he established a fair set of standards for contracting with laborers to assist in military construction. He streamlined a postal service that delivered 50,000 letters daily to his soldiers. He set up branches of the Adams Express Company at Fort Monroe as well as at other points along his department's line of operations. By March 1865 the branch at Bermuda Hundred, Virginia, was relaying 2,000 parcels to the front every day, bolstering morale throughout the Army of the James.[7]

Butler assisted agents of the U.S. Sanitary Commission and U.S. Christian Commission in ministering to the physical and spiritual needs of his troops. By war's end, scores of Sanitary Commission representatives were providing extra rations, reading and writing materials, and personal-care items to soldiers at the front, at the department's support bases, and in its hospitals. With Butler's blessing, the Christian Commission operated seven stations and numerous chapels in the field, supervised by fifty "delegates" and dozens of assistants. The historian of one of Butler's cavalry regiments recalled that "at Bermuda Hundred, as well as elsewhere, the kindly ministrations of the Sanitary and Christian Commissions, called forth grateful acknowledgments from many a . . . soldier." In other commands, the two agencies did not always work in tandem, but no such friction complicated their year-and-a-half-long association in Butler's department.[8]

Soon after reaching Fort Monroe, Butler cultivated good relations with the press. He closely involved himself in newspaper coverage of his command, seeking not only personal publicity but also a means of informing his troops of the big picture of operations and making their service familiar to the folks at home. Especially early in his tenure, Butler went out of his way to accommodate reporters whom he considered useful. He assured Charles C. Coffin of the *Boston Journal* that "of all things I should desire to have an intelligent, loyal, observing, discreet, and faithful correspondent of the press within my Department."

The operative words were "loyal" and "faithful." Correspondents who printed favorable stories could expect preferential treatment. Horace Greeley's *Tribune,* which sometimes promoted Butler for high office, was always in favor at Fort Monroe. Greeley's people got to travel on the *Greyhound,* Butler's private steamer, which was outfitted with every comfort. Occasionally they partook of food and drink from Butler's commissary. It was a symbiotic relationship, for newsmen realized that by staying in Butler's good graces they would gain access to inside information as well as to a commander who made good copy. A *New York Herald* reporter advised his editor on the eve of Butler's assumption of field command in the spring of 1864: "As General Butler takes chief command of operations of this Department, it might be better not to offend him.
. . . In fact your promise and that of Mr Bennett to me, was to the effect that nothing should be said against him."[9]

Reporters who did not share this philosophy were unwelcome in Butler's department. The *New York World,* which had accused the general of corruption at New Orleans, was barred from fielding a correspondent. Butler attempted to have certain critical journalists, including the *Herald*'s Sylvanus Cadwallader and Oscar G. Sawyer, kicked out of his department. Newsmen who remained were not always appreciated by objective-minded, fact-seeking readers. General Hawley, another of the department's nonprofessional

Brigadier General Joseph R. Hawley.
U.S. Army Military History Institute.

soldiers and himself a former editor, complained about those unprincipled reporters in Butler's hip pocket who "lied downright about some of his operations . . . [and] claimed as successes what were notorious defeats."[10]

If not always accurately covered, Butler's operations were scrutinized by a formidable phalanx of reporters. At least two dozen journals, mostly published in New York, Philadelphia, and Boston, maintained correspondents at headquarters. The *Herald* alone employed six full-time newsmen at Fort Monroe and various outposts. Every day the *Herald* featured at least one dispatch—sometimes three or four—to cover the movements, or the stasis, of Butler's command. Since the latter condition seemed to predominate, the reporters generated a great amount of minutiae. Still, their persistence made the Department of Virginia and North Carolina one of the most publicized commands of the war.[11]

When Butler was not monitoring Northern newsmen, he was spying on Southern military and political officials. Through an early alliance with Elizabeth Van Lew, an eccentric Unionist living in Richmond who ran a well-appointed spy ring, Butler mounted one of the most resourceful secret services of the war. A devotee of conspiratorial operations, he also ran his own network of detectives, spies, and scouts. Though some of his agents proved to be of little value (two of his most trusted spies spent most of their time and pay in Norfolk bars and brothels), other agents provided reliable information on enemy dispositions, numbers, and movements. In sharp contrast to the Pinkerton detectives who spied for the Army of the Potomac in 1862, Butler's operatives gathered some remarkably accurate intelligence on the strength and intentions of the Army of Northern Virginia. Through the efforts of his own and Van Lew's operatives, Butler also monitored the status of Union prisoners in Richmond. Word of the impending transfer of thousands of captives to South Carolina had played a role in his decision to launch Wistar's raid.

Butler also maintained a civilian spy ring in Norfolk, Portsmouth, Hampton, and elsewhere to supply him with fact and conjecture about the mood of the citizenry, the extent to which the locals were aiding Rebel forces, and efforts to disrupt Butler's regime. Butler's greatest coup came when, with the aid of Van Lew, he placed two informants, a cook and a gardener, in the Confederate White House in Richmond. The black servants supplied headquarters with an intermittent flow of information from war councils and political discussions held in Davis's parlor, study, and dining room.[12]

To this intelligence Butler added sometimes invaluable information from two units in his command that he took great pains to maintain. The first was a highly talented corps of signal officers headed by Captain Lemuel B.

Norton and his successor, Captain Henry R. Clum. The signalmen built a series of towers along the Richmond-Petersburg front, some of them 150 feet high, that in good weather enabled Butler to keep visual tabs on his enemy. The second unit was an enterprising band of telegraphers who worked the winding communications route between Fort Monroe and Butler's field of operations. These resourceful "brass pounders" tapped enemy circuits to bring Butler news of Confederate movements that otherwise would have been unobtainable.[13]

The telegraph was but one technological innovation whose military applications Butler exploited. A Yankee tinkerer, the department commander experimented with many contraptions of potential wartime utility. Some were plainly the work of crackpots, but others appeared promising, even revolutionary, in their implications. More than any other Civil War commander, Butler touted the machine gun. On several occasions he personally tested two early types: the hand-cranked Gatling gun and the Billinghurst Requa Battery. One of his officers described the latter as a carriage "carrying 25 gun barrels somewhat heavier and shorter than the common rifled musket, arranged horizontally, between the wheels of the carriage . . . breech loading and [capable of firing] 150 shots per minute . . . with great precision."[14]

Though neither weapon proved acceptable for widespread use, Butler was not deterred. He experimented with Greek Fire, a combustible substance applied by hose against flammable targets; armor-piercing artillery, which he hoped to use against Rebel gunboats; movable signal towers; portable cameras for use with reconnaissance balloons; railroad-mounted artillery; and dredging machines for undermining enemy defenses. This last contraption moved a visiting officer to comment that Butler "never is happy unless he has half a dozen contrivances on hand. . . . He has an auger that bores a tunnel five feet in diameter, and he is going to bore to Richmond, and suddenly pop up in somebody's basement, while the family are at breakfast!"[15]

At times Butler may have become carried away, but because he never lost his enthusiasm, vision, or willingness to experiment, he maintained one of the finest medical systems of any Civil War command. Near Fort Monroe were two army general hospitals, the Hampton and the Chesapeake. The first predated the war; the second had been converted in 1862 from a girls school. Nearby were two smaller hospitals, the Balfour at Portsmouth and Ferry Point on the outskirts of Norfolk. These ministered to the most sickly and severely wounded of Butler's command. Thousands of patients passed through their wards every month during the campaigns of 1864–65.

Of the four, only Chesapeake Hospital—which employed civilian surgeons as opposed to the other institutions, staffed mainly by Butler's

Signal Tower, Bermuda Hundred, June 1864. LIBRARY OF CONGRESS.

military doctors—was criticized. Its operating conditions, which lay beyond the jurisdiction of Major Charles McCormick, medical director of the department, were frequently horrid. One patient told of bloody and dirty bedding, ubiquitous bedsores, sick patients forced to serve as attendants, and a daily ration consisting of half-baked bread, two slices of pickled beets, and foul-tasting beef tea. This critic found the hospital's "contract surgeons" to be only half trained and drunk on medicinal whiskey. As a result, wounded men were butchered: "Amputation, hemorrhage, and death was the usual order of events."[16]

Whatever the accuracy in these observations—and they appear to be overdrawn—conditions at the Chesapeake improved after a military surgeon, Major Ely McClellan, in charge of the Hampton Hospital, added the civilian facility to his authority late in 1864. Thereafter, both hospitals were favorably described by a contributor to *Harper's New Monthly Magazine*. The writer applauded the "abounding comforts which the Government has provided for its stricken soldiers—comforts generally vastly greater than could possibly be enjoyed at home." He was especially impressed by the scope and variety of the facilities in Hampton Roads. Butler once boasted to Edwin Stanton that those institutions could, if necessary, care for fully half of his command at one time.

Proud of his hospitals, Butler zealously maintained their efficiency. He secured able, humane supervisors such as McCormick and McClellan. He continually repaired, refurbished, and expanded facilities. He helped establish innovative programs such as kitchens that catered to patients requiring special diets. And he maintained nine specially equipped transports to speed the sick and wounded from the front to the wards in the rear.[17]

When Butler's command began active operations, it supported a wide network of field hospitals. Both of its infantry corps maintained hospitals behind the lines, allowing for quick short-term treatment and decisions for further care. The command even pioneered a system of transportable dressing stations, forerunners of the mobile surgical wards of the twentieth century. Patients and observers alike praised the surgeons manning these stations; Butler had decreed that only the most skillful and caring should operate there.

Butler's command also benefited from one of the war's most efficient nursing corps. Clara Barton, a Massachusetts-born former Patent Office clerk who in June 1864 became chief of nurses in the department, filled that demanding position with such resourcefulness and fidelity that she became—with the possible exception of Dorothea Dix—the most famous nursing supervisor of her time. Given her talents, those of the surgeons at the front and at army headquarters, and the unflagging support all received from

their commander, a wounded or ill member of Butler's command stood to
benefit from some of the finest medical care available to the Civil War soldier.[18]

<hr />

When not ministering to the needs of his department, Butler nurtured the
personal ambitions that always animated him. He could not profit from
Wistar's raid, but his political prospects remained bright through the winter
of 1863–64. As a result, he had to weigh opportunities for a cabinet or vice
presidential berth against the prospect of winning higher office through
military achievement.

Prominent people in and out of government had long advanced the
Massachusetts general for secretary of war or state, especially after his New
Orleans regime. In the spring of 1863 Lincoln's postmaster general, War
Democrat Montgomery Blair, considered supporting Butler as Stanton's
successor. After much deliberation, Butler let it be known that if he was
returned to active duty, he would happily pass up a cabinet post.[19]

Early in 1864, with Butler ensconced at Fort Monroe, the influential
Horace Greeley began promoting him for president on a Republican or War
Democrat ticket. The effort caught Butler's fancy; soon he was dispatching
emissaries, including his chief of staff, Colonel Shaffer, and a civilian associate,
J. K. Herbert, to probe the depth of his political support in Washington.
Although inconclusive, the venture encouraged Butler.

About the time Greeley began to sound the trumpet for Butler, Lincoln
made a major overture. In January 1864 the president dispatched his private
secretary, John Hay, to confer with Butler at Point Lookout, Maryland.
Ostensibly interested in gaining the release of political detainees in Butler's
realm, Hay really was sizing up Butler as a potential rival to his boss. On
that occasion and during a meeting three months later, Hay found the general to be shrewd, possessed of a facile mind, and conversant on many "queer
matters." Apparently he also viewed Butler as devious and mysterious
enough to be dangerous. Hay's initial report may have alarmed Lincoln, for
the president called Butler to the White House soon afterward for a series
of heavily political interviews. Though Lincoln heard repeated assertions
of support, he continued to fear a Butler candidacy.[20]

In March Lincoln determined to place Butler behind him by offering
him a position on the Republican ticket as successor to Vice President
Hannibal Hamlin. Political boss Alexander McClure believed that Lincoln
acted because although Butler "had not achieved great military success . . .
his administration in New Orleans had made him universally popular

throughout the North, in which the vindictive vituperation the Southern people heaped upon him was an important factor."[21]

Lincoln conveyed the offer through his former war secretary, Simon Cameron, who visited Fort Monroe shortly before the spring 1864 offensive got under way. The vice presidential bid came wrapped in florid praise, but the general wasted no time in rejecting it. While Butler appreciated "this act of friendship and the compliment" thus paid him, "with the prospects of the campaign, I would not quit the field to be Vice-President . . . unless he [Lincoln] will give me bond with sureties, in the full sum of his four years' salary, that he will die or resign within three months after his inauguration." While he spoke facetiously, Butler was adamant in his refusal: "Tell the President I will do everything I can to aid in his election if nominated" but in a military capacity only.[22]

There the matter rested, though Butler maintained contact with Lincoln, in person and through Colonel Shaffer and other emissaries. The nature of the business discussed at these meetings remains unknown, but the pair may have reached an accommodation. Butler agreed to support Lincoln in public and to do nothing to hinder his renomination. In turn, the president upheld Butler's departmental rule, however controversial his policies. At one point the clamoring of Governor Peirpoint and other critics prompted Butler to seek Lincoln's written support. The president responded with a declaration that "Genl Butler has my confidence in his ability and fidelity to the country and to me and I wish him sustained in all efforts in our great common cause."[23]

Butler displayed his gratitude and loyalty by rejecting a vice presidential offer from Lincoln's Treasury secretary, Salmon P. Chase. A contentious Ohioan whose political ambition dwarfed even Butler's, Chase did not hesitate to use the influence of his office to further his candidacy. Though impressed by Chase's talents at self-promotion, Butler doubted his ability to gain the Republican nomination. Thus, when one of Chase's people visited Fort Monroe and offered him the second spot on a Chase ticket, Butler not only demurred but opined that if he were Lincoln, he would fire the Treasury official. As he informed the emissary, "I am but forty-five years old; I am in command of a fine army; the closing campaign of the war is about beginning, and . . . I should not, at my time of life, wish to be Vice-President [even] if I had no other position."[24]

━━━━━◆━━━━━

Butler's prospects for a field campaign laden with political opportunities had been strengthened shortly before the Chase campaign came calling.

Lieutenant General Ulysses S. Grant. LIBRARY OF CONGRESS.

Originally, the department commander feared being shunted onto a side-track while Meade's army took the through route to glory. General Halleck had ignored hints from Butler that he needed reinforcements before active campaigning resumed. In the second week in March, however, Ulysses S. Grant arrived in Washington as general in chief. From the first Grant made it known that his plan included an offensive by an enlarged force in Butler's area.

The news came sweetly to Butler's ear. By now Butler had decided that his prospects depended on the once-destitute drunkard who had become the most celebrated soldier in the Union. Believing Grant a political innocent, Butler resolved to guide him through the thicket of civil-military relations in a manner that would profit both of them. Despite the Illinoisan's celebrity, Butler was confident that given a little luck on the road to Richmond, he could win enough renown to compete successfully with Grant, the soldier.

Had Butler known the strategy Grant originally intended for the Virginia theater, he would not have welcomed his new superior so enthusiastically. In late January, while still in command of the Military Division of the Mississippi, Grant had suggested that the War Department abandon plans to take Richmond in favor of attacking coastal and inland strongholds in North Carolina. Though such a course appeared tailored to Butler's command, Grant believed that fully 60,000 troops should conduct it—a force that could have come only from Meade's army. Butler's involvement would have been limited to raiding railroads leading toward Raleigh.[25]

Fortunately for Butler's ambitions, this plan conflicted with political realities. Soon after Grant accepted command of all the armies, his civilian superiors impressed on him that a large advance south of Richmond would leave Washington vulnerable. At the government's urging, Grant revised his plan to emphasize the related objectives of protecting the capital, threatening Richmond, and overwhelming Lee.

On April 1, 1864, following a series of visits to Meade's army in middle Virginia, Grant called at Butler's headquarters. A fifteen-gun salute by shore batteries heralded his arrival at Fort Monroe. At their first meeting, guest and host scrutinized each other and for the most part liked what they saw. Grant's narrow military outlook confirmed Butler's hope that the commanding general would not vie with him for political power. Butler was also pleased to learn that his command would play an important part (though subsidiary to Meade's) in the coming campaign; moreover, he would be reinforced substantially. For his part, Grant was surprised by Butler's professional demeanor, his obvious efficiency as an administrator, and his apparently sincere desire to contribute to Grant's strategy.

Major General William Farrar Smith. U.S. ARMY MILITARY HISTORY INSTITUTE.

Before the generals got down to cases, Butler met Grant's retinue, which included his chief of staff, Major General John A. Rawlins; Elihu B. Washburne of Illinois, Grant's hometown congressman and political patron; and an officer who would soon become Butler's second in command, Major General William Farrar Smith.[26]

Butler was intrigued by Smith, with whose colorful and checkered career he was doubtless familiar. A fellow New Englander, the forty-year-old Smith had graduated from West Point, where prematurely thinning hair had given him the nickname "Baldy," though he remained more hirsute than many who addressed him that way. An exceptionally talented engineer, Smith had helped Grant restore supply lines to besieged Chattanooga, Tennessee, whose relief had sent his superior on his triumphal journey to Washington. Prior to his service in the Military Division of the Mississippi, however, Smith's once-promising career as a division and corps leader in the Army of the Potomac had collapsed. Unable to shake the chronic delusion that he was a genius surrounded by cretins, Smith had criticized his superiors and intrigued against them so shamelessly that he lost his field command early in 1863 and Congress had rejected his appointment to major general. Smith was not chastened. He stuck to an inflexible code of behavior, which he summarized in a letter to a colleague: "I hold it my duty as an honest public servant and an honorable man to denounce inability, inefficiency or a lack of virtue wherever . . . any of them may be injurious to the public service."[27]

Smith's teaming with Butler would have seemed a disaster in the making. By April 1864, however, Smith appeared to have learned the virtues of silence, patience, and cooperation. His low-key competence in Tennessee had won Grant's appreciation and regard; the future general in chief had written Edwin Stanton that Smith possessed "one of the clearest military heads in the Army. . . . No man in the service is better qualified than he for our largest command." Such an endorsement had restored Smith's second star and apparently his field career as well. Grant had brought Smith east to take an important position under Meade, only to discover that Smith's old associates in the Army of the Potomac had neither forgotten nor forgiven his indiscretions. Unwilling to make enemies in an army he would accompany in the field, Grant determined to find Smith another command in Virginia. His presence at Grant's side at Fort Monroe indicated which way the commanding general was looking.[28]

Butler wished to make the best impossible impression on his new superior; thus, he quickly agreed to Grant's wish that he take on Smith as his senior subordinate. Butler's plan to assign Smith to command the XVIII

Corps was one reason Grant decided he could get along with Butler, which was not the attitude he had expressed before leaving Tennessee. Though Grant had originally questioned the advisability of giving a nonprofessional soldier a large field command, he had bowed to the wishes of Lincoln and Stanton. The political realities troubled Grant, but he was reassured by the knowledge that a West Pointer of great competence (perhaps brilliance) would serve at Butler's right hand.

During their April 1 meeting, Grant touched lightly on the issue of grand strategy; he had yet to flesh out the role Butler would play. Instead, Grant got to know the lord of Fort Monroe and his commanders and satisfied himself that these men—so few of whom had military training or experience—could handle the task ahead.

Following a sumptuous dinner, cigars, and brandy, Grant prepared to leave; he would describe his strategy on a return visit. Suddenly, a gale blew into Hampton Roads, delaying his departure for twenty-four hours. The extended stay had fateful repercussions for the coming campaign, for early the next day Butler put before his guest some strategic ideas of his own as well as recommendations for implementing them.[29]

Butler represented himself as the sole author of these plans. In reality, they were heavily based on unsolicited suggestions made six weeks before by Major General Samuel P. Heintzelman, a former corps commander in the Army of the Potomac now confined to a desk in the Department of the Northwest. Heintzelman's plan may have had antecedents of its own, for proposals similar to his had appeared anonymously in the widely read *Army and Navy Journal*.[30]

Whatever their origin, the various plans coincided in their overall objective—the dispatching of a sizable expedition from Fort Monroe up the James River to Richmond. A swift movement along that route would lessen the possibility that troops from Lee's army or the Carolinas would reinforce the capital before the invaders could strike it from the rear. Under the portection of gunboats, troops would debark on the south side of the James near the Appomattox River, within easy marching distance of Richmond. Landing parties would seize bridges from the south, dooming Richmond to a sudden strike or, should obstacles arise, to a slow death by siege.

Butler and his strategists counted on light resistance by those Confederates able to challenge the move. Richmond was defended by a few thousand heavy artillerists, a scattering of infantry and cavalry units, and militia and home guards, all soon to be commanded by General Elzey's successor, Major General Robert Ransom, Jr. Fairly close by were the 13,500 troops of General Pickett, guarding southside Virginia and sections of North Carolina. Farther off were thousands of other Confederates under General Pierre G. T. Beauregard, hero of Fort Sumter and First Manassas. Having fallen from favor with Jefferson Davis and other political officials, Beauregard now commanded the backwater known as the Department of South Carolina, Georgia, and Florida. If approached stealthily but rapidly, Richmond would lack the time to gather supports from Pickett or Beauregard.[31]

In promoting his plan to Grant, Butler displayed an unexpected grasp of logistical and tactical detail. He proposed to land most of his expeditionary force at Bermuda Hundred, a peninsula enclosed on the east and north by the James and on the south by the Appomattox, fourteen miles below Richmond. At Bermuda Hundred as well as on the other side of the

General Pierre Gustave Toutant Beauregard. NATIONAL ARCHIVES.

Appomattox at the steamboat landing known as City Point, Butler intended to secure a base before launching an overland movement against Richmond via Drewry's Bluff. The proposed route marked a departure from Heintzelman's concept, which called for an amphibious landing five miles nearer the capital. Doubtless Butler knew that the enemy had strewn the upper reaches of the James with battery-activated torpedoes, pilings, and other obstacles. Butler knew little, however, of the difficulties of moving up the James against heavy works and heavy guns—difficulties that Heintzelman had foreseen.

Baldy Smith was not at the April 2 meeting, but the previous evening Butler had disclosed to him the proposal he would lay before Grant. Having only recently met Butler, Smith hesitated to criticize the plan, though he later admitted to having serious misgivings about it. Soon "it was manifestly too late . . . for me to criticize it, and remain in the confidence of Genl Butler."[32]

Smith's principal concern was Butler's intention to advance on Richmond without first neutralizing the outposts along the North Carolina line. Smith, who had initiated Grant's plan to operate around Raleigh, believed that no invasion could succeed unless it included at least a strike against Pickett's headquarters in Petersburg, twenty-two miles south of the capital, to block any Rebels en route from the Carolinas. Smith's chagrin increased when Grant, who appeared to be impressed by Butler's strategy, substantially approved it without consulting Smith.

The spires of Petersburg, Virginia. NATIONAL ARCHIVES.

The commanding general did tinker a bit with the plan. Later that day, when he put his thoughts on paper for Butler's behalf, Grant made no mention of Bermuda Hundred, though he did endorse the idea of entrenching at City Point. Smith believed that by instructing Butler to dig in on the south side of the Appomattox, Grant intended that Petersburg, not Richmond, should be his initial objective. Later, however, Butler claimed that his superior had accepted the need to debark on the north side of the Appomattox with a view to an early advance on Richmond. Smith was forced to agree; as he wrote years later, Butler interpreted Grant's directions "as indorsing his plan entirely, and so I thought and still think from the text of them."[33]

Grant's written guidance was broad and rather vague; he believed that the tactical details could not be fixed "at this time." Still, the outline was set: Butler should move against Richmond as soon as he secured a base of operations, "holding close to the south bank of the James River as you advance." Based on what he could learn of Meade's operations, Butler should coordinate his movements with those of the Army of the Potomac. If unable to seize Richmond outright, he was to besiege the city until Meade could come down from the north, driving Lee's army before it. At that point, Meade's and Butler's troops "would become a unit."[34]

Although Smith considered Grant's instructions to Butler seriously flawed, it is possible that he failed to understand Grant's intentions. General Rawlins, Grant's closest confidant, believed that the commanding general wanted it that way. Two weeks after the Fort Monroe conference, Rawlins wrote his wife that neither Smith nor anyone else was privy to the extent of Grant's thinking as it involved Meade's and Butler's forces. Thus, it is not surprising that Butler, Smith, and others later offered diverse interpretations of what Grant intended to accomplish at the outset of the campaign in Virginia.[35]

In the month following his visit to Hampton Roads, Grant elaborated on the instructions he had given Butler. On April 16 he wrote to allay Butler's concern over a rumor that his army would operate simultaneously against Richmond and Petersburg. The rumor may have originated with Smith, who preferred a dual line of operations in southeastern Virginia. Grant assured Butler, "You were entirely right in saying there should be but one movement made south of the James River. At no time has more been intended."[36]

In the same communiqué Grant offered specific suggestions as to how Butler might advance from City Point. He recommended that a cavalry force be sent down the railroads from Richmond to a point near the North Carolina line. This movement would draw enemy attention well south of the capital and, if the troopers damaged enough track, would stanch the flow of reinforcements from Beauregard. Grant also suggested that Butler begin collecting in Hampton Roads the transports he would need, doing so in increments to avoid alerting Rebel signalmen. Butler should also solidify his relationship with Admiral Lee to ensure the navy's cooperation.

The starting date remained undefined. On April 18 Grant informed Butler, "At present the roads are in such condition that the time could not be fixed earlier than the 27th." Even so, Butler should start from Fort Monroe as soon as he learned that Meade was crossing the Rapidan River above Lee's winter quarters near Orange Court House. Grant still hoped to create a single siege force around Richmond, Meade's right flank to connect with Butler's left "as far up the south side of the [James] river as . . . possible." He urged Butler to launch vigorous attacks against the capital "if you hear of our advancing" from the north "or have reason to judge from the action of the enemy that they are looking for danger to that side."[37]

Coupled with Grant's earlier instructions, these orders impressed forcefully on Butler the need to conform his operations to Meade's. This impression had an undesirable side effect: Butler came to believe that his movements were to be governed by Meade's. The undefined nature of Butler's venture with the Army of the Potomac—coupled with a lingering ambiguity concerning whether both Richmond and Petersburg, or Richmond alone, constituted Butler's objective—would complicate Union operations in a way neither general could have foreseen.

While attempting to refine his plans for the Army of the James, Grant strove to fulfill his pledge to provide Butler with more troops and capable leadership. To help fill vacancies in the XVIII Corps, Grant sent two infantry commanders and a cavalry leader. Brigadier General William T. H. Brooks, a forty-three-year-old West Pointer and a veteran of the Seminole and Mexican Wars, had built a commendable record in the Army of the Potomac; one of his former soldiers called him "as modest and devoid of self-seeking as he was conspicuous for skill and personal bravery in action." Glad to have him, Butler gave Brooks command of Smith's 2nd Division. The department commander was also enthusiastic about the addition of Brigadier General Hiram Burnham, a forty-year-old volunteer officer. He was a lumberman from Maine who had served capably in regimental and brigade command on many fields, most notably at Antietam. Burnham would prove to be one of Brooks's most dependable subordinates.[38]

The reputations of Brooks and Burnham had preceded them, but Butler knew little about the cavalryman, Brigadier General August Valentine Kautz, who had served mainly in the western theater and thereafter in the War Department. The thirty-six-year-old Ohioan had graduated near the bottom of his West Point class but had served honorably in the prewar dragoons and in 1863 had helped capture the Confederate raider John Hunt Morgan. Butler had made no effort to recruit Kautz; instead, he had lobbied for the services of Kautz's boss in the Cavalry Bureau, Brigadier General James Harrison Wilson. Grant, however, had promised Wilson, one of his Illinois protégés, a more prestigious command under Meade. In accepting Kautz Butler was definitely settling for second best, for the Ohioan was something of a plodder, effective only when closely supervised. Moreover, he was affected by seizures of malaria, which often left him groggy, disoriented, and sometimes incapacitated. Knowing nothing of Kautz's infirmities, Butler named him, as senior cavalry officer, commander of the department's mounted division, initially with four regiments.[39]

August V. Kautz.

On his own Butler secured the talents of Brigadier Generals Israel Vogdes and Godfrey Weitzel. Vogdes, a West Pointer and Mexican War veteran, had served in Florida and South Carolina. At best, he was a mediocre field commander but was, like Butler, an excellent organizer and administrator, and that was how his new commander intended to employ him. Weitzel was marked for a combat command. Having graduated from West Point second in the Class of 1855, the young officer had been a favorite of Butler's since the New Orleans expedition, on which he had served as chief engineer. In August 1862 Butler had been responsible for Weitzel's almost unprecedented leap from first lieutenant in the Regulars to a brigadier general of volunteers and brigade commander in the Army of the Gulf. Weitzel had remained in Louisiana after his patron's ouster, serving under Major General Nathaniel Banks in the Port Hudson Campaign and during the subsequent expedition to Sabine Pass. Although Weitzel had demonstrated only moderate competence in the field, Butler was determined to give him another chance at the head of a brigade or division.[40]

None of the new commanders brought troops with them. This was unfortunate, for Butler's command, which was critical to Grant's strategy, lacked the numbers to ensure success on the road to Richmond. In mid-April Grant transferred 10,000 members of the X Corps, then operating along the South Carolina coast, to Butler's department. Butler received the news

Major General Benjamin F. Butler (seated, left of center) and staff, including Brigadier General Godfrey Weitzel (seated, right of center). U.S. ARMY MILITARY HISTORY INSTITUTE.

enthusiastically, though he knew that the corps, under Major General Quincy
Adams Gillmore, had failed in its months-long mission to overcome the
Charleston defenses. Butler also realized that malaria and other lowland
maladies had taken a toll on the command. Still, he hoped that treated to
a new venue and a new departmental commander, Gillmore's people would
campaign more successfully.

Toward the close of April, only two weeks before Butler's offensive began,
the advance elements of Gillmore's command reached Hampton Roads.
Butler encamped the troops across the York River at Gloucester Point,
where Vogdes reorganized and outfitted them for the field. Most of the
corps and its commander were slow to reach Virginia, denying Butler an
opportunity to confirm Grant's assurances that the newcomers were worthy
additions to his department.[41]

In fact, the general in chief's evaluation had been faulty: neither Gillmore
nor his officers and men were close to peak operating condition. Along with
thousands of wounded and sick men, the corps had lost its morale on the
beaches outside Charleston as well as the confidence it once had in its commander. A year earlier, the forty-year-old Gillmore, a West Pointer, learned
engineer, and field officer of some promise, had enjoyed almost universal
trust and admiration. Since then, he had fallen so far in his troops' estimation,
largely from tactical miscalculations,
that some of his closest subordinates
scorned him.

Failure and frustration had in-
fected Gillmore with a moody aloof-
ness that repelled all about him. A
sensitive person, he agonized over the
thousands of lives that had been lost
in a campaign doomed from the outset. He blamed his civilian superiors,
whom he believed had forced upon
him an ill-considered offensive policy.
He was determined never again to
sacrifice his men to the vagaries of
War Department strategy.[42]

As much unaware of the X
Corps' limitations as he was of the
shortcomings of some of his new
subordinates, Butler immersed himself in preparations to leave Fort

Major General Quincy Adams Gillmore.
U.S. ARMY MILITARY HISTORY INSTITUTE.

Monroe for his first field campaign in a year and a half. As May brought better weather, he contemplated sweeping down on an unsuspecting enemy and dealing decisive blows to the nerve center of the Confederacy.

While Butler reveled in this vision, supporters throughout the Union were poised to wave his standard. One of his agents in Washington wrote to assure him that the Lincoln administration felt "more uneasy about your hold upon the hearts of the people than of aught else." The informant said it had become difficult to suppress public demonstrations in support of a Butler presidency: "We do not hesitate to avow our preference, and distinctly affirm that when the time comes we are more than ready to act."[43]

Butler could take pleasure in such assurances because, at last, he had the muscle to realize his dream of military glory and high office. He had begun his stint at Fort Monroe in command of a vast department dotted with minuscule outposts. Now, less than five months later, he commanded nearly 40,000 veterans whose strength and sense of purpose promised to make the next campaign the last.

CHAPTER THREE

Anatomy of an Army

THE ARMY OF THE JAMES WAS THE QUINTESSENTIAL YANKEE COMMAND. Among all Union armies, it boasted the highest percentage of units recruited in New England. That region, plus New York, Pennsylvania, and New Jersey, provided over 60 percent of the army's manpower. In contrast to the Army of the Potomac, many of whose troops hailed from the big city, the Army of the James drew largely from the towns, villages, and small cities of the Northeast. Conversely, Butler's command contained the fewest regiments raised in the Old Northwest. Four of the 146 regiments and batteries that served, at one time or another, in the Army of the James were raised in Ohio, two each in Illinois and Wisconsin, and one in Indiana. Most of these did not join the command until the winter of 1864–65, in time to participate in only one campaign.

More than any other Federal army, the Army of the James was a bastion of Republican and Union Party sentiment. While Lincoln enjoyed the support of most troops in every Union command, he had a special confidence in voters in Butler's force. When the 1864 presidential contest heated up, Stanton confided to one of Butler's staff officers that although Lincoln was not so confident about Meade's army, he had no doubt as to the loyalty of the Army of the James. The president's faith was not misplaced; support for Lincoln and his running mate, Governor Andrew Johnson of Tennessee, exceeded 90 percent in many of the regiments that voted in the field.[1]

The politics of the Army of the James were apparent in the large number of commanders with Union Party connections or loyalties. As the most prominent politician in uniform, Butler went out of his way to fill his ranks with prewar officeholders, editors of partisan newspapers, and political hangers-on. Of course, politics dominated every Union fighting force; each had to answer continually to political influences. Even so, the Army of the James appears unique in the richness of its political coloration. Butler was far from the only officer in the army who hoped to trade military success for political gain. Many seemed to spend as much time vying for power as they did fighting the Confederacy.

Partially because of its political roots, the Army of the James was a true citizen army over which trained soldiers exercised limited influence. For every West Pointer like Smith, Gillmore, and Kautz, the army boasted dozens of high-ranking officers with little or no experience. Not only did it feature the fewest trained soldiers of any Civil War army of its size or smaller, it contained the fewest Regular Army units: eight batteries of light artillery, no artillery or cavalry regiments. The lack of trained leadership and the fact that many of the units had not been part of a cohesive command posed organizational and operational problems. On the other hand, given the preponderance of regiments raised in the Northeast and the high percentage of native-born soldiers, the Army of the James appears to have been unusually homogeneous.

Despite the aura of unity, the army's components had distinct personalities. These differences were never more apparent than at the corps level. The men of the X and XVIII Corps brought unique identities to the Army of the James that remained largely intact throughout its existence.

The older organization by nearly four months—established on September 3, 1862, from forces in the Department of the South—the X Corps brought Butler a heritage of tribulation. Its people had undergone some of the bloodiest, most difficult service of the war during their eighteen months in South Carolina. The corps had endured numerous amphibious operations as well as the seemingly interminable siege of Charleston. A few of its components had also participated in an equally frustrating and fruitless incursion into northeastern Florida.[2]

More than common adversity bonded the members of the X Corps. To an even greater extent than their new comrades in the XVIII Corps, they shared a regional background: nearly 80 percent of the corps hailed from New York and New England. The troops were also linked by a maritime heritage few of them treasured. After the war one of their officers remarked, "The only objection we had to that corps was, that it went to sea too much. . . . Sometimes we used to wish we had gone into the navy instead of the army, so that we could stay more on shore." Yet another shared influence was frail health. Due mainly to its service on the water and along the marshy lowlands of South Carolina, the corps wore a feverish look, even if, as one observer commented, many of its men appeared "brown as Bedouins from exposure to a Southern sun." One of Grant's aides stated, "I have seen that entire corps unwell," the result of typhoid, malaria, fevers, sunstroke, and other maladies that produced long sick lists and frequent burials devastating to survivors as well as to victims.[3]

The mental health of the corps had also suffered from the lopsided battles and long-shot assaults to which Gillmore had committed it. His efforts to capture Morris Island below Charleston, to overwhelm Battery Wagner at the island's northern tip, and to reduce Fort Sumter in Charleston Harbor involved offensives against well-defended positions. The attacks against Battery Wagner on July 11 and 18, 1863, had taken an especially heavy toll—almost 20 percent of the command's strength. By early 1864 several regiments, notably the 48th New York and the 6th Connecticut, had been whittled down to company size.

In February Gillmore had sought a more promising arena by transferring 6,000 troops to Jacksonville, Florida, to seize Rebel supplies, liberate and enlist slaves, and strengthen Unionist enclaves. Expecting to enjoy an unobstructed passage along the Florida, Atlantic & Gulf Railroad, five Union brigades were halted by far fewer defenders near Olustee Station and Ocean Pond. In a day of bitter fighting, the Confederates inflicted nearly 2,000 casualties and routed the survivors.

The X Corps' service at Charleston and in Florida earned it a dubious reputation. When it reached Virginia, its new comrades greeted it warily, suspecting that the command would prove effective only at siege warfare. Observers began to refer to entrenching tools as "Gillmore's rifles" and to jest that "spades were trumps in the hands of the veterans from Morris Island."[4]

The men of the X Corps insisted that they had done more fighting than most of the Virginia-based soldiers who derided their lack of conventional field experience. A member of Grant's staff who had served in the corps informed the commanding general early in 1864 that "the Tenth Corps knows nothing of war but attacking fortifications, and that is what they have been doing now for years." Shortly before leaving Charleston, a semiliterate veteran of the 76th Pennsylvania complained that "we must . . . take them [the Confederates] by the Point of our Beyonets and charge them from behind Batteries, their entrenchments and their fortifications and their is where we loose our Most Men."[5]

If the troops of the X Corps were unified by hardship and defeat, the XVIII Corps remained an aggregation of disparate elements. Composed largely of garrison and outpost units never grouped under one leader, the command lacked a corporate identity. Its men included veterans of McClellan's shambling advance on Richmond, former members of Major General Ambrose E. Burnside's North Carolina coastal division, and troops that had braved the spring 1863 siege of Suffolk. More than a score of its regiments had never smelled battle smoke; others had not campaigned actively for well over a year.

Like the X Corps, the XVIII had a history of poor health. Those units that garrisoned the peninsula had been ravaged by respiratory diseases. In Isaac Wistar's district alone, the winter of 1863–64 produced three acres of soldiers' graves. The men had been rendered so susceptible to certain illnesses that quinine had become their daily ration.[6]

Another factor that sapped the fighting strength of the XVIII Corps was an abundance of soldiers who would fight only under duress, if at all. Especially among its New England regiments, unit effectiveness was compromised by the many men dragooned into service by unscrupulous agents employed by states anxious to enlist enough volunteers that they would not have to submit to federal conscription. Many of these unfortunates were recent immigrants, "mostly speaking foreign languages," who had been "drugged and kidnapped . . . then heavily ironed [shackled], confined in boxcars, and shipped like cattle" to designated regiments. Wistar, whose district contained hundreds of unwilling recruits, noted that in one New Hampshire regiment alone, eighty men deserted during their first night in Virginia. Other XVIII Corps outfits were found to contain an even less desirable brand of recruits. In the course of a few weeks, a couple hundred "bounty jumpers" deserted and returned north to enlist in distant cities under assumed names and collect additional money.[7]

If many of the white troops were unreliable, the army's contingent of black troops, untested in battle, did not inspire widespread confidence. To many of their white comrades, the blacks were an unamusing novelty, a social experiment gone too far, and a source of unease and concern. Many were liberated and runaway slaves, used to lives of docility and subservience. Could they display the martial skill, the initiative, the fidelity of whites? In the spring of 1864 most whites thought not.

Composed as it was of infantry regiments that had long been fragmented into small detachments, the XVIII Corps had little familiarity with or trust in its generals. Baldy Smith had not served in the command before his assignment to lead it. Many of his subordinates, including Generals Kautz, Brooks, Burnham, and Weitzel, were veterans of other armies and distant theaters; their names evoked little recognition in the corps. Other generals previously associated with the corps, including Wistar and Wild, had not seen field service in months.

The cavalry and artillery units of the Army of the James were of uneven quality. During its early stages, Kautz's command won praise from newspaper reporters as a "magnificent division of cavalry" and Kautz himself as a "terror to the rebels." Military observers were less flattering. James H. Wilson called Kautz's troopers "the wildest rag-tag and bob-tail cavalry I ever saw." Colonel Edward H. Ripley of the XVIII Corps complained of "this villainous Cavalry of Kautz's Division which has been so blowed about and exalted to the skies by toadying reporters" but that appeared more effective at looting than fighting. Even Butler, who defended the cavalry against all critics, privately acknowledged its low caliber.[8]

Part of the cavalry's problem was its strength: Kautz's command was too small to generate staying power against opponents either mounted or afoot. Whereas the Army of the Potomac maintained a suitable number of troopers— about 15 percent of its total force—Kautz's command amounted to only 8 percent of Butler's army. This limitation was only partially offset by the modern, effective firearms the regiments wielded: the 3rd New York and 5th Pennsylvania were armed with Spencer repeating carbines and the 1st District of Columbia Cavalry with Henry repeating rifles.

Butler continually sought to upgrade his mounted arm, but despite his influence with the War Department, the Army of the Potomac got top priority in the allocation of remounts and horse equipment throughout 1864. Only toward the close of his tenure could Butler secure enough additional troopers for a third brigade. The aggregate force was still so small that during the Appomattox Campaign, when Butler's command was absorbed into the Army of the Potomac, the Army of the James's horsemen were reduced to the status of a brigade. Not until that final offensive of the war did the cavalry of the Army of the James acquire a leader, Brigadier General Ranald S. Mackenzie, who knew how to exploit his command's potential.[9]

The strongest link in the army's body armor was its artillery. Provided with a nucleus of experience by its several Regular batteries, that arm also boasted the 1st Connecticut Heavy Artillery, the largest and most effective siege train in any army. Butler's command benefited from the talents of several outstanding artillerists, including Lieutenant Colonel Richard H. Jackson, longtime artillery chief of the X Corps, and Colonels Henry S. Burton and Alexander Piper of the XVIII Corps. Another effective cannoneer—when sober—was Lieutenant Colonel Freeman McGilvery, Jackson's immediate predecessor, who met an early death, apparently from cirrhosis of the liver, in the summer of 1864. Another cannoneer with a drinking problem was Captain Samuel S. Elder of the 1st U.S. Artillery. In June 1864, while temporarily commanding the batteries of the XVIII Corps, Elder became so drunk that he rode by mistake into the Confederate lines outside Petersburg. He spent several months as a prisoner of war, certainly a sobering experience.[10]

⬩➤◉◄⬩

Benjamin F. Butler was an equal-opportunity commander. He had made his legal and political reputation as a champion of the underclass, especially Irish and German immigrants. He carried into the service his credo that ethnic groups deserved an even chance to prosper in their new land. It is probably no coincidence, then, that the Army of the James contained thousands of recent arrivals and second-generation Americans. All found Butler an unfailing source of support and solicitude.

Several regiments had strong ethnic identities. Native-born Irishmen and Americans of Irish ancestry were heavily represented in several New York, Pennsylvania, and Massachusetts outfits as well as in the 3rd and 10th New Hampshire Infantry, the 23rd Illinois, and the 3rd Rhode Island Artillery. German-Americans predominated in several infantry outfits including the 41st, 52nd, and 103rd New York, the 9th New Jersey, the 39th Illinois, and the 67th Ohio, as well as the 5th Pennsylvania Cavalry. The last-named regiment, which contained many emigrant Jews, was the first military unit in U.S. history with a rabbi as its chaplain. In contrast to the Irish volunteers, most of whom entered the army from civilian life, numerous German recruits had been professional soldiers in their native land. The 41st New York boasted 23 officers and nearly 700 enlisted men who had served in the Prussian ranks.[11]

Still, not too much should be made of the ethnic composition of the Army of the James. Although Butler promoted the careers of foreign-born officers and men and ensured that no minority group was discriminated against, his command drew its identity from the native-born Americans of Anglo-Saxon descent who predominated in its ranks. Certainly the army's ethnic roots were less extensive than those of the Army of the Potomac and other commands that drew more heavily from the big cities of the North, havens to immigrants.

On the other hand, minority representation gave the Army of the James one of its most visible distinctions. No other Union command contained as many regiments of African-Americans or gave them so much attention, care, and support. An advocate of recruiting freedmen since his early days in New Orleans, Butler devoted his career in Virginia to the belief that a black soldier—properly armed, clothed, fed, trained, and led—was in every sense the equal of a white man in uniform.[12]

Company E, 4th U.S. Colored Troops, Army of the James. U.S. ARMY MILITARY HISTORY INSTITUTE.

In contrast to other army leaders, Butler assigned his black troops major responsibilities—spearheading assaults, holding front-line positions, and defending the army's most vulnerable sectors. He provided them with the best available rations and materiel; he maintained regiments of black cavalry and recruited black cannoneers despite War Department disapproval; and he devoted time and energy to maintaining the spirits of black units. His efforts to strengthen morale ranged from designing medals commemorating black troops' heroism to providing for their dependents through the army's Office of Negro Affairs.

No fewer than thirty-five units of African-Americans served in Butler's army—twenty-six of them additions to its initial contingent, secured through Butler's personal efforts. But the army leader's commitment to black troops went further. From departmental funds he paid a small but much-appreciated bounty to each recruit despite the government's aversion to awarding enlistment money to nonwhites. He crusaded for the equalization of pay between white and black troops, which became Federal law in mid-1864 as much because of his exertions as anyone's. He publicly vowed that "every enlisted colored man shall have the same uniform, clothing, arms, equipments, camp equipage, rations, medical and hospital treatment, as are furnished to the United States soldiers of a like arm of the service." Furthermore, he established a system to register and rectify blacks' grievances.[13]

Butler was careful to secure the best available officers—whites as mandated by Federal law—for his black troops. He urged promising subalterns and enlisted men who had demonstrated leadership in white regiments to accept commissions in the U.S. Colored Troops (USCT). He also was quick to discard officers whom he regarded as incompetent, lax, or lazy. Butler came down especially hard on alcoholics, declaring that "drunken officers are the curse of our Colored soldiers and I will reform it in this Department . . . in spite of . . . the Devil." In his eyes only a cruel or malicious officer was more reprehensible; such men he cashiered or disciplined harshly. Officers in any unit who disparaged or ridiculed black soldiers he tongue-lashed and barred from promotion. To counter the racial prejudice officers and men in black regiments experienced from some superiors, Butler decreed that Colored Troops could be court-martialed only when the tribunal consisted predominately of USCT officers.[14]

Butler was preoccupied with the physical, intellectual, and moral condition of his "sable arm." He kept fast to his pledge to provide black soldiers with medical and surgical care on a par with that furnished to white troops, and he certified that inspectors-general and regimental commanders promoted hygiene and sanitary conditions in their camps. A welfare worker who in mid-1864 visited the Balfour Military Hospital at Portsmouth raved about the "excellent care the colored soldiers received. . . . I have seen in no hospital such genuine, direct, and gracious courtesy as the hired nurses in the Balfour show to their colored patients." As a result, Butler declared, "the negro soldiers in this department are by far the healthiest troops I have. . . . the sick are not one & a half percent [of the USCT force]."[15]

Aware that ignorance and illiteracy hinder military proficiency, Butler cooperated with missionaries and relief workers to educate ex-slaves in uniform. With his moral and material support, the U.S. Christian Commission established camp schools for all who wished, when off duty, to better their lot. By early 1865 every black regiment had a schoolhouse. One regimental officer remarked after the war:

The men came to us ignorant of books, ignorant in manners, and with little knowledge of and less interest in anything outside their own little plantation world. Few could read—none scarcely could write their names. When the regiment was disbanded nearly all could read; a large percentage could write fairly, and many had acquired considerable knowledge. . . . What was of even greater importance, they had learned self-reliance and self-respect, and went back to their homes with views enlarged, sympathies quickened, and their interest in the outside world thoroughly awakened.[16]

Most of those who schooled the black soldiers were dedicated to their calling. One civilian declared that she could "devote my whole time in giving them spelling and reading lessons." Applauding this selfless commitment, Butler fed the teachers from his commissary and allowed them to requisition materials and laborers to build schoolhouses. He also facilitated the shipments of primers, writing materials, chalkboards, and other supplies.[17]

Butler supported the spiritual role of the Christian Commission as well as that of the army's clergymen. He and many of his subordinates considered African-Americans innately religious as well as responsive to the evangelism of the day. At least one officer of black infantry noted the overflowing religious services conducted in his regiment. To care for so large a flock, Butler took steps to ensure that dedicated, energetic chaplains were appointed to black outfits. Shirkers were sternly admonished, often in orders sent throughout the command. They made it clear that clergymen in the Army of the James answered to more than one higher authority.[18]

Butler also strove to promote the welfare of black troops outside the range of his authority. Having gotten himself appointed commissioner for the exchange of prisoners in Virginia, he tried to persuade Confederate authorities to treat black prisoners of war on a par with captured whites. His most celebrated effort was his October 1864 retaliation for the enemy's decision to force captured black troops to build fortifications within range of Union artillery at Petersburg. Hours after confirming the POWs' plight, Butler put an equal number of Confederate prisoners to work on the Dutch Gap Canal, a James River excavation project under daily bombardment. Infuriated by this development, the Confederates agreed to release the blacks from labor if Butler removed the prisoners from Dutch Gap. The general complied, satisfied that he had forced the enemy into tacit admission of the racial equality of prisoners of war.[19]

Butler's efforts extended to black soldiers' families. He had eliminated the ghettos on the Virginia Peninsula, known collectively as "Slabtown." Later he publicly encouraged white troops to do all possible to assist fugitive slaves in reaching Union lines and in finding a place to live, whether or not the runaways were considered prospective recruits. Any soldier who obstructed, insulted, or abused fugitives was punished. Aid to dependents was not limited by the soldier's term of service; it continued after he was killed or disabled.

Butler prohibited recruiters for other commands from taking enlistees out of his department without providing for their wives and children left behind. He asked business acquaintances to provide factory jobs for indigent blacks, informing one New England industrialist that "although darker skinned they are quite as intelligent as the green Irish help which you take into your mills." In August 1864 he even paid to send 160 widows and orphans of black troops to New York, Philadelphia, and Boston, where benevolent societies promised them jobs and homes.[20]

Though ever eager to recruit, Butler worked hard to prevent brokers in his department from hiring black civilians to take the place of white draftees, a practice that paid the substitutes a pittance while netting the brokers exorbitant commissions. Butler also employed blacks who had no intention of entering the army. To skilled workmen suited to military construction, he paid as much as $16 per month plus a daily ration. Conversely, he banned idleness among civilians, declaring that "no subsistence will be permitted to any negro or his family, with whom he lives, who is able to work and does not. . . . Any negro who refuses to work when able, and neglects his family, will be arrested, and reported to these headquarters . . . where he will be made to work."[21]

Blacks in mufti enjoyed many of the same educational benefits available to those in uniform. At Butler's urging, the Freedmen's Aid Society, the Christian Commission, and other welfare agencies established school-building programs throughout his department. Here, too, Butler tried to persuade Northern friends to help, even requesting his old school district in Lowell to contribute discarded benches, desks, and other furnishings.[22]

Perhaps the most ambitious project designed to aid Colored Troops benefited their families as well: a freedmen's savings bank was established in Norfolk late in 1864, in which pay and bounties could be invested. Administered by an experienced financier well known to Butler, the bank proved an unqualified success. By war's close one black regiment alone had contributed $90,000 to the bank's assets. Although critics accused the institution of financial irregularities, government auditors found "all its transactions systematic and honest."[23]

Finally, Butler's Office of Negro Affairs, headed by one of his most trusted aides, Lieutenant Colonel J. Burnham Kinsman, oversaw the feeding, clothing, and housing of thousands of dependents. The office also employed black civilians at fair wages, regulated contracts between them and their white employers (usually local plantation owners of Unionist sympathy), allocated government land to tenants who paid one-quarter of their harvest as rent, and audited blacks' accounts against the government.[24]

Everything considered, Butler established an unprecedented paternalistic system. Although latter-day critics viewed him as an elitist dispensing gifts (and sometimes punishment) to social inferiors, his efforts on behalf of a disadvantaged minority were truly groundbreaking for his time. Perhaps only under the conditions of civil war could they have flourished. To a certain extent, his promotion of black troops stemmed from political expediency (such gain motivated Butler's every endeavor), but in championing the cause of black troops and their families, he went far beyond what was required to maintain his identity as a friend of the African-American. Though it is always difficult to distinguish between Butler the idealist and Butler the opportunist, the conclusion is inescapable that a humanitarian impulse animated him throughout his tenure in Virginia.

To be sure, Butler received a fair return on his investment in social engineering. Fair-minded observers acknowledged that Colored Troops carried their share of the burden in camp, on the siege lines, and on the battlefield. At the outset few of Butler's white soldiers would have predicted this outcome; many, if not most, considered it a dreadful mistake to place white men's lives in the hands of former chattels. One target of criticism was the blacks' dearth of schooling. Late in 1863 a New Hampshire infantryman remarked that Butler's black troops "are all escaped slaves and a poor miserable ignorant set. They are far inferior to the nigger of the North in intelligence."[25]

Other critics decried what they saw as Butler's politically motivated favoritism toward black troops. A disgusted officer from the commander's home state believed that "the 'nigger' in this dept is supreme & it is policy for those who desire to bask in the smiles of official favor to be its very devout worshippers. . . . The attempt to mix [African-Americans] up with white soldiers & people is productive of mischief. They are very arrogant & insolent presuming altogether too much on their social position." Some white soldiers regarded the blacks as pampered children exempt from the more onerous duties of army life. A Pennsylvanian selected for fatigue duty complained, "We as [white] soldiers have to do the work & the infurnel Blacks lying low in the shade . . . laugh at us working."[26]

Most white soldiers did not regard their African-American comrades as fighting men. Many agreed with Wistar's evaluation of Colored Troops as the playthings of radical politicians. These soldiers claimed to know that in combat blacks "will charge when highly excited, but will not hold what they take." Even those who meant to praise the endurance of black troops ascribed to them stereotypical characteristics. A veteran of the 13th New Hampshire, coming upon a field of battle, found "a number of dead negroes . . . lying about—and a dead negro is the most ghastly corpse ever seen; and their wounded are coming back in all sorts of ways, [shot] in legs, arms, heads and bodies, but hobbling along and bringing their guns with them. Negroes will keep on their feet, and move on with wounds that would utterly lay out white men."[27]

Some criticism came from the blacks' own officers. A few complaints had some basis in fact, such as the educational deficiencies that Butler was determined to overcome. The commander of the army's single battery of black artillerymen observed that it was "impossible to [teach] the gunners how to point a piece with even tolerable correctness, or to . . . cut fuzes or fit them correctly, as those who can count must do so, so slowly as to be too often incorrect."[28]

Other strictures reveal more about the critic than the criticized. The colonel of a black cavalry outfit complained that his men "lack pride, spirit and the intellectual energy of the whites." In his view, a black soldier "cannot stand up to adversity. A sick nigger, for instance, at once gives up and lies down to die, the personification of humanity reduced to a wet rag. He cannot fight for life like a white man." Whereas many observers including Butler considered blacks, especially ex-slaves, to be deferential and obedient, other officers viewed them as inherently rowdy and undisciplined as well as lacking in respect for authority. A few treated their men with outright contempt, refusing to take them seriously as fighting men. An officer in the 27th U.S. Colored Troops complained that the "Negro soldier [is] a perfect nuisance, a mere imitation of a soldier."[29]

Such officers appear to have been a minority. Most had faith in the rank and file; otherwise, they would not have opted for commissions in black units. By early 1864 they were aware that blacks had served well in other theaters for months. There appeared no reason to suspect that black troops in the Army of the James were inferior.

In fact, the average USCT officer found that his troops quickly learned military movements, imitated the bearing of experienced troops until proficient themselves, and adapted well to roughing it. They displayed other praiseworthy traits, too, as Colonel James Shaw, Jr., of the 7th U.S. Colored Troops was quick to point out. In two years of service Shaw claimed to have seen none of his soldiers drunk, to have heard only a handful use profanity, and to have witnessed one fight among them. Furthermore, "in drill I never saw their equal. They took pride in their work and their sense of [close-order] timing is perfect." Even the Massachusetts officer who blasted black troops as arrogant and insolent conceded that they "make good soldiers enough," and the cavalry colonel who had impugned their stamina concluded that "properly officered, [they] would I believe be as effective as any [troops] in the world."[30]

Few observers could question the commitment of the black soldiers in the Army of the James. The sergeant major of the 4th U.S. Colored Troops put it simply: "A double purpose induced me and most others to enlist, to assist in abolishing slavery and to save the country from ruin." Another noncommissioned officer, when asked if he had received a bounty for enlisting in the 36th U.S. Colored Troops, shook his head indignantly: "I wouldn't 'list for bounty. . . . I wouldn't fight for money; my wages is enough. . . . Them big-bounty men don't make good soldiers. . . . Dey comes in for money; dar's no Country 'bout it, an' dey hasn't no stomach for fightin' and diggin' and knockin' roun', like soldiers has to."[31]

A black enlisted man in the Balfour Hospital was heard to say of his amputated arm: "Oh I *should* like to have it [back], but I don't begrudge it." A second amputee exclaimed: "Well . . . 'twas [lost] in a glorious cause, and if I'd lost my life I should have been satisfied. I knew what I was fighting for."[32]

With the usual exceptions, their leaders were similarly idealistic. Only a commitment to racial equality could have nerved a man against what Ben Butler termed the "stupid, unreasoning, and quite vengeful prejudice" a USCT officer was likely to encounter. As General Wild remarked shortly before war's end, "I was one of the very earliest to start the raising of negro troops; and for more than two years I have been identified with their cause. On this account I have had nothing but prejudice, jealousy, misrepresentation, persecution and treachery to contend against."[33]

Some of those who persisted tried to explain why. Brigadier General William Birney, son of a prominent abolitionist, took satisfaction in battling "the preconceived idea on the part of many that a negro has no rights whatever, and that he and his family" should remain invisible members of society. A lieutenant in the 2nd U.S. Colored Cavalry believed that fighting for minority rights was "a glorious and ennobling" cause. And a lieutenant in the 5th U.S. Colored Troops declared, "I did not enter this service from any mercenary motive but to assist in removing the unreasonable prejudice against the colored race; and to contribute a share however small toward making the negro an effective instrument in crushing out this unholy rebellion."[34]

The lieutenant's wish was granted. From Fort Monroe to Appomattox the blacks of the Army of the James gave their full energy and endurance toward final victory. They left their dead on every field, often heroically; of the ninety Medal of Honor recipients in the army, nearly thirty hailed from USCT outfits. After one battle, Butler rode among rows of black corpses and wrote his wife that "the man who says the negro will not fight is a coward. . . . His soul is blacker than the dead faces of these dead negroes, upturned to heaven in solemn protest against him and his prejudice." To honor the sacrifice of these men and those who followed their example, Butler designed a medal, modeled on the Victoria Cross, that bore the legend

"U.S. Colored Troops . . . Distinguished for Courage, Campaign Before Richmond."[35]

By war's end, the black troops of the Army of the James could take satisfaction in having helped lower centuries-old barriers of prejudice and discrimination. In the only manner permitted them, they had proven themselves the equal of white men by proving themselves the equal of white soldiers.

Toward the end of April 1864, with active campaigning only weeks away, Butler restructured his command into the form it would take in the field. Stripping outpost garrisons to the minimum and calling in outlying detachments, he massed the XVIII Corps at and near Yorktown, where he organized it into divisions and brigades. Taking Grant's unsubtle cue, he conferred corps command on Baldy Smith, whose reputation for brilliance Butler was willing to concede and whose penchant for bashing superiors he was able to overlook.

Working closely with Smith on the selections, Butler had placed the first division of the corps under General Brooks; it consisted of the infantry brigades of General Marston (the 81st, 96th, 98th, and 139th New York), General Burnham (the 8th Connecticut, 10th and 13th New Hampshire, and 118th New York), and Colonel Horace T. Sanders of the 19th Wisconsin Infantry (made up of Sanders's outfit plus the 188th Pennsylvania). The 1st Division also included a light artillery brigade commanded by Major Theodore H. Schenck and composed of Batteries K and M, 3rd New York; Battery L, 4th United States; Battery A, 5th United States; and the 4th Wisconsin Artillery.

Although he was not entirely comfortable with Wistar, Butler conferred on him, in recognition of his seniority, command of Smith's 2nd Division. Wistar's force contained the brigade of General Heckman (the 9th New Jersey and the 23rd, 25th, and 27th Massachusetts) and that of the young and promising Colonel Griffin A. Stedman, Jr. (the 11th Connecticut, 2nd and 12th New Hampshire, and 148th New York). The 2nd Division also consisted of Captain Frederick M. Follett's brigade of artillery: the 7th New York Light Battery; Battery A, 1st Rhode Island; and Battery D, 4th United States.

Butler had designated his black soldiers as the 3rd Division, XVIII Corps. He tendered command of this force to thirty-three-year-old Brigadier General Edward W. Hinks, a former Massachusetts legislator who had demonstrated competence and gallantry on many fields despite health problems dating from his severe wounding at Antietam. Hinks's brigade leaders were General Wild, whom Butler had permitted to retake the field at the head of the 1st, 10th, and 22nd U.S. Colored Troops; and Colonel Duncan, who led the 4th, 5th, and 6th regiments. The black artillerists that Butler had struggled to organize and retain, Captain Francis C. Choate's Battery B, 2nd U.S. (Colored) Light Artillery, rounded out Hinks's command.[36]

Butler had grouped Kautz's cavalry at Getty's Station, outside Portsmouth. Minus detachments assigned to support the main army, the little division remained south of Hampton Roads until the spring offensive, when it rode up the railroad to Petersburg as Grant had recommended. The command consisted of two brigades, led by Simon Mix (the 3rd New York and 1st District of Columbia) and Samuel Spear (the 5th and 11th Pennsylvania). Kautz's force included a two-gun section of horse artillery from the 8th New York Battery, under Lieutenant Peter Morton.

In addition to this field force of 23,000, other troops assigned to the XVIII Corps remained on garrison and guard duty at various stations. These included Colonel Joseph Roberts's 3rd Pennsylvania Heavy Artillery, the host unit at Fort Monroe; Graham's Naval Brigade, now four companies strong, in Hampton Roads; two regiments of black infantry and detachments of white cavalry and foot troops under Shepley at Norfolk; and detachments of all arms at Portsmouth, nominally under Vogdes. Unbrigaded troops were stationed at Williamsburg, where West led three mounted regiments (two composed of blacks) and two batteries; at the fortified camp at Newport News (a single battery); at Eastville, Virginia (one cavalry company); and within the District of Saint Mary's (one white and one USCT infantry regiment, detachments of regular cavalry, and a battery, all under Draper). Rounding out Butler's department were "unattached troops," including Colonel Edward W. Serrell's 1st New York Engineers, perhaps the finest military construction unit on either side. In addition to this wealth of field and support troops, Butler continued to exercise remote control over the 8,000 troops in Peck's District of North Carolina, temporarily under Brigadier General Innis N. Palmer.[37]

When the advance contingent of the X Corps reached Hampton Roads in mid-April, Vogdes, working closely with Butler and Gillmore's staff, produced a field-ready organization of three divisions under Brigadier Generals Alfred H. Terry, John Wesley Turner, and Adelbert Ames. If the corps commander was a question mark, each of his ranking subordinates was a solid, dependable leader. The thirty-seven-year-old Terry, a Connecticut

Brigadier General Alfred H. Terry.
U.S. ARMY MILITARY HISTORY INSTITUTE.

Brigadier General John W. Turner.
U.S. ARMY MILITARY HISTORY INSTITUTE.

Brevet Major General Adelbert Ames.
U.S. ARMY MILITARY HISTORY INSTITUTE.

native and a law graduate of Yale University, was the preeminent member of the trio despite his lack of prewar military experience; from First Bull Run through the Charleston campaign he had maintained an unblemished record and the ability to impress observers within and outside the army. A *New York Times* reporter considered Terry "as affable, intelligent and polished as he [is] . . . distinguished in the art of war." A New Hampshire veteran characterized the division leader as "a general favorite, a very efficient officer" whose troops "would go wherever he said." Those troops included three brigades under Colonels Francis B. Pond (the 39th Illinois, 62nd and 67th Ohio, and 85th Pennsylvania), Harris M. Plaisted (10th Connecticut, 11th Maine, 24th Massachusetts, and 100th New York), and Joseph Hawley (the 7th Connecticut plus the 3rd and 7th New Hampshire). Terry's division was supported by the 1st Battery, Connecticut Light Artillery, and the 5th New Jersey Battery, grouped under Captain Alfred P. Rockwell.[38]

Turner's division was the weak link of its corps, though the fault was not its commander's. The thirty-one-year-old Turner, a West Pointer and veteran of service in such disparate venues as Kansas and Georgia, was a polished artilleryman and adroit infantry commander. The bravery of this multitalented officer was legend; one observer spoke for many others in calling Turner "the coolest officer I have ever seen under fire." His fearlessness inspired "the utmost confidence of his men." A modest and unassuming man, he had turned down a chance in early 1864 to serve in the more prestigious Army of the Potomac, insisting that "a mere puddle is big enough for me to wriggle in."[39]

While Turner inspired confidence, the same could not be said of his brigade commanders, both of whom would lose their jobs before midway through the coming campaign. Colonel Samuel M. Alford, who led the 40th Massachusetts and the 3rd, 89th, 117th, and 142nd New York, was a physical coward as well as an incompetent. The other ranking subordinate, Colonel William B. Barton, commander of the 47th, 48th, and 115th New York, was prone to lose his head. Turner could depend at least on Captain George T. Woodbury, who commanded the efficient 4th New Jersey Battery and Batteries B and D of the 1st U.S. Artillery.[40]

The commander of Gillmore's 3rd Division was another distinguished veteran of both infantry and artillery service. A West Pointer whose gallantry in command of a regular battery at First Bull Run brought him a Medal of Honor, Adelbert Ames subsequently whipped a rabble of Down-Easters into one of the finest volunteer infantry regiments of the war, the 20th Maine. A brigade leader since Fredericksburg and a division commander since Gettysburg, Ames was a dedicated martinet. His dour demeanor and volatile temper antagonized many of his troops, although one veteran found "no more efficient and gallant leader in the armies of the Union." Ames commanded two brigades, Colonel Richard White's 9th Maine, 4th New Hampshire, and 55th and 97th Pennsylvania; and Colonel Jeremiah C. Drake's 13th Indiana, 8th Maine, and 112th and 169th New York. The division also included two artillery units under Captain A. M. Wheeler: the 33rd New York Battery and Battery E of the 3rd United States.[41]

⇒∘◉◦⇐

Not until April 28 could Grant set a date for the start of active operations. "If no unforeseen accident prevents," he wrote Butler that day, "I will move from here [the Culpeper Court House vicinity] on Wednesday, the 4th of May." He urged Butler to depart Fort Monroe the previous evening, "so as to be as far up the James River as you can get by daylight [on] the morning of the 5th, and push from that time with all your might for the accomplishment of the object before you." Grant was to keep Butler informed, as much as possible, of the movements of the Army of the Potomac. Reports were to be relayed to the Army of the James via the long, winding telegraph circuit from Fort Monroe up the banks of the James. In turn, Butler was to keep the War Department "advised of every move of the enemy so far as you know them."[42]

The cooperative nature of the coming campaign, deceptively simple on the face of it, was complicated by Butler's and Meade's inability to obtain intelligence directly from each other's headquarters. Each commander learned of the other's progress belatedly, often by second- and thirdhand information derived from newspaper accounts, rumor, and speculation. Instead of facilitating cooperation, such communication confused and misled the commanders.

Once apprised of Grant's timetable, Butler attended to the duties involved in a change of base. Already choked with ships of all types, Hampton Roads received dozens of new arrivals every day—mostly transports ready to carry upriver thousands of troops, staff officers, signalmen, engineers, hospital crews, and other personnel. Regiments and brigades prepared to break camp at Yorktown, Gloucester Point, and elsewhere along the York River preparatory to the run to Fort Monroe. Teamsters carted ammunition and food, while stevedores hauled the cargo aboard ship. The brawniest deckhands loaded the more unwieldy items, including artillery pieces, pontoon trains, and baggage wagons.

Such activity might have harried many leaders, but not Ben Butler. On May 4 a *New York Herald* reporter observed the general at his desk: "If he feels the anxiety which only a general upon whom so great a responsibility rests can experience, his outward demeanor does not indicate it; for his countenance is as serene as if he were on the point of attending a festive party, instead of going to the scene of strife."[43]

Butler's composure reflected the confidence that his army was on the verge of accomplishing great deeds, of writing its own glorious history. Many of his troops appeared to share his view, sensing the approaching end to a long, bloody road. A cavalry captain wrote his father from Norfolk that how the army "can help going into Richmond . . . I cannot understand." Taking Meade's command into account, the officer declared that "numbers are in the Army now in Virginia such as have never been massed on this earth since Napoleon Bonaparte entered Russia." This allusion to a doomed campaign raised the remote possibility of defeat: "If we fail now we can scarcely hope to succeed except by a war so long it may bring us [to] exhaustion."[44]

Other soldiers anticipated disaster. A hospital steward commented, "We cannot tell what calamity may be in store. . . . I fear, however, that the bones of many of my companions will be left to bleach on the soil of Virginia." Equally pessimistic was Baldy Smith, who in letters to army friends feared that Grant's plan was defective, that Butler was not enough of a strategist to repair it, and that Butler's army was too small, too weak, too heterogeneous, and too poorly led to accomplish anything significant on the road to Richmond. Admittedly a worrier, Smith may have had good reason to shudder. Grant's strategy had its flaws, but an even greater problem was that Grant and Butler appeared unable to agree on what the plan called for.[45]

The question of Butler's primary mission was a case in point. Although Grant believed he had made clear that Richmond should be taken in one swift, decisive operation, Butler saw his initial objectives as securing a base between Richmond and Petersburg, fortifying both sides of the Appomattox, cutting the railroad to the capital, and thrashing any Confederates who tried to interfere. These chores attended to, the army would finally head north to confront the Richmond defenses.

Another misunderstanding concerned the cooperative nature of Grant's operations in Virginia. The commanding general expected Butler to take Richmond on his own while Meade battled Lee's army far above the city; only if Butler's attack failed would the armies join in besieging the capital. Butler, however, had come to view his army as one jaw of a pincers aimed at Richmond. In his memoirs he argued that "it was never contemplated by them [Grant's instructions] or by me, that any attack or assault should be made upon Richmond, except in cooperation with the Army of the Potomac." Though the Army of the James was to reach the capital well ahead of Meade, it was to make only a limited assault—a demonstration to determine the strength and positions of the defenders—until the Army of the Potomac arrived, driving Lee before it.[46]

Years later, Butler offered some dubious evidence to bolster his contention that his army was not to attack Richmond by itself. He declared that Grant had given the Army of the James a ten-day timetable in which to operate against the city. What appears to have happened is that while at Fort Monroe, Grant expressed doubt about Meade's ability to push Lee toward Richmond before May 15. This comment led Butler to assume that if he left Hampton Roads on the fourth or fifth, as Grant directed, he would have ten days in which to secure a base of operations at Bermuda Hundred and City Point, to operate against the railroad, and to prepare to march on Richmond. Although no objective observer ever corroborated Butler's claim of such a schedule, he either believed it to be the case at the time or later convinced himself of its actuality. There is some evidence that he mentioned the timetable to subordinates during the campaign, but he wrote about it only after the war and then solely to defend his course of action. Thus he may have invented the story to cover himself, something a man of his flexible integrity was not above doing.[47]

Baldy Smith's other concerns about the coming campaign had some validity as well. The Army of the James appeared to lack a solid leadership base. Many of its field officers had been in service for two years or more, but few had distinguished themselves. In several of the regiments that had seen hard service, by April 1864 the most competent officers had been lost to wounds, diseases, transfers, or other causes.

The most conspicuous deficiency in leadership was at the top. His field service dated to June 1861, but Butler remained a novice at warfare. To ease the potential for disaster from his inexperience, Grant had bracketed Butler with well-educated subordinates presumably capable of saving him from folly. Yet neither of Butler's senior lieutenants would prove worthy of Grant's faith. Smith and Gillmore were not selfless, cooperative types dedicated to teamwork. In fact, their temperaments and prejudices conspired against the cooperation Grant sought. Grant could not have known this, since the corps leaders had never served together or been subordinate to a political general. Not only did Smith and Gillmore fail to rise above their inherent disdain of Butler; they did not, in the end, trust each other. Although at the time he insisted otherwise, in his memoirs Smith stated that it was impossible for the two corps leaders, "with the best intentions, to work together—we did not belong to the same school [of thought]." This, Smith realized too late, made for "a very ill assorted team." Grant had belated regrets as well; in his own memoirs he second-guessed himself for not having assigned steady-going and highly competent veterans such as Terry or Mackenzie as Butler's ranking subordinates.[48]

Another valid concern of Baldy Smith was the caliber of the tactical units assigned to Butler. Implicitly at least, Grant had promised him the best forces available. Instead, Butler had acquired a corps, under Smith, whose members had not seen recent field service, and a corps, under Gillmore, that had been victimized by a debilitating, demoralizing campaign in the Deep South. Butler also had a meager, nondescript cavalry arm. Moreover, Butler had not been permitted enough time to integrate his troops into a cohesive command. As the Army of the James prepared to take the field, most of the X Corps was just arriving in Hampton Roads. Such a haphazard effort at army formation ensured that weeks would pass before its major elements could pursue common goals smoothly.

Under the circumstances, it was little wonder that Smith and others felt a gnawing trepidation on the eve of their maiden campaign in the Army of the James. A few days before he broke camp, Smith penned an especially anxious letter to his friend and former superior, Major General William B. Franklin: "I am here in an anomalous position under Butler with a Campaign . . . before us which I dread as being full of unnecessary risks & of the kind that may produce the most terrible disaster."[49]

CHAPTER FOUR

On to Richmond?

THE X CORPS' TARDINESS MEANT THE ARMY OF THE JAMES LEFT ITS BASE A day later than Grant had suggested. At 4:00 A.M. on May 5 the first members of Butler's flotilla—three of Graham's gunboats—cast off from Old Point Comfort and entered the James. Then came a half dozen vessels of Admiral Lee's squadron: his flagship, *Malvern,* followed by the gunboats *Dawn, Osceola, Commodore Jones, Commodore Morris,* and *Shawseen.* Next were what one New Hampshire soldier referred to as "transports, transports, transports." These ships carried, in order, Hinks's division (the black soldiers would be the first to debark), the 15,000 white soldiers of the XVIII Corps, and the part of the X Corps that had arrived ahead of Gillmore. Then came barges carrying siege equipment, followed by dozens of cargo and hospital ships. Lee's ironclads—the *Roanoke, Onondaga, Tecumseh, Canonicus, Sagus,* and *Atlanta* (the last being a captured ship of the *Virginia* class)—chuffed along in the rear, accompanied by a score of double-ender gunboats and armed tugs.[1]

The integration of army and naval vessels suggested a close cooperation between the services. Butler and Lee, however, differed on what the navy could and should do in the campaign. Butler figured a landing at Bermuda Hundred and City Point required the fleet to penetrate as far up the James as possible, guarding the army's flanks and protecting its works and troops from Rebel warships. The problem was that while the broad, deep, and unobstructed Appomattox could easily accommodate Lee's ships, the upper reaches of the James were dicey. Above the Appomattox, the James was winding and narrow—less than 600 feet in some places. Near Richmond the river ran quite shallow and contained treacherous shoals. Moreover, light-draught gunboats patrolled the upper reaches of the stream, which was also thought to be thick with torpedoes (underwater mines detonated electrically from the bank) as well as with pilings sunk to gash the hulls of incautious vessels.[2]

Butler appeared oblivious to these hazards. To enable his army to gain a foothold near the capital, he wished Admiral Lee to take station off Farrar's Island, a misnamed peninsula formed by a loop of the James about ten miles below the capital. The enormity of this request took Lee aback; though he promised to do what he could to secure Butler's flanks, the flag officer doubted the advisability of passing beyond Trent's Reach, some miles downriver from Farrar's Island. Butler was nettled by what he considered to be Lee's timidity. He later wrote, "The admiral also doubted whether it was possible to make the movement a surprise, and argued strenuously against an attempt by the joint expedition to go above City Point." On his part, Lee complained to his superiors in Washington not only about Butler's cavalier attitude toward maritime threats but also about the short notice—less than a week—Butler had given the navy to prepare for the expedition. Navy Secretary Gideon Welles was sympathetic, noting in his diary that Butler's "scheme is not practical. . . . Certainly there have been no sufficient preparations for such a demonstration and the call upon the Navy is unreasonable."[3]

Interservice friction notwithstanding, the force made good progress upriver. Baldy Smith sneered at Butler's "motley array of vessels," but others marveled at the size and speed of the armada. A member of the 81st New York Infantry was struck by the sight of "so many transports, loaded with troops, and the Stars and Stripes floating from so many mastheads." A comrade in the 117th New York took in the panorama—flag-draped steamers, decks filled with waving soldiers; schooners and tugs lining the river, their whistles shrilling—and pronounced it "one of the finest and most stirring scenes imaginable." Butler also seemed caught up in the excitement. As his flagship, the *Greyhound,* passed to the head of the procession in the early light, he was seen on the hurricane deck, shouting and gesturing as if urging the other ships onward. Several times he shouted down at the pilothouse, "Give her all the steam you can, Captain!"[4]

Despite the complexities of the embarkation, Butler's movement had gotten off to a gratifying start. Only a single snag had developed, and Butler was not to blame. Grant had promised that the balance of Gillmore's troops would reach Hampton Roads by April 18, but the pledge could not be kept. Despite Butler's repeated urging that the X Corps hasten its departure from South Carolina, the last of its troops reached Gloucester Point only hours before the fleet cast off. By dawn of the fifth, with the XVIII Corps already well under way, many of Gillmore's men lingered about on York River wharves. When finally transferred to the transports, the troops embarked in a hodgepodge, with infantry regiments and artillery batteries, combat troops and support units intermingled without consideration of landing priorities. Moreover, many of the late arrivals were forced to board smaller, slower, less seaworthy vessels than those Baldy Smith had commandeered for his corps.[5]

The delays vexed Butler. Just before casting off, he had complained to Gillmore that, having waited so long for him to reach Virginia, "I am not a little surprised at waiting" still. Gillmore shot back a reply that must have rankled his superior, who had taken great pains to provide adequate transportation for his army: "The miserable conveniences for embarking troops have been a cause of great delay." The exchange suggested that the Butler-Gillmore relationship would be no love feast.[6]

That encounter aside, Butler could take satisfaction in knowing that not only had most of his army moved out smartly, so had three forces assigned to divert enemy attention from the fleet. Late on April 30 and early the next day, Alford's brigade of Gillmore's corps, under the temporary command of Colonel Guy Henry of the 40th Massachusetts, had gone up the York by transport from Gloucester Point, landing at 10:00 A.M. May 1 at West Point, the terminus of the Richmond & York River Railroad. The brigade spent hours rebuilding and expanding the partially dismantled wharf there as though to accommodate the balance of Butler's command. Henry's people also dug rifle pits to make it appear they planned to stay; they even improved the breastworks that had been built along the river the previous summer during Dix's failed offensive against Richmond. Henry, however, remained at West Point only until the fifth, when his brigade reboarded its ships and headed back to the James for a reunion with Butler's main army.[7]

Butler had entrusted the second diversionary mission to a pair of black cavalry regiments under Colonel West. Shortly before the army shoved off from Fort Monroe, these troopers started up the Peninsula from Williamsburg, scattering Rebel pickets and burning the camp of a Virginia cavalry regiment. After crossing the Chickahominy River at Jones's Ford, the black troops turned south toward the James, heading for Turkey Island Bend, six miles upriver from City Point. On May 8 they crossed the James to unite with Butler at his new base of operations within range of Richmond.[8]

The third diversionary effort was the largest and had the fullest itinerary. On the morning of the fifth, with Butler's armada well up the James, 2,500 cavalry under Kautz left the Portsmouth area and trotted toward Suffolk and points south and west. They were aiming for the Blackwater

River and a railroad that crossed it, the Petersburg & Weldon. Kautz was to strike the line at several points, dislodging track and burning bridges. This not only would draw enemy attention and resources from Butler's path but also would stymie efforts by Pickett and Beauregard to reinforce Richmond.[9]

Even before it began, however, Kautz's effort appeared certain to fall short. Days before, the cavalry leader had informed Butler that the objectives Grant had established for the raid were unattainable. The Blackwater River, which the troopers would parallel, was not fordable at any point that gave direct access to the Meherrin River bridge at Hicksford. With Butler's consent, Kautz concentrated instead on destroying less strategic bridges over Stony Creek, eighteen miles below Petersburg, and the Nottoway River, five miles farther south near Jarratt's Station.[10]

On the first day of the journey, Kautz led his 3rd New York, 1st District of Columbia, 5th and 11th Pennsylvania, and a two-howitzer section of the 8th New York Battery on a thirty-three-mile jaunt toward the Blackwater. Early on the second day, troopers and gunners crossed the river at Birch Island Bridge. After a brisk skirmish with Confederates who had moved too slowly to dismantle that span, Kautz pushed on to Wakefield, where his men cut an important communications link to Lee's army, the Norfolk & Petersburg Railroad.

Throughout the day the raiders continued westward, destroying supply depots and storehouses and setting forest fires. A reporter accompanying the division noted approvingly that "the country was lighted up in every direction by countless columns of luminous smoke." When passing the homes of civilians, many troopers dismounted to loot barns and springhouses and to steal horses and mules. The animals "'neighed and brayed' in welcome," wrote one officer, "showing that they were good Union beasts unjustly detained." Although Kautz would deny charges that his men were thieves and marauders, his protestations had a hollow ring on this occasion.[11]

On the afternoon of the seventh, having come almost 100 miles from Portsmouth, the troopers swept down on the Stony Creek Bridge along the Weldon Railroad, which they found guarded by a detachment of the 59th Virginia Infantry. The raiders compelled the defenders to surrender but only after three attacks, mounted and afoot, in which they had several casualties, including the severe wounding of Mix. After rounding up his prisoners, Kautz demolished the 110-foot bridge as well as two water tanks, three freight cars loaded with lumber, two wood bins, a culvert, and some turn-pits.

For a time Kautz feared that he had reached Stony Creek too late: three troop trains had recently crossed the span heading for Petersburg. Later, however, he learned that his depredations had prevented five additional trains from making the journey from North Carolina. If Butler struck Richmond before the bridge could be repaired, its destruction might have major strategic effects.

But Kautz's bridge burning was not done. Before completing his work at Stony Creek, he sent Spear with his old regiment, the 11th Pennsylvania, down the tracks to Jarratt's Station and the Nottoway River. After deciding against wrecking a third, well-guarded bridge over Rowanty Creek north of Stony Creek Station, Kautz led his main body to Jarratt's, where he found Spear destroying depot buildings and rolling stock. This work complete, the reunited command advanced on the Nottoway bridge, defended on both sides of the river by the main body of the 59th Virginia under Colonel William B. Tabb. After shelling both banks, Kautz sent Spear, with his 5th and 11th Pennsylvania, on a dismounted charge that drove the nearest defenders across the covered bridge in what Kautz termed "handsome style." From the south bank of the Nottoway carbineers kept Tabb's troops at bay while comrades piled combustible materials on the bridge and lighted them. Twenty minutes later the 210-foot span crashed into the river.

Gathering up his wounded and 130 prisoners, Kautz turned for home. He led his division across Allen's Bridge over the Nottoway, then northward along the Jerusalem Plank Road, across the Norfolk & Petersburg (another section of which he then destroyed), and reached City Point early on the tenth. After a brief rest within Hinks's lines, the division crossed to Bermuda Hundred, where Kautz sought out Butler to report his mission accomplished.[12]

But was it? Kautz had destroyed a pair of bridges along the only railroad that could bring reinforcements directly to Petersburg and Richmond from the Carolinas. Within days, however, repair teams would restore most of what his troopers had demolished. Until then, Confederates heading north from Weldon would leave their trains to march around broken sections of track and ford bridgeless streams—a mere inconvenience.

Kautz could have done more. He had failed to extend his bridge burning to Rowanty Creek on the north or to the Meherrin River on the south. Nor had he struck quickly enough to cut off a number of units that were en route to the Rebel capital, which would cause severe problems for Butler's main army. Those troops might have been delayed for many hours had Kautz's main priority been to reach the Weldon Railroad as quickly as possible rather than to spread destruction and terror through the countryside.[13]

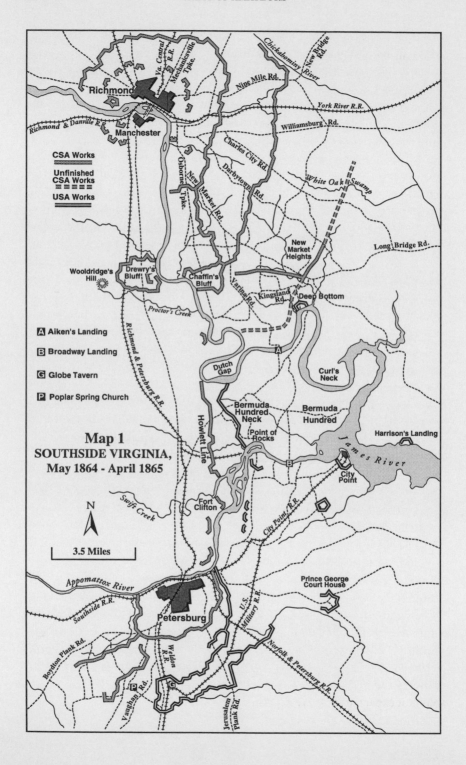

CSA Works

Unfinished
CSA Works

USA Works

Richmond

Manchester

Richmond & Danville R.R.

Via. Central R.R.

Mechanicsville Tpke.

Nine Mile Rd.

Chickahominy River

New Bridge Rd.

York River R.R.

Williamsburg Rd.

Charles City Rd.

Darbytown Rd.

White Oak Swamp

Osborne Tpke.

New Market Rd.

Long Bridge Rd.

New Market Heights

Wooldridge's Hill

Drewry's Bluff

Chaffin's Bluff

Varina Rd.

Kingsland Rd.

Deep Bottom

Proctor's Creek

Richmond & Petersburg R.R.

A Aiken's Landing

B Broadway Landing

G Globe Tavern

P Poplar Spring Church

Dutch Gap

Curl's Neck

Bermuda Hundred Neck

Bermuda Hundred

Harrison's Landing

Point of Rocks

James River

City Point

Howlett Line

**Map 1
SOUTHSIDE VIRGINIA,
May 1864 - April 1865**

N

3.5 Miles

Swift Creek

Fort Clifton

City Point R.R.

Prince George Court House

Appomattox River

Southside R.R.

U.S. Military R.R.

Petersburg

Weldon R.R.

Boydton Plank Rd.

Norfolk & Petersburg R.R.

P

G

Vaughan Rd.

Jerusalem Plank Rd.

Early on the afternoon of May 5, Butler's seagoing soldiers at last saw action on shore. The initial landing party, two of Wild's regiments supported by some field guns, captured Wilson's Wharf on the north bank of the James about fifteen miles east of City Point. The rest of Wild's brigade, two regiments and four cannon, landed at Fort Powhatan, a colonial-era earthwork on the opposite bank five miles farther west. Meeting no opposition at either point, the men entrenched while the rest of the army sailed past.[14]

The balance of Hinks's division encountered light resistance at its next destination, City Point. By early evening thousands of black troops were splashing ashore at the landing where prisoners had been exchanged over the past several months. In contrast to the teeming port it would become, City Point was described by one officer as "a few shabby houses ranged along two or three short lanes or streets" at the foot of a fifty-foot-high bluff. Atop the bluff sat a Confederate signal station, whose thirty inhabitants surrendered moments after a salvo from one of Graham's gunboats splintered their observation tower.[15]

With Wilson's Wharf bare of defenders and those at City Point captured, no one could spread the news of the incursion to Richmond or Petersburg. This was an unusual dividend for the less-than-stealthy Yankee army; one veteran noted that "the move took us quite as much by surprise" as it had the Rebels. "We expected to move," the man added, "but . . . up the York River instead of the James. I think it is the first that we ever made [an advance about which] the enemy was not as well posted as ourselves."[16]

The unexpected rapidity of the movement also served the army well at Bermuda Hundred. By 9:00 P.M. the white troops of the X and XVIII corps were pushing inland from the southeastern tip of the peninsula above the Appomattox and their commander was reporting the operation to Grant. The inexperienced Butler called his unopposed landing "a hazardous service— in [the] face of the enemy."[17]

The lateness of the hour did not prevent the army from entrenching on the southern edge of the peninsula. The work dramatized Butler's preoccupation with establishing a foothold on both sides of the Appomattox. But even during stationary operations, he considered taking the immediate offensive. As he wrote in his memoirs, no sooner had the *Greyhound* anchored than a member of Elizabeth Van Lew's spy ring sought him out at Bermuda Hundred. The operative reported Richmond to be virtually unprotected: all but a few infantry and artillery units at Drewry's Bluff had been sent to reinforce Lee. Replacements from the Carolinas under General Beauregard were not expected to arrive for another day or two.

This new led Butler to reconsider his priorities. Captivated by the thought of sauntering into the capital, he consulted his maps and found that he could move out an old stage road to the Richmond-Petersburg Turnpike, then up the pike to Drewry's Bluff. A full moon lit up the night and his soldiers were eager for action. But when he broached his plan to Generals Smith and Gillmore, they balked. By his account, "One of them intimated that he should feel it his duty to refuse it even if it were ordered. I said I should not order it for I could have no hopes of an expedition made against the will of the commander."[18]

Smith and Gillmore later denied there was such an exchange, and Butler eventually decided that if a night disembarkation was dangerous, a night time advance through unknown territory posed even greater risks. The army spent the balance of the night entrenching rather than marching.

By the morning of the sixth, however, the Army of the James was doing both. With all but a few late elements on dry ground, Butler ordered detachments of both corps on a seven-mile march westward from their landing site. The journey brought the columns to Bermuda Hundred Neck, a three-and-a-half-mile-wide expanse of ravine-bordered grassland, studded with patches of timber, that stretched from opposite Farrar's Island on the James to Port Walthall, a coal depot on the Appomattox. There the men halted and began to erect works heavier than those they had built the previous night. Before day's end, a vast wall of earth, its approaches guarded by rifle pits, had begun to stretch from one end of the peninsula to the other. Over the next few weeks, this position would be made virtually impregnable through the addition of redoubts, redans, bastions, revetments, and embrasures to accommodate dozens of heavy and light artillery pieces.

While Butler's soldiers labored with picks and spades, their navy comrades tried to secure their northern flank. Lee's warships and some of Graham's gunboats ventured gingerly up the James, probing for Rebel infantry and artillery and dragging the stream for torpedoes. The work was arduous, nerve-racking, and far from foolproof. About noon on May 6, the *Commodore Jones* struck a mine near Farrar's Island. The torpedo, which contained a 400-pound charge, destroyed the vessel and killed seventy-five of her crew. The following day the navy gunboat *Shawseen,* while engaged in the same hazardous duty, was shelled from Turkey Island Bend. Forced to run aground, the gunboat was boarded, twenty-seven crewmen were taken prisoner, and she was burned to the waterline.[19]

Sobered, Butler reconsidered his demands on the navy. He now believed that the bank near Farrar's was so elevated that defenders could menace any vessel that attempted to support his troops. As Lee had notified Welles, Butler had come to see that a push as far upstream as Curl's Neck, a few miles north

General Butler's headquarters, Bermuda Hundred. NATIONAL ARCHIVES.

of Turkey Island Bend, "will afford the army all the protection that it requires." So the navy played a negligible role in the balance of the campaign. The outcome appeared preordained: Butler's ultimate goal was Richmond, where Admiral Lee could not accompany him.[20]

Except for amphibious support, Butler's plan seemed to be progressing smoothly. By midday of the sixth he had fulfilled what he considered his initial objective—the securing of a strategic expanse of enemy territory. Then he turned to the railroad that ran north to Richmond. He ordered Smith and Gillmore each to send a brigade toward Port Walthall Junction, three miles west of the lower end of Bermuda Hundred Neck. If enough track could be taken up there, about fifteen miles from Richmond and six miles above Petersburg, any Confederates not cut off by Kautz's raiders might still be prevented from threatening Butler's army.

The first offensive of the campaign got off to a poor start from failures by Butler's corps leaders. Though ordered west by early morning, Smith's troops—Heckman's so-called Star Brigade—did not move out until 4:00 P.M., while Gillmore's troops did not move at all. Neither general explained his lapse, although Gillmore informed Butler that he had ignored the order "for what I consider good and sufficient reasons."[21]

Fuming over Gillmore's disobedience, Butler lashed out at him, if indirectly. While he did not press his subordinate for answers, the next day he wrote the chairman of the Senate Military Committee, asking that Gillmore's pending confirmation as major general be rejected: "General Gillmore may be a very good engineer officer, but he is wholly useless in the movement of troops." Though Butler had cause for anger, his public criticism appeared an overreaction, albeit one in keeping with his nature. General Hawley noted that whenever Butler "turns against a man as against Gillmore he means to make a sure thing of it and to smash him utterly."[22]

The lack of cooperation among the army's triumvirate doomed the May 6 mission against the railroad. By the time Heckman's soldiers came within view of Port Walthall Junction, they found Confederates dug in about 300 yards east of the tracks, barring their way. Heckman outnumbered his enemy three to one, but the mere sight of defenders appears to have frightened him. A fierce little skirmish broke out, resulting in almost seventy casualties (one being Heckman himself, injured when tossed from his wounded horse), but it ended in Federal withdrawal. No track would be dislodged this day.

The unexpected presence of defenders along the Richmond & Petersburg —some 600 members of the 21st and 25th South Carolina Infantry under Colonel Robert Graham, recently arrived from their home state—suggested that Butler had already lost the element of surprise. Graham's men were the advance of a force under Beauregard en route to Richmond in response to the recent buildup in Hampton Roads. Fearing for its life, the Confederate government had appointed Beauregard to head all the forces in the potential area of operations, including those at Petersburg under Pickett and those at Richmond under Ransom.

Neither Beauregard, Pickett, nor Ransom was responsible for Graham's presence at Port Walthall Junction. Having come up from the south before Kautz's raiders could block their path, these members of Brigadier General Johnson Hagood's brigade had moved to Richmond in response to War Department orders, before retracing their steps, at the behest of General Braxton Bragg, Jefferson Davis's military adviser, to the point where they were needed most. Later, a second force sent from Petersburg to Richmond, Brigadier General Bushrod Rust Johnson's Tennessee brigade, returned south to confront the invaders.

Behind Hagood's and Johnson's brigades came thousands of other troops from the Carolinas. In less than two weeks, Beauregard commanded no fewer than seventy-five regiments of infantry and cavalry at Richmond and Petersburg plus thirty-six artillery units, including the heavy batteries of the James River defense line. Due to combat attrition, his total force amounted to 30,000 effectives, slightly fewer than what Butler commanded. Still, considering their fortifications—especially the three lines of defenses that ringed Richmond—the Confederates enjoyed a decided advantage.[23]

Butler must have sensed that his opportunity to take Richmond was slipping away, for he ordered a return to the railroad early on the seventh. For this mission he told off three X Corps and two XVIII Corps brigades. Reacting to Gillmore's inertia of the previous day, Butler placed the entire force under Baldy Smith, who delegated field command to Brooks. Gillmore immediately protested the informality of the arrangement, forcing Butler temporarily to assign Gillmore's brigades to Brooks. One result was that not until midmorning did the combined force—8,000 infantry; one battery; and the 1st New York Mounted Rifles, the only cavalry outfit currently serving with the main army—start for Port Walthall Junction.

When it reached its destination, Brooks's advance guard found that Johnson's brigade and the balance of Hagood's had arrived to reinforce Graham. The still-outnumbered Rebels appeared eager to fight. Until Beauregard and the rest of his command came up from Petersburg, these troops alone stood between Butler and Richmond. They were determined to prevent the fall of their capital.

This day the Confederates were dug in both east and west of the railroad. Every sector of their line opened fire, preventing Brooks from flanking the position on the north with the X Corps and on the south with the XVIII. The oncomers fell back, then rallied and held their ground, setting the stage for hours of skirmishing. Late in the day, Brooks finally got up enough momentum to press both of his enemy's flanks. The attackers made greater progress to the north, where Plaisted's brigade, supported by Barton's, forced the defenders to give ground. This enabled Plaisted's 24th Massachusetts and 100th New York to reach the railroad and begin demolishing it.[24]

The destruction was not all it might have been, for the Federals lacked the specialized tools, including levers and claw crowbars, to do a thorough job. Then, too, miscommunication between Brooks and Plaisted resulted in a premature withdrawal from the railroad. Damage estimates ran from 100 to as many as 500 feet of track. This was less than Butler had hoped for; even the downing of some telegraph wire failed to cheer him up.[25]

To add to his dismay, late in the afternoon General Heckman suspended his drive against the enemy's lower flank, prompting Brooks to retreat. He made no second attempt to destroy tracks and ties. The withdrawing troops considered themselves outfought and statistics bore them out: Brooks had suffered almost 350 casualties against fewer than 200 for the much smaller force that had brought him to a standstill. A chagrined staff officer in the XVIII Corps called the day's work a "stationary advance" and asked himself,

"How long will it take to get to Richmond if you advance two miles every day and come back to your starting point every night?"[26]

As if the day's outcome had not been enough to concern Butler, by evening he had new worries. Since the previous afternoon he had been sitting by the telegraph from Fort Monroe. The wire had begun to hum with important messages, including a rather ominous one from Secretary Stanton.

On the morning of the fourth, Grant and Meade had launched their campaign against the Army of Northern Virginia. Butler had been told that their route ran through the Wilderness, an enormous tract of second-growth pine and tangled thicket about sixty miles north of Richmond. The generals hoped to clear the trees before Lee could hasten up to engage them on terrain that would neutralize their numerical superiority. Butler had learned—apparently during the April 1 conference at Fort Monroe—that whatever the short-term outcome, Grant expected the Army of the Potomac to keep moving by its right flank, threatening Lee's left and forcing him back upon Richmond.

Alive to the implications of a battle in the Wilderness, Butler was alarmed to hear from Stanton on the seventh that hard fighting had been going on in the forest for the past two days. The report came from a *New York Tribune* dispatch that Stanton had wired to Fort Monroe late on the sixth. This turn of events made Butler question the careful timetable by which the Armies of the Potomac and the James were to coordinate their operations. Moreover, should Meade bog down in the heavy timber, Lee might feel comfortable enough to detach troops to strengthen Richmond or attack Bermuda Hundred. Those prospects convinced Butler that he ought to concentrate on finishing his defense line across the neck of the peninsula. Not long after Brooks's expeditionary force trooped back to base late on the seventh, Butler sent a somewhat cryptic message to Baldy Smith: "No bad news . . . but hurry up your defences anyhow." A similar note went to Gillmore, who had halted work on his sector of the line to permit his men a late supper. "Work first," Butler told him, "eat afterwards." In a wire to Stanton, Butler was less circumspect. He reported Brooks's fight along the railroad (which he magnified into a substantial success) and announced that he was "intrenching for fear of accident to the Army of the Potomac."[27]

Butler's preoccupation with entrenching extended well into the eighth. His decision to defer a new advance proved to be a grave error. Every hour brought reinforcements to the Richmond-Petersburg area by the railroad, which connected with the Petersburg & Weldon, the artery that Kautz had damaged in only a few places. Although troops from Beauregard's department had to hoof it for as much as ten miles at a stretch, they lost only a single day in their journey to Richmond. By the eighth, in fact, Ransom was reporting that Beauregard's rear guard, along with its commander, would reach the capital shortly. Already Ransom considered the capital's defenses well manned: "I am now ready for the enemy."[28]

The realization that time was running out hit Butler late that day. Rankled by reports that barely 5,000 Confederates occupied the country between Petersburg and Richmond, he complained to Gillmore that "it is a disgrace that we are cooped up here." He ordered the corps leader to take four brigades back to the railroad the next morning, mangling it "at any place where you may strike it, and along as much of it as possible." He instructed Smith to "take all the troops that can be spared" and attack in conjunction with Gillmore. Given recent events, Butler was justified in emphasizing that the order for "this movement . . . is imperative."[29]

When the sun rose on May 9 two large columns started westward. Butler, unwilling to entrust another important expedition to a less-than-determined subordinate, accompanied them. To the south marched the greater part of Smith's corps, retracing its path to Port Walthall Junction. The 1st New York Mounted Rifles had the advance, followed by Brooks's division, then by the division formerly entrusted to Isaac Wistar and now commanded by Butler's old protégé from Louisiana, recently arrived at Bermuda Hundred, Godfrey Weitzel. Farther north, Gillmore's column headed for Chester Station, a depot almost four miles above Smith's objective. White's brigade of Ames's division led the way, with Alford's brigade of Turner's division following and with two-thirds of Terry's division, the brigades of Joseph Hawley and Colonel Joshua Howell, in the rear.

Making better time than their comrades, the men in the upper column reached the railroad first. By 8:00 A.M. Gillmore's troops were tearing up track for a good distance on either side of Chester Station. An articulate member of Alford's command noted, "We seized upon rails and poles for levers and working in unison the multitude heaved up 200 feet of iron rails and wooden ties together and forced the unwieldy masses over the side of the road and down the steep embankment. Sometimes the track was merely hoisted, flop[ped] over and left to be used by Johnny Reb with the ties up."[30]

While Gillmore's command labored, Smith's wing passed over the littered battlefield of the previous day and in midmorning came within sight of the rail line. After detailing parties to bury dead soldiers and horses, Smith and a few staff officers reconnoitered Port Walthall Junction. The corps commander had a penchant for long, careful tours of observation; one of his aides wrote that Smith "seemed to think that the whole art of war consisted in making reconnaissances, and that time was not an element that entered into it." On this day the general's eyesight was as poor as his sense of timing. A handful of Rebels lingering near the junction convinced Smith that he was facing the vanguard of the force that had given Brooks's division all it could handle two days before.[31]

Suspending his advance, Smith dispatched a message to Gillmore to cut short his demolition, move south by his left flank, and assist him. With Butler's approval, Gillmore moved to comply at about 10:30 A.M., heading toward Port Walthall Junction with Turner's division followed by Hawley's brigade. Meanwhile, Howell's brigade moved eastward to set up a flanking position at Ware Bottom Church. Before any of these commands could assist Smith, however, the Confederates vanished from his front. For nothing, Butler had lost his hold on the railroad that he had spent three days gaining.

Confounded by the enemy's disappearance, Smith sent scouts galloping down the railroad. By early afternoon he received word that Johnson's and Hagood's brigades, apparently reinforced by troops out of Petersburg, had taken up a line south of Swift Creek, a deep stream that flowed a couple of miles below Port Walthall Junction. In minutes, Smith's troops, followed by the X Corps brigades of White and Alford, were surging along the turnpike toward Petersburg. Sweltering heat bedeviled the marching men—the mercury was climbing above 100 degrees—and scores collapsed by the roadside.

By midafternoon the rest of the column approached the turnpike and the railroad bridges over Swift Creek. The invaders found most of Hagood's South Carolinians dug in below the stream near the footbridge, with two regiments on the north bank as an advance guard. Johnson's Tennesseans and other troops lay behind earthworks on the far bank near the railroad span. Cannon protruded through the breastworks at strategic points along the south bank of the creek.[32]

At Smith's order, Weitzel and his division prepared to rush the defenders of the upper bank. The preparations took hours and the oppressive heat and a scarcity of drinking water took a toll. One Federal recalled that "scores more were prostrated by the sun. Many lost their reason. Some filled the air with their insane yells. Some needed force to prevent them from dashing alone upon the enemy. Others, it is said, turned their weapons upon themselves."[33]

Shortly before Weitzel could strike, one of Hagood's regiments suddenly crossed the turnpike bridge to reinforce its comrades on the north side. Soon all three outfits were charging up the turnpike to strike Heckman's brigade, which held the Union center near Arrowfield Church. The Star Brigade kept its composure, unleashing a volley that swept the pike clear of attackers. Taking advantage of the confusion in the Confederate ranks, Heckman counterattacked with the 9th New Jersey and 23rd Massachusetts. As the Federals came on, the surviving Rebels stampeded for their works, in the process suffering almost 140 casualties.

Greater damage would have been inflicted had Heckman sent more than two regiments against the bridge. From behind its breastworks Hagood's main body shredded the small attack force and sent its pieces flying back to Arrowfield Church. The repulse chastened Heckman; the balance of the day on Swift Creek was spent in desultory skirmishing at long range. Baldy Smith later asserted that only a lack of suitable fording points prevented him from renewing the attack. After the war one of his aides insisted that neither Smith nor anyone else ventured closer than 100 yards from the stream, which was "fordable at many places."[34]

The day's action was not quite over. During the fight along the turnpike, one of Smith's brigades, temporarily assigned to the recently arrived Brigadier General John Martindale, moved against Fort Clifton, a Confederate earthwork along the lower bank of the Appomattox near Swift Creek. Martindale's advance was made in conjunction with an overland movement from City Point by 1,800 troops under Hinks as well as with a run down the Appomattox by army gunboats supported by one of Admiral Lee's ships. None of these supposedly cooperative efforts achieved anything, for the artillery strength of Fort Clifton (which was responsible for sinking a gunboat), the fort's elevation, and the narrowness of the river made attacks from any direction difficult. When long-range shelling of the fort proved ineffective, Martindale, Hinks, and their maritime supports withdrew in disgust.[35]

———⊶⊷———

The repulse at Fort Clifton ended a miserable day for Butler's army. Not only had it failed to sever the railroad to Richmond, but it had been kept well short of Petersburg by an understrength foe. Still, Butler was not ready to quit. He began to hunger for another offensive, this time toward Petersburg. He decided that his advance on Richmond could wait until he neutralized the troublesome little garrison to the south. While his troops exchanged artillery fire with their opponents below Swift Creek, Butler met with his corps commanders to plan a morning assault across the stream. He hoped to gain the line of the Appomattox as well, destroy the railroad bridges on both sides of the water, and attack Petersburg. To exploit any breakthrough above the "Cockade City," Butler sent word to Hinks, who was returning to City Point from Fort Clifton, that he should strike Petersburg from the east.

Early in the evening, confident that he had secured his corps leaders' approval of a morning assault, Butler left Swift Creek for Bermuda Hundred. At his field headquarters near Point of Rocks on the Appomattox, he perused recent dispatches from Washington. Unlike previous telegrams, these reported dramatic advances by Meade's army in the Wilderness. According to Stanton, Lee's forces "had been driven at all points" and as of May 8 were "in full retreat for Richmond." The most recent wire, which Stanton had sent at 4:00 P.M. on the eighth, informed Butler that Grant was "on the march with his whole army to form a junction with you" but that Grant "had not determined his route."[36]

Again, Butler permitted himself to be diverted from the work at hand. He had moved toward Petersburg believing that time permitted him to defer his advance on Richmond, Meade having been slowed if not stopped in the Wilderness. Now, with the Army of the Potomac back on the move and the ten-day timetable of cooperation presumably again in effect, Butler had been caught looking in the wrong direction. As he wrote years later, it was then clear that "I should carry out my instructions, secure my base at Bermuda Hundred, and move as far up the James as possible, to co-operate with the Army of the Potomac in its investment of Richmond. No time was to be lost in attacking Petersburg." He therefore countermanded the order to Hinks.[37]

Butler was preparing a similar message for Smith and Gillmore when a courier reached headquarters with a note from both corps leaders. Soon after Butler had left them, the generals had reconsidered their course of action against Petersburg. They rejected Butler's plan to attack across Swift Creek in favor of building a pontoon bridge over the Appomattox to City Point, which they considered a better line of advance. "Such a bridge can readily be constructed in one night," they instructed their superior, "and all the work of cutting the [rail]road and perhaps capturing the city can be accomplished in one day, without involving us in heavy losses."[38]

The message ignited all the hostility and resentment that had been gathering around Butler since the campaign began. Thus far from Gillmore he had gotten recalcitrance and insubordination; from Smith he had gotten none of the helpful, well-meaning advice Grant had led Butler to expect.

Even on paper, the generals' condescending attitude came through. Butler was not alone in blaming his corps commanders. Many in the ranks believed that Smith and Gillmore delighted in seeing Butler "thwarted and defeated in his plans, even though the enemy would be greatly benefited thereby."[39]

Butler poured out his rage. At about midnight Smith and Gillmore received separate copies of his reaction to their recommendations: "While I regret an infirmity of purpose which did not permit you to state to me, when I was personally present, the suggestion which you make in your written note . . . I shall [not] yield to . . . a change of plan made within thirty minutes after I left you. Military affairs cannot be carried on, in my judgment, with this sort of vacillation." He recounted the changed situation that necessitated canceling the move against Petersburg. The army was to retire from Swift Creek early the next morning and return to Bermuda Hundred to prepare for a march on Richmond. As for the generals' suggestion to shift operations to City Point, Butler had no intention of "building bridges for West Pointers to retreat over."[40]

Although stung by the tone of Butler's remarks, Smith and Gillmore did not dare disregard his orders. But even as they prepared to leave the Swift Creek line, they revealed anew their inability to cooperate and obey. Despite Butler's demand that some of Gillmore's brigades trade places with Smith's to permit the latter to disengage first, Smith had to repeat the order three times before his associate complied. And though Butler had stipulated a return to home base on the morning of the tenth, the main body did not start up the turnpike until shortly before noon. Not until late in the afternoon did Gillmore's rear guard clear Swift Creek.[41]

Once in motion the blue column made passable progress, but not toward Bermuda Hundred. Instead of heading northeastward, the troops found themselves hustled directly north in response to sounds of battle from Chester Station, where part of Terry's division was reported to be "hard pressed by the enemy." That

Major General Robert Ransom, Jr.
U.S. Army Military History Institute.

pressure had come from an unexpected quarter, the Richmond defenses. The previous afternoon Ransom had ventured down from Drewry's Bluff at the head of two infantry brigades, recently arrived in the capital. Nettled by the Federals' efforts (spasmodic though they were) to sever the railroad to Petersburg, the garrison commander had probed Colonel Howell's position near Ware Bottom Church, and this day he had struck Colonel Alvin C. Voris's 67th Ohio, which Howell had stationed at the intersection of the turnpike and the road from Bermuda Hundred to Chester Station. Isolated from the rest of his brigade and Terry's main force near Port Walthall Junction, Voris occupied a highly vulnerable position.

Though outnumbered almost ten to one, the colonel put up a stiff fight, especially when reinforced by two regiments and a battery sent up from Swift Creek with uncharacteristic dispatch by Gillmore. Thanks to his own inspired leadership and a lack of cohesion among his enemy, Voris held the crossroads until Terry's division came to his aid. Terry's arrival widened the fight, which took on a dreadful aspect when artillery rounds started a fire in tinder-dry foliage—a fire that engulfed several wounded men. One Union officer wrote that he had "visited many fields of carnage, but never before saw . . . so many horrors" as on this occasion.[42]

Once the vanguard arrived from Swift Creek to strengthen Terry's position, Ransom broke off the fight and withdrew north. He also recalled a detachment that had continued to oppose Howell's presence at Ware Bottom Church. Ransom's retreat left the Army of the James with the only combat victory it was to gain during this campaign. Casualties ran close to even—280 for Terry, Howell, and Voris; 250 for Ransom—but the Federals held the field.

Afterward the victors tended to the wounded, gathered up their prisoners, buried the slain, and withdrew to Bermuda Hundred, tearing up a short stretch of railroad as they went. The rear guard joined the rest of the army inside its peninsula defense line by nightfall. On the surface, Butler's command had turned in a commendable performance. Many of his men admitted, however, that by evacuating the railroad without leaving so much as a detachment behind, they had forfeited much of their gain.[43]

⟫●⟪

Giving up the railroad was bad enough; Butler compounded the error by spending an entire day, the eleventh, inside his works, preparing for the march on Richmond. While his people sat idle, Beauregard dispatched several brigades, recently arrived at Petersburg, to Richmond. He joined them in the capital on the thirteenth after placing one of his most trusted North Carolina subordinates, Major General William H. C. Whiting, in command at Petersburg. Whiting thus relieved Pickett, whose nerves had given way under the weight of thousands of invaders rampaging through his bailiwick.

Throughout May 11 Rebel infantry and artillery moved up the railroad where rails and ties remained intact and up the turnpike where broken track intervened. Their passage was audible at Bermuda Hundred. The sounds of train whistles and tramping feet chilled the hearts of many listeners who feared they would pay for "the folly of retreating from the railroad." An officer in Hinks's division viewed that mistake as the most recent in a long series of blunders, miscalculations, delays, and hesitations:

I am afraid there has been a fine opportunity for decided advantages lost here by inexcusable tardiness. I will always be of the opinion that on the night on which we landed at City Point . . . [Petersburg and Richmond] could have been taken without serious trouble by our Division alone. Our arrival here was entirely unexpected and they [the Confederates] were comparatively destitute of both men and arms. We lay here for days without advancing a step, and then on making a feeble attempt yesterday we found them prepared for us. Very courteous in us not to take them unawares.[44]

CHAPTER FIVE

Debacle at Drewry's Bluff

At 4:00 a.m. on May 11 the Army of the James filed out of its defenses and began its long-deferred march to Richmond. Under a gloomy drizzle—it would rain intermittently during the next few days—Weitzel's XVIII Corps division took the road to Chester Station, then turned north onto the turnpike to Richmond. Behind him came the division of William Brooks, which was so slow to clear its works that it did not reach the pike till late in the morning. On Weitzel's left, Turner's division of the X Corps, temporarily attached to Baldy Smith's command, made better time northward, while to the left and rear of Smith's column, close to the Richmond & Petersburg Railroad, trudged Terry's division, accompanied part of the way by the division of Adelbert Ames. At a predetermined point Ames angled toward Port Walthall Junction; from that oft-occupied depot his men could cover the rear of the expeditionary force.[1]

Although he was at last bound for Richmond, Ben Butler had an imperfect understanding of what he was in for and what he was supposed to do. His interpretation of Grant's orders was that he should demonstrate against the capital but not attack with the intention of entering and occupying it on his own. By all accounts, however, Grant expected the Army of the James to make a determined effort to penetrate the Richmond defenses or, failing that, to invest the city until Meade's army could join it there.[2]

If this miscommunication boded ill for his army's fortunes, so did Butler's tactical plan. He had made Drewry's Bluff, the most formidable of the many defensive positions along the James, his first objective. The heavy cannon and the numerous troops stationed there had already thwarted one major

effort against the capital, a naval offensive launched two years earlier almost
to the day. Since then, no Union commander had been foolish enough to
confront the position.

Butler would have been better advised to cross the James east of Drewry's,
putting the defenses behind him, or to remain on the lower bank of the
river but move far enough westward to bypass the bluff. Having rejected
those options, he needed as much naval support as he could get. Yet he had
failed to notify Admiral Lee of his advance from Bermuda Hundred—
testimony to his low regard for the North Atlantic Blockading Squadron.

Another problem with Butler's route was the likelihood that should he
secure a foothold near Richmond, he would soon have to relinquish it. The
flat, open country that lined his chosen path provided easy access for any
Confederates striking the army's rear or interposing between Butler and
his base at Bermuda Hundred. If they could concentrate in force, the
Confederates would find Ames's division at Port Walthall Junction a minor
obstacle.[3]

Whatever the limitations of Butler's strategy, at least he had gotten off
dead center. Not only was his main army in motion, he had ordered his
cavalry off on another raid, this time on the Richmond & Danville Railroad,
which Beauregard and Ransom might use to gain last-minute reinforcements.
Breaking the R & D would also assist Grant by keeping supplies from a city
that might have to be starved into submission. These considerations had
prompted Butler to override Kautz's protest that his men were too tired to
mount a second expedition so soon after the first.[4]

After briefly accompanying the main army toward Drewry's Bluff, the
cavalry struck cross-country, heading westward. Kautz reached the railroad
at Coalfield, ten miles southwest of Richmond, at about 11:00 P.M. Since his
troopers still did not have demolition tools, they took picks and axes from
the nearby mines that gave the place its name. Under a moonlit sky, they
cut the telegraph, burned depot buildings, destroyed a water tower and
wood bin, and tore up a respectable amount of track.

Butler had encouraged Kautz, once at Coalfield, to strike the nearby
James River Canal, which brought barge traffic into Richmond from the west.
Making not even a token effort in that direction, Kautz led his men down
the Danville line early on the thirteenth, seeking more desirable objectives.
He found one at Powhatan Station, five miles below Coalfield, where his
column wrecked track and telegraph lines and destroyed or confiscated food
bound for Lee's army.

Kautz's next objectives, Mattoax Bridge over the Appomattox and the
unnamed bridge over Flat Creek near Chula Station, were guarded by

regiments and batteries undaunted by the horsemen's approach. The raiders made a feeble attempt to thrust the 30th Virginia Infantry away from Mattoax Bridge before turning south in defeat. At Chula Station, unwilling to order another retreat, Kautz made a succession of attacks against earthworks that the 17th Virginia had built along the stream. The Rebels repulsed every assault in a matter of minutes. He finally called off the effort and guided his column down to the Southside Railroad, which carried into Petersburg provisions every bit as valuable as those the Danville road brought to Richmond. Although he had inflicted minimal damage to the Richmond & Danville, Kautz considered his work along that supply artery completed.[5]

The troopers struck the Southside at Wilson's Station, twenty-five miles southwest of Petersburg, late on the fourteenth. There and at nearby Wellville they accomplished little, but farther south at Black's and White's Station they demolished depot facilities, freight cars, and miles of track. As though afraid to tarry at this scene of destruction, Kautz departed the Southside early the next morning and headed back to the Weldon Railroad. On the sixteenth he detoured around the twin villages of Belfield and Hicksford to avoid defenders reported there. In so doing, Kautz passed up the chance to wreck the railroad bridge over the Meherrin River that Grant had brought to Butler's attention.

At 5:00 P.M. May 16 the raiders stopped at Jarratt's Station, scene of their recent depredations. Everyone from Kautz on down was flabbergasted to find that the damage inflicted on the eighth had been repaired and the Nottoway Bridge was back in service. The troopers angrily sacked the depot but Kautz considered it imprudent to try again to burn the well-defended bridge. Instead, he sent his weary men and mounts over the Nottoway River via a partially dismantled footbridge east of the railroad that had been replanked by a unit of Maine timbermen. Circling eastward around Petersburg, the Federals struck and, for the second time in two weeks, damaged a section of the railroad to Norfolk. This final chore completed, they passed inside General Hinks's lines at 6:00 P.M. on the seventeenth, ending a six-day, 350-mile circuit of southside Virginia.[6]

Kautz's second raid was less fruitful than the first. His division had damaged all four of the railroads it crossed but none for more than a few miles at a stretch. As the raiders' return to Jarratt's Station had demonstrated, Kautz's troopers could not inflict long-lasting damage. Even as the cavalry headed for City Point, railroad gangs were repairing track, ties, rolling stock, and telegraph lines; the last line to be restored was fully operational by May 26. More serious was Kautz's inability to disable any bridges that could convey troops and supplies to Richmond. Butler had expected much more from his horsemen; he came to see that if the present campaign was to succeed, his infantry and artillery would have to do the job.[7]

After its late start on the morning of the eleventh, the army moved at a glacial pace up the turnpike to Richmond. In large measure, its slowness was the result of well-positioned sharpshooters on both sides of the road. The Rebels blasted the head and flanks of the column, fled north before they could be cut off, dug in again, and reopened fire.

The most stubborn resistance was less than a mile above the upper flank of Bermuda Hundred Neck. At the point where the road crossed Redwater Creek, a phalanx of skirmishers, backed by field pieces, halted Butler's advance. During the delay Baldy Smith conducted a long reconnaissance that enabled Weitzel's division to find a weak point in the defenders' position. Coming up in force, Weitzel dosed the Rebel line with musketry, then bulled his way across the creek, permitting the advance to resume.

The next major barrier was Proctor's Creek, a deep stream skirted by an intricate network of earthworks held by infantry and cannoneers. Along the south side the defenders again stopped Weitzel's division. His front swept by rifle and artillery fire, Weitzel this time sent back for assistance. Smith, in response, dispatched six of Brooks's regiments to Weitzel's left flank and used Turner's division to extend Weitzel's right toward the James River. For hours artillery and marksmen flailed away at each other, seeking an advantage but finding none. At the height of the standoff one of Turner's men observed "a jolly little bird . . . perched in a tree over our heads, hidden in a cloud of smoke but chirping away as though he were singing for dear life."[8]

Union strength finally asserted itself; late in the afternoon, Smith's reinforced line pressed forward on either side of the turnpike. The enemy then took up a line north of Proctor's Creek, about four miles from Drewry's Bluff. Though gratified by this belated success, Butler permitted his men to advance only as far as the creek, beside which they lay on their arms through a rainy night.[9]

On the morning of the thirteenth the army's rear echelon, less Ames's division, closed up on Proctor's Creek and traded skirmish fire with the enemy across the water. Sometime before 9:00 A.M. Smith's vanguard began to ford the stream and found that the Rebels had abandoned their new earthworks. Snaking through a clotted forest, the XVIII Corps reached the edge of a clearing slashed by a line of rifle pits a mile or so long. Smith curtailed his advance until he could make another reconnaissance, which lasted so long that no further movement was possible until the next day.

On Smith's left the X Corps had made greater gains. At about 6:30 A.M. 5,000 of Gillmore's troops probed toward the western end of the line beyond the Richmond & Petersburg Railroad. This force consisted of Hawley's brigade of Terry's division, bolstered by White's brigade (detached from Ames's division at Port Walthall Junction) as well as by Marston's brigade of the XVIII Corps. By detouring along a secluded road that crossed a branch of Proctor's Creek, Hawley's brigade found itself facing the rear of the Rebel right flank, anchored upon Wooldridge's Hill. Terry attacked, with Hawley's men in advance, at about 4:00 P.M.

Although surprised and turned about, the well-entrenched enemy threw back the first wave, taking an especially heavy toll of the lead regiment, the 3rd New Hampshire. Hawley's brigade regrouped and started forward, only to learn that the enemy, fearful of being cut off, had retreated to Drewry's Bluff. As General Gillmore noted proudly, the X Corps occupied the Rebel position, "obtaining possession of about a mile of their line."[10]

The lodgement above Proctor's Creek encouraged the right wing to resume its advance. Shortly after dawn on the fourteenth, Smith moved against the works in the clearing. Like Hawley at Wooldridge's Hill, he found the defenses abandoned. The Federals occupied and strengthened their position, while skirmishers probed the next line of defenses along the southern rim of the fortified complex at Drewry's Bluff. Advancing cautiously "under cover of stumps and huts," the skirmishers found that position held by Confederates intent on staying put.[11]

Smith would not commit himself to a further advance until he could appraise his opposition. He held his position, waiting for the X Corps to take the initiative. Dutifully, Gillmore moved up his right flank, consisting of Turner's division (now returned to X Corps control), until he was able to connect with Smith's left between the railroad and the turnpike.

The men of the Army of the James spent the rest of the day consolidating their gains, pondering their next move, and arguing among themselves. Butler lost his temper late in the afternoon when Gillmore asked for tools to construct a walled trench to protect his corps against counterattack. Butler sharply reminded him that the army was on the offensive. The corps commander said nothing more about entrenching, but the exchange displayed, as Gillmore's signal officer put it, "the usual hard feelings natural between a technically instructed officer . . . [and] a civilian political general."[12]

Butler's preoccupation with offensive operations also precipitated a clash with Baldy Smith. Late on the fourteenth, when updating Butler on his position, Smith explained that the defenses facing him were formidable but did contain a weak point or two. Hearing what he wanted to hear, Butler approved Smith's nonexistent plan of attack and scheduled it for dawn on the fifteenth. Smith saw a trap being set for him. As he told Brooks, "If I go in without orders and should get whipped Butler will saddle me with the failure. If I carry the works only his name will appear in the result." Smith informed Butler that he had proposed no assault but would "cheerfully and to the best of my ability endeavor to carry out any orders which may be given to me."[13]

According to Smith, Butler cursed his response and suspended the attack. The records, however, suggest that Smith himself called off a planned advance after learning that Gillmore could not support it. Whatever the facts, the exchange was another illustration of the distrust and acrimony that pervaded the army's hierarchy.[14]

Despite Butler's desire to keep moving, Smith spent the next day preparing to defend his position. Troops all along his line—from the left flank west of the turnpike to the far right along the bank of the James— improved their entrenchments and built breastworks facing Drewry's Bluff. Smith acted from fear of impending disaster. He had no confidence that Butler would mount a successful attack; rather, he believed that the local topography, "with its creeks and ravines, [and] with Petersburg in the enemy's hands . . . was impracticable for an aggressive campaign against Richmond with the force General Butler could command." On May 15 the corps commander went so far as to tell Major General Philip H. Sheridan—who had reached Turkey Island Bend at the head of 10,000 cavalrymen after cutting loose from Meade's army on a raid toward Richmond— that Butler's command was in mortal peril. Smith asked Sheridan, upon returning north, to advise Grant that the Army of the James should be withdrawn to Bermuda Hundred. Grant should leave Butler and a skeleton force to hold the peninsula and transfer the balance, under Smith's command, to the Army of the Potomac.[15]

Despite Smith's preoccupation with fortifying, he failed to make his position impregnable. By late on May 15 a gap perhaps three-quarters of a mile long lay between his right flank, which had been entrusted to Heckman's brigade, and the James River. To occupy that stretch, Smith posted 150 members of the 2nd U.S. Colored Cavalry, recently returned from Colonel West's expedition to the Chickahominy. The troopers, however, were spread too thinly and were impeded by swampland and underbrush.[16]

Always innovative in defense, Smith strengthened his works farther west, those held by Brooks's division, with wire stripped from telegraph poles along the turnpike. Brooks's men stretched the wire from stump to stump and limb to limb a few feet off the ground, forming a cunning obstacle to enemy advance. Enough wire was available to create entanglements along part of Weitzel's front as well. For unexplained reasons, however, none was used to close Heckman's open flank. Butler later criticized Smith for this lapse, though the army commander admitted that he had decided against protecting the far right, which he did not recognize as vulnerable.[17]

A belated effort by Smith to protect that flank only aggravated the situation. Before nightfall he called up several regiments from the rear to occupy works freshly improved by Heckman's men. Most of the Star Brigade was forced to take up positions on open ground farther east. The terrain left the displaced troops, especially the 9th New Jersey on the extreme right, dangerously exposed. Despite the realignment, the critical gap remained. During the night, enemy units probed the position and vowed to exploit its weakness.

Not only did Smith's repositioning fail to solve the problem, it drained Butler's limited reserves. Smith's call-up of troops and similar action by Gillmore so depleted the rear guard at Port Walthall Junction that by the morning of the sixteenth General Ames was left with just two regiments of infantry, a battery, and a scattering of horsemen.[18]

Smith's and Gillmore's calls for reinforcements underscored their unease, a feeling they seem to have communicated to their soldiers. As darkness came and sounds to the north heralded enemy movements near Drewry's Bluff, anxiety gripped Butler's command. Given the formidable Confederate position, no one expected Butler to attack, but many feared their opponents would prove more restive. One of those who worried, the colonel of the 39th Illinois, told anyone within earshot that "the rebels are going to give us h-e-l-l."[19]

Early on the fifteenth Sheridan, who had placed his raiders in camp east of Drewry's Bluff at Haxall's Landing, visited the front. Shortly before his arrival, Butler had received new dispatches from Stanton, reporting success by Meade in breaking Lee's lines at Spotsylvania Court House, which had been the Army of the Potomac's location since exiting the Wilderness on the seventh. As Butler recalled, "These telegrams strengthened me still further in the view that it was necessary to invest Richmond as closely as possible, and prepare to meet General Grant around the intrenchments above [west of] the city, to which point I supposed he was marching."

Then, however, Sheridan visited Butler's headquarters and the army commander's perception of the situation changed markedly.[20]

The meeting of the two strong-willed generals was not uniformly cordial. Troubled by his inadequate cavalry support, Butler urged Sheridan to guard his flanks at Drewry's Bluff. He was chagrined when Sheridan refused, pleading an inability to comply due to his horses' exhaustion. Butler considered compelling Sheridan's people to remain with him indefinitely. But on May 17, as Kautz's troopers returned from their second raid, Sheridan rode north, tired horses and all, to rejoin the Army of the Potomac.

Before he departed, however, the cavalry leader gave his host a startling bit of firsthand information that told Butler he had been naive in accepting the earlier reports from Washington. Instead of marching by its right flank toward a junction with Butler west of Richmond, Meade's army was swinging far to the southeast along a route toward City Point.

In his memoirs Butler emphasized the shock he felt, apparently a genuine reaction. Sheridan's report forced him to activate a contingency plan he claimed Grant had outlined to him at Fort Monroe: "I judged that it was impossible for him [Grant] to do otherwise than to take the alternative in the plan agreed upon between us, in case he failed to turn Lee's left and drive him back into Richmond. . . . Evidently Grant was not coming to Richmond but . . . [intended] to continue his operations on the south side. . . . I concluded that I would not continue to hold my position more than a day or two longer . . . [and would then] retire and finish the intrenchments at Bermuda Neck."[21]

Butler may have distorted, and perhaps fabricated, this "alternative" strategy. If such a plan existed, it was never put on paper and Grant never mentioned it. Even so, Butler's decision to pull back to Bermuda Hundred was proper, given the changed situation as he understood it. He had to place his base of operations beyond the possibility of capture, and this mission was magnified if the Army of the Potomac was heading his way. It seems logical, too, that Butler should wish to group his command inside its defenses well before Meade's arrival. Such reactions were inevitable given Grant's insistence that Butler conform his movements to Meade's.

Thus, by midday on May 15, Butler had gone on the defensive. As soon as he could, he would break contact with the enemy and return home, hoping the Rebels would not turn aggressive.

His hopes were doomed by the grandiose vision of Beauregard. Late on the thirteenth the Creole general had ridden north from Petersburg with a small escort. Detouring west of the Federals holding the turnpike, the band made its way shortly after dawn through the city that Confederate

Secretary of War James A. Seddon had recently declared to be in "hot danger."[22]

Reports from scouts and front-line troops had convinced Beauregard that Butler's army was lying quietly around Drewry's Bluff. Before the picture changed, he determined to seize the initiative through an along-the-line assault. He had almost 18,000 infantry and artillery, most of whom had reached the capital during the past ten days. This force Beauregard rapidly organized into divisions under General Ransom, Major General Robert F. Hoke, and Brigadier General Alfred H. Colquitt. A fourth division of 5,300 was taking shape twenty miles south of Richmond under General Whiting. Beauregard believed this force could deal Butler a stunning blow, especially if it could be masked by morning fog, a common condition in eastern Virginia in mid-spring. Beauregard had only a rough idea of enemy strength, but he based his plans on the assumption that he was handily outnumbered. The disparity, however, was not as great as he supposed. Subtracting the troops left behind at Bermuda Hundred, City Point, Port Walthall Junction, and outposts along the James, no more than 25,000 Federals held the captured works south of Drewry's Bluff.

Beauregard was akin to Baldy Smith in believing that he alone knew how to use men and arms in the manner of the great captains. He did not dwell on earlier performances that had fallen short of expectations. One student of the Bermuda Hundred campaign speculated that Beauregard "used up so much energy in conceiving and writing out his sanguinary plans . . . that his harvest of promise was never realized."

Past failures long forgotten, Beauregard sought permission from Jefferson Davis to transfer several thousand soldiers from Robert E. Lee's department to his own; with so many reinforcements he would not merely drive Butler away but smash him utterly. Beauregard's enlarged command could then march to Lee's headquarters and crush the Army of the Potomac. This accomplished, Beauregard "felt sure of . . . open[ing] the way to Washington where we might dictate Peace!"[23]

Displaying, perhaps, better sense (certainly more discretion) than their subordinate, President Davis and General Bragg rejected Beauregard's scheme. Beauregard should have realized that his superiors never would have depleted Lee's army in the face of Meade's continuing advance. Beauregard would have to dislodge Butler with his force on hand.

Disappointed but not devastated, the Louisianan planned anew. Having probed southward from Drewry's Bluff, he appreciated the weakness of Butler's right flank. He decided that at dawn on the sixteenth, Ransom's 6,400-man division would hit that vulnerable sector and slice between Heckman's brigade and the river. General Hoke would then assail Butler's center and left with his 7,100-man division. Colquitt's 4,000 men would stand ready to reinforce either wing. The set piece of Beauregard's strategy was a carefully timed strike against the Federal rear by Whiting's division. If coordinated with the main effort, that attack would destroy Union cohesion and morale, sending Butler into rapid, headlong, panic-stricken retreat.[24]

——❧——

In answer to Beauregard's prayer, dawn of May 16 brought down on Drewry's Bluff a cold mist that thickened as hours passed. A veteran of the 24th Massachusetts later asserted that "one who was not there cannot form any idea of the density of the fog." A horse and rider could be swallowed up fifteen yards away.[25]

The fog and chill only added to the discomfort of soldiers who had endured more than a few hardships over the past several days. Many also suffered from an oppressive dread, knowing almost anything was possible from an enemy that had surprised them so often before. Surely the Rebels would not allow them to remain indefinitely on Richmond's doorstep. Searching for the word to describe the army's condition, one veteran settled on "skittishness."[26]

Just before five o'clock, with the fog clinging tightly to trees and foliage, troops along the Union right heard the spine-raking Rebel yell, faintly at first, then at high volume. Before anyone could react, Ransom's men burst through the cloud of vapor and plunged into the Yankees' trenches—screaming, shooting, and flailing about with their bayonets.

The fog both hindered and abetted the attackers. Dozens fell sprawling, victims of the "damned rascally contrivance" Baldy Smith had fashioned from the local telegraph. The mist was so thick, however, that Ransom's easternmost brigade, under Brigadier General Archibald Gracie, passed undetected around the swamp on Smith's right. Brushing aside the cavalry pickets, the Rebels fell upon Heckman's ill-protected infantry, most of whom were soon heading in all directions. Hundreds of Federals were shot down by unseen assailants; hundreds of others, including Heckman, were taken prisoner. As the enemy began to roll up the flank from east to west, Smith and Weitzel rushed in reinforcements. These troops eventually halted the onslaught, but not until midmorning. By then, Heckman's brigade and a portion of Wistar's had gone under.

A little over an hour after Ransom attacked, Hoke charged the Union center. For a time, Hoke's command, which included the troops under Johnson and Hagood who had so stoutly protected the railroad to Petersburg, made headway. But after sending XVIII Corps pickets into retreat and reaching Smith's main line, these attackers also ran afoul of the telegraph cable, while taking a crossfire from Brooks's division and the left flank of Weitzel's broken command. The Rebels halted and milled about in confusion until Beauregard sent in some of Colquitt's reserves. After a time, the advance resumed but Brooks's well-positioned regiments held their ground. Their resistance prevented Hoke and Ransom from cooperating as envisioned in Beauregard's plan.[27]

As the Union center stiffened and reinforcements tried to shore up the right flank, a portion of Hoke's division swung into line to strike the X Corps divisions of Terry and Turner east of the railroad as well as the XVIII Corps brigade of Gilman Marston west of the tracks. At first inclined to rush forward and beat the foe to the attack, Gillmore hesitated, with visions of the slaughter outside Charleston numbing him into indecision. He finally decided to receive an assault. Just before it struck home, however, Gillmore found it necessary to shift eastward to fill a long-overlooked gap along Smith's left. In motion when Hoke slammed into its line, Gillmore's corps was caught flat-footed. Gillmore made matters worse by prematurely ordering a counterattack. Leaving the security of its trenches, Turner's division charged piecemeal, absorbing heavy firepower. Alford's brigade took the fiercest beating; when a part of it retreated in unseemly haste so did Alford—the victim, one of his men suggested, of "a severe attack of discretion." A few days later the colonel was cashiered from the service.[28]

The need to coordinate movements with the XVIII Corps drove Gillmore to yet another confrontation with Butler. With the fog lifting at about 9:00 A.M., Gillmore received the unexpected news that Brooks and Weitzel were withdrawing a short distance south of their trench lines, where they hoped to regroup. Although concerned by his comrades' fallback, Gillmore held his ground with Terry's division and what remained of Turner's, while stationing Marston's brigade farther south to secure a route to the rear if needed. In reporting these actions to army headquarters, Gillmore inadvertently gave the impression that he was retreating. Butler sent him a sharp note questioning the need to fall back. Despite Gillmore's attempts to explain the situation, Butler dated the X Corps' withdrawal from the hour Gillmore's misleading communiqué reached him.

The X Corps remained in position for another hour or more until it became obvious that Smith had fallen back and the Rebels were closing in. When Turner reported his right was about to collapse, Gillmore saw no alternative to retreat. Although he pulled back mainly because his comrades had already done so, Gillmore later found his tenacity questioned by his commander. Butler forever believed that the X Corps had started to the rear before anyone else.[29]

It was Smith, not Gillmore, who lacked a good reason for retreating. The XVIII Corps pulled out because of its commander's loss of nerve. Prevented by the fog from making one of his patented reconnaissances, Smith felt vulnerable. Following Heckman's disintegration, he considered the entire corps on the verge of dissolution. As early as 8:00 A.M., when General Weitzel reported the Rebels probing his jury-rigged right flank, Smith thought the end was near. Weitzel had not meant to suggest that an irresistible attack was imminent, but by the time he realized Smith had misinterpreted his message, it was too late. Not long after eight o'clock Smith ordered Brooks and Weitzel to fall back and concentrate east of the turnpike. Neither subordinate protested, though a staff officer found the air "sulphurous" with words expressing Brooks's distaste for retreating.[30]

Not until the move was well under way did Smith reconsider his hasty decision and try to countermand it. Some time after 9:00 A.M., when the fog had thinned enough to permit him to observe the terrain in his front, Smith realized that Ransom's offensive had spent itself and that neither Brooks nor Weitzel had been in danger of being cut off. Rather sheepishly, one imagines, Smith ordered Weitzel to reoccupy his position. The division leader attempted to obey, but only a couple of his regiments were well enough in hand to countermarch. The balance of the division and Brooks's command were well to the rear and beyond quick recall. Realizing that two regiments could not hold any ground they retook, Weitzel resumed his retreat.

Left with no feasible alternative, Smith led his reunited command well down the turnpike, where his men built works strong enough to foil pursuit. They remained there until early afternoon, when Gillmore's regiments left their fallback position to join the XVIII Corps well south of Proctor's Creek.[31]

At this juncture an anxious and uncertain Butler conferred with his lieutenants and tried to develop some options. At first he wished to return to the scene of his repulse and test whether renewed resistance was possible. A directive to advance northward, however, resulted only in recovering some of the dead. Then, heeding Smith's repeated assertions that the army was vulnerable, Butler ordered everyone back to Bermuda Hundred.

The retreat, slowed by a downpour such as accompanied many battles, took all afternoon and much of the evening. Long before they reached their peninsula home, the survivors of Drewry's Bluff—wet, weary, sullen, and dispirited—sensed that they had come as close to their enemy's capital as they were going to get for quite some time.[32]

As confused and difficult as the retreat was, things could have been worse. Had Beauregard's strategy worked, Whiting's division would have cannoned into the Union rear even as its comrades at Drewry's Bluff struck the head of Butler's line. The gray pincers failed to close due in part to the postbattle cloudburst, which made roads muddy and slick, but primarily because of Whiting's inexplicably feeble advance against Port Walthall Junction.

By the time he neared the Union-held depot, about 8:00 A.M., Whiting's 5,000-plus troops confronted perhaps one-fifth as many Yankees, the rest of Ames's division having gone north to reinforce Smith and Gillmore. For whatever reason—some critics alleged drunkenness, others drug abuse, while the general himself cited chronic fatigue and lack of sleep—Whiting performed as if in a daylong stupor. Magnifying the size of Ames's force and interpreting its confused movements as a trick to lure him into a trap, Whiting barely drew within shooting distance of the junction. From that point he dithered so long, despite the urging of officers who saw opportunity fading, that the day slipped past before Whiting realized it. The division leader capped his performance by returning to Petersburg, having suffered barely thirty casualties. With the Confederates gone, Ames remained along the railroad only long enough to gather up his men before leading them at the double-quick toward Bermuda Hundred.[33]

Spared Beauregard's contemplated one-two punch, the Army of the James continued its unhappy trek back to base. As the men plodded south, grumbling and cursing spread through the ranks. Other soldiers were morosely quiet, contemplating their defeat and trying to understand how it had come about. Their conclusions were predictable enough. Some cited the lack of cooperation among the army's major components. A diarist in the 13th New Hampshire put it succinctly: "the two Corps did not work well together." Other men singled out the high command for blame: a New Jersey soldier attributed the shameful defeat to "treachery and imbecility" at the top.[34]

Such theories are too fragile to bear scrutiny. The army's failure was not simply a matter of disharmony or the shortcomings of two or three of its generals, although such factors undeniably contributed to the outcome. The command had been hamstrung by flaws in the strategy conceived by Grant and interpreted and implemented by Butler. The most serious misconception was that Butler's army could coordinate its movements with those of the Army of the Potomac based on a steady flow of accurate intelligence from Meade's headquarters. In fact, Washington had sent Butler vague, misleading, inaccurate, and false information that left him, at critical times, torn between courses of action. Butler's vacillation ensured his inability to make a long-range contribution to the overall Union strategy. Much of the blame goes to Grant, who should have seen the hazards in tying the Army of the James to a cooperative venture that hinged on uncontrollable factors of time, distance, and communication.

Of course, Grant had also failed to provide Butler with helpful, energetic, and cooperative subordinates who had the best interests of their army at heart. For his part, Butler had been distrustful and resentful of his corps commanders. The upshot was that the army lacked cohesive guidance— a force that might have overcome Butler's obsession with entrenching, his tendency to relinquish strategic positions as quickly as he occupied them, his confusion over multiple objectives, and his poor choice of points of attack.

The most significant example of a lack of high-level cooperation and mutual understanding involved not Butler and his lieutenants but Butler and Grant. Despite ample opportunity to resolve differences of perception, the two field leaders had failed to establish the basic objectives and priorities of the campaign. Throughout, the gap between what Grant wished Butler to accomplish and what Butler believed Grant expected of him was so wide that Butler's failure is not surprising. Indeed, the failure of their minds to meet doomed the maiden effort of the Army of the James long before the first transport cast off from Hampton Roads.

CHAPTER SIX

Death in the Meadows

UNIMPEDED BY A CLOSE PURSUIT, THE ARMY OF THE JAMES COMPLETED ITS return to Bermuda Hundred by 10:00 P.M. on May 16. The XVIII Corps, which had led the withdrawal from Drewry's Bluff, took position along the lower flank and center of the defense line across the neck of the peninsula, while the later arrivals of the X Corps went into place along the northern flank.

The troops set about to improve their earthworks. Overnight a fresh complex of redoubts, redans, abatis, palisades, and ditches indicated Butler's intent to hold his base of operations against all comers. But if this work reflected the army's determination to remain within striking distance of Richmond, it also illustrated an attitude that had already caused many problems. Ordered to build a common perimeter in advance of the main defenses, Smith and Gillmore fortified along divergent lines, which required construction of a third wall of defense to cover the disconnected line.[1]

General Beauregard's decision to postpone renewed combat gave the Army of the James time to reflect on its travail. The general mood was disbelief, disappointment, and bitter regret. A USCT officer spoke for many in reporting himself "very much disgusted with the result of our first advance." Joseph Hawley informed his wife, "I lose no faith nor hope but the agony of these days is awful." A captain in the 118th New York saw "a great many long faces" in his regiment; he did not expect them to brighten for some time.[2]

The inevitable finger-pointing went on for weeks. While some soldiers attributed their defeat to the corps commanders, Butler absorbed most of the blame. An enlisted man from New Hampshire wrote that Butler had engineered "a great disaster," and a Massachusetts officer closed a diary entry about Drewry's Bluff with the notation "Butler's Blunder." An enlisted man from New York declared that "Butler may be a very smart man in some things, but if I have got to fight I want to do it under a man that knows more about war than he does." Colonel Hawley decided that "Butler failed as a great general. Our position [at Drewry's Bluff] was weak and [our] line thin. Most of the leading officers in our corps felt the defeat coming for two days." Hawley hoped that one of Meade's stalwarts, such as Major General Winfield Scott Hancock, would take over the army because "Butler will not do."[3]

For the first time since he took the field in Virginia, Butler was also pilloried by the mainstream press. To some extent this reaction was the angry response of editors who regretted having assured their readers that the Army of the James was on the verge of a great victory. Before Drewry's Bluff many papers had dressed up the command in glowing headlines, such as the *New York Herald*'s banner of May 17: "BUTLER—One Small Work to be Stormed—and then on to Richmond!"

Following the army's return to Bermuda Hundred, many newspapers turned against the general they had long supported. The *Herald* and the *Times,* which early in the month had hailed Butler as a hero-to-be, now portrayed him as a blunderer, a military novice whom the Union could not afford. On May 22 a *Herald* correspondent called the army leader a man of "high administrative abilities" but one who lacked "the same ability for field operations." An editorial by James Gordon Bennett in the same edition called for the general's immediate relief. A few days later a *Times* reporter asserted that "General Butler has made one or two capital mistakes. . . . Many a good and true man among us doubts seriously whether his right place be to have command of military operations in the field. I suppose that nobody will pretend that General Butler was educated a soldier. And it seems tolerably clear that he was not born one." Commentary from Philadelphia, Boston, Baltimore, and other metropolitan areas ran in this same vein.[4]

For Butler, who yearned for favorable publicity, the pain and embarrassment of such condemnation must have been excruciating; still, he made no show of emotion. He tried to put the best face on his fallback, which he refused to describe as a retreat. In fact, when he reported to the War Department on the seventeenth regarding his recent operations, he shunned candor like a poor relation. Instead of portraying his advance on Drewry's Bluff as the independent operation it was, he implied that it had been only a feint to prevent the Richmond garrison from turning against Kautz's raiders. Butler explained that as soon as he learned of his cavalry's arrival at Mattoax Bridge, where it appeared to be beyond pursuit, he had deliberately marched back to Bermuda Hundred.

The most Butler would admit was that early on the sixteenth, due to the fog as well as to reinforcements that made the Rebels "equal to my command," Beauregard surprised the XVIII Corps and drove it from its position "in some confusion and with considerable loss." Once the fog lifted, Butler insisted, Smith reestablished his line and checked the assault. Smith's success enabled Butler to carry out his planned withdrawal "at leisure." The army leader also implied that he had returned to Bermuda Hundred out of concern for his men, who had been "on incessant duty for five days, three of which were [spent] in a rainstorm." His orderly and unhurried withdrawal—made possible when Ames "handsomely repulsed" a "heavy attack" against the rear— enabled the army to "hold the railroad between Petersburg and Richmond."[5]

How much of Butler's report was outright falsehood and how much he believed to be true is impossible to determine. Certainly he begged the question by failing to admit that his original intent was to cooperate with the Army of the Potomac in besieging Richmond. And whether or not his decision to withdraw from Drewry's Bluff predated Beauregard's attack, Butler's claim that he did so because of his troops' fatigue is specious. So too is his claim to having held the railroad after he retreated; by May 17 only a few pickets remained west of Bermuda Hundred Neck, none of them near the rail line.[6]

However blatant Butler's effort at deception, the War Department appeared willing to accept it. On the nineteenth Edwin Stanton replied to Butler's initial telegram as well as to a request for reinforcements. Instead of reproving the general, Stanton informed him that "great interest is felt by the President and this Department in the success of your operations, and by holding the enemy in front of you, Grant is to that extent relieved, and you will contribute greatly to the success of the campaign. Nothing in our power will be spared to support you, and add to the important results you have already achieved."[7]

About the time Washington learned of Butler's return to Bermuda Hundred, so did Grant. The commanding general had been dismayed by the lack of headway against Lee in the Wilderness as well as by the bloody and indecisive fighting near Spotsylvania Court House. Grant had recently learned of a setback in another theater, the Shenandoah Valley, where on the fifteenth an army under Major General Franz Sigel had been whipped by a much smaller force at New Market. Added to such gloomy news, word of Butler's defeat would have made a lesser man despondent. Yet Grant had anticipated rough going on more than one front when he and Meade broke winter camp on May 3. According to one of his staff officers, "The general was in no sense depressed by the information [of Butler's repulse], and received it in a philosophical spirit." The fact that Grant was seeking new ways to circumvent Lee's southern flank suggested that he was not about to revamp his strategy in response to his subordinates' setbacks.[8]

———⊷⊶⊷———

Besides trying to explain away his recent reverses, Butler spent much of May 17 reorganizing his forces and making good the losses they had suffered. His shuffling of commanders changed the face of the XVIII Corps. Ostensibly out of disgust for his corps leaders' inability to entrench along a common line, he relieved Weitzel from field command, named him the army's chief engineer, and empowered him over higher-ranking officers. Three days later Butler assigned his protégé's division to General Martindale, a forty-nine-year-old West Pointer whose apparent competence was compromised by recurrent bouts of typhoid fever and a long period of inactive service after a checkered performance during the Peninsula Campaign.[9]

Butler also replaced a number of brigade commanders; in every case, the new man was a political appointee. To succeed the captured General Heckman in command of what remained of the Star Brigade, Butler appointed Brigadier General George J. Stannard, a crusty Vermonter just off the disabled list following his wounding at Gettysburg, where his heroics had helped repulse Pickett's Charge. Another recently arrived brigadier, Charles Devens, Jr., a Harvard-educated lawyer from Boston who had accumulated a distinguished record as well as several wounds in the Army of the Potomac, replaced Colonel Horace Sanders at the head of the 3rd Brigade, 1st Division. And to take the place of Wistar, hospitalized with dysentery, Butler selected Colonel Griffin Stedman of the 11th Connecticut, a courageous young officer with a penchant for risk taking that would cost him his life.[10]

Many good men under Butler had preceded Stedman to an early grave. The campaign had cost the army 5,000 casualties, nearly 15 percent of its effective force. The Confederates had lost 2,500 men killed or wounded while routing the enemy and capturing five artillery pieces, nearly 4,000 small arms, more than 60,000 rounds of ammunition, and 1,400 prisoners. Butler was justified in pleading for reinforcements. Such losses would not cripple his command but would prevent it from launching another major offensive for weeks to come.[11]

Beauregard, however, could not trust his enemy to remain aloof from Richmond. On the morning following his victory, he led his regrouped forces south from Drewry's Bluff. That night his advance guard drew within artillery range of Bermuda Hundred, initiating five consecutive days of fighting.

The first clash, on the evening of the seventeenth, was mainly between picket lines. The following morning Beauregard attacked the same position, the sector of the right flank held by Plaisted's and White's brigades. This time the Rebels came in heavy force, scattering one of White's regiments and capturing a stretch of the Bermuda Hundred defenses. Its first urge was to flee, but White's main body turned and counterattacked, spearheaded by the 97th Pennsylvania under its nineteen-year-old lieutenant colonel, Galusha Pennypacker. Making a spirited charge across a farmstead known as Foster's Place, Pennypacker's outfit regained most of the ground and then, backed by other elements of its brigade, pursued the Confederates westward. The energetic assault gave Butler reason to hope that the repercussions of Drewry's Bluff would be short-lived.[12]

During the pursuit, Pennypacker's skirmishers spied Beauregard's main body digging in about two-thirds of a mile beyond Bermuda Hundred Neck. Word went back to Gillmore that the Rebels were in force along a line about four miles long, with their upper flank anchored on the James opposite Farrar's Island and their lower flank resting near Port Walthall Junction. In mid-afternoon Gillmore informed Butler that the heaviest enemy concentration appeared to be opposite his right.

The enemy had established an out-post at the Howlett house, a plantation home on a bluff along a bend in the James, as well as perhaps a half mile farther south at Ware Bottom Church, site of the skirmish of May 10. Doubtful that he could crack Beauregard's northern flank, Gillmore ordered Kautz to probe the other end of the enemy line. Butler, however, recalled the horsemen before they could accomplish more than a hasty reconnaissance.

The enemy's labors spelled trouble for the Army of the James. By early evening Butler knew that Beauregard not only was fortifying Bermuda Hundred Neck but also was erecting two heavy batteries

Brigadier General George J. Stannard.
U.S. ARMY MILITARY HISTORY INSTITUTE.

opposite the Union right. The first gun emplacement, on the Howlett estate, soon began to pound Gillmore's position. The other, on the northeastern tip of Farrar's Island at a point where the James formed a neck known as Dutch Gap, had opened on some of Admiral Lee's ships. At Butler's urging, Gillmore sent fifty sharpshooters from Terry's division to neutralize the Dutch Gap battery. Gillmore also brought up two twenty-pounder Parrott gun batteries to shell both positions.

Butler did not fully understand Beauregard's intentions, but he tried to prepare himself for anything. While the defenses going up opposite Bermuda Hundred seemed to indicate stationary operations, Butler did not rule out another Confederate assault. He warned his corps leaders to "take measures to effectually prevent a surprise tonight or in the fog in the morning."[13]

Beauregard intended only a limited attack because he had begun to plan another master stroke of strategy involving his and Lee's troops. Only four days before, he had proposed to Confederate Secretary of War Seddon that the Army of Northern Virginia join with him near Drewry's Bluff. Now, late on the eighteenth, he suggested the transfer of 15,000 men from Richmond and Petersburg to Lee's front, "thus rendering Grant's defeat certain and decisive in time to enable General Beauregard to return with re-enforcements from General Lee to drive Butler from . . . his present position in advance of Bermuda Hundred." Beauregard added a dire prediction: "Without such concentration nothing decisive can be effected, and the picture presented is one of ultimate starvation" for Richmond and two Confederate armies.

Elements of Beauregard's strategy appeared feasible. With 22,000 troops on hand and two days' worth of entrenchments in his front, he could afford to send 15,000 to Lee and still hold his position. On the other hand, as Bragg advised Davis, so large a transfer might enable Butler to break out of his peninsula, cut the railroad he had failed to destroy in previous weeks, entrench at Richmond's doorstep, capture Petersburg, and ravage territory "on which we must depend for supplies in future." Bragg considered Beauregard's current force "ample for the purpose of crushing that under Butler, if promptly and vigorously used."[14]

Bragg's objections, and Seddon's endorsement of them, persuaded Davis to reject most of Beauregard's plan. The president did like his suggestion about reinforcing Lee. He directed the Louisianan to send as many men as he could spare to the Spotsylvania front. On the nineteenth, an unsmiling Beauregard detached four infantry brigades, one artillery battalion, and a cavalry regiment; a few days later a fifth brigade of infantry headed for Richmond and beyond. Each unit was badly understrength; the transfer involved no more than 5,000 troops. The loss was partially offset when Beauregard called up from Petersburg the equally undermanned infantry brigade of Brigadier General William S. Walker. The latter move was a calculated risk: Walker's transfer left the city defended by two infantry regiments under Brigadier General Henry A. Wise, a few hundred cavalrymen under Brigadier General James Dearing, Jr., and a small, unreliable force of militia.[15]

The subtractions and additions left Beauregard with about 18,000 men. He resolved to make the most of his reduced resources. If his superiors considered him strong enough to break Butler's hold on Bermuda Hundred and the line of the James, he would test their belief.

Late on the nineteenth, a day of rain and mud, Beauregard's artillery opened on the X Corps to cover the detaching of troops to Lee. The Federals replied with rifle and artillery fire, and the gunboats above Farrar's Island joined in. The shelling produced an infernal racket but few casualties on either side. Work aimed at making Butler's formidable defenses impregnable continued through the night as they had throughout the day.

The lack of enemy pressure may have convinced the Federals they had plenty of time to improve their works, especially after deserters and captives told of Beauregard's loss of men to Lee. But if the Army of the James supposed its enemy had been critically weakened, it received a shock early on the twentieth. Just after dawn, Gillmore's advance works came under heavy shelling, followed by an infantry attack. Beauregard had hit what he considered Butler's most vulnerable point, the sector running from the James to Ware Bottom Church, where the divisions of Ames and Terry abutted. Other Confederate units gave covering fire, but because a deep ravine fronted the XVIII Corps' position, no troops penetrated south of Ware Bottom Church.[16]

At first Beauregard's offensive—aided by a smokescreen from a fire set in underbrush and fallen timber—was a smashing success. The attackers gobbled up Ames's picket posts as well as his first line of rifle pits. Chased out of their holes by screaming Rebels, the Federals were bombarded with shells from the Howlett house battery as they ran for the cover of their main line. Confederate troops then seized the abandoned pits and, with rapid shovelfuls of dirt, reversed their parapets. Soon Gillmore was wailing to Butler, "I find the enemy in strong force and am losing heavily." About noon Butler sent a curt reply, suggesting that Gillmore at once retake his evacuated position: "It was too easily lost."[17]

While Ames's forward position caved in, Terry's line farther north remained intact. Thanks to the support of Turner's division, Terry repulsed repeated assaults, inflicting dozens of casualties. Finally, about

5:00 P.M., Butler ordered Smith to send two brigades to the embattled flank. Smith failed to obey. After the war, Butler asserted that the corps commander cursed the messenger who brought the order, adding: "Damn Gillmore; he has got himself into a scrape,—let him get out of it the best way he can." Butler claimed he had to ride to the front and personally dispatch Brooks's division to the X Corps' relief.[18]

Smith later denied Butler's charge, claiming that if he had disobeyed the order he would surely have been court-martialed. Even so, he admitted refusing to aid Gillmore until Butler sent a second order to that effect. Conversely, Butler probably overdramatized Smith's obstinateness. No evidence confirms that he ordered Brooks into the fight. If he did, the division arrived too late.

Left to his own resources, Gillmore in the early afternoon supervised an attempt by Ames to regain his line. First, part of Jeremiah Drake's brigade rushed the captured pits, spearheaded by the 13th Indiana. The Hoosiers went in with determination but, as an onlooker remarked, they were "received by a thundering volley from the whole rebel [line] . . . and almost annihilated."[19]

When the first wave receded, Ames sent in White's brigade, led by the 9th Maine—the regiment that had been routed on May 17—backed by Colonel Pennypacker's feisty Pennsylvanians. Despite a blanketing fire from Gillmore's artillery, the men of Maine and Pennsylvania were roughly handled. A New Hampshire soldier noted that the Rebels permitted them to get near the captured pits, then "opened their artillery and musketry fire all along the line, and we saw puffs of smoke belch forth and the line immediately broken. . . . [Soon] nothing could be seen of any men except as they were either crawling on hands and knees or running in a crouching manner to some rock or stump or . . . lying flat on the ground as they had fallen." Pennypacker was wounded three times. Unable to bear additional punishment, White's survivors joined Drake's in retreat.[20]

At this point Terry assumed responsibility for recapturing the trenches. Because of Hawley's and Plaisted's tenacity, his sector had held firm. Thus secure, Terry detached Joshua Howell's brigade, reinforced it with two regiments, and sent it to flank the Rebels in the pits. The white-haired Colonel Howell attacked what proved to be Walker's brigade; bitter fighting swirled around, above, and in the rifle pits. At the height of the melee, General Walker galloped up to the 67th Ohio Infantry, which amid the smoke he mistook for one of his own regiments. Realizing his error, he wheeled and galloped away but got less than fifty yards before a volley brought him down. Rushing forward, the Ohioans captured the severely wounded officer and confiscated his possessions, including a photographic map of the Petersburg area.

Walker's fall signaled the end of Beauregard's attempt to hold the position he had seized. By late afternoon the captors of Ames's rifle pits had drawn off into the woods between the lines and the fighting had become an artillery duel. Casualties amounted to 800 Rebels, 700 Yankees.[21]

The outcome should have told Beauregard he could gain only a temporary advantage by assaulting Bermuda Hundred Neck. On the evening of the twenty-first, however, he made yet another attempt to demolish Butler's upper flank. Under cover of the dark, a few infantry brigades crossed the ground in front of the X Corps and dislodged another sector of Ames's picket line, this one held by the 4th New Hampshire of White's brigade. Ames retaliated with an artillery barrage. "How our batteries crashed and roared and rattled out their crossfire of solid shot and shell and whirling grape," a New Yorker wrote two days later, "drowning alike the hearty cheers of our men and the yells of the chivalry. The chivalry went back to look into the cost of the [attack] . . . and have not troubled us since."[22]

This repulse convinced Beauregard he stood little to gain by throwing men against the Union right. Since the natural obstacles on the other flank intimidated him, the Rebel commander took a breather during which he extended his own works as far south as Swift Creek, four miles from the Howlett house.

While the Bermuda Hundred front quieted, action heated up along Butler's line of communications with Fort Monroe, defended by Hinks's division. To the surprise of many white troops North and South, the USCTs, who had been confined to fatigue and sentry duty since their landing at City Point on the fifth, gave excellent accounts of themselves on several occasions.

On May 18 a force out of Petersburg—600 cavalry, two companies of infantry, and two twelve-pounder cannon—advanced against the fortified camp at Spring Hill. Duncan's brigade replused the attack with relative ease. Over the next few days other Rebels came out from Petersburg to shell gunboats and transports running down the Appomattox from City Point. Duncan's and other black units interrupted their work and put them to flight every time.[23]

On the afternoon of the twenty-first, a much larger force—Major General Fitzhugh Lee's cavalry division, detached from the Army of Northern Virginia initially to pursue Sheridan's raiders—made a demonstration against Fort Powhatan. Colonel Joseph B. Kiddoo's 22nd U.S. Colored Troops chased the horsemen away with "well-directed shots from our guns." The continuing pressure on his communications nevertheless drove Butler to place all of Hinks's outpost forces in a heightened state of readiness.[24]

Butler's decision was well timed. Following his repulse at Fort Powhatan, Fitz Lee crossed his division to the north bank of the James. At 2:00 P.M. on the twenty-fourth he moved against Wilson's Wharf, a dockside earthwork four miles east of his earlier target. Interposing himself between the wharf and City Point, Lee cut off the garrison, that day under the direct command of General Wild. He then called on the black troops, whom he outnumbered two to one, to surrender. General Wild refused in a sarcastic note. The one-armed abolitionist was confident that his troops and their horseshoe-shaped earthwork—eight feet tall, protected by heavy abatis and a ditch six feet deep—would withstand a great deal of pressure. So too was Ben Butler, who had assigned the black soldiers to that isolated and vulnerable position: "I knew they would fight more desperately than any white troops, in order to prevent capture, because they knew . . . that if captured they would be returned into slavery. . . . There was no danger of surrender." The possibility of a worse fate hung over the garrison, though: according to rumor, Lee had executed two of Colonel Kiddoo's men captured on the twenty-first.[25]

Annoyed by his opponent's reply, Lee opened with his artillery, then launched a series of dismounted attacks against the earthwork. In their first test of combat, Wild's troops held still until their opponents were almost upon them, then sprayed the air with rifle fire. As one of Wild's officers reported, the enemy charged "with a yell, but our boys gave a louder yell, (which must have been <u>heard</u> to be appreciated,) and poured so much lead among them, that they broke and ran like sheep, leaving a number of dead and wounded on the field."[26]

Three hours later, after additional attacks had failed, Lee sullenly departed before reinforcements could reach Wild. The cavalry had suffered 20 killed, more than 100 wounded, and 19 captured against 22 Union casualties. The stunning victory earned the African-Americans an outpouring of praise from Butler, white comrades, and civilian observers. Newspapers began to counter the prevailing wisdom that the USCT would be found wanting in a crisis: "With good officers the negroes would make good soldiers," wrote a *New York Times* correspondent. "An old adage, and true of any men of any color."[27]

Butler's people had proven themselves formidable on defense, but their actions were insufficient to satisfy their commander. He believed that, far from being trapped inside its defenses (as Beauregard appeared to believe), the Army of the James could launch a potent offensive. The same day that Wild's men prevailed at Wilson's Wharf, Butler informed Stanton that within a few days "I shall resume offensive operations."[28]

Butler was not planning an assault against Beauregard—he would not mimic his adversary's mistakes. Instead, he focused on the strategic significance and continuing vulnerability of Petersburg. His abortive assault of the tenth, and the lost opportunity it appeared to represent, preyed on his mind. Yet if Petersburg had been a worthy objective then, it was no less important now, for it remained the supply hub of Richmond and the main link between the Confederate capital and its support from the south. A simple crossing of the Appomattox—something Beauregard could not prevent—would carry Butler's army to Petersburg's doorstep before its tiny garrison could cry for help.

Although Baldy Smith later denied that Butler organized such an expedition, the record indicates that by May 26 the army leader had set in motion a plan to strike Petersburg with about 17,000 men. But at the eleventh hour he again postponed a promising offensive to comply with an order from Grant.

The chain of events that brought this about began early on the twenty-third, when two distinguished visitors arrived at Bermuda Hundred on an ominous errand: Brigadier Generals Montgomery C. Meigs, the Union's quartermaster general, and John G. Barnard, chief engineer of the Washington defenses. Grant had sent these technical specialists to inspect Butler's peninsula enclave and to speculate on the Army of the James's prospects for active campaigning.

Grant was concerned that Butler's force—holed up at Bermuda Hundred—was beginning to lose its physical and emotional strength. In a recent letter to his friend James Harrison Wilson, Smith had characterized the command as demoralized and restive; as Smith probably hoped, the letter was brought to Grant's attention. Subsequently Grant wrote to Henry W. Halleck, the army's chief of staff, who gave Meigs and Barnard their orders, that "there is some difficulty with the forces at City Point [and Bermuda Hundred] which prevents their effective use. The fault may be with the commander, and it may be with his subordinates," especially the commander of the XVIII Corps. Grant added pointedly: "General Smith, whilst a very able officer, is obstinate, and is likely to condemn whatever is not suggested by himself."[29]

Sensing that his military career lay in the hands of these visitors, Butler greeted them warmly and granted them every courtesy throughout their three-day visit. Butler and his staff escorted the generals from below Dutch Gap on the James to Point of Rocks along the Appomattox and as close to Beauregard's lines as possible. Butler could be a charming host and on this occasion he outdid himself.

At first the red-carpet treatment appeared to work. Meigs and Barnard composed two reports to Halleck, who forwarded them to Grant. In the first report, dated the day of their arrival, the inspectors declared that "General Butler's position is strong; [it] can be defended, when works are complete, with 10,000 men, leaving 20,000 free to operate" elsewhere. By coordinating his operations with Meade's army, then fighting Lee along the North Anna River twenty-five miles north of Richmond, Butler could retake the offensive. Therefore, his army should be kept intact: "A skillful use of it will aid General Grant more than the numbers which might be drawn from here." Meigs and Barnard added that the army was abundantly supplied and in "good spirits" and that the reports of demoralization and disharmony appeared groundless.[30]

The following day, however, Butler's guests sent Halleck a second set of suggestions. They proposed that Butler be relieved by an officer "of military experience and knowledge" who should assume the offensive or that 20,000 troops be detached from Butler and sent to where they could make their numbers felt.

In this second letter the visitors evaluated the command situation at Bermuda Hundred. They termed Butler "a man of rare and great ability, but he has not experience and training to enable him to direct and control movements in battle." If Butler was politically untouchable, they recommended that he be kept in his present position; that Gillmore, whom he so obviously disliked and distrusted, be relieved; and that Smith be given field command of both corps, with Brooks and Weitzel exercising corps command, "unless you can send here better officers." This arrangement would produce a more cohesive command under an officer to whom Butler would probably defer, although "success would be more certain were Smith in command untrammeled, and General Butler remanded to the administrative duties of the department."[31]

These recommendations were painful enough to Butler, but a few days later Barnard dealt his ego a harder blow. Meigs returned to Washington on the twenty-sixth while his colleague reported to Grant in person. Barnard described the terrain around Bermuda Hundred, drew a rough sketch of Butler's and Beauregard's lines, and coined a phrase that haunted Butler for years: "It's like a bottle, General, but the enemy has corked it!" Grant thought the description so apt that he inserted it into his campaign report, ensuring it a wide circulation.[32]

Grant came to regret the characterization, for he saw, as Butler had, that the Army of the James was not doomed to stationary operations. Beauregard may have blocked the army in front, but it enjoyed easy access to the James, the Appomattox, and the country beyond. With this in mind, Grant determined to enlarge upon one of the options his emissaries had outlined. He had Halleck instruct Butler to retain only enough troops to hold Bermuda Hundred, City Point, and the outposts on the James. "All available forces" were to be placed under Smith, shipped to Fort Monroe, then up the York and Pamunkey Rivers to link with Meade somewhere below the North Anna. Integrated with Meade's force, the transferees could aid Grant's overall strategy. Despite his misgivings about Smith's temperament, Grant considered him the ablest officer along the Appomattox. Rescued from a situation he loathed, Smith might render effective, even outstanding, service.[33]

When Halleck relayed Grant's decision to Bermuda Hundred early on the twenty-sixth, the local response was predictable. Butler grew depressed at the thought of losing more than half his command. "It is the worst sign I have seen of the movements of Grant," he wrote his wife, "that he is looking to get his reinforcements from here." Butler was further chagrined by a second cable from Halleck, specifying Smith as leader of the expeditionary force and suggesting that Gillmore or Weitzel, not Butler, command the troops that remained on the peninsula. Smith viewed the order as a reprieve from hell. He had just written to his family expressing the fear that he was being left to rot in "this hole," where "we are in a regular muddle." The Army of the James had fallen so low in strength and morale that "it is now a perfectly useless command . . . and nothing will set it right" but a change at the highest level.[34]

Despite his pique, Butler expedited Smith's detachment. Within hours he began to concentrate the troops to be sent north and to fill the gaps their departure would create. For the expedition he selected the XVIII Corps divisions of Brooks and Martindale, which were positioned nearest the Appomattox landings. To round out the number Grant had requested, he detached several regiments from the X Corps divisions of Ames and Turner. Turner would not accompany this force; Ames would, but not to command it. Butler formed the X Corps contingent into a provisional division under his newest subordinate, General Devens. Four additional X Corps regiments he attached to the XVIII Corps, three to Martindale's division and one to

Brooks's. Although Smith stated that the thirty-seven regiments assigned to him totaled 12,500 effectives, the number was probably closer to 15,000. Its departure would leave Terry's reinforced division to hold Bermuda Hundred while Hinks's division would continue to garrison City Point and the James River forts.

While Smith waited for transports, Butler shifted Terry's division, along with the remnants of Ames's and Turner's, southward until they stretched across the center of the Bermuda Hundred defenses. To augment the southern flank, Butler called up dismounted troopers from Kautz's division, infantry from Hinks's, ambulatory wounded, and heavy artillerymen from the recently arrived siege train of Colonel Henry L. Abbot. To divert Beauregard's attention from the operation, Butler ordered part of Martindale's division, waiting to embark at Bermuda Hundred landing, to move against the Confederate right. The advance merely added to Butler's casualty list, the most prominent fatality being Colonel Arthur H. Dutton of the 21st Connecticut, who had been widely considered to be general officer material.[35]

Despite Butler's best efforts, Smith's departure was chaotic. An insufficiency of ships, stevedores, and support equipment slowed the embarkation; although the force began to sail on the morning of the twenty-seventh, most of the troops did not leave Bermuda Hundred for another two days. Some did not board ship until the thirty-first. When finally under way the troops found themselves crammed aboard aged, creaky vessels soiled with manure from previous passengers: cavalry mounts and beef cattle. The conditions provoked much complaint, as did the indiscriminate manner in which cargo was loaded. Critical supplies such as rations and medical stores were stacked at the bottom of the holds, while many of Smith's sixteen cannon and almost all his ordnance stores remained on a wharf along the James long after the transports left.[36]

Other problems concerned Smith. Although Grant had ordered him to land at White House, near the head of the Pamunkey River, the expeditionary leader feared he would encounter detachments of Lee's army there. He had petitioned Grant to permit him to debark instead at West Point, where Henry's brigade had landed at the outset of the Bermuda Hundred campaign. Grant refused, believing that a landing there would place Smith's men on the wrong side of the Pamunkey and require an extensive ferrying operation. But as Smith's main force cast off from Bermuda Hundred, it was preceded by the brigade assigned to Ames, which Smith had ordered to West Point. After landing, Ames was to march to the north bank directly opposite White House, guarding Smith's landing site. As Grant had warned Halleck, Smith would substitute his plan for another whenever he could get away with it.

Smith worried in vain, though things could have been even worse than he imagined. Under gunboat convoy, Ames made an unmolested trip up the James and the York, went ashore early on the twenty-ninth, and tramped northwestward to White House. This was remarkable, for only fifteen miles west of White House, near a country crossroads known as Cold Harbor, Lee's army had been gathering since the previous day. At the last minute, Grant feared for Smith's safety; he went so far as to order Meade to send Sheridan's cavalry to White House on escort duty. Smith was lucky that the usually vigilant enemy failed to detect his presence along the Pamunkey until he secured a foothold there.[37]

Soon, however, he encountered real trouble. When he left Bermuda Hundred he knew nothing of Meade's location—merely that the Army of the Potomac was preparing to cross the Pamunkey—and so he could not guess where a linkup would take place. Not until the evening of the thirtieth did Smith receive a telegram (two days old) announcing that Meade was concentrating at Hanover Town, several miles northwest of White House. The message ordered Smith to New Castle, halfway between the first two locations. Against his better judgment—he felt exposed without his guns and supply train—Smith started his men northwestward. They carried enough ammunition for only a few hours of fighting.[38]

The last day of May brought baking, breezeless heat; stragglers soon littered the road to New Castle. To worsen matters, when the head of the column neared its destination late in the day, no comrades were in sight. The reason became known soon after daylight on June 1, when a messenger from Grant reached Smith with word that the troops were supposed to march to New Castle *Ferry*, several miles to the north and west. There they would find Major General Horatio G. Wright's VI Corps of the Army of the Potomac; Smith was to fall in on Wright's upper flank.

Grant subsequently urged him to hurry up. An irritated Smith moved quickly on from New Castle without allowing his men time for breakfast. His advance echelon reached the ferry late in the morning. As at New Castle, no one was on hand to greet Smith; one veteran found that "nothing but [the] muttering of distant artillery gave sign of war." Smith and many of his troops were disgusted; others felt lost and anxious, beset by an "awful sense of coming danger."[39]

Repressing his anger and frustration (something not easy for him to do), Smith sent a staff officer to locate Meade. Before he could return, Lieutenant Colonel Orville Babcock of Grant's staff galloped up to confirm that an egregious mistake had been made. Through the carelessness of someone at Grant's headquarters—a telegrapher, perhaps—the Army of the James had marched far to the north of its intended destination, Cold Harbor.

Smith, foreseeing a long countermarch under the sun, was furious, but nothing could be done. He turned his column about and had it trudge southeastward until it met a thoroughfare that Babcock assured Smith led to Cold Harbor via the old battlefield of Gaines's Mill. Soon after the march resumed, the troops had to endure a new discomfort—the stench of dead horses. Carcasses along the road attested to recent fighting outside Cold Harbor between Sheridan's men and the cavalry of Major General Wade Hampton, successor to the late J. E. B. Stuart. The head of the column next passed an intersection and a sign that read, "Twelve Miles to Richmond." Men shouted in exasperation: "If that's the way to Richmond, what the devil are we going to Gaines's Mill for?"[40]

A few miles shy of Cold Harbor blue troops appeared along parallel roads: Smith's men had finally found the Army of the Potomac. As the columns exchanged greetings, Smith rode forward to confirm that his men were marching beside the VI Corps. Sometime after noon, still a few miles from his destination, he met a courier from Meade, who delivered a dispatch that told Smith his hard marching would be followed by hard fighting: "As soon as General Wright opens the road from Old Church to Cold Harbor, you will follow him, and take position on his right, endeavoring to hold the road from Cold Harbor to Bethesda Church. General Wright is ordered to attack as soon as his troops are up, and I desire you should co-operate with him and join in the attack. The enemy have not long been in position about Cold Harbor, and it is of great importance to dislodge and, if possible, to rout him before he can entrench himself."[41]

From his knowledge of the local topography—he had fought nearby during the Peninsula Campaign—Smith suspected that both armies were being drawn to a certain road junction north of Richmond. Doubtless Grant was going to use the crossroads as a jumping-off point for the final leg of his drive on the capital. Lee would strive to block Meade's path, forcing the Federals to swing wide around his lower flank as they had done time and again during the past month. Smith wondered if Grant had enough room to do so, hemmed in as he was by the James, Chickahominy, and Pamunkey Rivers.

Sometime after 3:00 P.M. Smith's long, hot, and circuitous journey came to an end. About a mile and a half northeast of Gaines's Mill, his soldiers went into line of battle just above the VI Corps, a part of which was already engaged with Rebels toward the west. While awaiting further orders, Smith recon-noitered enemy positions and identified points of concern. He feared that an enemy concentration near Bethesda Church, three miles to the northwest, commanded the ground he would have to cover during an assault. To protect his right flank, Smith sent toward the church several regiments he had intended to attack with. His intent had been to strike in three ranks, backed by a substantial reserve; now he would have to go forward in two lines, with a meager contingent in the rear.[42]

As his column closed up, Smith prepared it for action. On the left, connecting with Wright's command, he placed the weakest of his divisions, the provisional organization under Devens, which was missing the better part of Ames's brigade, left near White House to guard the far rear until relieved by Meade. He formed Brooks's division, like Ames's, into two ranks and positioned it in the center, "with half a line in reserve." Along the right flank he posted Martindale's command, its upper echelon at a right angle to the rest of the line and connecting with the troops sent to Bethesda Church. Barely had Smith moved his units into position when, at about 5:30 P.M., Meade directed him to advance in cooperation with the VI Corps. By driving the enemy, Smith and Wright would purchase time for the bulk of the Army of the Potomac—the II, V, and IX Corps—to reach the field.[43]

Devens's and Brooks's troops started forward, with Martindale's remaining behind to provide cover fire. As rifle balls spattered out of the woods that shrouded Lee's forward works, the Army of the James broke into a trot across the sun-drenched meadow. The crash of cannonfire suddenly sounded from the woods and men crumpled under a spray of shell and case shot.

Most of Smith's troops kept moving for the trees, their only hope for shelter. Martindale's sharpshooters prevented the enemy from applying unbearable pressure against the north flank, but on the other end of the line the VI Corps took a heavy beating. Greater opposition and rougher terrain than Smith encountered stopped Wright's troops from keeping pace with the Army of the James. The resulting gap in the attack formation permitted the Confederates to concentrate their fire against Smith's left, taking a heavy toll of Devens's division.

Despite the onslaught, most of Smith's troops made it into the woods, where they came upon a hastily dug and imperfectly fortified line of earthworks. The attackers vaulted over the works and fired into the trenches. Shocked and demoralized, many Confederates raced for the rear. "There, boys, see those devils run!" shouted Colonel Drake of Devens's division. "Didn't I tell you you'd drive them out?" But not every Rebel had fled; a minute later one drilled a bullet into the colonel's skull.[44]

Despite the loss of its commander, the brigade made it into the woods in good order. William Barton's brigade, however, was hit so hard that many

men, utterly demoralized, fled back to their lines before making it halfway
across the meadow. In the center, only a provisional brigade under Guy
Henry reached the trees; the rest of Brooks's division was halted short of its
objective by a deep marsh undetectable from the starting point of the
attack. Henry's brigade, however, did enough good work for all, chasing
away hundreds of the enemy and capturing a length of rifle pits.

After securing the trenches just inside the woods, Drake's and Henry's
survivors pressed on. A few hundred yards farther west they encountered
a much stronger line of trenches inside a grassy clearing. Defended by artillery,
this position was formidable, and the attackers could not withstand the
firepower. The Federals wavered and fell back to the works they had captured,
where they were joined by comrades up from the rear.[45]

Studying the situation through field glasses, Smith decided against
a further advance. While his men in the woods improved their confiscated
defenses, the expeditionary commander had his reserves build a defensive
perimeter in case a further retreat proved necessary. As darkness came on,
trench diggers extended Smith's line across the grassy plain till an elongated
V appeared, its arms stretched so thin that Smith feared it would not withstand a counterattack, especially now that he was running low on ammunition.
Hours earlier he had asked for some cartridges from the Army of the Potomac
till his ordnance wagons arrived from White House but had received no reply.
He later learned that upon receiving his request, Meade had exclaimed,
"Why the hell didn't he wait for his supplies to come up before coming here?"[46]

Such discourtesy was more than enough to infuriate Smith. The morning's
exertions and hardships had left his temper fiber-thin, and the afternoon's
carnage had done nothing to improve it. Smith may have been tactless,
brusque, even insolent with peers and superiors, but he treated his officers
and men courteously and was ever concerned with their well-being. Thanks
to Meade's tactics, those men had endured an assault across a long expanse
of ground bristling with natural obstacles and bereft of flank support.
Smith would never forgive Meade for the 1,000 casualties that had resulted.

His wrangling with Meade was not over. During the night Smith's men
in the woods withstood four limited counterattacks against their reinforced
position. About midnight, shortly after the final repulse, Meade ordered
Smith to renew his offensive at sunrise "with your whole force and as vigorous[ly] as possible." The message closed with an implied rebuke: "I have had
no report of your operations this afternoon." The criticism was unmerited,
for Smith had sent couriers to army headquarters throughout the day,
updating his situation. Now he let out his anger in a reply rushed to Meade:
"I have endeavored to represent to you my condition. In the present condition

of my line an attack by me would be simply preposterous; not only that, but an attack on the part of the enemy of any vigor would probably carry my lines more than half their length. . . . Deserters report the enemy massing on my right for an attack early in the morning."[47]

Though perhaps unduly concerned about a counterassault, Smith was right to consider his command in no condition to retake the offensive. Not only was ammunition low, but he would not be at full strength for days. Only now were his rearmost regiments debarking at White House, along with his supply train. Confusing orders and logistical problems prevented these troops from starting for Cold Harbor until early on June 3; some would not reach the battlefield until the fifth. Nor was the whole of Meade's army on hand; suspecting that any support from the Army of the Potomac would be severely limited, Smith regarded a renewed assault as suicidal. His belief communicated itself to his men, who feared that just such an assault would be ordered. One veteran wrote of "the hopeless look which many of the soldiers wore" that night.[48]

To their great relief, June 2 passed without a general engagement. Meade postponed his desired assault until 5:00 P.M. When he learned that his rear elements were still on the road to Cold Harbor, he rescheduled the attack for dawn on the third. The respite permitted Smith to strengthen his position by moving fresh troops up to the hard-pressed brigades in the woods while relieving other units with a newly arrived division of Wright's corps. Smith also helped distribute ammunition that Wright graciously offered him.

By late on the second, Meade's now-intact army had joined Smith's command along a six-mile line running south from Bethesda Church to Barker's Mill on the Chickahominy. The Union force totaled 114,000, opposed to Lee's 78,000. Regardless, the Confederates, protected by earthworks they had been allowed twenty-four hours to improve, enjoyed the tactical advantage. Fully aware of the fact, Smith realized that an assault would have to be executed with extreme precision, requiring the utmost cooperation among the corps.

For this reason Smith was incredulous when he learned of Meade's plan for the third, which called for an assault along the entire line, with each corps to fight without reference to the others. If Smith went forward on his own, he stood to suffer at both ends of his line. He could not count on Wright's corps to cover his left flank, and his right was separated by almost two miles from the nearest element of Meade's army, the V Corps of Major General Gouverneur K. Warren. Smith believed that an uncoordinated attack forfeited "the few advantages belonging to the assailants" and increased

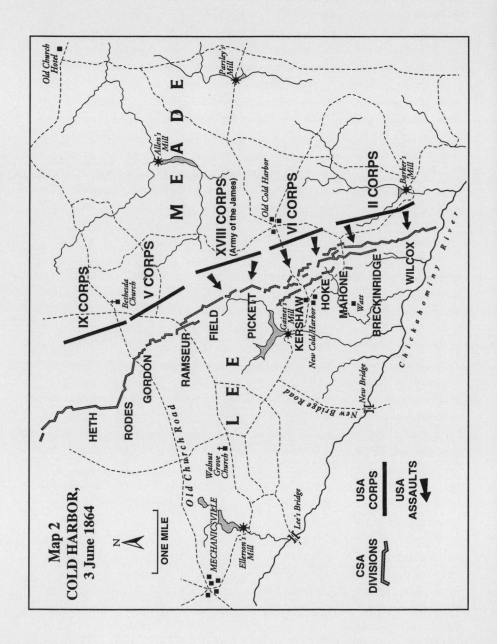

Map 2
COLD HARBOR,
3 June 1864

N

ONE MILE

CSA
DIVISIONS

USA
CORPS

USA
ASSAULTS

"largely the chances of [a] successful defense." As an experienced construction engineer, he appreciated the strength of the works to his front. This may have escaped Meade, whose experience was largely in topographical engineering, and Grant, who had won many of his campaigns through siege operations or frontal assaults against relatively weak positions.[49]

Smith realized that his objections, however valid, were futile. His men joined him in fearing the worst. As they had on previous occasions prior to assaulting well-entrenched positions, they attached handwritten name tags to their uniforms so that their bodies might be identified and given a proper burial. That night a steady drizzle came down, making many a soldier's sleep miserable.

At 4:30 on the morning of the third, Meade's artillery opened and then the infantry lurched forward all along the line. This time it was Devens's division, now on the northern flank, that remained behind to try to cover the gap between Smith's corps and Warren's. The troops under Martindale, in the center of Smith's position, and those of Brooks on the left rushed forward in the hope that a speedy advance would enable them to overcome the obstacles before them.

At first the cannonade shielded the divisions, but as soon as they outdistanced their artillery support, both encountered heavy fire that obliterated the head of the attack force as well as large portions of both flanks. "It seemed more like a volcanic blast than a battle," recalled a New Hampshire officer, "and was just about as destructive." Those who reached the heavily defended clearing fell so rapidly they formed human breastworks behind which men in the rear took refuge. The clearing became carpeted with so many bodies that for yards in every direction the ground appeared to turn from green to blue.[50]

Despite the carnage, some of Smith's troops progressed toward the enemy line. Part of Brooks's division advanced far enough to drive Rebel infantry away from the cannon they had been supporting. Some of Martindale's men took shelter in a ravine halfway through the clearing, from which they poured volleys into the woods beyond, flushing out Rebel reserves. These accomplishments notwithstanding, progress was measured in a few feet at most points.

Treading a careful path to the front in midmorning, Smith huddled with Martindale. They concluded that little more could be done on the right flank; the ravine was as far as Martindale's division could push. Smith then made his way south, dodging sharpshooters' bullets, to see if he could get things moving on the other end of the line. He could not, for Brooks had been pinned down by a new outbreak of cannon and rifle fire. While in that sector, Smith observed a renewed assault to the north, undertaken to support what Martindale mistook for an offensive by Brooks. When a barrage from the clearing sent Martindale's veterans scurrying to the rear like rookies, the disheartened Smith realized that the day was lost.

His colleagues were not so prescient. At eleven o'clock, with Smith's troops still immobilized, Meade ordered yet another attack. Smith rejected the order and treated Meade's courier to a burst of profanity, an act for which he expected to pay. To his surprise, at about 2:00 P.M., Meade's headquarters announced meekly that "for the present all further offensive operations will be suspended."[51]

Smith immediately recalled his troops. Those able to disengage made their way gingerly to the rear, many on hands and knees; others wormed their way back to escape streams of bullets overhead. Hundreds did not dare attempt to withdraw until dark. Toward evening Lee's barrage finally slackened, with only a few artillery pieces keeping up a measured response. Union cannon replied to the desultory cannonade, and in this fashion, a tragic day ended.

For Smith the day ended on a fitting note. At sundown a circular from Meade's headquarters reached his hands: "The commanding general directs you to report the condition of affairs in your front, and what it is practicable to do to-morrow." Smith could only conclude that Meade was

Charge of Smith's XVIII Corps at Cold Harbor, June 3, 1864. ENGRAVING FROM *FRANK LESLIE'S ILLUSTRATED NEWSPAPER.*

deluded. Again, he sought to bring Meade back to reality: "In reference to the condition of affairs in my front, I would respectfully state that I now hold and have held all that I have gained. . . . In reference to what it may be practicable to do to-morrow on my front, I can only say, that what I failed to do to-day—namely, to carry the enemy's works on my front by columns of assault . . . I would hardly dare to recommend as practicable to-morrow with my diminished force."[52]

Ultimately, Grant as well as Meade came to share this view; there were no further assaults at Cold Harbor. The progress the Federals had achieved on the first and third remained fixed: an average of perhaps 100 yards of open and wooded terrain. In gaining so little, the attackers had suffered nearly 13,000 casualties, most of them in the first half hour of fighting and roughly a quarter of them in Smith's command. More costly battles lay ahead, but for concentrated carnage and sheer futility, the assaults at Cold Harbor would stand as unique.

By the close of June 3 Baldy Smith was feeling very much the effect of those losses. With tears in his eyes, he directed efforts to inter the dead, tend to the wounded, and rescue men still trapped between the lines. At intervals he swore aloud, cursing Meade for engineering such butchery and Grant for permitting it. The bitter feelings Smith would harbor against those commanders—feelings more virulent than any he had toward Ben Butler—would redound to his detriment. But as long as he lived he would not permit himself to forgive the architects of the disaster at Cold Harbor.[53]

CHAPTER SEVEN

The Petersburg Follies

ON THE DAY SMITH'S EXPEDITION LEFT BERMUDA HUNDRED FOR COLD Harbor, a downcast Benjamin F. Butler wrote to his wife at Fort Monroe, "Grant has sent all my troops to move over on the other line and help him. This is a sign of weakness I did not look for, and to my mind augurs worse for our cause than anything I have seen." Of course, he was also concerned about the blow to his military and political career that Smith's detachment had dealt him. He realized that in the mind of the Northern public, the loss of 15,000 men to a more active operation dramatized what the newspapers had been proclaiming: his campaign in Virginia was a failure.[1]

The resourceful and supportive Sarah Butler tried to cheer her husband by dismissing anonymous enemies: "So, they have shorn you utterly at last! Never heed it. You will yet go beyond them. In their wish to kill they will o'erleap the mark, and stumble to their own downfall." She then turned toward future ventures: "If you could hold your command complete, now would seem to be the time when you could win glory for the country and yourself, but even [with the army] divided . . . with your active mind in expedients, you could inflict more injury upon the enemy and give greater aid to Gen. Grant than to be swallowed up in his immediate command."[2]

Mrs. Butler knew how to enliven her husband. Her words made Butler realize that he could still contribute significantly to the war effort. The 15,000 or more troops left at Bermuda Hundred and City Point were more than enough to hold those positions, especially against Beauregard's thinned ranks, and still continue to carry out active operations elsewhere. Butler might have deferred his plan to attack Petersburg but he had not abandoned it.

The military and political rewards of attacking the city appeared enormous. Its capture might doom Lee's army and the Confederate government, and Benjamin F. Butler would move swiftly from failure to success and adulation. The Republican Party's nomination for president, to be conferred in June, remained attainable. If Butler had not benefited from the recent operations in Virginia, neither had Abraham Lincoln. In fact, the president's popularity was noticeably weakening; even party stalwarts had begun to work actively against his renomination. One of the most visible indications of this disaffection was an impending convention in Cleveland at which radical Republicans—dissatisfied with the president's military, political, and social agenda—would choose an extremist alternative to Lincoln. Butler believed that neither Lincoln nor the radicals' candidate would win in November; perhaps only a military hero could save the party from disaster.

As Butler concentrated on Petersburg's possibilities, his spirits took flight. By the last day in May he was his old, optimistic self. He wrote Sarah that "the tide of deep, bitter disappointment has rolled over, and most sharply has the wrong done as well to the country as myself been felt, but it has been borne as well as may be. At least, none have heard outward sign of complaint. My time will come, and that not long delayed. . . . Do not think me sad and complaining—far from it. I was never more quietly calm, cool, or determined. Two days will decide whether we are to be pounced upon here or not. I think not, and then I take the offensive."[3]

He wired General Hinks that same day, inquiring how many black troops could be spared from City Point and Spring Hill ("infantry and cavalry alone wanted") for a drive on Petersburg. He then asked General Wild how many defenders might be detached from Wilson's Wharf and Fort Powhatan for the mission. Their replies convinced Butler that within two days, he could assemble 2,000 black troops plus about half as many white soldiers from Bermuda Hundred. He tentatively planned to move on June 2.[4]

At first it appeared that Beauregard would not ruin this timetable. For several days after Smith began to leave the James for the Pamunkey, the lines along Bermuda Hundred neck saw little activity. The twenty-seventh was quiet but for an hour's worth of Rebel sharpshooter fire. The next day an artillery barrage appeared to signal an impending assault, but after going on alert to no purpose, the Federals relaxed. A Massachusetts infantryman found the next two days dull and boring: "We lie and glare at each other, and do nothing but skirmish a little on the picket-line." One of General Kautz's subordinates, serving dismounted at the front, called the daily routine a "sad farce." Kautz himself began to wonder if Beauregard had pulled out.[5]

The proceedings livened up on May 30, when a new round of artillery fire gave way to a small attack against the far right. Some ground was lost, but it was quickly regained; as Gillmore informed Butler, the fracas did not "amount to anything serious." The following day, however, Confederates attacked not only Bermuda Hundred but Spring Hill as well. Bermuda Hundred stood firm, but Hinks's garrison, which had been weakened to augment the works on the peninsula, was in peril for a time. The threat passed as soon as the USCTs at Bermuda Hundred returned to their old post via the pontoon bridge Butler had thrown across the Appomattox at Point of Rocks.[6]

On June 1 Butler broached his Petersburg plan to Hinks and Kautz. As they mulled it over, a new assault struck Bermuda Hundred. After an hour and a half, part of the right flank gave way and was restored only after support hustled there from the south. Once the fighting subsided, however, Butler said no more of Petersburg. Kautz, for one, believed he had dropped the project.[7]

Butler had not, but he postponed the operation yet again after Beauregard, early on the second, made his most aggressive attack in two weeks. Not even during the week after Drewry's Bluff had the Rebels struck in two widely divergent sectors as they did on this occasion in an attempt to determine how many troops had left Butler's front. On the northern flank the brigades of Matt Ransom and Henry Wise (the latter minus its commander, still at Petersburg) rushed the pickets of Terry's 7th Connecticut and 39th Illinois. Ransom's men shot up both regiments, snatched up more than 100 prisoners, and drove off the rest. The Yankees' flight left a third regiment on the picket line, the 11th Maine, easy pickings for Wise's brigade, which captured the outfit virtually intact. The entire flank was threatened with collapse until troops from the main line, led by the 3rd New Hampshire, regained most of the lost ground in a spirited late-morning counterattack. Some captured sectors of the picket line proved unrecoverable, and Butler readjusted his positions accordingly.[8]

Meanwhile, on the other end of the Union line, a South Carolina regiment previously in Walker's brigade pounced on other pickets of the 7th Connecticut, supported by Kautz's troopers. In what one participant called "scrappy and disconnected" fighting, both sides gained and then lost the advantage. As on the upper flank, the tide turned with the arrival of reinforcements, including the 1st District of Columbia Cavalry with its Henry repeaters. The South Carolinians drew off, having suffered 172 casualties, including their mortally wounded colonel, O. M. Dantzler. In honor of his energetic assault, Dantzler's name later graced the battery at the Howlett house.[9]

Some of Butler's subordinates, including Gillmore, feared the two-pronged attack was the prelude to an all-out offensive. Butler, observing from the rear, did not share their concern. Indeed, there was no further pressure on his line that day, and on the third day only skirmish fire came from the enemy position. Most of the day was so quiet that the sounds of battle drifting south from Cold Harbor, twenty miles away, were more audible than Beauregard's musketry.

The racket from the north left the Army of the James worrying about the result on Meade's front. Not until the sixth did Butler's people get an inkling of the disaster above Richmond, thanks to a flag-of-truce exchange of newspapers with Rebel pickets. Unhappy details trickled into Bermuda Hundred over the next several days, casting gloom everywhere.[10]

The news depressed Butler less than it would have under normal circumstances. A major failure by the Army of the Potomac would partially offset his own recent setbacks in the mind of the public while further devaluing Lincoln's political stock on the eve of the National Union convention in Baltimore, to be attended by mainstream Republicans and War Democrats. On June 4, three days before the convention opened, Butler's chief of staff, Colonel Shaffer, went to Baltimore with the hope of starting some logrolling in his superior's behalf.

On the fifth Butler again sought military success to support his candidacy. Now certain that his defenses could be held by 5,000 troops, he readied an equal number for a move against Petersburg. He dispatched 200 of Kautz's men in advance to reconnoiter the approaches to the city. What they found was not recorded, but two days later a deserter came inside Butler's lines to proclaim that a single infantry regiment, supported by unreliable militia, guarded Butler's objective.[11]

As he drew up plans to strike south, Butler received an unexpected telegram from Cold Harbor. Written on the sixth, it reported that Grant had decided to cross the James at an early but unspecified date. To facilitate the crossing, he was sending Lieutenant Colonel Cyrus Comstock of his staff to collect bridge-building materials at Fort Monroe. Comstock and others would select the crossing points in consultation with Butler's engineers.

Butler feared that his Petersburg offensive was in jeopardy. Grant's telegram indicated that he and Meade were heading for Petersburg, too. With them on the scene, Butler could be denied credit for the capture of Richmond's support center. Thus, he resolved to launch his assault before the Army of the Potomac could reach his front. Late on the seventh he directed Kautz to ready an expeditionary force; similar orders went to Hinks at City Point. Although Hinks did not record his reaction, Kautz believed "the expedition can only succeed" given its "impudence and [the] want of fore-sight on the part of the enemy" in protecting the city. One day later, however, the cavalry leader decided that the mission "looks uncertain but it may possibly succeed."[12]

By the time he modified his opinion, Kautz had been briefed on the operation. The northeastern side of Petersburg was to be attacked by 3,500 USCT members, who would hold in place those defenders along the road from City Point. Meanwhile, Kautz's force of 1,400 would enter the city from the south, moving up the Jerusalem Plank Road and burning rail and foot-bridges over the Appomattox. That done, Butler predicted, "the rest of the town will be at our mercy." The Federals would hold the city until Lee sent reinforcements or would withdraw after completing their destruction.[13]

The plan appeared simple and viable. Had it been implemented as drawn up, it might have succeeded. Unfortunately for Butler it became unacceptably complicated through the intrusion of Gillmore, who, smarting from the criticism of his recent performances, saw the project as an oppor-tunity for redemption. As Butler recalled, Gillmore "became very strongly impressed with the great probability of its [the operation's] success, and insisted that he ought to command it, being senior officer. He . . . claimed it as his right and as a matter of military courtesy." Butler added ruefully: "I was fool enough to yield to him."[14]

Gillmore's involvement prompted a change in plans. Something of a negrophobe, the corps commander would not entrust Hinks's troops with critical responsibilities. He persuaded Butler to allow only Wild's brigade to operate northeast of Petersburg, primarily in support of four white regiments of Hawley's brigade. Kautz was authorized to take only about two-thirds as many troopers as originally envisioned, principally Spear's brigade. No artillery would accompany the expedition. The combined force would cross the pontoons at Point of Rocks at about midnight on June 8, camp below the Appomattox till daylight, and head south in a single column. At dawn Gillmore would push across the City Point and Jordan's Point Roads, allowing Kautz to proceed south. Once the cavalry was in position fifteen to twenty miles below the infantry, it would attack from that direction while Gillmore struck from his sector. He would also destroy the railroad bridges above the city, especially the Government Bridge, which, as Butler informed Gillmore, "formed the only link of railroad of the proper gauge on which the transportation of Lee's army could be sent south."[15]

Gillmore assured his commander that he would adhere faithfully to the plan. Seven hours before leaving Bermuda Hundred, however, he asked Butler's permission to take a battery. While agreeing to allow a two-gun section to go, Butler cautioned that "this is not to be artillery work, but a quick, decisive push." He must have wondered if Gillmore knew the meaning of those last three words.[16]

In addition to seeking artillery when none was authorized, Gillmore took a fifth infantry regiment, the 62nd Ohio of Howell's brigade, without informing Butler. This addition further compromised the mobility of the column.

Gillmore also failed to adhere to the timetable. He was to have his troops on the river's south bank by midnight, but his rear guard did not straggle across at Point of Rocks until 2:30 A.M. on the ninth. The expeditionary leader's excuse was that he had lost his way in the dark. Afterward, a sarcastic Butler suggested to Gillmore that "as the pontoon bridge is on the left of your line of intrenchments, it would seem that your regiments got lost within their own lines." How this was possible, Butler had no idea. His anger only increased when Gillmore's chief of staff "woke me up at 2 o'clock in the morning to inquire the road . . . to the pontoon bridge, which . . . should have been as familiar to him and to you as the path to your bed."[17]

Gillmore was not solely to blame for these miscues, however. Having intended to take the direct road to the bridge, at the last minute he was informed by General Terry that the route was in full view of the enemy. To preserve surprise Terry suggested a road farther to the rear but one less familiar to Gillmore. Unknown terrain and a dark night resulted in the head of the column stumbling into a swamp, "with mud reaching nearly to their knees." After that, as Butler subsequently commented, the troops wandered about "like sheep without a shepherd" till early on the ninth. Butler added a final dollop of sarcasm: "If it took five hours and ten minutes to get out of your lines, how long would it take you to get into the enemy's?"[18]

Gillmore's travail did not end when he located the bridge. Bales of hay had been placed on the pontoons to muffle the sounds of tramping feet, but when the mud-spattered troops reached the bridge they used the hay to clean the muck from their uniforms. Unaware of his troops' actions, at 3:40 A.M. Gillmore complained to Butler that "I have no doubt that the enemy are fully apprised of our movement by the noise of the bridge. It is not muffled at all, and the crossing of the cavalry can be heard for miles."[19]

Instead of resting on the south bank, Gillmore's men hurried down to City Point. There they united with Hinks and Wild, who had been waiting almost three hours. Under the supervision of Butler's staff, the USCTs had readied themselves for the march precisely on time. Muttering about the unexplained delay, they fell in behind their white comrades as the long column lurched southward.

At about 5:00 A.M., after perhaps two hours on the road, Kautz's troopers passed to the front of the column, as planned, and moved south by another road. Kautz had informed Gillmore that by 9:00 he would be in position for their coordinated assault. Hinks's infantry followed the horsemen till they reached the Jordan's Point Road. The black troops turned west and took position a few miles from the city, where they were to remain until they learned that Kautz had reached his jumping-off point. Gillmore had assigned Hinks to penetrate and seal off the defenses on the Jerusalem Plank Road, then move northwestward to seize and destroy all "the public buildings, public stores, bridges across the Appomattox, depots, and cars" that crossed their path.[20]

After Kautz and Hinks left him, Gillmore led Hawley's brigade westward on the City Point Road. Moving cautiously, the advance guard of the expanded brigade made contact with some Confederate cavalry at about six o'clock. Shoving the mounted pickets aside, Hawley's 7th Connecticut pressed forward. Meanwhile, on the lower road, Hinks's men gouged Rebels from advanced positions and made parallel progress. By 7:00 A.M. Hawley's brigade had halted before Lunettes 2 and 3, two of the fifty-five detached forts that defended the city along a semicircular line ten miles long. To the south, Wild's men pushed to within fifty yards of Lunettes 4 through 7.

Other than sending his chief engineer frequently to confer with Hinks, Gillmore apparently spent the next three hours staring at the works facing him and fretting about their strength. Hinks filled the time with short-range skirmishing. The enemy put up unexpectedly stiff resistance, and at about ten o'clock Hinks was forced to withdraw from his original position. Reconnoitering the works before him, the division commander concluded that they prevented a successful assault unless Gillmore advanced to distract the artillerists along the Jordan's Point Road.[21]

Gillmore was not certain he could help the USCT. Lunettes 2 and 3, bristling with artillery protected by heavy works, began to look as foreboding as Battery Wagner outside Charleston. He decided he would not attempt to take the positions until he learned that Kautz had attacked on the south. Throughout the morning and into the afternoon, however, no sounds of fighting drifted up from Kautz's sector, leaving Gillmore uncertain that the cavalry had gotten into position. He began to rationalize his inactivity and convinced himself that even if Kautz carried his part of the line, a successful penetration in the infantry's sector was not guaranteed.

After 1:00 P.M. Gillmore began to fear that Hawley and Wild were too far apart to provide mutual support in a crisis. Perhaps remembering Beauregard's attack at Drewry's Bluff, which had threatened to drive a wedge between

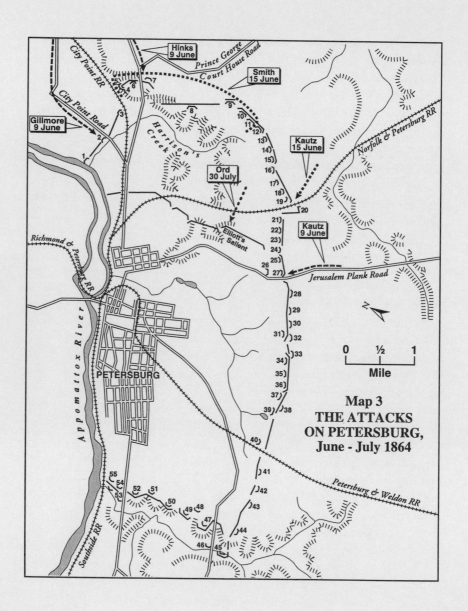

Hinks
9 June

Smith
15 June

Prince George
Court House Road

Gillmore
9 June

City Point RR

City Point Road

Harrison's
Creek

Kautz
15 June

Norfolk & Petersburg RR

Ord
30 July

Elliott's
Sallent

Kautz
9 June

Richmond & Petersburg RR

Jerusalem Plank Road

N

0   ½   1
Mile

PETERSBURG

Appomattox River

Map 3
THE ATTACKS
ON PETERSBURG,
June - July 1864

Petersburg & Weldon RR

Southside RR

the X and XVIII Corps, Gillmore asked his subordinates whether a limited withdrawal was warranted. Colonel Hawley favored a pullback: his men were boxed in by the Appomattox to the north and on the south by the roadbed of the Petersburg & City Point Railroad and a sixty-foot ridge parallel to the tracks. Gillmore then learned that Hinks's command was taking enfilading fire from Lunette 7. He conferred hurriedly with Hinks and was supposedly told that to attack the works was to risk a "slaughter." Here was a word calculated to chill Gillmore's blood. Mounting concern that the infantry was in a tight spot persuaded him, at about 1:30 P.M., to retreat. Later he claimed he withdrew merely to link Hawley's brigade with Wild's, but he could have accomplished that without pulling back. The City Point and Jordan's Point Roads converged a short distance to the west, safely in front of the Rebel works.[22]

After reuniting the black and white troops beyond range of Petersburg's guns, Gillmore marked time for another two hours. Hearing nothing from Kautz, the expeditionary commander suspected that the cavalry had gone raiding instead of attacking the southern approaches. Supposedly he had heard Butler approve such a mission in the event Kautz found no opportunity to attack Petersburg.

Gillmore did not intend to shoulder the whole load. After three o'clock he moved farther to the rear, halting by a sawmill several miles from Petersburg but still, in his opinion, within earshot of Kautz. The wait at the mill consumed another hour; by 4:00 P.M. Gillmore was certain that Kautz had taken his troopers off the board and that nothing more could be accomplished east of Petersburg. He led his troops northward, refusing to take the more westerly route that would have enabled him to seize the bridges Butler had directed to his attention.

Gillmore also ignored Butler's injunction against returning home unblooded. The army leader had stressed this by providing Gillmore with an estimate of acceptable casualties: "The advantage [of seizing Petersburg] would be cheaply purchased at 500, and not too dearly with the sacrifice of 1,000 men in killed and wounded." By the time he headed back to Point of Rocks, Gillmore had suffered a couple dozen casualties. Even worse, opposition had been astonishingly light. Throughout the day Hawley's 2,200 troops had been held inactive by a handful of cannon supported by militia, while 500 regulars had kept Hinks's 1,300 men at bay.[23]

While Gillmore headed home, Kautz was trying mightily, if erratically, to meet his obligations south of Petersburg. Though displaying greater fortitude than

Gillmore, the cavalry leader seemed destined to fail in this mission just as he had on his railroad raids. One reason was the lack of a set time for a cooperative attack. Kautz also had no way to keep Gillmore informed of his progress, a fatal oversight. Another factor was that Kautz's force was too small to ensure a successful assault even against a similarly underweight enemy. But the most serious obstacle was Kautz's inability to adhere to his timetable. In his report he reduced the matter to a single sentence that explained nothing: "The circuit proved greater than I expected, and we did not reach the enemy's lines till midday."[24]

The nature of the difficulty appears to have been twofold. First, Kautz either underestimated the distance to be covered or found the terrain rougher than expected. His misjudgment, however, is difficult to reconcile with his long familiarity with the region. In preparation for his railroad raids, one of which carried him through this same area, he had spent weeks acquainting himself with every road, trail, and landmark outside Petersburg. The second factor was the stubborn resistance he encountered. He had to drive one enemy force (he identified it as the 62nd Georgia Cavalry) from its camp along the road to Prince George Court House. At many other points Kautz's outriders clashed with mounted pickets who fought and fell back and fought again, several times bringing the Union column to a standstill.

The result was that the troopers did not reach the Jerusalem Plank Road, the designated path of assault, until well after noon. By then the city had received ample warning of their approach. Brigadier General Raleigh Colston, Wise's ranking subordinate, noted that "the alarm-bell was rung in the city about 9 o'clock, and every man able to shoulder a musket hurried out to the lines."

The works confronting Kautz on the Jerusalem Plank Road—Lunettes 27 and 28—were held by 125 militiamen under Major Fletcher H. Archer. Most of the defenders were second-class reserves, boys below conscription age and men exempted from active service because of age or infirmity. Some oldsters lacked the teeth to open the paper cartridges to load their firearms. As Colston remarked, "Very few of them wore a uniform, and they were armed with inferior muskets and rifles, for all the best arms had to be reserved for troops in the field."[25]

Upon arriving south of the city, Kautz observed that the works "were not strongly defended." He estimated that he was opposed by 200 Confederates, including many regulars, backed by several pieces of artillery. In reality, not one gun confronted the cavalry upon its arrival; only after Gillmore retreated, freeing the defenders on the northeast side of the city for service elsewhere, did reinforcements (including a single howitzer) hasten south to oppose Kautz.

Hoping to stun the defenders with a quick blow, Kautz sent dismounted detachments of the 1st District of Columbia and 11th Pennsylvania toward Lunette 27 on the right side of the road. While these units drew Archer's fire, the 5th Pennsylvania aimed a mounted attack at the other fort. Several troopers topped the low parapet and dosed the militia's right flank with carbine and pistol fire. Though Colston claimed the Pennsylvanians were repulsed, a number of horsemen circled around the militia and captured Lunette 26, in rear of the main line. From that sheltered position they laced the enemy's rear, forcing many to abandon their works, then drove forward and captured scores of old men and boys as well as the recently arrived howitzer. By one o'clock the defenders were fleeing fortifications on either side of the road, escaping through a ravine so deep it stymied pursuit.

Kautz considered the day won. Apparently, however, he did not think to inform Gillmore nor was he troubled by the lack of battle sounds from the northeast, which should have alerted him that something had gone wrong on Gillmore's front. Instead, he called in his detachments, slowly formed a column, and prepared to enter the city in triumph. This latest in a long series of delays ensured Kautz's failure. Given time to react, General Wise shifted defenders from Lunettes 2 through 7, along with support sent down from Bermuda Hundred Neck by Beauregard, to the Jerusalem Plank Road. By the time Kautz passed through the breached defenses, pausing at the base of the ravine through which Archer's survivors had fled, "several hundred muskets suddenly opened from the opposite crest." In support were elements of two batteries—one drawn from Beauregard's front. The formidable-looking force persuaded Kautz's vanguard to fall back and diluted its commander's confidence. "The prospect of entering the city," he wrote, "was here suddenly defeated."[26]

Kautz contented himself with burning some supplies that belonged to the local garrison, then withdrew. As he moved off down the plank road with forty-two captives in tow, his enemy inflicted a further indignity by scrambling from their works to capture a horse artillery gun and two caissons.

So ended a tragicomic succession of events that probably constituted the sorriest performance ever turned in by the Army of the James. The litany of errors was appalling: an unconscionable lack of cooperation among the attack forces, no resolution on the part of any commander involved, a general disregard for the importance of speed and surprise, a chronic hesitancy to commit troops although ordered to do so, and a disregard of secondary objectives once the primary goal had been declared unattainable. Kautz was guilty of most of these sins, but Gillmore was more culpable. For inspired ineptitude, his performance northeast of Petersburg dwarfed any of the blunders he and Baldy Smith had concocted to frustrate and enrage their superior during the Bermuda Hundred campaign.

Aware of Butler's low opinion of him and of the high hopes Butler had for the expedition, Gillmore must have dreaded returning to army head- quarters. If so, his fear was not misplaced; when Butler learned of the mag- nitude of Gillmore's failure, the army leader erupted. After interviewing several subordinates, including Hinks, who claimed to have argued against a retreat as unnecessary and even cowardly, Butler became convinced that Gillmore had thrown away an opportunity to win the war in a fell swoop.[27]

Butler decided he needed an airtight case of Gillmore's culpability. He interrogated and sometimes browbeat other participants for damning testimony against the expeditionary commander. One interviewee was amused by the hanging-judge antics of the general, "who puffed out his cheeks at intervals, put on a portentous grin which one might suspect to be a sign of mirth until it dissolved into sobriety; and looked both ways until I was at a loss to know when he was looking at me." When Butler attempted to bully Colonel Hawley into criticizing his superior, the brigade leader rose up in anger. Butler then changed his tack and "cunningly coaxed" damaging testimony out of him.[28]

To strengthen his case against Gillmore, Butler decided to exonerate other participants in the fiasco. He had nothing but kind words for Hinks and Kautz upon their return. As the latter noted in his diary, Butler ranted and raved against Gillmore but "seems well pleased with what the cavalry did. He says we accomplished all that was expected of us."[29]

Butler berated Gillmore to anyone within earshot. On June 10 Kautz met Colonel Comstock, just down from Cold Harbor to prepare for Meade's crossing of the James. Comstock noted that as soon as he reported to Butler the latter burned his ear with criticism of Gillmore's generalship, doubtless hoping the staff officer would convey his displeasure to Grant. Butler's performance may have had the intended effect, for that night Comstock wrote in his diary of Gillmore's ineptitude and the inevitability of his relief.[30]

Butler was less vituperative in his correspondence with the War Department. The night of Gillmore's return to camp—even before Kautz's men had reached Bermuda Hundred—the army leader informed Stanton that Gillmore had failed to crack the city's defenses despite having suffered "no considerable loss." Next day he was even less critical of his subordi- nate, terming his failure to exploit Kautz's breakthrough "a misfortune."

Apparently Butler was reluctant to condemn Gillmore publicly until he had perused the latter's report of the expedition. Early on the tenth he ordered the corps leader to furnish him, within four hours, a comprehensive account of the operation, with pertinent times, forces involved, casualties suffered, damage inflicted, and plans followed, appending to it copies of every order issued to Kautz, Hinks, Hawley, and other ranking subordinates.

The best Gillmore could do was a three-page report replete with evasions, half-truths, and special pleading. He ascribed his retreat to the unexpected strength of the works northeast of the city, to Hinks's limited withdrawal on the Jordan's Point Road, and to Kautz's failure to report his progress. Gillmore's major premise was that no assault would have succeeded without a diversion by Kautz. He claimed that unnamed "principal officers" concurred in his belief that "the works could not have been carried" by infantry alone.[31]

The report was more or less what Butler had expected. He tore into it with gusto, terming it "entirely unsatisfactory" and the expedition itself "dilatory and ill-judged. The demonstration, too feeble to be called an attack, was in direct disobedience to orders. The whole affair, in view of the forces known to be opposed, was most disgraceful to the Union arms." On the eleventh he sent Gillmore a critique of the report, three times the length of the original document. Butler the barrister lodged a point-by-point rebuttal of every excuse behind which Gillmore tried to hide his "humiliating failure." On the fourteenth he finally forwarded Gillmore's report to Grant along with additional commentary brimming with invective and sarcasm. In the same mail Butler enclosed copies of Richmond and Petersburg newspapers whose accounts of the mission mentioned only Kautz, proving that "the enemy never discovered that Generals Gillmore and Hinks with the real attacking column came against them at all."[32]

By the time he dispatched these materials to Cold Harbor, Butler had worked off most of his anger and frustration. By then, too, he had relieved Gillmore from command and had ordered him to report to Fort Monroe to await further orders. Apparently he did so because Gillmore, objecting to Butler's characterizations of him, had asked for an inquiry into the expedition, which allowed Butler to remove him from the field till the investigation was completed. Gillmore protested that he had not sought his own relief, only an investigation, but he complained to no avail: Butler had already placed the X Corps under the temporary command of Alfred Terry. The only concession Butler made was to Grant, who may have wished to mute the reaction of Gillmore's political allies, including Treasury Secretary Chase. On June 17 Butler modified his removal order to make it appear that Gillmore had been relieved at his own request.[33]

Fittingly, Sarah Butler had the final word on the military enterprise she had planted in her husband's mind. "I suppose it was appointed to be," she wrote Butler on the twelfth, "that Genl. Gillmore is a valuable officer for the rebels. If he could manage . . . to inflict on the enemy a little of the mischief he has done our cause it might be a reason why he should not be court-martialed. Well, there is no help for it, so once more 'have patience, good people.'" This time, however, she could not lighten Butler's emotional burden. Her husband replied that he was "much dispirited and worn out with continual failures for which I see no remedy. True, I shall punish Gillmore, but that won't take Petersburg."[34]

The commander of the truncated Army of the James appeared to have ample cause for gloom. Not only had Gillmore cost him the Confederacy's most valuable city, but Meade's army was making final preparations to leave Cold Harbor for Bermuda Hundred. For a day or two after the fiasco of the ninth Butler considered another stab at Petersburg, using Hinks and Kautz. He even toyed with the idea of dispatching a special column of volunteers against the city but rejected the idea as impractical. Soon after Gillmore's retreat, Beauregard had reinforced Petersburg and further fortified all sides of the city. The critical element of surprise was lost.

Beyond these unhappy events, a steady flow of emissaries from Meade signaled the imminent arrival of his army. By June 14 what would become a 2,000-foot-long floating bridge began to stretch across the James a few miles upriver from Fort Powhatan. When Hinks begged his commander to undertake a second movement against Petersburg, vowing to resign his commission should he fail, Butler replied grimly that the next such attempt would be made by a force larger than his own.

Although he did not inform Hinks of the fact, Butler had gotten permission from Grant to attack the city before Meade's arrival but only if Butler could hold it until relieved. Uncertain that he could accomplish as much now that Petersburg had been strengthened, and unwilling to risk another failure, Butler elected to withhold the blow.[35]

The army commander had another reason to feel dispirited. The National Union convention at Baltimore had gone overwhelmingly in Lincoln's favor. Whether or not the president could prevail in November, his Republican supporters and their Democrat allies were not about to change horses. Although he had foreseen Lincoln's renomination, Butler must have been disappointed to learn that despite the best efforts of his backers, he had received only 28 votes at the convention against the president's 484.

Butler tried to keep up appearances; he wired congratulations to Lincoln and his running mate, Andrew Johnson, the military governor of Tennessee.

To every political acquaintance he professed his support for the president's reelection. In private he resorted to dark humor. "Hurrah for Lincoln!" he wrote Sarah on June 11. "That's the ticket! This country has more vitality than any other on earth if it can stand this sort of administration for another four years."[36]

If Butler was feeling low, the mood of his army at Cold Harbor was subterranean. To the thousands of losses it had suffered on June 1 and 3, dozens were added when Smith's command repulsed small-scale counterattacks on the fourth, fifth, and seventh. Even when the enemy stopped trying to recover what little ground it had lost, the Confederates kept the Federals pinned inside rifle pits and behind breastworks. Smith's survivors were constantly on the alert, their nerves tensed against sudden attack.[37]

The picked units of the X and XVIII Corps had to endure dangers and discomforts in addition to near-constant sharpshooter and artillery fire. Their rations were so poor and available water so brackish that many, including Baldy Smith, got sick. For more than a week they roasted under the glowing sun. Held on the firing line hour after hour, they had no opportunity to bathe or change clothing. Not until the seventh did the Confederates agree to a truce in order to bury the dead that lay between the lines. Thus, for four days and more, rotting corpses befouled the air while bored Rebels took target practice at the fallen, including wounded men unable to crawl to safety.[38]

The conditions drove Smith to caustic exchanges with Meade, Grant, and their staffs over sundry aspects of command relations. These clashes, on top of bad water and sleepless nights, left the corps leader not only sickly but "utterly worn out." But even as his physical and emotional strength waned, Smith composed biting commentaries on how his superiors had managed the recent fighting. Criticism of his old patron Grant was rather circumspect, but he did not mask his conviction that Meade was to blame for every casualty the Army of the James had suffered on the first and third.

If Smith was imprudent in putting his accusations on paper, his principal correspondent, James Harrison Wilson, was indiscreet in forwarding them to Grant's headquarters. Wilson, a tireless critic of Meade, hoped Smith's critique would cost the army leader his job. Instead of hurting Meade, however, Smith's letters lowered his own standing. Grant admired and trusted Meade—he had upheld the army leader in the face of earlier criticism from within and without—and resented the strident, bitter tone of Smith's observations.[39]

Fortunately, Smith's ordeal at Cold Harbor was nearly over. Grant had informed his staff on the sixth that he intended to break contact with Lee, concentrate toward the rear, and cross the James and Appomattox to City Point. Smith learned that his troops would have the advance, returning to White House and taking ship to their old position on the peninsula. Smith, however, had no inkling of his ultimate destination.

To ensure that preliminary arrangements were fully attended to, Grant did not implement the withdrawal for six days—days of additional discomfort, frustration, and jangled nerves throughout Meade's and Smith's ranks. By the afternoon of June 12, when the Army of the James was directed to file to the rear, many were at the limit of their endurance. They realized, however, that their hazardous duty was not done: the pullback, if detected, would provoke a violent reaction from the enemy. "How thankful I will be to God," wrote a private in the 9th New Jersey, "if we are not shelled when we withdraw."[40]

They were not shelled, thanks to the rapidity and stealth of their retirement. At 8:00 P.M. Guy Henry, who supervised the movement, guided Devens's division (now under Ames, Devens having been felled by rheumatism) to the rear. The troops secured their equipment to mute telltale sounds. Noises that could not be muffled were drowned out by regimental bands, which Henry ordered to keep playing long and loudly. The deception worked; as one of the colonel's aides observed, "The Johnnies either didn't know what we were about or knowing didn't care to take advantage."[41]

Once beyond sharpshooter range, Ames's division moved rapidly on the road to White House. The exhausting gait was kept up for almost a mile, inducing, as a Massachusetts officer recalled, "profuse perspiration, which, forming a combination with the dense, suffocating dust, literally encased the men in an earthen armor, and the horrible odors from the dead mules and horses scattered along the road were such as to make an occasional breath of fresh air a heavenly luxury."[42]

When Ames had cleared the field, Colonel Henry placed the men of Brooks and Martindale on the moon-washed road. Despite Meade's assurance that the pullout would be unobstructed, it was brought to a standstill by the supply trains and artillery teams of the Army of the Potomac. There was crowding at the head of the column and the two divisions withdrew less rapidly than their comrades in the X Corps. Even so, by 4:00 A.M. on the thirteenth the Army of the James had departed Cold Harbor.

A few hours later, Ames's command reached White House, where the men crowded aboard the steamers that had run them up from Bermuda Hundred two weeks earlier. By midday the transports were churning through the brackish waters of the Pamunkey. That evening they rounded Old Point Comfort, and by early on the fourteenth they arrived at Bermuda Hundred Neck. The men expected to file inside the works quickly, but after several hours of waiting, they disembarked and were marched toward the Appomattox. A rumor began to circulate that they were heading for Petersburg!

Their commander was just as surprised by the unexpected turn. Not until his steamer hove to at sundown did Baldy Smith learn why the survivors of Cold Harbor had turned south and why other forces—the infantry of Hinks, Kautz's horsemen—were massing around City Point. Barely had the ill and weary commander set foot on dry ground when Butler broke free from a crowd at the landing and pulled him aside.

Smith soon learned that Grant had launched a multipronged campaign to take Petersburg. The main effort would be made by Smith's Cold Harbor force, augmented by the cavalry, the black troops from City Point, and—as soon as they completed their water and overland journey from Cold Harbor—elements of the Army of the Potomac. Stunned by the magnitude and secrecy of the movement, Smith was staggered to learn that he had been chosen to spearhead the critical assault, scheduled to begin immediately.[43]

CHAPTER EIGHT

Four Days of Frustration

EARLY ON JUNE 15 FIVE SEGMENTS OF THE ARMY OF THE JAMES—KAUTZ'S cavalry, Hinks's infantry, the just-debarked divisions of Brooks and Martindale, and a X Corps detachment under Colonel Louis Bell of the 4th New Hampshire—cautiously approached the northeastern environs of Petersburg. Having crossed the Appomattox on a new pontoon bridge near Broadway Landing, eight miles above the enemy stronghold, the Federals neared their objective in two elongated columns. Most of the invasion force—Kautz in front, followed closely by Hinks, Brooks, and Bell—moved down the City Point Road. Martindale advanced along the River Road, which hugged the south bank of the Appomattox, two miles above the main body.

These same roads had led Gillmore's brigades to Petersburg six days ago. Though the earlier operation had ended in defeat and disgrace, the man leading this day's advance, Baldy Smith, had no intention of soiling his hard-won reputation. Like Gillmore on June 9, Smith hoped to restore to his career the luster it had lost during the nightmarish campaigning of the past six weeks. He was determined to succeed where his X Corps colleague had failed.[1]

A single concern beset Smith: he had not been fully apprised of what was expected of his 9,000-man force. The fault was Grant's. While planning Meade's and Smith's withdrawal from Cold Harbor, he had envisioned a wide, converging advance on Petersburg, culminating in its capture and occupation and the quick destruction of its communications. But Grant had failed to define fully the roles to be played by the Armies of the Potomac and the James. Based on the orders sent from Grant to Butler and then to Smith, Smith supposed he was to force the garrison on Petersburg's northern and eastern outskirts, now under Beauregard, inside the city. Smith had only the vaguest notion of how the Army of the Potomac was to support him and how the two commands would cooperate in making a breakthrough.

Smith, out of necessity, improvised a plan of approach. While Martindale protected the north flank of the main body, Brooks and Bell would make the primary effort along the road they shared. As the white infantry struck the enemy works, Hinks's troops would shift a mile or more to the southeast, regaining their recent position on the Jordan's Point Road and from there launching a secondary attack. Kautz would extend the line farther south and east, anchoring the left flank along the Norfolk Road. If all went as envisioned, the attackers would penetrate the city along a line three and a half miles long, engulfing Lunettes 1 through 11.

Smith's plan benefited from a preponderance of numbers; he was opposed by fewer than 2,200 Confederate regulars, backed by the same oldsters and youths Kautz had scattered on the ninth. But to be effective Smith's advance had to be rapid and decisive; otherwise Beauregard would have time to call down the four brigades opposite Bermuda Hundred. Already the time element was posing problems. In giving Smith his sketchy instructions, Butler had suggested a crossing of the Appomattox shortly after daybreak—about 3:30 A.M. But not until almost four o'clock did Kautz's horsemen lead the march to Broadway Landing, and when they reached the far bank they moved slowly and spasmodically. In their rear the infantry spent an idle hour, waiting for the road to clear. Hinks's division, which joined the main column at City Point, was also delayed by the slow-footed cavalry. It was after 5:00 A.M. before the infantry got under way.[2]

Unanticipated trouble arose when, a good two miles in advance of the works, Smith's vanguard encountered resistance from outposts along the City Point Road. When Kautz and Hinks came up to a line of abatis and earthworks on steeply rising ground near Baylor's farm, they found they had to approach the position via an almost impenetrable thicket a quarter of a mile wide, beyond which lay a 400-yard-long plain cleared for artillery fire. The position was held by a provisional brigade under Brigadier General James Dearing: two infantry regiments, several companies of cavalry, and four twelve-pounder cannon.

Although the works were far from impregnable, their location astride the invaders' route meant trouble for Smith, who now had to give battle well in advance of his objective. Moreover, he would have to use forces whose steadfastness he questioned: Kautz's troopers and Hinks's USCTs.

While the cavalry was too puny to mount much of an offensive, the African-Americans had yet to prove themselves. One of Hinks's officers acknowledged that "we had considerable experience in marching, some in throwing up earthworks, and were fairly well trained in company, regimental, and brigade drill, but in fighting we were novices."[3]

Without great expectations, Smith attempted to break Dearing's line with cavalry alone. Kautz dismounted the better part of his command and sent it through the thicket and across the open ground. When the attackers were halfway to the enemy position, the Confederates opened fire, sending the troopers scrambling behind a hill that shielded them from harm but kept them from their target.

Disappointed if not surprised, Butler's senior lieutenant called on Hinks's infantry. Moving up quickly on the left, the troops displayed dash and enthusiasm—at least until their commander was thrown from his horse, reopening the wound received at Antietam. With Hinks incapacitated, command passed to Colonel Duncan, who had not led a charge in his career. Duncan's inexperience showed in his choice of a unit to lead his assault: a dismounted cavalry regiment made up of raw recruits and only recently attached to the division. Willing to do its duty, the 5th Massachusetts Colored Cavalry slowly cleared the thicket and then, without waiting for Duncan's signal to break cover, rushed onto the open ground beyond. In the clearing they met the fate of Kautz's men; under the accurate shelling of Dearing's twelve-pounders, the dismounted troopers broke for the rear in panic.

Part of the 4th U.S. Colored Troops, stationed in rear of the panicky regiment, was caught up in the Bay Staters' retreat. The 4th stampeded in its turn, breaking through the ranks of the next regiment in line, the 6th USCT. The commander of the 6th, Colonel John W. Ames, halted the snowballing effect of the retreat and, according to some accounts, tried valiantly to resume the advance. Another observer described Ames as giving way to the general panic, making himself look "more like a fool than anything else." Colonel Duncan claimed that Ames held his men in the thicket for the balance of the day, where they were "of no avail for an immediate charge."[4]

The difficulties experienced by Hinks's force produced an unanticipated benefit. The Confederates had concentrated so heavily on stopping Duncan's advance on the left that they permitted two other black regiments, the 5th and 22nd, to strike almost unopposed against the opposite flank. Too late, Dearing redirected his artillery barrage, but before they could be halted, both regiments crossed the field, scaled the works, and cut down the defenders with rifle blasts and bayonet thrusts.

U.S. Colored Troops of Hinks's division, with captured Confederate gun, June 15, 1864. ENGRAVING FROM *THE SOLDIER IN OUR CIVIL WAR.*

Astounded by the speed and ferocity of the assault, Dearing's men abandoned the flank along with one of their guns. As they raced off, their assailants celebrated the first successful charge by African-American soldiers in the eastern theater of operations. The victors tossed caps into the air and shouted at the tops of their lungs. Members of the 22nd USCT capered about the cannon they had seized as though it were a trophy beyond price. Hobbling painfully to the captured works, an incredulous Hinks inquired of one soldier: "What has become of the Johnnies?" "Well, sah," came the reply, "dey jes' done lit out; didn't car' to make close 'quaintence!"[5]

White troops watching from the rear were impressed. One New York soldier extended his grudging admiration: "The Niggers charged on our left and did well." Others were more effusive; one declared that "the problem is solved. The negro is a man, a soldier, a hero." Even Smith praised their charge, though he criticized the troops' postbattle celebration, which he believed rendered them useless for further service.[6]

Fittingly, on this day, Congress addressed the implications of what one of Smith's white troops called blacks' "equal value" in battle. Heretofore black soldiers had been paid $2 a month less than their lighter-skinned comrades. Heeding the words of commanders such as Butler ("the colored man fills an equal space in ranks while he lives, and an equal grave when he falls"), legislators passed a pay equalization bill, retroactive to January.[7]

———————

By 10:00 A.M. the Federals were marching in the direction Dearing's men had fled, toward Petersburg's outer works. Martindale's troops continued to shuffle down the River Road while Brooks's and Bell's advanced along the adjacent road from City Point. Hinks's division had regained the Jordan's Point Road, and Kautz's men were cantering along the Prince George Court House Road on the far left. The columns converged between Lunettes 3 and 11, two miles northeast of the city.

Dearing's opposition had provided Beauregard with time to reinforce the outer works. Even so, the garrison was not much stronger than it had been on the ninth, and the Creole knew he could not hold it against as many Yankees as he suspected were coming his way. Already he had rushed couriers above the James to petition Lee for help. None appeared to be forthcoming. Having failed to detect the extent of the Union withdrawal, Lee refused to admit that Grant and Meade had stolen a march on him; apparently he assumed that a detachment from Bermuda Hundred was threatening Petersburg. He did agree to return Hoke's division, which Beauregard had given up following the victory at Drewry's Bluff, but he would do no more until he ascertained Union whereabouts and intentions.

In the interim Beauregard hunkered down behind his works, planning to make maximum use of his few infantry and artillery regiments along with whatever support he could get from the militia. He considered withdrawing part of Bushrod Johnson's division from opposite Bermuda Hundred, but because such a move would permit Butler to wreak havoc above the Appomattox, Beauregard decided it would have to remain a final resort.[8]

Not until eleven o'clock did Brooks's division come within view of Petersburg's outer line. The works confronting Brooks, Lunettes 4 through 7, formed a deep salient directly opposite the junction of the City Point and River Roads. The face of the salient ran south from above the Petersburg & City Point Railroad to the Jordan farm, about a half mile north of the Jordan's Point Road.

Sizing up the position, which he considered the key to Beauregard's line, Brooks worried that it might be impregnable. Another officer described the salient as consisting of "redoubts connected by breastworks, all of earth and perhaps twenty feet thick at the base and six feet at the top. In front . . . was a dry ditch perhaps fifteen feet wide and six feet deep, and still [farther] in front of it was the slashing which had been formed by cutting down the trees a quarter of a mile to the front."[9]

When he pushed to within sight of the salient, Baldy Smith was just as daunted as his subordinate. Still anguished by the mismanaged assaults at Cold Harbor, he refused to commit himself to an attack until the position had been reconnoitered thoroughly. Since Butler had not provided him with an engineer, Smith secured one himself. He would not have understood the logic of one critic who later suggested that Butler had refused Smith an engineer for the same reason he had denied Gillmore artillery on June 9: he wanted a rapid, decisive push into the city.

While Brooks's men traded long-distance skirmish fire with the defenders of the salient, Smith started on the errand he considered a prerequisite to any assault. Alternately crouching and crawling, he moved slowly through woods and underbrush, showing no regard for the occasional sharpshooter fire he drew (coolness under fire was Smith's long suit) and getting ever closer to the nearest defenses. It was midafternoon before he concluded what he called his "long and painful operation," returning to his starting point unhurt except for scrapes and scratches. Next, he made circuitous trips to apprise Brooks, Hinks, and Martindale of his findings. By five o'clock he was ready to align his attack columns, which took another half hour or more. Smith then moved to position his batteries to provide effective cover fire. As he ordered up one brace of cannon, he discovered that his chief of artillery, Captain Frederick Follett, had sent many of the battery horses to the rear for watering. Although Smith would later blame Follett for this additional delay, as expeditionary leader Smith was responsible for keeping his support well in hand.[10]

It was almost 7:00 P.M., less than half an hour before sunset, before the assault column was ready. Smith's plan, based on his reconnaissance, was to strike simultaneously along the line between Lunettes 5 and 11, which encompassed the salient and a mile's worth of auxiliary works. The tactics Smith had devised were innovative, even revolutionary. Instead of columns of assault, loose-order skirmish lines would carry the attack. By spreading out the charging troops, Smith hoped to avoid the mass casualties he had suffered on June 1 and 3. Smith also wanted Brooks's division, chosen to lead the assault, to be sheltered somewhat by a ravine that he had discovered between Lunettes 6 and 7.

The plan appeared inspired, but it had potential drawbacks. By widening his path of attack, Smith risked a failure to bring sufficient pressure to bear at any one point. Though he accorded Brooks and Martindale a major role, he relegated Hinks to a minor one in support of Brooks. Smith either failed to note or did not care that Martindale's troops, who would have the most ground to cross, would have little natural cover. Moreover, a wide ditch blocked Martindale's access to the nearest works; the division commander later contended that his men "could not have crawled across it."[11]

At the heart of the matter was the time factor. Smith had delayed so long that his attack would be made in gathering darkness, a chancy undertaking for troops unfamiliar with the terrain. Even if they broke through, the lateness of the hour would complicate exploitation of the success. Smith had no right to expect the attackers to push on in darkness to seize the Appomattox bridges by which Beauregard's garrison could be reinforced.

Martindale's skirmishers went forward at about 7:15 P.M. They advanced only a few hundred yards before being halted by the ditch. Farther south, Brooks's division made greater headway. Inspired by the bravery of leaders such as Colonel Aaron F. Stevens of the 13th New Hampshire, commanding the skirmishers of Burnham's brigade, the troops sprinted across the open ground, poured through the strategic ravine, and interposed neatly between Lunettes 6 and 7, blasting the flanks of both forts before the defenders could wheel their guns about. One attacker recalled that the movement was "easier than expected" and was accomplished "with a comparatively small loss."[12]

Above and below Lunette 7, the Federals had a rougher time, ramming into obstructions and tumbling into dry ditches where they became easy targets. Smith's skirmisher tactics did, however, prevent the defenders from using close-quarter ammunition such as canister. Some of the artillerists did not bother to fire, doubting they could inflict much damage to troops advancing in loose order.[13]

When Brooks's division led out, the skirmishers under Louis Bell charged farther to the right. They made such progress that they beat the other columns to the enemy line. A sergeant in the front of Bell's advance recalled, "With yells that might have raised the dead, we rushed like a whirlwind over the broad plowed field, thickset with big stumps, and breasted the hills. . . . Three minutes later we were inside the rebel works, taking prisoners and behaving like wild men." About 100 members of a New York regiment penetrated the curtain connecting Lunettes 5 and 6. With the aid of friends farther south, the New Yorkers captured Lunette 5 from the rear, taking four cannon, one battle flag, and 211 prisoners, including 16 officers. "Secesh made tracks at a fearful rate," wrote one captor, "and we pumped him as he ran." The fellow added, "Had we been purposely supported and our rear protected we could have rushed at once into Petersburg—all our prisoners agreed on that point."[14]

The white troops had captured three redans, containing ten cannon. Their success, while significant, was far from decisive. But it did not represent the extent of Smith's gains this evening. Although directed to confine himself to a demonstration on behalf of the whites, Hinks led his USCTs in a full attack on and south of the Jordan's Point Road. His 4th and 22nd Regiments veered toward Lunette 7, the capture of which would leave Lunettes 8 and 9 vulnerable. At the same time, the 5th and 6th Regiments angled toward Lunettes 10 and 11, whose heavy fire Hinks was determined to suppress.

Shouting patriotic slogans, Hinks's men charged across the plain in massed ranks, not in the skirmisher formation their comrades had adopted. Packed so tightly, the attackers suffered 500 casualties, two-thirds of Smith's loss in this engagement. The carnage failed to deter the black phalanx; after cutting through a nearly impassable ravine leading to the upper forts, detachments under Colonel Kiddoo and Lieutenant Colonel George Rogers raced up a forty-five-degree incline strewn with felled trees. Surmounting these obstacles, they flooded over the redans, helping Brooks capture Lunette 7. Turning abandoned cannon southward, they helped white units force the evacuation of Lunettes 8 and 9.[15]

As Hinks had anticipated, Lunettes 10 and 11 offered stiffer opposition. Their heavy artillery and intricate abatis stymied the 5th and 6th Regiments for nearly an hour and a half. At that point elements of the 4th and 22nd Regiments left the works they had captured and charged the rear of Lunette 10. The fort fell after brief fighting, surviving defenders hastening west along with the garrison of Lunette 11. Unaware that those forts had been abandoned, the 5th and 6th USCTs charged both from the front. Scrambling up the glacis, an officer of the 6th "felt sure . . . that as fast as a 'colored troop' would put his head above the level of the parapet it would be shot off. . . . Not a bit of it. We climbed into the fort or battery, only to find it empty. The last Confederate was gone, save one, a fair haired boy of 17 or 18 years, dead."[16]

By 8:30 P.M. the offensive had spent itself. Every work between Lunettes 5 and 11 had fallen, yielding sixteen guns and 230 prisoners. Blacks and whites alike were jubilant. A USCT officer, studying the captured positions, wondered "how our troops managed to take them," knowing that feat would have been "impossible if there had been a large force to defend them." Here was the key ingredient of Union success: despite their appearance, the redans had been too lightly held and lacked infantry support. Had the works been manned in greater force, Smith would have suffered much heavier losses no matter which assault tactics he used.

Smith had committed little more than two-thirds of his force on hand. Most of Martindale's division, blocked by the ditch and other obstacles, had seen little or no fighting. Only the brigade of George Stannard had been actively engaged, attacking and seizing works in advance of Lunettes 3 and 4. Even at that, Martindale had accomplished more than Kautz's cavalry. At Smith's direction Kautz had paid a return visit to the defenses he had tested on June 9, driving in another militia force. Following limited success, however, the cavalry leader marked time for several hours before making a half-hearted demonstration that carried his men no closer than 500 yards from Lunettes 19 and 20. The troopers skirmished with the Second Class Reserves for a few hours at long range, absorbing forty-three casualties, including the mortal wounding of the troubled Colonel Mix, who had exposed himself suicidally. The horsemen turned about late in the day and trotted north as though content with their effort. As General Smith noted tersely, they "retired behind the infantry without my permission, so that we had no support from them."[17]

In the aftermath of victory, Smith's force reveled in its achievements. When he rode past the captured works in the moonlight, Bell's command gave "Old Baldy" a chorus of cheers. The general "took off his hat and smiled from ear to ear," wrote one onlooker, "but remonstrated by waving his hand gently as does an orchestra leader when he means 'pianissimo.'"[18]

Despite rejecting any accolades, Smith was quite satisfied with his performance this evening—so satisfied that he had no immediate intention of exploiting his breakthrough. Although Grant and Butler had envisioned one continuous, decisive sweep through the city, Smith was not about to lumber ahead blindly. From his observation tower near Point of Rocks, Butler messaged him at 7:20 P.M.: "Time is the essence of this movement. . . . Push and get the Appomattox between you and me. Nothing has passed down the railroad to harm you yet."[19]

But Smith was not so sure. He strongly suspected that the city had been reinforced. His skepticism was justified: soon after Brooks and Hinks cracked Petersburg's defenses, Robert Hoke's division had begun to pass through the city and out to the firing lines. By now Beauregard had inserted Hoke's force into the defense line he was hastily constructing along Harrison's Creek, a half mile or so west of the captured lunettes. Before the end of the night Beauregard would begin to strip the works opposite Bermuda Hundred and rush the troops across the bridges Smith was supposed to have destroyed.

As yet Smith had no proof that support had reached Beauregard. He would always claim, however, that after dark on the fifteenth he received a warning from Butler that Hoke's troops were arriving and that Smith should halt and dig in rather than press on. Butler denied this assertion, and since Smith presented no evidence to prove his contention, historians have upheld Butler. Many years after the war, Smith's case was supported by one of Butler's signal officers, Sergeant Maurice S. Lamprey, who recorded in his diary that late on June 15 he signaled "Gen Smith to entrench at once and hold his position." Lamprey added a personal observation: "Guess Gen. B. is getting rattled over the dust that the rebs are kicking up" on the road to Petersburg. Thus Smith had ample authority to suspend his drive until he could ascertain the strength and position of his adversaries.[20]

Smith maintained that this uncertainty was only one factor—and not necessarily the primary one—in his reluctance to push on after initial success: "My white troops were exhausted by marching day and night, and by fighting most of the day in the excessive heat. My colored troops, who had fought bravely, were intoxicated by their success, and could hardly be kept in order." This excuse—a lack of fresh resources—was invalidated well before midnight, however, by the appearance east of Petersburg of Winfield Scott

Hancock's II Corps. Grant had wanted Hancock to reach Petersburg soon after Smith's attack and expand upon any success of the Army of the James. In the manner of Smith's difficulties on the road to Cold Harbor, sloppy staff work and logistical foul-ups had slowed and misdirected the II Corps—mistakes that Hancock, who, like Smith, was in poor health on this occasion, could not overcome. From his observation post Butler had located the errant corps and guided it toward Smith, but it was close to eleven o'clock before Hancock's leading divisions, under Major General David Bell Birney and Brigadier General John Gibbon, came up the Jordan's Point Road in rear of Duncan's brigade.[21]

Another hour passed before Hancock's vanguard negotiated the shadowy road to the captured lunettes. Then arose what has traditionally been portrayed as an Alphonse-and-Gaston act by the high command—Smith and Hancock exchanged pleasantries, each deferring to the wishes of the other as to how their commands should cooperate, neither willing to usurp the other's authority, while critical hours slipped past. Smith is usually depicted as the culprit, for both Grant and Butler later claimed that Hancock, who was senior to Smith, deferred to him in the belief that Smith was better acquainted with the situation and especially the topography—a belief apparently borne out by Smith's midnight boast to Butler that he held "the key to Petersburg" and was about to turn it. Smith argued afterward that Hancock had not surrendered his authority as senior field commander. This assertion appears to be true; no one in the II Corps, Hancock included, ever disputed it.

Even if Hancock did not subordinate himself to Smith, he asked Smith for advice on how to proceed. The latter told him, as he had already told Butler, that nothing of consequence could be accomplished before daylight. Apparently, Hancock concurred. He also agreed to Smith's request that the II Corps relieve the troops holding the captured works on the City Point and Jordan's Point Roads, permitting them to shift toward the Appomattox. Thus Hancock was responsible for what was accomplished—precious little. Instead of directing Birney and Gibbon aggressively to reconnoiter the ground in front, he advised them to strike a blow only if they found the enemy holding positions that must be neutralized. Fearing to do anything precipitate, the division commanders failed to strike out for Harrison's Creek until sunup.[22]

In this way one of the most critical days of the war in the east came to a close. Smith and Hancock allowed their people to rest on their arms while Beauregard's troops strengthened the new line and Hoke's reinforced division prepared to occupy it. If the Confederates were too busy to sleep, their opponents, who could hear the digging and chopping, were too upset to close their eyes. "The most bloodcurdling blasphemy I ever listened to," one of Hancock's soldiers recalled, "I heard that night, uttered by men who knew they were to be sacrificed on the morrow. The whole corps was furiously excited."[23]

In addition to monitoring Smith's and Hancock's progress at Petersburg, Butler was closely observing events on his own line. About 10:00 P.M. on the fifteenth the officer in charge of the pickets of the 10th Connecticut, which held the far right of the Bermuda Hundred defenses, reported enemy troops "moving in their works, and crawling forward on . . . hands and knees close up to their pickets at different points." Similar reports flowed back to Point of Rocks from other posts along the neck of the peninsula. "Soon after midnight," observed a member of another Connecticut outfit, "word came to the reserve that the enemy had planted cannon so as to sweep the main road across which was the picket line, that he was massing troops for an attack at the right, and that he had advanced his vedettes as if to make room for an attacking column."[24]

Thus Butler expected a heavy cannonade and an assault along the banks of the James. Aware that Hoke was en route to Petersburg, Butler probably feared that other Confederate detachments were heading for Bermuda Hundred. But if he took any precautions, he left no record of them.

By dawn of the sixteenth the crisis appeared to have passed and a strategic opportunity beckoned. Shortly before four o'clock Colonel Voris, officer of the day in the 1st Division, X Corps, reported to Brigadier General Robert S. "Sandy" Foster, temporarily in command, that the Confederates were evacuating their works. After relaying the intelligence to Terry, provisional commander of the corps, the thirty-year-old Foster, an Indiana native who had risen through the ranks during service in western Virginia, South Carolina, and Florida, ordered the leader of his pickets to probe the lines opposite them. If they had been abandoned, he was to occupy them at once.[25]

By 5:00 A.M. Butler, suspecting a Confederate withdrawal, ordered a heavy demonstration—only to be thwarted, he claimed, by General Terry, who feared the imminent arrival of Lee's army from Cold Harbor. If Terry was concerned, he did not stop Foster's pickets, who chopped through the abatis that sealed off part of the works across Bermuda Hundred Neck. Soon afterward, informed of Butler's desire for a full-scale demonstration, Foster's men rushed the breastworks in front of them as well as those at the Howlett house. Miscommunication between the troops and their gunboat support in the James nearly proved fatal when Admiral Lee's fleet sent a couple of 100-pound shells toward the Howlett battery. The embattled infantry waved handkerchiefs in lieu of white flags and in that manner surrendered to the navy.[26]

Once convinced that the Rebels were gone from his front—at least from his right flank—Butler realized that he enjoyed one final opportunity to accomplish something dramatic at Bermuda Hundred. By now Grant and Meade were nearing Petersburg, the commanding general having established his headquarters at City Point. Most of the Army of the Potomac, however, was still above the James or only now crossing it. Any success Butler gained at Bermuda Hundred would be his alone. If he helped topple Petersburg, he would win the fame and glory so cruelly and repeatedly denied him over the past six weeks.

Having squandered so many chances to sever the railroad between Richmond and Petersburg, Butler determined not to fail this time. With the railroad broken, Lee would have a much more difficult time reinforcing Beauregard. The lost hours might prove critical. Butler directed Terry to head west with a force of about 4,000—two-thirds of the troops available at Bermuda Hundred—and destroy as much track as time permitted.

Soon after, Butler reasoned that a larger force might produce a more sweeping success. He wired City Point, seeking the assistance of Meade's army crossing the James near Wilcox's Wharf, seventeen miles upriver from Petersburg. Any element of that army "in conjunction with the troops of this line . . . could I think advance on the railroad and isolate Petersburg, and as only a part of Lee's army has passed down, cut it in two and hold it cut." He added that a cooperative movement might also envelop Richmond from the south.[27]

Grant's reply did not address the suggested move against Richmond, but he did order the VI Corps from Wilcox's Wharf to

Brigadier General Robert S. Foster.
U.S. ARMY MILITARY HISTORY INSTITUTE.

Bermuda Hundred. He could not predict how long it would take Wright to reach Butler—it might be several hours. Until then, the troops opposite Beauregard's abandoned works were on their own.

Like his superior, Terry was determined to make the most of the break-out from Bermuda Hundred. He formed two columns and sent both to the railroad, a mile west of the abandoned works. The upper force, led by Foster and consisting of six regiments from his division, started at about 8:00 A.M. toward Chester Station. Foster left behind a number of other outfits, including several units of Ohio militia recently attached to Butler's army for three months' service. Butler had them level captured works that blocked the line of fire from Bermuda Hundred. Meanwhile, the lower column, under Ames, moved toward Port Walthall Junction; it consisted of the main body of Turner's division, a few hundred of the militiamen, detachments of Kautz's cavalry, and the dismounted 1st U.S. Colored Cavalry, on loan from Hinks's division.[28]

Reaching the railroad at about ten o'clock, Ames's wing set to work. The extent of track destroyed was variously estimated as one to four miles. Ames's troops might have done more, but by about 12:30 P.M. their attention had shifted northward, where sounds of battle indicated that Foster's wing had become engaged.[29]

In fact, Foster had not even reached the right-of-way before an unidentified enemy force plowed into his column near Ware Bottom Church. The Rebels drove Foster's advance guard upon his main body, which consisted of two regiments each from Howell's and Hawley's brigades. At first Foster believed he was tangling with Beauregard's troops, returning to their abandoned lines. He belatedly came to share Terry's concern about the proximity of the Army of Northern Virginia. The newcomers were members of Major General George E. Pickett's division of Lee's army, the first element sent from Cold Harbor following Hoke's detaching.[30]

Pickett had not expected to give battle short of Petersburg. "It was a delightful day," a South Carolinian recalled of the march down the pike. "There was no more expectation of encountering the enemy than . . . of finding him in the streets of Charleston." But when they encountered Foster's column less than a mile from Chester Station, the Confederates immediately attacked, intent on maintaining Lee's rail connections.[31]

Foster's soldiers resisted gamely, but within minutes the fast-arriving Rebels outflanked them on the right. A well-timed blow from Voris's 67th Ohio restored the balance of battle. Still, as more of Pickett's units arrived, it appeared unlikely that Foster could hold his position unless heavily reinforced. At Terry's order, Ames rushed up from the south to provide that support.

The fighting west of Bermuda Hundred would have escalated greatly had not Grant learned of it and ordered Butler's troops to withdraw. "Whilst the body of the troops are engaged at Petersburg," he informed Butler rather cryptically, "I do not think it advisable to make an attack in the center of the enemy's lines. . . . It [Terry's resistance] would detain a force from going to Petersburg, but would attract attention to a point where we may want to make a real attack some day hence."

Although disappointed, Butler at about 3:30 P.M. recalled both columns to Beauregard's old defenses, which he directed to be improved and held until further notice. By about four o'clock both forces had returned to the works, behind which they skirmished briskly with their pursuers, who had taken up positions near the Howlett house and Ware Bottom Church.[32]

To increase his troops' staying power, Butler had the artillery at Bermuda Hundred, including some thirty-pounder Parrott rifles, hurl shells toward Pickett's new line, to little effect. Most of the newcomers continued on to Petersburg to aid Beauregard, but a healthy number turned east to pressure Terry. The captured works, most of which had been leveled, offered the Yankees little protection, and many, including scores of militiamen, were driven out by the incessant Rebel fire. Most of Terry's command held the position until after dark, but by 1:00 A.M. on the seventeenth the division commander, aware that his dislodging was only a matter of time, ordered a withdrawal to Bermuda Hundred. The operation was conducted so quickly and stealthily that well before sunrise all of Terry's troops were safely within Butler's defenses.[33]

The army's effort to exploit Beauregard's stripping of Bermuda Hundred Neck had come up short. A few miles of broken railroad—repaired within four days of the Federals' retreat—constituted Butler's only achievement. This was truly a hollow feat in view of Lee's decision to march his army to Petersburg instead of hauling it there by train.

The outcome should have been foreseen. Given the enemy's easy access to the battlefield, it seems unlikely that Butler could have held the railroad long enough to inflict substantial damage. Even so, he could have accomplished more. Had Butler chosen his objectives more carefully, Lee's advance might have been checked. Instead of trying to cut the railroad, Butler could have seized and fortified the lower reaches of the turnpike. Strong works thrown up there could have denied reinforcements to Beauregard for twenty-four or even forty-eight hours. The delay might have enabled Smith and Hancock to quit dawdling, push westward, and secure the most important city, just then, in North America.

Backed by Hoke's division and the troops from Bermuda Hundred, Beauregard held the Harrison's Creek line throughout June 16. He now had 10,000 men, four times as many as the day before. The Louisianan was still outnumbered by a wide margin, especially after Major General Ambrose E. Burnside's IX Corps of the Army of the Potomac joined Smith and Hancock east of the city at 10:00 A.M., bringing Union strength to almost 50,000. But the new arrivals, who went into position on the right of the II Corps, appeared just as reluctant to assume the offensive as their predecessors. Not even Grant, now on the scene, could mount a decisive push westward. Instead of directing an assault, Grant ordered his commanders to reconnoiter Beauregard's new line and determine if it could be attacked at about 6:00 P.M.

The day was given over to maneuvering. In addition to shifting cautiously westward, the three Union corps moved to the north, closing up to make room for the rest of Meade's army—Warren's and Wright's corps—which would extend the line southward. As Smith's command moved close to the Appomattox, it provoked a barrage from the northernmost redans. Brooks responded by sending a few regiments to determine if the works "could be cheaply taken." They could not, and the division leader discarded the idea.[34]

Late in the day the Army of the James launched the reconnaissance Grant had ordered as well as a limited offensive. The 97th Pennsylvania of Bell's command made a dash on a detached work in advance of Harrison's Creek, capturing it after brief fighting and bagging 200 prisoners, half the size of the attacking force. At about the same time, one of Martindale's outfits, the 2nd Pennsylvania Heavy Artillery, a convert to infantry service, captured an outpost along the River Road. Elsewhere along Smith's line, elements of Brooks's and Hinks's divisions pressed close to the creek, studying Beauregard's position. Comrades working the guns in the forts captured the previous evening gave them covering fire.[35]

Beyond these activities Smith's command lay relatively idle throughout the day. By 4:00 P.M. its leader, at last concerned that time was short, reported to General Meade, "I have in the neighborhood of 8,000 men for an attack, in good fighting trim and good spirits, and will be ready to make an attack in my front at any hour which may be indicated by your order." No such order came. Just before six o'clock Meade's artillery started in, apparently softening up the enemy for an assault. The Army of the James expected to go forward at any minute. "It was an hour of anxiety," recalled a man in the 112th New York, "for all supposed that bloody work was before them." But when, promptly at six, the II Corps moved to the attack, supported by Burnside's command, Smith's soldiers listened for bugle calls that never sounded.[36]

Reduced to spectators, the men of the Army of the James stared westward at what a New Hampshireman called "a grand but terrible spectacle,"
featuring fighting "exceedingly fierce." A member of the 98th New York
"could see our troops run to the charge, and hear them yell and fire. Three
times we saw them advance and retire. . . . All night long the battle lasted,
and all night long we stood to arms. In the woods and fields, along the
fences, hedges, all that summer's night [the] roar of volley and crash of shell
were incessant."[37]

Despite the action, there were no additional gains. Morning found the II
and IX Corps holding a few hundred yards of new ground in front of Harrison's
Creek, but Beauregard's line remained intact. A frustrated Grant then ordered
dawn assaults by elements of Hancock's, Burnside's, and Warren's corps, the
last just up on Burnside's left. This time, too, Smith's command was held in
reserve. The attackers took high ground near the Hare and Shand houses,
below the Jordan's Point Road. As at Cold Harbor, however, the movements
of the several corps were so poorly coordinated that they failed to breach
the Rebel line.

By now time was almost up for the attackers, for Lee, at last convinced
that Grant and Meade were at Petersburg, was marching in force to relieve
Beauregard. Alert to his arrival, Grant at 9:15 A.M. on the seventeenth directed
Butler to retake the ground that Foster and Ames had held briefly the day
before along with the all-important turnpike to Richmond. Butler was to
add to his force two VI Corps divisions, commanded personally by Wright,
then arriving on the north bank of the Appomattox hours after Butler had
expected them.[38]

Wright's delay in reaching Bermuda Hundred by transport dismayed
and upset Butler. Interpreting Wright's tardiness as a sign he would rather
not fight beside the Army of the James, Butler shortly after 10:00 A.M. asked
Grant to send him Smith's command instead. Grant replied that Smith would
be returned to Bermuda Hundred as soon as he could be spared from Petersburg; for now, Butler should use Wright.[39]

It was late in the afternoon before the VI Corps could support the troops
at Bermuda Hundred. Shortly before its arrival, Pickett, still holding Beauregard's old works, had attacked the center of Butler's line, capturing Foster's
sector and gouging three veteran regiments, the 39th Illinois, 6th Connecticut, and 85th Pennsylvania, out of their rifle pits. The 24th Massachusetts,
holding the far right of the threatened position, saved the day by forming a
pivot on which supporting units swung back into position, closing most of
the gap that Pickett's advance had created.[40]

The fighting died down by 7:00 but the Confederates held part of Foster's advance picket line. Butler ordered Terry to make the "most strenuous efforts" to regain the position. He also directed Wright to support the counterattack with the divisions of Brigadier Generals David A. Russell and James B. Ricketts. Wright promised his hearty cooperation.

But no cooperative movement took place. Over the next three hours Wright and Terry inched westward, but only to reconnoiter. At length they reached the conclusion that Pickett's remaining foothold was too firm to dislodge. When ten o'clock passed without any counterattack, Butler was furious. His mood did not improve when Grant asked about the result of the offensive.

When Wright sent Butler a communiqué at 10:30 P.M. questioning the feasibility of an assault, the army commander exploded. Once again, a timid, textbook-bound soldier, an engineer masquerading as a combat leader, had presumed to question Butler's orders. His first reply was terse: "It is impossible to get on if orders are not obeyed." Soon afterward he sent Wright a note that better conveyed his frustration: "At 7.10 this evening I sent an order to you and Gen. Terry to do some fighting. At 10.30 I get no fighting but an argument. My order went out by the direction of the Lt. General." Butler then apologized to Grant that "nothing has been done, or even a vigorous attempt made."[41]

Predictably, Wright took offense, calling the rebuke "entirely unmerited." He declared that "every man I have will at once be put in to do some fighting." For his part, Terry complained to Colonel Hawley that Butler's behavior showed him to be "an incompetent . . . [who] must go at all costs." Hawley mentioned the incident two days later in a letter to his friend Gideon Welles, apparently hoping the navy secretary would convey to Abraham Lincoln that "Butler will not do in the field. . . . He will sit miles off and Napoleonically order charges and movements without any of that personal 'sensing' of the ground & force before you that the successful general must have."[42]

Butler made a clumsy attempt to soothe Wright ("no reproach is given, a fact is stated") while suggesting that a joint attack be made at dawn on the eighteenth. But at 1:00 A.M. Grant ordered the army leader to withhold his blow and stand ready to "take advantage of any weakening of the enemy in your front that may be caused by their withdrawal of troops to re-enforce Petersburg, against an attack that will be made by Meade in the morning." Yet another chance to achieve something important had passed Butler by. Grant's decision was all the more disappointing because by the time Butler relayed it to Wright and Terry, the generals were reporting themselves as "ready to move forward."[43]

Doubtful that the VI Corps would be of further use anywhere but Petersburg, Grant directed Butler to send Wright and his two divisions to Meade in exchange for Smith's command. Already, in fact, Brooks's and Bell's troops had begun their return to Bermuda Hundred, although Martindale's division would remain outside Petersburg until further notice. Sometime after 2:00 A.M. Brooks's column reached the defenses it had left almost three weeks before. At that hour, in response to a suggestion from Grant, Butler detached Brooks from the XVIII Corps and placed him in command of the X Corps, relieving Terry. Unaware of Grant's involvement, Terry probably added another black mark against the name of a certain political general.[44]

<hr>

All elements of the Army of the James saw action on June 18, the last day in which the Federals at Petersburg enjoyed an overwhelming superiority. In conjunction with an assault by most of the Army of the Potomac, Martindale guided his own division and the VI Corps division of Brigadier General Thomas H. Neill—the only portion of Wright's command that had not been shunted to Bermuda Hundred—against the northernmost sector of the Harrison's Creek defenses. Although elements of Meade's army began to press the enemy line at 4:00 A.M., Martindale was not ordered westward until noon. By then he had formed his composite force into three columns: Duncan's USCT brigade on the right, covered in rear by the rest of Hinks's division; Stedman's and Stannard's brigades in the center; and Neill's division on the left, with Brigadier General Frank Wheaton's brigade in the vanguard.[45]

The advance was initially successful; by 12:30 P.M., against little opposition, the attackers occupied a strategic crest in front of the creek. From there Martindale made plans to penetrate Beauregard's main line, half a mile farther west. Positioning most of the USCTs and Neill's troops to secure the flanks, he sent forward Stedman's brigade, followed by Stannard's.

Martindale quickly found himself in a situation dismayingly reminiscent of Cold Harbor: the Army of the Potomac failed to cover his advance. Facing heavier works than Martindale confronted, Hancock's II Corps could not advance alongside the Army of the James as Meade had directed. The result was that Stedman and Stannard took a murderous enfilading fire. Members of the already decimated Star Brigade, especially the 25th and 27th Massachusetts, took the worst beating; casualties in the latter regiment included dozens of enlisted men and every officer but one. When Martindale hustled up two black outfits to provide belated support, they too "suffered considerably."[46]

The parallels with Cold Harbor sharpened when Martindale halted his advance and petitioned Meade for help. As on the third, Martindale was told "to advance my command without any regard to my connection with my left." The division commander attempted to resume his movement, only to attract such a fusillade that his brigade leaders, two of the most combative officers in the army, begged him to desist. Again importuning Meade for help, Martindale was told to cease his movement and hold the 300 yards or so he had gained.[47]

Martindale had failed because time had finally run out on the Union armies. Lee's vanguard had reached Petersburg late that morning; for the balance of the day the defenders numbered about 20,000 men, more than enough to hold Harrison's Creek. Grant's plan to overthrow Beauregard had collapsed under the combined weight of delay, poor timing, uncertainty, hesitation, failure to coordinate offensive operations, and a frantic defensive effort.

No single factor loomed quite so large as Baldy Smith's several-hour delay in attacking on the fifteenth. Had he nerved himself to strike in midafternoon—even if he had been forced to use conventional tactics—it seems likely he would have overwhelmed everything in his path within a few hours. He could have begun penetrating to the heart of Petersburg before dark, destroying the foot and rail bridges that Lee eventually used to reinforce Beauregard. With those objectives attained, Meade, upon arriving at Petersburg, might have joined Smith in securing the city beyond hope of recovery.

Each of these possibilities fell victim to Smith's inability to strike until he could make a painstaking reconnaissance, mature his plan of attack, and maneuver carefully into position. Years later, one of Hinks's officers would surmise that the delay "cost us ten months of fighting in front of Petersburg" and thousands of lives on both sides.[48]

CHAPTER NINE

Regular Approaches

ALTHOUGH FRUSTRATED BY HIS INABILITY TO CRACK THE PETERSBURG defenses, Grant refused to brood over his misfortune. By June 19 the commanding general was planning simultaneous drives against both ends of the enemy's line. On Lee's south flank he would send cavalry to destroy three railroads that sustained the city, even as Meade's infantry tried to seize one of the lines, the Petersburg & Weldon. If successful, the foot soldiers would sweep westward across the Boydton Plank Road in rear of the Confederate flank.[1]

Grant hoped that in countering the twin movements Lee would stretch his lines paper-thin to the south. To force him to do the same on the other flank, Grant scrutinized the territory north of the James River for a similar purpose. The Confederate line above the river had already been reduced to oppose Butler at Bermuda Hundred and Meade at Petersburg, leaving Richmond vulnerable. Grant increasingly viewed that city as a worthy objective. While the loss of Petersburg would imperil the enemy's physical strength, the capture of his seat of government might fatally weaken his morale.

Given its position between the Appomattox and the James, Butler's reunited army was the logical choice to strike toward Richmond. Grant felt certain that the Army of the James was strong enough to hold its peninsula defenses and also operate miles away; it had done so at Cold Harbor and during the early assaults against Petersburg. The command had just demonstrated this ability on June 18. While Martindale and Hinks attacked at Petersburg, the rest of the army repulsed two attacks by Pickett's division, reinforced by Lee, against the right flank of the Bermuda Hundred works. Pickett's decisive setback suggested that Butler's enclave was secure.

Grant's first task was to choose a site on the upper bank of the James from which Butler could operate northward and westward. He and Butler decided on Jones's Neck, about ten miles southeast of Richmond. From there the James flowed north for about a mile before forking to create Four Mile Creek, which led westward, and Bailey's Creek, which continued north across the New Market and Darbytown Roads toward New Market Heights, a long, high plateau directly south of Richmond. The capital's outermost defenses lined both creeks. Grant and Butler determined to secure a foothold on the west side of the river below another of its tributaries, Three Mile Creek.[2]

Grant directed that a relatively small force—1,200 men from the X Corps under Foster—should make the effort north of the James. Foster was to quickly secure and expand his position, which engineers would link with Bermuda Hundred via pontoons. After extensive planning by General Weitzel, Butler's chief engineer, and Weitzel's counterpart in the Army of the Potomac, Brigadier General Henry W. Benham, Grant decided to lay the bridge just west of a swampy creek mouth known as Deep Bottom, where the James was only 575 feet wide. A potential drawback was the terrain on which Butler had to entrench—so hard and grainy as to be, in Weitzel's words, "most unfavorable for excavation and embankment."[3]

Just after dark on June 20, as elements of Meade's army left the Petersburg trenches for the Weldon Railroad, Weitzel put his engineers in motion. His assistant, Lieutenant Peter S. Michie, placed the pontoon boats in the river and 100 of Foster's men boarded them, a dozen or more to each boat. Soon the unlikely armada was making for the north bank, thought to be defended by a picket force that stretched to within 300 yards of the future bridgehead. After grounding at the appointed site, the troops cautiously debarked and turned the boats over to Michie's pontoniers, who would fashion them into a floating bridge.

The operation came off almost flawlessly. Neither the initial crossing nor the work of Michie's troops—including pioneers who felled trees and cut roads to the bridge—alerted the Rebel pickets. Everyone worked with speed, stealth, and purpose. On the south bank a member of Foster's command watched as the engineers "divided into details to carry the string-pieces, to place them in position on the boats, to bring plank[s], to lay them in place, and all with wonderful celerity and precision, so that a little after midnight the bridge was complete."[4]

When the Rebels on the north bank finally responded, just after daylight on the twenty-first, it was too late: Foster's brigade had scooped out trenches in the hard ground by the water, and some of his men were pressing inland.

They drove away the largest band of pickets, which had held an advance post at the Grover house, about a mile northwest of the bridgehead. Later in the day other Confederates appeared near Grover's, but Foster's marksmen kept them away from the bridge. That afternoon Admiral Lee's gunboats churned upriver to Jones's Neck and shelled enemy snipers. While the fighting continued, other Federals fortified the bridgehead, cleared fields of fire for artillery, and established outposts toward Richmond.

Initially, some of Foster's men believed they were making a diversion to aid Meade's movement south of Petersburg; they expected to remain north of the James for a few hours at most. But before nightfall most realized that their stay would be an extended one. In fact, the Army of the James maintained a presence north of its namesake river for the remainder of the war. Foster's move was a prelude to operations that eventually placed several thousand troops within reach of the Richmond defenses.

The foothold so threatened the capital that it forced the Confederates to erect a fourth line of defense south of the city. It ran east from Chaffin's Bluff, along the James, to just above Foster's position, then north across the New Market, Darbytown, and Charles City Roads toward the Chickahominy River. The perimeter, however, was not impregnable: in a little over three months it would collapse during a major offensive by Butler's army.

Foster's dash above the James had succeeded through a combination of speed, surprise, favorable timing, and the efficiency of all involved. The success ensured that Grant's armies would exert continuous pressure against both Petersburg and Richmond, preventing Lee from quickly shifting his forces from one flank to the other for offensive or defensive purposes. Conversely, the lodgement increased Grant's tactical options and demonstrated the mobility of the Army of the James. Rather than being trapped inside Bermuda Hundred, that army could travel virtually anywhere opportunity beckoned.[5]

For his movement against the Weldon Railroad, to run concurrent with Foster's advance above the James, General Meade selected the II and VI Corps. The former, now under General Birney, headed down the Jerusalem Plank Road, preparing to strike westward toward Reams's Station, seven miles below Petersburg. Wright's corps swept south along Birney's right flank, then angled toward the Southside Railroad.

The departure of these commands uncovered both flanks of the Army of the Potomac. To secure the left end of the line, Meade's remaining forces sidled southward. Meade needed outside help, however, to plug the gap on the right. At Grant's suggestion, Butler offered the XVIII Corps, backed by Kautz's cavalry. In so doing, Butler acted with good grace in a difficult situation; he would not be compensated for the loss of those several thousand troops, and no one could say how long he would be without them. Once they left Bermuda Hundred, Brooks would extend the left of his newly acquired X Corps to cover the vacated sector.

The return of Smith's corps to Petersburg on June 21 began well enough but ended on a sour note. Brooks's old division, now under George Stannard (back with the army after recovering from a wound received at Cold Harbor), crossed the Appomattox at Point of Rocks, took position on the far right of the Petersburg works, and relieved a portion of the VI Corps. Next to cross was Kautz, whose troopers occupied trenches well in the rear of Stannard's command. Then Hinks's and Martindale's divisions crossed the pontoons, moving into place on Stannard's left, between the River and City Point Roads.

The detached force was augmented two days later by two brigades of the 2nd Division, X Corps, under Colonel Bell. Upon Bell's arrival the Army of the James had three distinct segments: Foster's infantry, supported by militia and mounted riflemen, at Deep Bottom; most of the X Corps (the brigades of Howell, Hawley, and Colonel N. Martin Curtis, plus additional militia units) at Bermuda Hundred under Butler and Brooks; and the XVIII Corps, Bell's infantry, and Kautz's troopers, all under Smith, outside Petersburg. The army would hold all three positions until war's end.[6]

Although Butler hated to lose so many regiments from Bermuda Hundred, Smith's departure did not proceed briskly enough to suit him. At 9:00 A.M. on the twenty-first Butler observed Martindale's men pass his headquarters, several miles from the bridge. Apparently unaware that other elements of the XVIII Corps had already reached Petersburg, he assumed that Smith had not begun the transfer early in the morning, as directed. Rather hastily, Butler sent his subordinate a reminder that "the great fault of all our movements is dilatoriness." This was bad enough, but he made the mistake of adding, "I have found it necessary to relieve one general [Gillmore] for this among other causes."[7]

Poorly worded but probably well intentioned, the communiqué struck a nerve. Taking the reproof personally, Smith shot back an ill-tempered reply. He rejected Butler's reproof ("a reprimand can only come from the sentence of a court martial, & I shall accept nothing else as such"); he denigrated the critic ("I have some years been engaged in marching troops, and I think in experience of that kind, at least, I am your superior"); and he refused to be intimidated ("your threat of relieving me does not frighten me in the least").[8]

Butler appeared surprised and hurt. He dashed off a second message: "When a friend writes you a note, is it not best to read it twice before you answer it unkindly?" His gesture at conciliation accomplished nothing. Suffering still from the intestinal ailment he had contracted at Cold Harbor, short on sleep, and discomfited by a hot, dusty march, Smith sent Grant's headquarters a copy of Butler's first note accompanied with a request to be transferred from Butler's army. Grant chose not to respond, and the storm blew over. Still, the incident intensified Grant's concern that the Butler-Smith relationship might never pan out.[9]

While Smith's infantry took position outside Petersburg, Kautz's horsemen headed for Mount Sinai Church. There, some miles south of the city, they joined a larger force of horsemen—Brigadier General James Harrison Wilson's 3rd Division, Cavalry Corps, Army of the Potomac—for what Butler called "an expedition to cut the lines of communication south."[10]

The assignment would return Kautz to some old haunts. At Grant's behest, he and Wilson were to operate in remote cooperation with the II and VI Corps against the Weldon Railroad. That attended to, the cavalry was to help demolish the Southside and the Richmond & Danville Railroads. If all three lines were cut, Lee might abandon Petersburg for lack of supplies, wandering about in search of a nonexistent haven.[11]

While the raid was bound to be difficult, there would be few pursuers. Shortly before he left Cold Harbor for Petersburg, Grant had sent Sheridan, with two-thirds of Meade's horsemen, toward the Shenandoah Valley to operate against the Virginia Central Railroad and the James River Canal. If successful, Sheridan would not only deprive the Army of Northern Virginia of food from the "Breadbasket of the Confederacy" but also would divert Rebel cavalry from Grant's path. As the lieutenant general had hoped, a proportional amount of Lee's cavalry, under Wade Hampton, pursued Sheridan; only the small division commanded by General Lee's son, Rooney, remained at Petersburg to oppose Wilson and Kautz.

The Federals appeared to be more than a match for Rooney Lee. To the 3,300 troopers under the brash, headstrong Wilson, his erstwhile bureau assistant added 2,000 riders of uneven quality who were nonetheless familiar with the country to be visited. Wilson believed that as long as potential pursuers were kept to a minimum, he and Kautz would destroy enough track, rolling stock, and support facilities on all three railroads to cripple Lee's army.

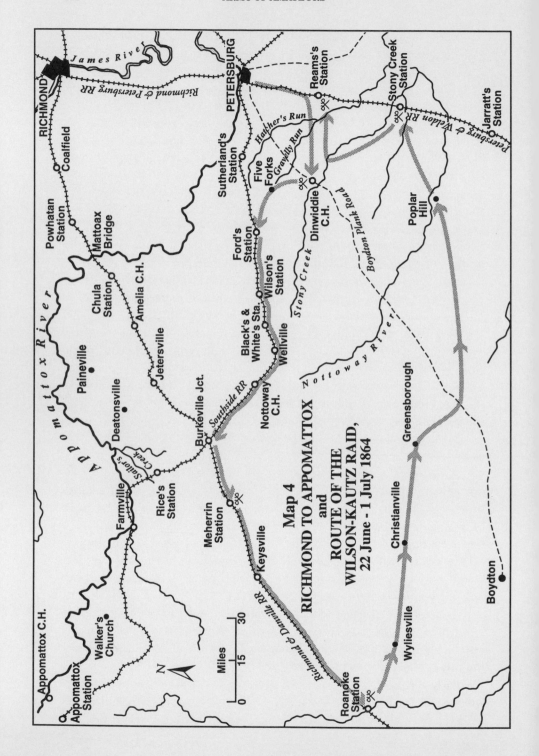

Map 4
RICHMOND TO APPOMATTOX
and
ROUTE OF THE
WILSON-KAUTZ RAID,
22 June - 1 July 1864

Wilson also was promised the kind of support he wanted. Meade's chief of staff, Major General Andrew A. Humphreys, assured him not only that Sheridan would detain Hampton but also that a day or two after the raiders started out the II and VI Corps would seize much of the Weldon line, then stretch toward the Southside. Such a lodgment would help cover Wilson and Kautz by opening an avenue of retreat in a crisis.[12]

Hopeful of great things, the raiders broke camp at Mount Sinai Church at 2:00 A.M. on June 22 and started down the Weldon line. The original plan had been to make an early exit from the railroad and cut west to hit the Southside. But when word came that Rooney Lee was entrenched near Sutherland's Station on the Southside, Kautz, who was in front, continued south to Reams's Station. There Kautz inflicted his first railroad damage in six weeks, tearing up track and again demolishing the Nottoway River Bridge near Jarratt's Station.

Late in the morning Kautz finally veered west, passing through Dinwiddie Court House and reaching the Southside some miles beyond Rooney Lee's camp. Heading southwest along the right-of-way, Kautz chased a small force out of Ford's Station, wrecked two trains, and burned several miles' worth of rails and ties, making the "sky blood-red with light" well into the evening.[13]

Wilson was not as fortunate in eluding Rooney Lee. Nettled to learn that the Yankees had detoured around him, Lee rushed up to batter the rear of Wilson's column soon after it cleared Reams's Station. Wilson repulsed two attacks in brigade strength and continued westward, if more slowly than before, hoping to reunite with Kautz at Burkeville Junction.

Riding well in advance of the 3rd Cavalry Division, Kautz pushed on through rising temperatures and clouds of dust. He reached Burkeville, where the Southside crossed the Richmond & Danville, at about 3:00 P.M. on the twenty-third. There his troopers pried up track in four directions. Supervised by Colonels Spear and West (the latter having replaced Colonel Mix in brigade command), the work continued into the night. Next morning at about six o'clock, Kautz's men followed the Richmond & Danville, dislodging sections as they rode. The rails of the R & D rested upon yellow-pine stringers, which burst into flames as soon as a trooper applied a sulfur match. Fires lighted the raiders' seventeen-mile ride to Keysville, where they were joined by Wilson, whose division had temporarily outdistanced Rooney Lee.[14]

Early on the twenty-fifth Kautz resumed his southwestward jaunt, wrecking not only the R & D but also sawmills that supplied the railroad's stringers. By 5:00 P.M., when the column halted at the Staunton River Bridge, just opposite Roanoke Station, the raiders had destroyed forty miles of track on three railroads—thirty miles on the R & D, Lee's principal supply line west of Petersburg. At that point Kautz and Wilson believed they had accomplished their mission.

It was well they had, for the raiders—figuratively, if not in fact—were at the end of the line. Sending skirmishers across the Staunton River Bridge, Kautz found the far side alive with more than 1,200 Confederate regulars, militiamen, and home guards. Well dug in and backed with artillery, the Rebels commanded both ends of the bridge.[15]

Though dubious of success, Kautz obeyed Wilson's order to charge the bridge, seize it, and burn it. He committed mounted and dismounted men from both of his brigades; none got very far. Under a barrage from two twenty-pounder Parrott rifles, the attackers rushed back to their starting point, minus several comrades dead, wounded, or captured. One of Kautz's subalterns rightly criticized him for attacking a fixed position using the same piecemeal tactics that had failed during his earlier expeditions.

Although frustrated by Kautz's repulse, Wilson decided the opposition was too formidable and ordered his colleague to pull back. The generals held the enemy in place until nightfall, then disengaged. Morning found both divisions in southeasterly retreat.

Throughout the twenty-sixth Kautz and Wilson made for the Weldon line as fast as jaded mounts could travel. Rooney Lee and local pursuers dogged the raiders' heels as they passed through Wyliesville, Christianville, and Greensborough, crossed the Meherrin River, and approached Jarratt's Station.[16]

As rations and feed dwindled, Kautz permitted his troopers to forage liberally. The historian of the 1st District of Columbia Cavalry recalled that "bread, and meat, and butter, and milk, and eggs, and cream, in a word, whatever the smokehouse, or the spring house, or the field, or garden, or stall, or pasture of a rebel contained . . . was remorselessly appropriated without waiting for either commissary or quartermaster process." Fortunate men exchanged winded horses for fresh ones or for the mules more readily available in those parts. Some raiders confiscated nonmilitary goods as well. At mission's end, one of Wilson's forage wagons was found to contain a communion service from an Episcopal church.[17]

With fatigue and straggling taking an increasing toll, Kautz and Wilson attempted to avoid a pitched battle short of the Union lines. On the afternoon of the twenty-eighth, as they neared the Weldon Road, Kautz suggested they bypass Stony Creek and Reams's Stations in favor of striking the tracks at Jarratt's Station, which he considered less likely to be heavily defended. Earlier Wilson had deferred to his colleague's judgment, but this time he rejected Kautz's advice. The result was that when the head of the column reached Stony Creek early that evening, it found thousands of Confederate infantry and horsemen dug in for a fight. The foot soldiers were locals, but the cavalry was from Hampton's command. As the raiders later learned, Hampton, after fighting Sheridan to a draw along the Virginia Central, had returned speedily to Petersburg in defiance of Grant's and Meade's calculations. Worse, Meade's infantry had not cleared a path of return for Kautz and Wilson.

The fracas that broke out around Stony Creek Station was spirited but did not take a critical toll of the raiders. Wilson remained on the scene, pinning the enemy down, while Kautz bypassed the depot and headed north to Reams's Station. Unfortunately, when the troopers of the Army of the James neared their objective early on the twenty-ninth, they stumbled into battle against Hampton's main body—two divisions supported by infantry under Major General William Mahone. The much more numerous enemy moved to surround the Federals, but Kautz himself, belying his reputation for mediocrity, mounted an inspired defense. Building breastworks under fire, he held them against several attacks (the firepower of his well-armed troopers served him ably) and even launched a counterassault that captured one of Mahone's brigades.[18]

Battering its way out of Stony Creek Station, Wilson's division, along with its supply and ambulance trains, reached the scene of Kautz's fight late in the morning. Quickly becoming entangled in the fray, Wilson sent one of his staff officers, escorted by forty members of Kautz's 3rd New York Cavalry, to find help. The little band slipped through a seam in the enemy line and by hard riding reached Meade's headquarters at Petersburg that afternoon. The aide persuaded Meade to order one of Wright's divisions to Reams's Station, though its commander doubted it would arrive in time to help. The relief column reached the scene of fighting at 9:00 A.M. on June 30 to find friend and foe long gone.[19]

Bereft of reinforcements, the raiders fought long and hard to escape encirclement, but by midafternoon of the twenty-ninth, with Hampton and Mahone closing in, Wilson ordered an every-man-for-himself retreat. Abandoning everything, including wounded and sick as well as several hundred slaves who had joined the column, Wilson spurred south at high speed. Kautz attempted to follow but found himself cut off by Mahone. Only a valiant charge by Spear's 11th Pennsylvania enabled Kautz to loop eastward below Reams's Station.

Kautz's chosen route led his men through woodlots and thickets ("shells from rebel batteries knocking the branches about our ears," as one of them remembered), then across creeks and into swamps so deep their artillery had to be abandoned. Despite all obstacles Kautz kept his troopers well in hand, and his knowledge of the countryside enabled most of them to keep ahead of their pursuers. Dirty, ragged, and exhausted, the main body staggered back to City Point that evening. Wilson was more closely pursued and more roughly handled; even so, the greater part of his division entered friendly lines along the James River on July 1.[20]

The results of the raid, as with most cavalry expeditions of this war, were mixed. The commands had suffered a combined loss initially estimated at 1,500 men (although several hundred eventually straggled back to their outfits), sixteen artillery pieces, and hundreds of supply and hospital vehicles. At such cost the raiders had rendered more than fifty miles of track on three railroads temporarily useless to the Confederacy. The raiders had also destroyed, as the historian of the 11th Pennsylvania noted, "every railroad station, water tank, wood pile, bridge, trestle, [and] sawmill, from fifteen miles [south] of Petersburg to the Roanoke River."[21]

The raiders had gathered spoils, the scope and nature of which infuriated Confederate officers, politicians, and editors. Virginia newspapers flayed the "mounted thieves" who over a week's time had indulged in "the pleasure of safely tormenting non-combatants" wherever they rode. Wilson sought to deflect such charges—which even Grant and Meade found difficult to ignore— but Kautz admitted that the Federals had laid a heavier hand than usual on the citizenry. Though Kautz's men had lived up to their reputation as banditti, most of the vandalism appeared to have been committed by the Army of the Potomac.

For all the damage it did, the expedition achieved no greater strategic success than Kautz's earlier raids. The R & D was back in operation by July 16, the Southside and Weldon Railroads before the close of August. Wilson's claims notwithstanding, the soldiers outside Petersburg and the civilians in the city suffered no long-term privation as a result of the demolition. Robert E. Lee turned to southward-running highways such as the Boydton Plank and Cox Roads, which could accommodate larger-than-usual supply trains. Much to the chagrin of the Union command, such make-do efforts enabled the Army of Northern Virginia to endure throughout the period required to repair the railroads.[22]

Like Kautz's independent expeditions against Richmond and Petersburg, his joint venture with Wilson pointed up a critical shortcoming of mounted raids. Due to its relatively small size and lack of staying power, a raiding column could inflict only short-term damage, thus the "window of opportunity" for exploiting its success would be brief. If the main army did not take the offensive at the same time, the expedition would likely degenerate into a nuisance raid. In the present instance, as soon as Meade's infantry failed to reach the Weldon Railroad, the raiders' contributions went by the board.

Though hopeful that the railroad raid would force Petersburg's evacuation, Grant hedged his bets. Two days before the cavalry started out, he called up the siege train of heavy artillery, ammunition, and support equipment that had been outfitted at the Washington arsenal. Butler had received an advance installment of this train at Bermuda Hundred in mid-May. At first Grant saw no use for the remainder, but now that he was facing the prospect of "regular approaches"—a long siege campaign—heavy guns figured to play an important role in his plans.

The balance of the train—several dozen thirty-pounder Parrott rifles, four-and-one-half-inch siege guns, and mortars large and small—arrived at Broadway Landing on the twenty-third. Over the next six weeks twenty-eight guns and fifty-three mortars were deployed to dozens of points along the lines outside Petersburg. Many were placed in the Army of the Potomac's sector, where they came under the control of Meade's artillery chief, Brigadier General Henry J. Hunt. Yet most of the train, including its most impressive member, a flatcar-mounted thirteen-inch seacoast mortar nicknamed "Dictator," supported the XVIII Corps. The train's commander, Colonel Abbot, was a West Pointer and an engineer by training.[23]

Well before the balance of the siege train reached Petersburg, Federal artillery had pounded away at the city in an attempt to reduce its forts, breastworks, and morale. On some occasions commanders such as Birney subjected Petersburg to five or six hours of shelling. The Confederates replied in kind. On the afternoon of June 23 Lee's artillery north of the Appomattox raked the Bermuda Hundred works for an hour or more, inflicting several casualties.

Then the Rebels looked southward for new targets. At 7:00 A.M. on the twenty-fourth guns on both sides of the river opened up at Smith's corps, raining what one Federal called "a perfect storm of shot and shell" on Stannard's division along the Jordan's Point Road. Colonel Edgar M. Cullen, commanding one of Stannard's brigades, told his men to hug the ground and not return fire: "When the enemy stops fighting, he'll charge upon us. He'll think he has killed us all. Then rise up and stand firm. . . . Don't let a man flinch, but up and at 'em, and by the living God we'll hold the line!"[24]

Cullen was prophetic. Once the barrage ceased, Hoke's division charged the embattled Yankees. When the attackers were 150 yards away, Stannard's men stood and let loose with a volley that cleared the field. Survivors rallied, reinforcements rushed up, and the Confederates came on again and again. For almost two hours Hoke tried to interpose between Stannard and the river before declaring the fight lost and drawing off. Early the next day he attacked again and was again repulsed. In two days of combat Stannard's well-entrenched command had suffered a few dozen casualties while inflicting three times as many.[25]

Over the next week those X Corps units temporarily under Smith's command planned offensives of their own, but each died quickly. On the twenty-fourth Smith prepared to strike a hilltop salient opposite his left flank, but General Turner, the on-scene commander, found the position so formidable that he called off the movement minutes before it was to begin. "We all thanked God with overflowing hearts," a soldier remarked. Butler was not as pleased with the turn of events. Believing that the salient could have been taken, he demanded to know why the movement had been called off. The army commander went so far as to complain of the outcome to Grant and to offer to lead the operation personally. Grant talked him out of

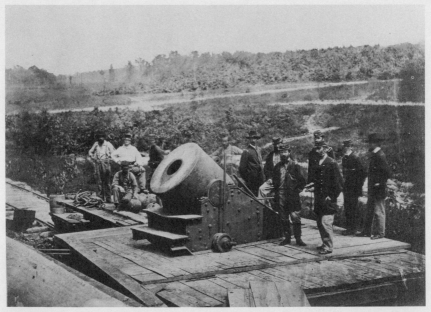

Seacost mortar "Dictator," with Colonel Henry L. Abbot, commander of the siege train of the Army of the James (fifth from right). LIBRARY OF CONGRESS.

the idea, but Butler and Smith exchanged words over the operation, planting new seeds of enmity between them.[26]

Still smarting from Butler's criticism, on June 30 Smith scheduled another attempt to take the salient. To improve its prospects, he directed Colonel William Barton to stage a diversion with his X Corps brigade. Barton, who lacked combat experience but appeared eager for the assignment, was to advance through woods that would mask his approach. He was then to rush the south flank of the fortified hill, deflecting enemy attention from Colonel Curtis's brigade, which would charge the position from another direction at the same time.

The plan had its points, but Barton's incompetence ruined it. Instead of moving rapidly to the shelter of the trees, the colonel formed his men on open ground within sight of the enemy. Before the brigade could move out, Rebel artillery and sharpshooters opened fire and pinned it down. Another supporting brigade, under Colonel Bell, advanced on Barton's flank to try to relieve the pressure, but the now-alert Rebels dosed it with shot and shell, wounding its leader.

A disgusted Smith called off the operation again. He arrested Barton and ordered an inquiry into his conduct. Barton was acquitted on a procedural point, but his career was over; he was replaced by the army's highest-ranking teenager, Galusha Pennypacker.[27]

The debacle of the thirtieth was followed by a long spell of monotony along the Petersburg lines. The more realistic soldiers realized that the chances of a dramatic breakthrough were slim. For them, the siege began to resemble an infinite tunnel.

Some aspects of life in the trenches would have made Job cry aloud. Dozens of soldiers perished every day from sniper fire and artillery barrages. When not dodging bullets and shells, the troops endured a spectrum of natural discomforts. "Heat! dust!! flies!!!" wailed a *New York Times* correspondent on June 28. "Suffocating heat! blinding dust! torturing flies! The thermometer reported at 98 to 100 under the canvas of our tents." The grime of trench life turned the complexion of white soldiers so dark they were mistaken for black troops. Only those who could get mosquito netting could sleep: a New Hampshire soldier remarked, "It was the only way one was sure of having any head [left] in the morning." By the twenty-eighth a veteran from Maine reported that "our army is pretty well used up." Not only were the soldiers tormented by weather, vermin, and enemy fire, they reeled from the memory of comrades "slaughtered [without] . . . much accomplished."[28]

Commanders suffered just as much. Writing to his father on June 27, General Turner declared that "this war of rifle pits is terrible. . . . The advance upon Petersburg so far has been a series of charges to dislodge the enemy from his rifle pits, with terrible cost to us; when driven from our lines, he retires to the next hill top and in a few hours is buried" in bunkers. Turner saw no hope for a quick change in this grim and frustrating mode of warfare, for the enemy had "fallen back now to a line that apparently we can make no impression upon—and the flank movements to me appear to be used up. Grant has no streams like the Rappahannock, York & James to furnish us a base for another flank movement." The brigadier added with a sigh: "I am entirely at a loss for an opinion what next to do, and I think it is bothering bigger heads than mine."[29]

The high command resorted to various expedients to prop up morale. One perhaps misguided effort was the issuance of a whiskey ration to troops at Bermuda Hundred and Petersburg, a gesture one New Englander considered just compensation for the "excessive duty" demanded of his regiment and others on the front lines. The liquor appeared not to harm the fighting ability of the Army of the James, but on June 29, when General Grant imbibed, the command went into convulsions.[30]

The most dramatic result of Grant's libation was its effect on Baldy Smith's career. By the twenty-ninth Smith was in a foul mood over recent tiffs with his least favorite political general. The two had most recently argued over Smith's charge that during the aborted operation of the twenty-fourth, the army's USCT division (temporarily commanded by Colonel John Holman) had been demoralized by cannon fire while forming in support of the antici-pated attack.

When Smith charged that elements of the division had proven themselves to be undependable and "totally inefficient," Butler, mindful of his status as protector of black troops, claimed that Smith's words reflected racial prejudice. The abolitionist also resisted Smith's subsequent attempt to persuade Grant to merge Holman's troops with the all-black 4th Division, IX Corps, Army of the Potomac. Butler sought to punish Smith by attempting to exchange white regiments of the XVIII Corps for Meade's African-Americans and to place the new arrivals in Smith's corps.[31]

His problems with Butler and continuing physical debility nearly destroyed Smith's morale. Sick, weary, and fed up, on June 29 he wrote to his wife, "I can stand as much as most men, but I cannot live under this man much longer." At the minimum, he would work hard to win a leave of absence, during which he would seek a command apart from Butler.[32]

Smith had a chance to speak to Grant about a furlough that day, but the situation was hardly conducive to asking favors. The circumstances of the meeting remain in dispute because Smith and Butler, both of whom were with the commanding general for much of that day, left conflicting accounts of what transpired.

According to Smith, Butler went to Grant's headquarters on the morning of the twenty-ninth with a request (which Grant approved) to inspect the lines outside Petersburg. Butler persuaded Grant to accompany him on the tour. The pair stopped first at IX Corps headquarters, where Butler prevailed on the convivial Major General Ambrose E. Burnside to offer Grant a glass of whiskey from his private mess. Afterward, Grant and Butler made their way to XVIII Corps headquarters where, in Smith's presence, Butler solicited another drink for Grant. After an awkward hesitation, Smith provided a little whiskey. As soon as the lieutenant general had drunk, Smith hid the bottle under his cot. To his exasperation, Grant snatched up a flask of brandy that Smith kept on hand for medicinal purposes, drank, and announced that the liquor was doing him "much good." With growing concern, Smith watched Grant drain the flask. Butler, as Smith recalled, looked on approvingly.

After about an hour, Grant and Butler prepared to return to City Point; by then Grant was drunk. As Smith told it, the general remounted with some difficulty, then rode off "in a most disgusting state after having vomited all over his horse's neck & shoulders." Appalled by the exhibition, Smith commented to one of his staff officers: "General Grant has gone away drunk; General Butler has seen it, and will never fail to use the weapon which has been put into his hands."[33]

Smith at once wrote down the incident in detail for General Rawlins, Grant's teetotaling adjutant general and self-appointed guardian. The next day, as Smith reported, he received a note from the staff officer, thanking him for his letter and accusing Butler of engineering the sorry episode. Supposedly, Rawlins closed by acknowledging the implicit threat to Grant's reputation and career: "Being thus advised of the slippery ground he is on, I shall not fail to use my endeavors to stay him from falling."[34]

As one might expect, Butler roundly disputed Smith's account of the twenty-ninth. In his memoirs almost thirty years later, the army commander wrote, "I never saw General Grant drink a glass of spiritous liquor in my life." It is tempting to dismiss Butler's assertion out of hand. Although Grant by 1864 had acquired a reputation for occasional intemperance, he drank sparingly and infrequently, and rarely during active operations. Butler further stated that had he urged Grant to drink as Smith charged, "I should have expected Grant to dismiss me from the service at once, as he ought to have done, and as I would have done to him under the same circumstances."[35]

Neither man's version of events is entirely credible. No disinterested observer ever charged Butler with providing liquor to Grant. On the other hand, several unimpeachable witnesses (including General Stannard and the visiting assistant secretary of war, St. John Tucker) testified to seeing Grant drunk. If Butler's declaration that he never saw Grant drink is difficult to accept, Smith's contention that Butler engineered the incident for personal gain is equally suspect. In Smith's view, the whole thing was an orchestration to blackmail Grant into relieving him from command of the XVIII Corps and reversing his unannounced decision to remove Butler from the field.[36]

While there is just enough truth in Smith's story to make it appear plausible, some aspects of it strain credulity. On July 1, two days after the incident at XVIII Corps headquarters, Grant wrote the War Department an extraordinary letter in which he proposed to revamp the command system of the Army of the James. Weary of the friction between Butler and Smith, Grant wished to remove one of them before the feud affected operations. Still doubtful that Butler was fit for field command, Grant asked the chief of staff, General Halleck, to devise a way to send Butler to "another field of duty" in Kentucky or Missouri. In such a theater Butler could concentrate on administrative duties rather than the tactical responsibilities that had so often involved him in disputes with his subordinates.

Halleck, whose opinion of Butler was much lower than Grant's, replied that to send the political general to a volatile border state "would probably cause an insurrection." He suggested instead that Grant restrict Butler to desk duties in his present theater. The commanding general readily embraced that idea, which would neutralize Butler without ravaging his pride and would save Lincoln from having to embarrass the general only a few months before a critical election. On July 6 Grant asked the War Department to remand Butler to Fort Monroe as departmental commander while placing Baldy Smith in charge of Butler's field troops.

The resulting order on the following day tried to do what Grant wanted but fell short of desired results. The order gave Smith command of that part of the Army of the James "serving with the Army of the Potomac in the field . . . [while] Maj. Gen. B. F. Butler will command the remainder of the troops in that department, having his headquarters at Fort Monroe." Since the order implied that Butler would retain tactical control over the troops not immediately cooperating with Meade, including those at Bermuda Hundred and Deep Bottom, it would have the effect of halving the Army of the James, a most unwieldy arrangement.[37]

On July 10 a dissatisfied Grant tried again to translate his wishes into words. Having recently ordered two divisions of the XIX Corps, Army of the Gulf, from Louisiana to Virginia, he hoped by month's end to add the former leader of the corps, William B. Franklin, to the Army of the James.

Grant proposed to make Franklin second in command of the army, neatly inserting him between Butler and Smith. Butler would serve as titular head of the army from his headquarters in Hampton Roads; Franklin would have tactical control of the X, XVIII, and XIX Corps; and Smith would exercise immediate command of those forces outside Petersburg.

The new arrangement may have been more unwieldy than the one it was supposed to improve, as its complexity allowed for misinterpretation. When Smith learned of the order around July 8, he supposed he was being named department commander and that Butler was being confined to a nebulous position that existed primarily on paper. Later, he came to believe that Butler, angry over the implications of the order, had stormed off to City Point, threatening to use his extensive contacts in the press and Congress to publicize Grant's recent fall off the wagon. Such a story, breaking as it would at a critical stage of the Virginia campaign, might have had devastating effects.[38]

Smith believed he had ample grounds for accusing Butler of blackmail, for on July 10 Grant suspended the order. Nine days later, to the astonishment of many, including Smith, Grant upheld Butler's authority as both tactical and administrative commander of the Department of Virginia and North Carolina while relieving Smith of command and directing him to New York to await further orders. Following this unexpected turnabout, a furious Smith spread his tale of chicanery and double-dealing via some of the same contacts that he had accused Butler of threatening to manipulate. To the end of his days Smith remained implacably convinced that Butler had done him in by exploiting Grant's weaknesses and fear of exposure.

Smith appears to have been wrong about Butler's motivations. He assumed that Butler got Grant drunk on June 29 because Butler knew that the order of July 7 was in the works. In reality, he was ignorant of the document up to July 9, when he expressed pleasure at what he took to be an affirmation of his authority over a soon-to-be-enlarged army. After conferring with the lieutenant general, Butler informed his wife that Grant intended to leave him in full command of the Army of the James. Any contrary references in the order had been "the work of Halleck, upon the application of Smith," and Grant had promised to strike them from the final draft. In sum, Grant "has vindicated me and my military operations."[39]

Smith failed to see that he, more than anyone, was responsible for Grant's suspension of the order. By early July the commanding general had come to blame Smith for the tension among the commanders of the Army of the James. Grant had often experienced Smith's prickly temper, especially after becoming an unwilling sounding board for Smith's condemnation of Meade.

Grant knew that neither of his army leaders was a genius, but he respected Meade and, as he told Halleck, "I have no difficulty with General Butler, finding him always clear in his conception of orders and prompt to obey."[40]

Thus Grant found it increasingly difficult to tolerate Smith's barbed references to Cold Harbor, one of the few subjects on which Grant himself could be touchy. Grant also must have winced when reading the presumptuous letter Smith sent him on July 2, advising Grant on how to conduct siege operations at Petersburg and asking in reference to Butler: "How can you place a man in command of two army corps who is as helpless as a child on the field of battle and as visionary as an opium eater in council?"[41]

As if his blasts at Butler and Meade were not sufficient, Smith was foolish enough to indirectly criticize the lieutenant general. Grant, Smith appeared to claim, had been criminally lax in keeping Butler and Meade in command. Grant also grew resentful of what he saw as Smith's intrusion into his private affairs. Grant suspected that Smith, not Butler, had publicized his drinking spree throughout the officer corps. Smith had also embarrassed Grant by bringing down on him the Calvinist wrath of John Rawlins.

Smith could not leave bad enough alone. He meddled again on July 8 when, in company with General Franklin, who had arrived in Virginia in advance of the XIX Corps, he met Grant at the City Point headquarters of Brigadier General Rufus Ingalls, chief quartermaster of the siege armies. First Smith berated Ingalls for providing Grant with a glass of whiskey. Then he tried to involve Grant in a debate over the battle of June 3. He later claimed he had made the commanding general admit that "there was a butchery at Cold Harbor & that he had said nothing about it because it could do no good." Finally, though Grant did not get drunk on July 8, Smith again tattled to Rawlins, who subjected his boss to another temperance lecture.[42]

Afterward, Smith left City Point by train. On July 2 he had submitted a leave request so that he and his ill wife might recuperate together at their summer home at Goshen, Vermont. Grant at first rejected the petition; he did not want such a high-ranking officer to depart the field just then. But a few days later, after Smith badgered him about the matter, Grant gave in.

Even before Smith's latest diatribe, Grant had begun to wonder if he had been trying to remove the wrong man. After the corps commander went on leave, the lieutenant general became convinced that Smith's inability to get along with Butler, Meade, or almost anyone else posed the greatest threat to high-level harmony. He therefore wrote out the order relieving Smith of command. He considered replacing him with Franklin until learning that the latter, a vociferous Democrat, was in disfavor with the Lincoln administration. Instead, Grant temporarily elevated General Martindale to the command of the XVIII Corps while casting about for an officer of sufficient rank, prestige, and political acceptability to become Smith's permanent successor.[43]

While in Vermont, Smith learned of Grant's action in a letter from Major George Suckley, medical director of the XVIII Corps. Suckley, an inveterate gossip who had long advised Smith on army politics, helped convince his superior that the suspension of the order of July 7 was Butler's doing. This reinforced Smith's initial impression that Butler had power over Grant, doubtless the result of entrapment.

Smith cut short his furlough, rushed back to Virginia, and on July 19 had a final audience with Grant. The lieutenant general made clear that deteriorating relations between Smith and his superiors, not Butler's machinations, had prompted the change of command. Smith refused to believe it. By hiding behind this fabrication, Grant "showed himself false and cowardly," he asserted. Unable to reason with Smith, Grant ended the interview by exclaiming, "You talk too much!"[44]

The following day, after cleaning out his tent and bidding farewell to his staff, Smith left the Army of the James. He did not again serve on active duty and was still awaiting orders at war's end.

Left with plenty of time to brood, Smith tried to convince anyone who would listen that he, a dedicated soldier and a man of integrity, had been railroaded. Until his death in February 1903, he held to his story of conspiracy and slander. He never realized the effects of his own arrogance, conceit, tactlessness, and (as Grant had diagnosed) big mouth.[45]

CHAPTER TEN

Action on the Northside, Action on the South

THROUGHOUT JULY FEW MEMBERS OF THE ARMY OF THE JAMES SAW BATTLE action, although the troops in the Bermuda Hundred works and the lines outside Petersburg did dodge shells and sniper fire. The regiments at Petersburg alternated between duty in the trenches and in sheltered camps in the rear, spending forty-eight hours at a stretch in each sector.[1]

Such warfare, at once tedious and hectic, chipped away at the men's physical and emotional endurance. As a member of the 118th New York remarked, siege duty left everyone, regardless of his proximity to enemy guns, "pretty well 'played out,' dirty, tired & sleepy." A Massachusetts veteran wrote to his wife from the Petersburg trenches that "I feel completely worn out, and I think I represent a good many others. . . . We have been kept on a jump ever since we have been here. . . . Night and day we have either a shovel or a Gun in our hand." A comrade in a less active section of the lines observed that "nothing can exceed the monotony of camp-life. We read and look after the duties of our office; we walk; we ride; we gaze at the sky, the stars, the sun, the moon; yet we are compelled to return to the same surroundings, camps, arms, intrenchments, and lines of defense. We become weary . . . of the pride and pomp and circumstances of glorious war."[2]

July produced large-scale activity only along the army's flanks. Threats to the Deep Bottom lodgement occupied not only Foster's infantry but also Kautz's cavalry and the foot and horse units of Meade's army. And in the closing days of the month, the salient that Baldy Smith had failed to capture in late June became the scene of a Union failure that would dwarf every lost opportunity of the campaign.

Foster's foothold north of the James, though attained relatively easily and cheaply, had not been easy to maintain. As early as June 22 two brigades of gray infantry, backed by cannon and cavalry, captured a section of his picket line; the position was retaken only with stubborn fighting and reinforcements from Bermuda Hundred. The Deep Bottom garrison repulsed several later attacks and endured barrages by batteries hidden to the north and east. Some shells reached as far as the river, damaging the pontoon bridge and the gunboats that guarded it. Despite the almost constant harassment, Foster's men hunkered down and awaited an opportunity to strike toward Richmond.[3]

A movement of some kind appeared imminent when, in late July, Deep Bottom was greatly reinforced by XIX Corps units. The initial contingent of the corps, two brigades under Brigadier General Henry W. Birge, reached Bermuda Hundred on the twelfth after an eighteen-day voyage from Louisiana. On the twenty-first they were temporarily attached to the X Corps and assigned a reserve position behind the main line. Two days later one of the brigades, led by Colonel Leonard D. H. Currie, crossed to Deep Bottom. Currie spent the next several days trying to help Foster neutralize an infantry-artillery force below Four Mile Creek opposite the right flank of the Deep Bottom line.

Instead of providing steady support, the new arrivals impressed Foster as unreliable. At daylight on the twenty-fifth two of Currie's regiments, posted in line of battle on ground that Foster had wrested from the enemy, stampeded under rifle fire and refused to rally. An angry Foster dispatched Colonel Plaisted's 11th Maine, with the 10th Connecticut in support, to chastise the Confederates. Despite heavy opposition, the veteran regiments not only regained the lost ground but carried a line of rifle pits along Four Mile Creek, gaining a strategic foothold on the New Market Road barely nine miles from Richmond. The fighting that won this position, which one participant described as "Indian style, man to man, from tree to tree," cost Foster several casualties, which he blamed on the XIX Corps in a caustic message to Butler. But even Butler found his condemnation "too sweeping, although I can well pardon the vexation of an officer at the loss of what he so gallantly won." One of Foster's men added that soldiers such as Currie's "will help us the most by staying away."[4]

The Army of the James did not have to put up with the visitors from Louisiana for long. Another 1,300 erstwhile members of the Army of the Gulf, the brigade of Colonel Edward L. Molineux, took position at Bermuda Hundred on the twenty-fifth. Three days later elements of this command moved over to Deep Bottom but spent only a day above the James before recrossing the pontoons and reembarking for Fort Monroe. Molineux's departure signaled that the Army of the James would not be permanently enlarged.

Grant's plan to add at least a part of the XIX Corps to Butler's siege forces had been dashed by the audacity of Lieutenant General Jubal A. Early, whose portion of the Army of Northern Virginia had begun a march from the Shenandoah Valley toward Washington. Responding to government concern, Grant detached Meade's VI Corps, sending it by water to Alexandria, Virginia. This force would prove to be insufficient to quell the fear of Washingtonians. As Grant informed Butler on July 26, "Everybody is scared and wants re-enforcements. Send all of the Nineteenth Corps that can possibly be dispensed with at once." Butler complied with good grace, dispatching most of Birge's division that day and the rest by the evening of the thirtieth. Butler would not see them again. Early was clear of the Washington area before the troops from Louisiana could challenge him, but after his return to the Valley, the VI and XIX Corps pursued "Old Jube," intending to curtail his depredations and distractions once and for all.[5]

<hr />

The troops above the James were compensated, if only temporarily, for the loss of their reinforcements. Late in July, in support of an operation planned by Burnside's IX Corps outside Petersburg, Grant launched an infantry-cavalry expedition against Richmond. The troops for this mission were to cross the river not at Deep Bottom but on a second pontoon span that General Weitzel's engineers constructed on the evening of the twenty-sixth to connect the Jones's Neck sector of Bermuda Hundred with Strawberry Plains, a grassy plateau directly east of the mouth of Deep Bottom.

Although most of the expeditionary force came from Meade's army—the II Corps, again under General Hancock, plus two divisions of Sheridan's cavalry—Butler's horsemen were to make the trip as well, while Foster's infantry mounted a diversion in support of the operation. As early as the twenty-fourth Butler informed Kautz that he should "get ready to move with everybody you can muster," plus six days of rations and full ammunition. Kautz spent the next two days outfitting his division and briefing his subordinates. Late on the twenty-sixth he led his troopers across the rear of Bermuda Hundred and bivouacked near the new bridgehead to await the arrival of the Army of the Potomac.[6]

The vigil extended well into the next morning because Hancock and Sheridan had trouble locating the path to the new bridge. Hancock complained to Grant that the road was poorly marked, though Weitzel insisted that his engineers had lit it with bonfires. Regardless, Hancock and his cavalry support did not cross until well after daylight on the twenty-seventh. Kautz passed over just after noon. Most of his command had never crossed a floating bridge; one trooper noted that "both men and horses reeled as if drunken" all the way across.[7]

For all the difficulties in getting over, those men and horses saw relatively little action. Hancock and Sheridan probed toward Richmond the next three days, sparring with defenders of all arms along its outer defense line. The Federals battled not only an aroused enemy but also heat, dust, and thirst.

As a diversion for Burnside, the expedition was a success, for in countering it Lee stripped the Petersburg works of all but three infantry divisions, some 20,000 men. The five divisions he rushed north of the James, however, ensured that Hancock would not get within shelling range of Richmond. Blocked near the Bailey's Creek crossing of the New Market Road, Hancock ordered Sheridan and Kautz to curve around the enemy's upper flank and reach the Darbytown Road, a thoroughfare to Richmond.

The combined cavalry force did so early on the twenty-eighth, but its foothold could not be expanded, thanks to the stubborn opposition of Major General Joseph B. Kershaw's division of Rebel infantry. Even so, by rapid use of their Spencer and Sharps breech-loading carbines and their Henry repeating rifles, Kautz's understrength division accounted for many of the 200 dead and wounded left on the field at day's end. Admitting stalemate, the troopers finally retreated to the New Market Road, where they spent the next day in long-range support of Hancock's futile effort to drive north.[8]

While Kautz saw action near Strawberry Plains, Foster made a successful foray from Deep Bottom. Attacking out of their riverside perimeter on the twenty-seventh, the 100th New York, 24th Massachusetts, and 11th Maine, supported by a section of the 1st Connecticut Battery, flushed a Confederate force from its defenses along the Kingsland Road, preventing it from fording Bailey's Creek and threatening Hancock's column. Two days later Foster resumed his advance, bolstered by four guns whose concentrated fire displaced part of the Rebel right flank along Four Mile Creek.[9]

The expeditionary force turned south on the twenty-ninth and headed back to the James. The timetable Grant had drawn up for the operation was at an end and the troops wanted to get back to Petersburg, where something big was brewing. That evening Kautz's cavalry recrossed the narrow, swaying bridge, returned to its old camp, and bedded down. Well before dawn on July 30, however, the troopers were shaken awake and led across the Appomattox to Petersburg, where they were to help Sheridan guard the south flank of the Army of the Potomac.

Kautz's bleary-eyed riders were brought fully awake at about 4:45 A.M. when a blast shook the earth for miles around. Its meaning escaped all but those few troopers who had heard reports of a mining operation southeast of Petersburg.[10]

———◦◦◦———

Edward Otho Cresap Ord was a forty-five-year-old Marylander, a graduate of the West Point Class of 1839, and a veteran of twenty-six years of active duty. By mid-1864 he had distinguished himself in action many times, most notably under Grant in the West as the major general commanding the XIII Corps, Army of the Tennessee. But despite gallant service throughout the Vicksburg campaign, Ord had been removed from corps command early in 1864 (partially because of his Democrat sympathies) and had been largely inactive since. Grant had come to his rescue: early in July Ord's old commander sought a new job for him, telling the War Department that "I would give more for him as a commander in the field than most of the generals" then opposing Early's raid through Maryland.[11]

Taking heed, fellow Democrat Ben Butler tendered Ord command of the X Corps. (William Brooks had failed to win Senate confirmation as a major general of volunteers and had resigned his commission in disgust.) But when Ord reported for duty at City Point, Grant assigned him instead to lead the XVIII Corps; General Martindale, temporary successor to Baldy Smith, had become so ill he had to take convalescent leave. Although unfamiliar with his new command, Ord was quite pleased by the assignment, which was announced on the twenty-first.[12]

Barely a week after taking over, Ord found himself assigned to exploit a remarkable feat of military engineering: a 511-foot-long shaft that had been dug under an enemy salient by a regiment of coal miners in Burnside's corps. Lateral galleries at the end of the shaft had been loaded with 8,000 pounds of blasting powder that was expected to blow a gaping hole in the Rebel defenses and allow the Union armies into the heart of Petersburg. An attack by part of the IX Corps, supported by Ord, would exploit the mine's success.

Originally, Burnside's single division of black troops had been selected to make the assault. Aware that if the attack failed they might be accused of sacrificing minority troops, Grant and Meade decided almost at the last minute that the blacks would go forward only after Burnside's white divisions attacked. Meanwhile, on the northern edge of Elliott's Salient, Burnside's objective, Ord was to mount a supporting attack toward Baldy Smith's previous objective, Cemetery Hill. That force would consist of Turner's

Major General Edward O. C. Ord.
U.S. ARMY MILITARY HISTORY INSTITUTE.

X Corps division as well as the 2nd Division, XVIII Corps, now under Adelbert Ames.[13]

After dark on July 29, about eight hours before the powder was to be touched off, Ord received Butler's permission to lead both divisions out of their trenches east of Petersburg. After being replaced in the line by the II Corps division of Brigadier General Gershom Mott, just returned from Strawberry Plains, Ord's troops headed south toward the position of the IX Corps, which they, in turn, occupied. Freed for mobile operations, Burnside's troops moved up toward the Rebel salient via a covered trench, a third of a mile long, that permitted them to get as close to the objective as possible without drawing fire. Shortly before 3:00 A.M. on the thirtieth Ord's corps gathered in Burnside's rear, with Turner's division filling the covered way and Ames's men in line farther east, near Burnside's headquarters.

The troops waited anxiously for dawn, many unaware of the reason why. When H-hour came and went, those who had heard of the tunnel decided it had been a bad joke. Informed of the attack plan, one of Ord's surgeons conceded that he and his colleagues "ridiculed the idea." But at 4:45 A.M., after Burnside's miners had spliced and relit a broken fuse, the tunnel exploded with an unearthly crash and a flash of light that turned the predawn gloom into day. One veteran watched as the enemy salient "rose up in the sky." Another noted that "the earth shook and quivered under our feet . . . with the smothered roar of an earthquake." For a moment the massive wall of soil that shot skyward threatened "to entomb our whole line."[14]

When the noise faded, it was replaced by the roar of cannon as Meade's guns started in, hoping to suppress what Rebel defenses remained near Elliott's Salient. With the cannonade at its height, Burnside's troops started forward, only to be stymied by the narrowness of the covered way, which permitted two men, at most, to go forward abreast. Many of the troops, who had not been drilled in the attack plan, filed into the hole that had replaced the salient, a smoking crater 170 feet long and 40 feet deep, at the bottom of which lay dead Rebels, shattered limbers and caissons, and overturned wagons. The crater quickly became a trap, for most of the Federals could not scale its steep walls.

By six o'clock only about half of the attack force had cleared the covered way, but Burnside, as on-scene commander, ordered Ord to commit his troops. A dubious Ord relayed the directive to Turner, who attempted to follow closely upon Burnside's rearmost division under Brigadier General Robert B. Potter. Within minutes Potter's advance slowed to a shuffle and Turner's division—Bell's brigade in front, followed by the brigades of Newton Curtis and Colonel William B. Coan—began to bunch up, intermingling with the IX Corps and spreading confusion along the trench line.

At half-past six Ord notified Turner to "move forward on crest of hill to the right of Potter, near or on Jerusalem Plank Road." Turner attempted to scale the north wall of the covered way, only to discover that despite Meade's barrage, "the enemy . . . held his line up to within seventy-five yards on the right of the crater, and any attempt to get out of our lines . . . would have been futile." The Army of the James could go nowhere until the Army of the Potomac got out of its way.[15]

Ord had just received Turner's reply when Meade ordered him to move Turner and Ames "rapidly forward to the crest of the [Cemetery] hill, independently of General Burnside's troops, and make a lodgement there." Ord forwarded copies of the directive to Turner and Ames, but neither could make headway. Ord complained of his predicament to Burnside, whom he held responsible: the IX Corps commander had not reconnoitered the ground over which he was to attack and had exaggerated his ability to cross it without delay. Stung by the accusation, Burnside spent the balance of the morning alternately criticizing Ord for not adequately supporting his troops and begging him not to complain to Grant or Meade about the clogged trench.[16]

About seven o'clock an agitated Ord made his way to the scene of action. He was appalled to find IX Corps units still piling into the crater, where they were being gunned down by Confederates who, having recovered from the shock of the blast, had come up in force to shoot fish in a barrel. Ord later told a congressional investigating committee that Burnside's men, in the hole, "were about as much use . . . as so many men at the bottom of a well."[17]

Turner's command at last began to emerge from the covered way. Ord was pleased to note that the head of the division advanced resolutely for perhaps 100 yards under a galling fire. Then, unexpectedly, Turner's main body collided with Burnside's USCT division, led by Brigadier General Edward Ferrero, which had interposed between Potter and Turner via a diagonal trench that fed into the covered way. Amid the crush of blue-clad bodies, Turner's men slowly sorted themselves out and tried to resume their advance.

Eventually the bulk of the division emerged from the covered trench and rushed toward the safety of some enemy works not shattered by the mine blast. Although unable to reach the crater, Coan's brigade dug in just short of it and held its position against tremendous pressure. Farther to the rear, much of Curtis's brigade rushed up in support while Ames's division, now grouped in the covered way, prepared to sweep forward.[18]

Shortly after 9:00 A.M. disaster befell every unit involved in the assault. Demoralized by steadily increasing opposition, Burnside's white and black troops suddenly wheeled to the rear and ran back to the covered way in "great confusion." When Ferrero's division absorbed the shock of this stampede, the USCTs became the most visible participants in the retreat. A member of Curtis's brigade recalled being brought to a halt by "terror-stricken darkies who came surging over [us] with a force that seemed almost irresistible. They insisted that the rebels were close on their heels and would gobble us all up—that their strength was twice our own. They yelled and groaned in despair and when we barred their progress [they began] to leap and scramble up the sides of the trench."[19]

A staff officer watched in horror as the African-Americans ran down Ord: "One of them, a burly black, carried him along for some steps by reason of the catching of their belts, and then threw him, in his wild career, and an indefinite number of hard-shod and light-heeled negroes fled over his body before he could arise." While the black troops received the most unfavorable publicity that day, one of Turner's officers later acknowledged that "white troops and black were indiscriminately mingled in this awful stampede."[20]

The rout of the IX Corps cost the Army of the James any hope of contributing to a successful attack. By ten o'clock most of Turner's troops were streaming back to the covered way. Unlike Burnside's men, however, they halted and rallied at Ord's urging and turned back toward the enemy. The bruised and dirty Ord was forming them into line for a new advance when Meade directed the XVIII Corps to return to its old camps in the rear. Frustrated and angry as well as aching, Ord turned his troops eastward. Well before noon the men were under cover in the rear, huddling beside Burnside's survivors. The attack had cost 3,800 dead or wounded in and around the crater. Though only partially engaged, Ord suffered more than 300 casualties.

The debacle had killed what Grant later called "so fair a chance" to take the Confederacy's most strategic city and cut Lee's army in two. As it was, the siege of Petersburg quickly returned to the monotonous, deadly pattern it had assumed following the botched attacks of June 15 to 18. The transition left virtually everyone frustrated and disappointed. "What an opportunity then was here presented," exclaimed an alliterative New Hampshireman, "and how wonderingly woeful was it misimproved." A USCT officer called the high command "criminally negligent and I hope [they] will receive the punishment which such conduct richly merits. By just such villainous carelessness about details, this bloody and ruinous war has been unnecessarily prolonged." Presumably this man was pleased when, a few weeks after the disaster, Burnside was relieved of command and sent home to Rhode Island.[21]

A few soldiers viewed the fiasco more philosophically. In a letter home, one of them expressed the sort of stoicism that enabled the Army of the James to keep moving on, stepping over the lost opportunities in its path:

> Man proposes and God disposes. A short delay of an hour, of a single hour, or the unaccountable panic that seized the niggers, lost us a battle, which if it had been gained by us, would have proved to be the most important and decisive one of the campaign either in this department or any other. But we have failed and must submit for it is the will of God, and He doeth all things well. It will only prolong the war for an additional length of time, but perhaps each delay will only serve to make our peace more lasting & complete when it does come.[22]

As if the lost opportunity were not painful enough, Ord's troops suffered cruelly in returning to their lines above the Appomattox. While part of his column disengaged and marched homeward in the evening darkness of July 30, other troops did not begin their march to Bermuda Hundred until the next morning. Torrid weather punished them at every step, taking a heavy toll in sunstroke and dehydration. The historian of the 115th New York noted that Turner's division "lost more men this day, killed by the sun, the want of water, and by hard marching, than it had in the terrible battle of the day before." When thirst-maddened soldiers drank from a polluted stream on the north side of the river, the casualty list lengthened: "In a few minutes nearly all [who drank] were lying prostrate. Dozens were taken thence to the Point of Rocks hospital, quite a large percentage of whom were permanently disabled, and some lapsing into sickness, from which they died."[23]

By the morning of August 1 the last of the troops sent to exploit the crater breach had returned to their old positions, Ord on the northeastern edge of Petersburg, Turner between the James and Appomattox. For Turner, additional discomforts loomed. Confederates attacked his segment of the Bermuda Hundred line late that day and drove against Foster's salient at Deep Bottom. The Federals withstood both efforts, suffering a number of casualties but dealing the attackers "severe loss."

Butler learned the next day that the Confederates opposite Ord were preparing to explode a mine charge of their own. The blast at 6:00 A.M. on the fifth fell short of Ord's left and, according to one witness, made "a great dust only." A fitful attack, easily repulsed, followed the explosion, as did what one New Englander called "one of the most terrific artillery duels we had ever witnessed." There were few casualties, but they included one the Army of the James could not afford: Griffin Stedman, who fell mortally wounded with a canister round in his chest. The entire army mourned the "faultless, peerless Stedman," while in Washington a family friend, Navy Secretary Gideon Welles, wrote in his diary that "so goes the great and brave of this 'cruel war.'"[24]

For four days after the Rebel mine fizzled, the Bermuda Hundred front was generally quiet. At Petersburg Ord's troops also enjoyed a respite of sorts until August 9, when a series of explosions rocked the wharves at City Point, sending fragments of ordnance, equipment, rations, cotton bales, and other debris through the air. Ammunition-laden barges in the Appomattox detonated one after another, turning the dock into a scene of "death and destruction all around." When the smoke cleared, 43 soldiers and civilians lay dead and 126 others had been injured. Most were from Butler's army— generally depot guards, deckhands, and stevedores. Grant, whose headquarters tent had been shredded, miraculously escaped injury. Rescuers eventually filled twenty bags with the fragments of the victims.

A court of inquiry pronounced the disaster a freak accident caused by careless soldiers unloading ammunition from the barge *Young America*. Almost a year later, however, Federal authorities learned from captured documents that Confederate saboteurs had planted and detonated a "horological torpedo," a disguised land mine rigged to a timer. The infiltrators defended their deed as "just retaliation" for Yankee barbarism, most recently reflected at the crater.[25]

⟶•◆•⟵

Early in August Butler turned his attention to an excavation that would surpass the Petersburg tunnel as the most remarkable engineering project of the war. The army leader had been troubled by the rigid confines of his position at Bermuda Hundred since early summer. He was also concerned about the range and power of the batteries that General Beauregard had constructed north, west, and south of Trent's Reach, above Bermuda Hundred Neck. Not only did those batteries help immobilize a major part of Butler's command, they prevented Admiral Lee's warships from advancing against Drewry's Bluff, Chaffin's Bluff, and Richmond. If Union gunboats could negotiate Trent's Reach, the enemy might have to weaken its lines opposite Butler to reinforce the capital. A manpower shift from his front might enable Butler to break free of his bottle.

Butler concentrated on a point two miles northeast of Bermuda Hundred Neck, where Trent's Reach doubled back upon itself in hairpin fashion. The prongs of the pin were separated at their narrowest point—the northeastern extremity of that misnamed peninsula, Farrar's Island—by 174 yards of earth. The strategic stretch of land lay almost two miles from the nearest Rebel battery. If those 174 yards were to disappear, gunboats could reach Richmond without exposing themselves to a cannonade. Transports might even carry Butler's troops to Jeff Davis's doorstep.

Butler was soon tinkering with a plan to dig a canal across the neck of Farrar's Island. He had studied a prewar effort with the same aim, the work of a Dutch engineer whose money had run out in midexcavation. However, the project had received so much publicity that the neck of land had become known as Dutch Gap. At length, Butler determined that he would succeed where the immigrant had failed. Already he had made calculations; as he informed General Grant, "the land is but 30 feet high as an average, and we should have for a fifty feet cut but about 55,000 cubic feet [cubic yards] of excavation or 10 days' labor for a thousand men."[26]

Butler's preliminary survey was flawed. As Assistant Chief Engineer Michie later pointed out, the tract was, on average, 43 yards wide at the top and 27 yards at water level, 31 yards deep at its northwest end, and 12 yards on the southeast. About 67,000 cubic yards of earth would have to be removed, and due to a relative scarcity of manpower, the project would take more than four months. Grant, who assumed that Butler's initial calculations were correct and believed that the work would take no more than a few weeks, gave permission for the project.

By August 3 Lieutenant Michie, now acting chief engineer of the army, was making a more thorough survey of the work to be done. His observations pleased Butler; the enterprise was manageable, given sufficient men and machinery, including a steam dredge. As work proceeded, the water would be held back by an earthen bulkhead 15 feet thick, to be removed by a controlled detonation such as the one at the crater. After consulting with Professor Benjamin Maillefert, a French-born specialist in maritime engineering now serving as an officer in Butler's 1st New York Engineers, Michie determined that the depth of the canal could be easily increased to admit heavy-draught ships. He concluded that by making Farrar's an island in fact as well as in name, Butler would save the Navy four and three-quarter miles on the water route to Richmond.

Not everyone shared the high command's enthusiasm. When he learned of the project, Joseph Hawley exclaimed that "Butler don't know what he is about." Lieutenant Colonel Theodore Lyman of Meade's staff predicted that "when Butler gets his canal cleverly through, he will find fresh batteries, ready to rake it, and plenty more above it, on the river." When Butler's plans came to their attention, Richmond editors ridiculed them, predicting that the canal would only expand Confederate commerce.[27]

Butler ignored his critics and on August 6 put out a call for laborers, hoping to get 600 volunteers from each of his corps. He now claimed the work would take twenty days to complete at a daily rate of seven and a half hours. Volunteers would receive eight cents of additional pay for each hour they put in, plus half a gill (two ounces) of whiskey (or its equivalent in pay) per diem. Preliminary work got under way on the ninth. That morning Lieutenant Colonel Benjamin W. Ludlow of Butler's staff led a party of X Corps troops to Farrar's Island; they built breastworks across its north-western edge to protect the diggers. At 5:00 A.M. the following day excavating began with the aid of a dredge appropriated from a local contractor.

Under the guns of the ironclad *Onondaga*, anchored in the James below Dutch Gap, hundreds of laborers—black and white, soldier and civilian—turned the first earth. No sooner had they begun, however, than enemy rams patrolling the western end of Trent's Reach opened on them. The initial barrage was ineffective, but Butler learned that the battery at the Howlett house would soon include long-range guns trained on Farrar's Island. He built a signal tower and placed a battery on the south bank of the peninsula, facing the Rebel position. A sentry kept constant watch on the Howlett house, shouting a warning "when a gun was fired so that the [laborers] . . . might run to cover."[28]

By August 14, with nearly 1,000 men working under Professor Maillefert's supervision, enemy rams ran upriver toward the head of the gap while the Howlett battery and two field guns near Cox's Ferry began to pound away at the peninsula. Laborers scattered in all directions, but not before thirty of them fell dead or wounded. Union artillery at and below Farrar's Island opposed the enemy land and water batteries for several hours. Late in the day the Federals got the range of both forts and ships; they sank one of the rams, drove the others back, and silenced the guns at the Howlett house and Cox's Ferry, dismounting one of them.

Work on the canal resumed the next day, though the volunteers labored more warily than before. In later days, shelling from ships and land halted work and damaged some equipment; one lucky shot sank the steam dredge, though the machine was repaired and returned to use. Perhaps cowed by the shelling, Maillefert gave up his supervisory position to Martin Winch, a civilian engineer. With Winch's arrival civilian laborers (most of them black) took over most of the work, supplemented by Confederate prisoners. Reluctantly, Butler decided he needed a full complement of troops back at the front. The loss of military workers ensured that the project would greatly exceed his timetable.

With passing weeks the Confederates lost interest in the canal. A barrage directed at Dutch Gap invariably drew heavy return fire that the Confederates found difficult to endure. General Pickett, in command of the troops opposite Bermuda Hundred, summarized his army's attitude: "I should encourage Butler and his River Improvement Company. . . . The canal will be an advantage to us, and Butler, in digging it for us, may in part atone for the many homes he has destroyed, mine among them."[29]

—⟫•⟪—

By the second week in August Grant had come to believe that Lee had thinned the Richmond defenses to reinforce Jubal Early in the Shenandoah Valley as well as the defenses of South Carolina. On the twelfth the commanding general informed Butler, "I have determined to see if we cannot force him [the enemy] to return here or give us an advantage." When reconnaissance parties brought word that as many as three divisions had left the works above the James, Grant planned an offensive along Bailey's Creek and the New Market Road, the same sectors attacked in late July.

As before, Grant assumed that much of Butler's army could be spared for the movement. He convinced Butler that the Bermuda Hundred defenses were "now so strong that with a very thin line they can be held. We have the further security that the enemy have shown that he feels no inclination to attack fortifications." Grant directed most of the X Corps to cross the river, test the strength of the works below Richmond, and if possible, capture them. The movement would also enable Meade to threaten Lee's southern flank and damage the Weldon Railroad, which was back in service.

Once again, Meade's II Corps spearheaded the movement on the Northside. Grant doubted that the X Corps alone could crack the defenses in that sector, which had been strengthened since the first operation, and General Hancock's command was the only other force "out of line [in reserve at Petersburg] and foot loose." Two of Meade's cavalry divisions, under Sheridan, had gone to Washington before joining the VI and XIX Corps in opposing Early in the Valley. The remaining division, led by Brigadier General David McMurtrie Gregg, accompanied the expedition over the James. Hancock again exercised overall command.[30]

As ever, Butler responded quickly and precisely to Grant's tasking. By early on the thirteenth he had positioned five brigades of white soldiers— Terry's division, plus two-thirds of Turner's—as well as a recently acquired brigade of African-Americans to cross to Deep Bottom, carrying three days' rations. As they advanced toward the defenses south of the New Market Road, less than 600 yards from the Deep Bottom perimeter, they were joined by General Foster's brigade. The combined force would strike the enemy at daylight, while Hancock, after advancing north on the other side of Bailey's Creek, would attack the extensive works in that sector.

Hancock stressed stealth and secrecy. To confuse the enemy, his soldiers would march north of the James only after boarding transports at City Point to make it appear that they were heading for some other theater of operations, such as the Shenandoah Valley. After churning down toward Fort Monroe, the vessels would abruptly turn, make for Deep Bottom, and unload.

Once on the north bank, infantry and horsemen would take a number of routes—the New Market, Darbytown, and Charles City Roads, among others—to further confound the enemy. At a certain point, the expeditionary force would divide, the infantry moving up the east side of Bailey's Creek and Gregg's riders cantering along more westerly roads to "threaten or attempt [to capture] Richmond, if practicable; if not to destroy the Virginia Central Railroad."[31]

The units from the Army of the James would advance via an even greater number of routes. After breaking through north of Foster's perimeter, they would push northwestward in two columns. The upper would take the New Market Road, the lower the Kingsland Road. When the latter reached the Varina Road, which led almost directly north into Richmond, it would move up that thoroughfare until able to resume a more westerly advance along the Mill Road. The lower column would turn north yet again onto the Osborne Turnpike, the westernmost of the several major routes to the capital.

For these intricate movements to succeed, the officer in charge of Butler's contingent had to be a skilled tactician and logistician. On this count Butler may have felt some concern because the expeditionary commander was an unknown to him: David Bell Birney, recently Hancock's senior subordinate

Major General David Bell Birney (standing, left); Brigadier General John Gibbon (standing, right); Major General Winfield Scott Hancock (seated).
NATIONAL ARCHIVES.

in the II Corps, Army of the Potomac. Son of a prominent Alabama abolitionist, now a resident of Philadelphia, the thirty-nine-year-old major general possessed tenacity, dependability, and a finely tuned combination of
prudence and aggressiveness. Even so, he had his limitations. As a brigade
leader in 1862 he had performed brilliantly; as a division commander in
1863–64 he had sometimes appeared beyond his depth. Now he held an
even higher position, having succeeded to the command of the X Corps
only days before the coming movement was drawn up. Like Ord, Birney
was Grant's choice, not Butler's, and the latter did not know what to expect.
He did know that Birney was afflicted by recurrent malaria and dysentery
and had a reputation as a tippler.[32]

When he joined Butler's command, Birney brought along his older
brother, William. A new brigadier general, the elder Birney was a rarity in
this or any other army—an intellectual as well as a zealous libertarian. Educated
at four colleges including Yale and fluent in thirteen languages, he had taught
English at the Lycée in Paris, had written on the arts for U.S. and European
journals, and had quit a lucrative law practice in Cincinnati to command
white troops, then blacks. He currently led an African-American brigade
attached to his brother's corps, consisting of the 7th, 8th, and 9th United
States and the 29th Connecticut Colored Infantry. Though there were few
more ardent supporters of union and liberty than William Birney, some
observers believed that as a combat commander, he was a fine linguist.[33]

The Birney brothers began their service in the Army of the James in
good form. By 10:00 P.M. on the thirteenth the X Corps had massed near the
Deep Bottom bridge; David Birney led them across the James just after midnight. Soon his brother's troops, along with the division of Alfred Terry, were
moving alongside and in rear of Foster's brigade, ready to hit the nearest works
come daylight.

While the X Corps prepared for action, Hancock's command boarded its
transports, with most of the men anticipating a transfer to a more promising
theater of operations. The embarkation was a logistical nightmare almost
from the start. Seaworthy vessels were few; those available were long delayed
in leaving City Point and in steaming about to return to Deep Bottom. When
the ships finally pulled in at Deep Bottom, inadequate wharfage kept the men
aboard for several hours, alerting enemy signal officers and defeating Hancock's
misdirection tactics.[34]

The long delay might have jeopardized the cooperative nature of the
operation, but David Birney refused to postpone his advance. At daylight
on the fourteenth he pushed forward in cooperation with Foster's troops,
striking for the Rebel defenses to the north and west of Deep Bottom. His

lead element, Terry's division, was engaged by about 5:00 A.M. Sharp skirmishing lasted until after 7:30, when Terry finally concentrated his elongated battle line and tore into a skirmish force from Brigadier General John Bratton's South Carolina brigade, astride the Kingsland Road. In this drive Foster's 24th Massachusetts and 11th Maine, which had performed so ably during the first excursion above the James, captured two lines of rifle pits, six guns, two mortars, and hundreds of prisoners. Farther west, the brigades of Joseph Hawley and Colonel Francis B. Pond, supported closely by William Birney's brigade, carried a third line of trenches "with trifling loss to us and with several prisoners from the enemy."[35]

By 7:00 A.M. the X Corps held a solid position at the base of New Market Heights, atop which sat the main Confederate line west of Bailey's Creek. Contrary to expectations, the ground appeared to be strongly held by infantry and artillery. David Birney, however, was certain it could be overrun by a powerful movement. The expeditionary commander was in lofty spirits; his troops had suffered more than 100 casualties but had inflicted even greater losses in captured Confederates alone. Eager for additional prizes, Birney hoped to move around if not through the defenses in front of him, the last major barrier to Richmond.

But he was denied a further advance. By 7:15, he was reporting to Butler that, at Hancock's order, he had suspended his movement. Until enough II Corps troops disembarked at Deep Bottom to launch the intended offensive, the X Corps would have to dig in. The word to advance never came. By late afternoon Birney's troops were digging earthworks along the Kingsland Road while exchanging sharpshooter and artillery fire with the enemy north of them.

After having worked so hard to get that far, Birney's men were ordered to abandon their position late in the day. The head of the II Corps, which had finally started north in midafternoon, had bogged down against unanticipated resistance. Mott's division had been pinned down along Bailey's Creek, while that of Brigadier General Francis C. Barlow had ground to a halt farther north at Fussell's Mill, near where the Darbytown Road crossed Bailey's Creek.

Rebel resistance had been formidable, and the II Corps had not demonstrated its customary aggressiveness this day. That quality had become critical because Grant's intelligence officers had failed him. Rather than weakening his lines on the Northside, Lee had strengthened them. The II Corps had encountered not only the defense force long stationed in that sector—Major General Charles W. Field's division, plus three infantry brigades and one brigade of horsemen—but also reinforcements from the Southside. The infantry brigades of Ambrose R. Wright, John C. C. Sanders, and Nathaniel

H. Harris, plus the cavalry of Rooney Lee and M. Calbraith Butler, had come up to bolster Field, obliterating the Yankees' manpower edge.[36]

Such opposition forced Hancock to revamp his plan for an offensive on both sides of Bailey's Creek. Late on the fourteenth as well as the following morning he ordered Birney to withdraw from the New Market line to the other side of Deep Bottom and from there to move to the immediate support of the II Corps. Disengaging under heavy pressure, the X Corps, led by Foster's brigade, crossed Four Mile Creek, marched back to Deep Bottom, crossed the pontoon bridge to Jones's Neck, then recrossed the James on a second floating bridge to a wide stretch of open ground known as Curl's Neck. The complicated movement was not completed until 9:00 A.M. on the fifteenth.[37]

Through the balance of that morning Birney's soldiers trudged along the northward-running Quaker Road, heading for Fussell's Mill and the Confederate left flank, which Hancock wished to turn. A heavy rain from the previous night had ceased, and the marching column kicked up thick clouds of dust. The day was inhumanly hot, and roadside fields soon teemed with panting men. Birney's route took more able-bodied troops across Strawberry Plains, then north of the Long Bridge Road. The thick woods of the area, the crooked and poorly marked roads, and the fatigue of the men caused much stopping and starting. Not until near nightfall were the exhausted troops in position to assist the II Corps (which had seen only desultory action that day) and to launch Hancock's new assault. By then dozens of soldiers were out of action from sunstroke and debility.[38]

About noon on the sixteenth—six hours behind Hancock's unrealistic timetable for the assault—Birney formed for a strike against Fussell's Mill. From Foster's brigade he fashioned a long skirmish line and backed it with the rest of Terry's command. A provisional division under William Birney supported this force from the rear with artillery. On its left the X Corps enjoyed additional support from Colonel Calvin A. Craig's brigade of Hancock's corps.

It was 10:00 A.M. before Foster's skirmishers initiated battle. The loose-order units crossed several hundred yards of timber and swamp before they came upon two lines of well-manned rifle pits. The Confederates poured such fire into the head of the Union line that the 100th New York and the 1st Maryland (Dismounted) Cavalry broke for the rear. The rest of the skirmishers surged over the enemy position, drove out any defenders they did not shoot or bayonet, and captured several pits. Exhilarated attackers pursued the escapees as far as the main Confederate position, a line of breastworks on the far side of an inundated ravine, protected in front by felled trees.

Despite the intricate nature of the defenses, Foster paused only briefly. About 1:00 P.M. the 11th Maine and two companies of the 24th Massachusetts cut through the slashing and crested the ravine under what one regimental commander called "the heaviest and deadliest fire I have ever witnessed. The first division went down like so many ten-pins." Those who remained standing jumped into the ditch, clambered up its rear slope, and scaled the elevated works. At the same time the remainder of Foster's command—the re-formed 100th New York and 1st Maryland, plus the 10th Connecticut and the other eight companies of the 24th Massachusetts—attacked along the oblique ravine. Within twenty minutes the multipronged attack had secured the position. Pond's brigade alone had captured six flags and several dozen prisoners.[39]

Foster's victors did not venture far from the ravine, permitting part of Terry's division—three of Hawley's regiments and two of Pond's—to chase the retreating foe into yet another woods before the pursuers took up a position in an open field 400 yards in front of Foster. Terry held his ground for an hour and a half while as many of his men keeled over from sunstroke as from bullets. Finally, at about 3:00 P.M., a reinforced enemy advanced against both of his flanks. Within minutes Terry's soldiers were falling back past the abandoned ravine to a line of captured breastworks. This position they held against several counterattacks, prompting David Birney to consider launching a second offensive at six o'clock. Only three minutes before the hour, after a reconnaissance suggested that too many Rebels confronted him, Birney opted to abandon the field.[40]

Despite their rising numbers the Rebels were not inclined to take the initiative. Perhaps they had been cowed by two Union movements in their rear. Early that day Grant directed Butler to arm 1,000 of his canal builders and, with the aid of Melancton Smith's warships, to occupy Aiken's Landing on the north bank of the James two miles southwest of Deep Bottom. At noon Lieutenant Colonel Ludlow guided the 4th and 6th USCT and some laborers northward from the landing toward where Three Mile Creek crossed the Kingsland Road. Bolstered en route by one of Newton Curtis's regiments from Bermuda Hundred and supported by fire from Smith's gunboats, Ludlow captured Signal Hill on the Cox farm and held it until the eighteenth, when he was driven off by a heavy attack and forced to sail back to Dutch Gap.[41]

The second diversion against the rear of Fussell's Mill was conducted by the 8th U.S. Colored Troops, one of two outfits William Birney had left to guard the Deep Bottom bridge. Under the bridgehead commander, Colonel William B. Wooster, the regiment moved a strong skirmish line toward the Three Mile Creek–Kingsland Road intersection. It did not reach its objective but did pry several companies of gray infantry from rifle pits along the center of the New Market line before returning to Deep Bottom at 9:00 P.M. on the sixteenth.

This partial success notwithstanding, Hancock realized by the evening of August 16 that he was not going to reach Richmond; the resistance encountered since the afternoon of the fourteenth forced him to recross the James. Not only had his main force been blocked at Fussell's Mill, but during the sixteenth the Rebels had repulsed an attempt by Gregg's horsemen to reach the capital by way of the Charles City Road. Gregg had penetrated as far as White's Tavern, seven miles from the city, where overwhelming opposition forced him to return to Hancock's side.[42]

Although resigned to withdrawing, the troops of the Armies of the Potomac and the James stayed near Fussell's for four more days. Though there was no heavy fighting during that period, it could have been otherwise. About 5:00 P.M. on August 18 the Confederates advanced in force toward David Birney's position. Their plans called for Rooney Lee to attack from the north while another cavalry column under Wade Hampton struck from the northeast. The Rebels intended to make Birney fall back by threatening his rear; if the scheme succeeded, Field's infantry would attack the Yankees while they were in motion. Nothing worked as conceived, however, for Birney's soldiers remained rooted despite a half hour of heavy musketry. The Rebel retreat marked the last concentrated action during Grant's second offensive above the James.

At sundown on the twentieth, under Grant's orders, Hancock led his corps and Gregg's division, followed by Birney's, over the pontoons to Bermuda Hundred. Foster's brigade then returned to its old stomping grounds at Deep Bottom, relieving Wooster. The balance of Terry's division and the troops under William Birney returned to the defenses astride Bermuda Hundred Neck.[43]

For a brief time it appeared that the work of the returning troops was not done. Grant, suspecting that Lee had stripped Pickett's division to man the defenses above the James, directed Butler to attack out of Bermuda Hundred. Obedient as always, Butler directed David Birney to mass 4,000 troops against Pickett's right flank near Port Walthall. If he broke through, Birney was to continue west along Bakehouse Creek and slip between the Confederates on the Northside and those opposite Bermuda Hundred.

Timing was critical, but Birney did not seem to understand. He slowly gathered troops and for some reason (perhaps because he remained unacquainted with his new corps commander) Butler did not press him. Birney was still forming his column on the evening of the twenty-first when Butler's signalmen concluded that Pickett's works were back to strength. When Butler informed Grant that Birney would not be ready to strike until early the following morning, Grant reluctantly called off the whole thing."[44]

With operations on hold, the troops recently returned from the North-side could assess their offensive. They had not seized Richmond, but the failure was more from timely enemy reinforcement than any lack of skill or aggres-siveness on their part. In later weeks, however, Hancock blamed his old sub-ordinate, Birney—specifically, Birney's inability to strike the Rebels at Fussell's Mill at dawn on the sixteenth—for the outcome. Such criticism appears mis-placed and unfair. The X Corps had been delayed in forming its attack by obstacles too formidable to be surmounted in the time available. Even so, on those occasions when Birney's troops attacked—on the fourteenth along the Kingsland Road and two days later at the mill—they displayed more speed and power than the vaunted II Corps had exhibited during the operation. Moreover, Hancock had no grounds for criticizing a colleague in view of the many delays for which his corps had been responsible.

Despite the strategic failure of this second campaign on the lower outskirts of Richmond, the Federals had forced the recall of M. C. Butler's cavalry, which had been en route to the Shenandoah Valley, and prevented Field's infantry from going there as well. The invaders had also lowered military and civilian morale by throwing Richmond into a panic and by killing several commanders, including Brigadier Generals John R. Chambliss, Jr., and Victor Girardey. Based as it was on defective intelligence, the expedi-tion might have ended disastrously. Instead, it had made contributions— small though they seemed at the time—to Grant's broad strategy.[45]

CHAPTER ELEVEN

A Taste of Victory

EVEN BEFORE HANCOCK'S COLUMN LEFT FUSSELL'S MILL, GRANT POISED TO attack the Weldon Railroad. Convinced that infantry must take up where Wilson and Kautz had left off, he selected the V Corps for the mission. Gouverneur Warren's troops moved south early on August 18 and, despite stout resistance, lodged near Globe Tavern about four miles from Petersburg. By nightfall the V Corps had dismantled several hundred yards of track.[1]

Warren's movement resulted in new assignments for Kautz. His troopers were weary, tattered, and in need of remounting. No matter; immediately after the fiasco at the Crater, Kautz had trotted south with his five regiments (one a recent addition, the 1st New York Mounted Rifles, which had been relieved of its infantry support mission). After scouting Lee's Mill, a strategic position in the rear of Meade's army, Kautz on August 1 had backtracked to Jordan's Point on the James. Two days later his riders had been sent south again, this time to man a thirty-mile-long picket line from Cocke's Mill, seven miles below Jordan's Point, across the Norfolk & Petersburg Railroad to the Jerusalem Plank Road half a dozen miles below Petersburg. The troopers of the Army of the James had to patrol such an extensive area because two-thirds of Meade's cavalry had left the Petersburg front for the Shenandoah Valley; Kautz's division and that of David Gregg were the only horsemen available below the Appomattox.

For two weeks Kautz, who was fighting not only weariness but malaria and, in consequence, a drug-induced stupor, tried to protect the rear of the Petersburg lines by stretching his already thin ranks, supported by Gregg's equally elongated command. Kautz's responsibilities increased exponentially after August 12, when Gregg left him to accompany Hancock and Birney north of the James. When Warren headed for Globe Tavern six days later, three of Kautz's regiments under Colonel Spear accompanied the V Corps.

For the first few days of the expedition, Spear kept the enemy from interrupting the railroad demolition. On the twenty-first he bested a large detachment of Rooney Lee's division, killing several, taking seventy prisoners, and burning Rebel supplies near Reams's Station. On August 22 he took an advance position west of that depot and held it with the recently returned Gregg. That day the II Corps reached Reams's Station to take over the work begun by Warren.

After three days of relative inactivity a large body of Hampton's cavalry, followed by a larger force of infantry from the corps of Lieutenant General A. P. Hill, swept down on Hancock's breastworks west of the station. Spear and Gregg worked frantically to protect the flanks and rear of the II Corps, which found itself fighting for its life. The attacks caused a retreat that quickly became a stampede. For the first time, the proud II Corps abandoned a fixed position in the face of approximately equal numbers. Spear and Gregg held their ground to the last, permitting most of Hancock's regiments to escape. As the demoralized foot soldiers fled northward, the cavalry screened them against pursuit. The next morning Kautz concentrated his division along the Prince George Court House Road southeast of the siege lines at Petersburg. There the command, which had suffered 140 casualties during the past several days, rested and tried to recoup its strength.[2]

The movements near Globe Tavern and Reams's Station resulted in a change of venue for virtually every element of the Army of the James. Warren's departure necessitated the southward shift of the IX Corps under Major General John G. Parke, successor to Ambrose Burnside. Parke's move created a gap that Grant filled with Ord's corps. The change of position involved a hard march that dropped an unusually high number of stragglers along the road. This emphasized the weakness and fatigue of the XVIII Corps, which from incessant skirmishing since late June had been reduced to fewer than 12,000 effectives. In contrast, the 14,200-strong X Corps, which enjoyed a relatively tranquil stay at Bermuda Hundred and Deep Bottom, had seen little action since returning from the Northside.[3]

To compensate, Grant and Butler decided to switch the corps' positions. On the evening of August 23 Ord's men filed out of their rifle pits within sight of Petersburg's steeples, passed to the rear, and crossed the bridge at Broadway Landing to Bermuda Hundred. Simultaneously, the troops on the peninsula headed for the pontoons at Point of Rocks. Most of the transfer was completed by the next morning, but some units were still changing position as late as the twenty-ninth.

The troops' reactions to the change were predictable. Veterans of the X Corps recoiled from the heavy picket firing they attracted almost from the moment they crossed the Appomattox and shuddered at the thought of daily doses of it. Meanwhile, the soldiers of the XVIII Corps felt they had gone to heaven. A Connecticut man recalled his deliverance: "We had fairly become round shouldered from stooping to avoid wounds, and now we experienced the unutterable relief of once more standing erect and fearless, for by tacit agreement there was no firing on the Bermuda Hundred front. So we rested . . . and grew clean and well-conditioned, and we had not a grumble in our hearts."[4]

When the transfer was complete, Terry held the left flank of the army at Petersburg, William Birney's newly designated 3rd Division, X Corps, covered the center, and Turner's division (temporarily led by Sandy Foster) guarded the right flank along the Appomattox. Above the river the XVIII Corps had been fragmented to take up several positions. Ames held the works along the neck of the peninsula, Stannard's division (now led by Brigadier General Joseph B. Carr, Stannard being on convalescent leave) was in reserve behind Ames, and Hinks's USCT division manned the Deep Bottom works.

This arrangement paid dividends for the black soldiers, for above the James their division could be massed for the first time. This concentration helped the division become a cohesive force under Brigadier General Charles J. Paine. The thirty-one-year-old Harvard graduate from Boston was a former attorney, a railroad developer, a yachtsman, and the great-grandson of a signer of the Declaration of Independence. One of Butler's many New England protégés and once a member of his headquarters staff, Paine found his new command "pretty well scattered," disorganized, and somewhat demoralized after its experience at the Crater. The new brigadier sought to establish order—a first step toward making his command as well disciplined, equipped, and led as any white troops.[5]

Writing to his wife in late August, Butler discussed his presidential ambitions, which the vicissitudes of military service periodically wounded but could never kill. Doubtful that he could secure a furlough on which to campaign in his own behalf, he mused about his quest for high office: "We must let it drift along as it will. There is nothing else to be done than duty here."[6]

In truth, Butler and his political henchmen (many of them members of his staff) were not content to ride out events. Throughout the spring and summer they tried to offer an alternative to Abraham Lincoln within the Democratic Party or through a third party. Their efforts bore some fruit; for a time, in fact, Butler's prospects appeared increasingly bright before winking out like a dying star.

Those prospects fluctuated in inverse proportion to the public's perception of the war effort. When spring ended with Butler's and Meade's armies mired in siege warfare, the outlook for Lincoln's reelection appeared bleak. Though the president had been renominated at Baltimore, his power base had shrunk alarmingly within a few weeks. Not surprisingly, when Lincoln visited his field armies in Virginia on June 21-22, he conferred in private with the Union's most prominent political general. Although their discussion was never publicized, there seems little doubt that Lincoln was sounding out Butler on his plans. At the same time or shortly thereafter, the president asked Grant's reaction to his naming Butler to succeed Secretary of War Stanton. Grant did not care much for the idea and nothing came of it, but clearly Lincoln was mulling over ways to remove Butler from the field of competition.[7]

Butler's standing in the national arena was given a boost during the first half of July. The stalemate at Petersburg continued, while in the West Major General William T. Sherman was advancing toward Atlanta at an excruciating pace. By now members of the president's own party were urging him to step aside in favor of someone who commanded the public's confidence, such as former Major General John C. Fremont, who was pressing his campaign to win the White House on an ultraradical ticket. Moreover, by mid-July the price of gold was nearing a spectacular $300 per ounce, an indication that investors had lost faith in the dollar that was financing the war.

It had reached the point that influential politicians such as Senator Benjamin Wade of Ohio had begun to work quietly behind Republican scenes to persuade both Lincoln and Fremont to bow out of the race in favor of Butler, a candidate behind whom hard-war voters could unite. An encouraged Butler soon was advising his chief of staff, then testing the waters in Washington, that "our time will come; watch, wait, and work."[8]

Butler was himself working; one day after writing to Colonel Shaffer he sent a fawning letter to Grant, ostensibly to convey tactical suggestions but actually to forestall the commanding general (whose political potential Butler still feared) from interfering with his presidential plans. "I desire to serve you," he professed, "in all things. My future is not in the army; yours is. Our paths can never cross." For that reason, the pair could never act callously toward each other despite "all the selfishness of life." Through this thinly veiled suggestion of quid pro quo—Butler foreseeing the day when he could help a certain soldier—the army leader hoped to show Grant (as Shaffer put it) the "necessity of trimming his sails for the storm."[9]

The rising clamor within Republican and War Democrat circles for Lincoln to step aside intensified in late July and early August. Repeated overtures were made to Fremont on Butler's behalf, and Shaffer relayed rumors that the "Pathfinder" would support Butler if the latter won the top position on a major party ticket. Before July ended a movement arose to organize War Democrats into a separate party. A convention was to be held in Chicago or Cincinnati in August to nominate a presidential candidate. Some, however, favored postponing the gathering until after the mainstream party's convention in Chicago late that month. When, as they anticipated, the regular Democrats put forth an antiwar candidate, War Democrats would bolt to select an alternative. Shaffer was certain that the alternative would be Butler.

Butler's chances, and hopes, continued to grow throughout August. Without leaving Virginia he secured pledges of support from representatives Henry Winter Davis of Maryland and James M. Ashley of Ohio as well as from New York political bosses Thurlow Weed and Roscoe Conkling. Other power brokers—including Senator Zachariah Chandler of Michigan, once an intimate of Lincoln—were reported to be falling in behind Butler, while influential editors such as Henry J. Raymond of the *New York Times* and George Wilkes of *The Spirit of the Times* praised Butler without formally endorsing his candidacy.[10]

War Democrats gathered at a rally in New York City's Cooper Union on August 17 "for the purpose of consultation and organization preparatory to the Presidential canvass." Though no summons for a convention resulted, many attendees clearly favored such a course. Within ten days, a committee of "Loyal Citizens" (War Democrats and anti-Lincoln Republicans) called for a convention at Cincinnati to oppose presidential candidates who lacked the support of the Northern public. Butler's legman, J. K. Herbert, who had attended the Cooper Union meeting and who had contacts among the Loyal Citizens, informed his boss that "every man I have met says 'give me Butler.'"[11]

Events continued to favor Butler for another couple of weeks. On August 23, dispirited by defections within his party, Lincoln wrote a memorandum on the likelihood of his defeat. Eight days later the regular

Democrats met in Chicago and adopted a platform denouncing the war effort and calling for a negotiated peace. This was what the War Democrats had been waiting for; a day later, they published a letter from their adherents in Ohio, "supporters of the National Government." The letter affirmed that "none of the Candidates for the Presidency already presented can command the united confidence and support of all loyal and patriotic men," and it invited such men to send delegates to a presidential convention to be held at Cincinnati on September 28. Herbert, one of the forces behind the call, believed he knew who the nominee would be. He assured Butler that "all goes charmingly—never was [there] a more center shot at public desire & aim." Unionists everywhere appeared to scramble over each other to board the Butler wagon.[12]

Encouraged, Butler nevertheless decided he must firm up support in Washington and New York. On August 25 he handed the army to General Ord and headed north on leave, intending to "come in contact," as his wife had urged, "with leading men." Officially, however, he was visiting Washington to settle "matters of business connected with my command and the exchange of prisoners."[13]

As he departed Virginia, Butler must have believed he stood within reach of more power than he had ever enjoyed in uniform. Even so, doubts nagged him. Union fortunes seemed to be improving on several fronts. On the eleventh Rear Admiral David G. Farragut had won a dramatic victory at Mobile Bay. The draft, which had begun at last to send great numbers of young men into the field, promised to swell Grant's armies. Decisive victory had not been won, but as Colonel Hawley informed his wife in early September, "we have touched bottom," and improvement was expected soon.[14]

Improvement came more quickly than even Hawley could have anticipated. On September 2 Butler was at Willard's Fifth Avenue Hotel, conferring with New York political and financial movers, when news of Sherman's capture of Atlanta swept Manhattan. The announcement created a sensation virtually everywhere in the North, while in Virginia it transformed Meade's and Butler's armies into ecstatic mobs. A *Philadelphia Press* correspondent at Butler's headquarters reported with almost biblical lyricism: "Regiments in camp . . . made the welkin ring with rejoicings and congratulations, until the spirit of enthusiasm reached the outermost pickets, who joined in the shouts of exultation."[15]

The cheering drowned out the previous clamor for Butler's presidential candidacy. Sherman's seizure of the industrial hub of the Deep South, a Federal objective almost as entrancing as Richmond, suggested that the restoration of the Union was a matter of time. Added to a trio of celebrated victories by Sheridan in the Shenandoah Valley in September and October, the fall of Atlanta would ensure Lincoln's reelection.

Butler watched the demise of his political dreams with a melancholy detachment. Even before the price of gold plummeted, before politicians and editors streamed back into the Republican fold, and before the War Democrat convention was canceled, the leader of the Army of the James sensed that he would come up short, once again, in the arena in which his most cherished dreams were played out. Three days before Herbert wrote to him that his candidacy had "failed for want of active friends," Butler was back in Virginia, feeling "sick and tired of it all." As he wrote to Sarah a few days after his return, "You speak of hopes for the future. I haven't any."[16]

His political aspirations dashed, Butler tried to devote full attention to his military duties. One indication was his response to Grant's latest and most ambitious effort to seize Richmond and prevent Lee from reinforcing Early in the Valley.

On September 28, only one day after Grant directed him to "prepare your Army according to the verbal instructions already given," Butler drew up a remarkable campaign plan. The culmination of months of study and contemplation, the multipage document, copies of which he sent late on the twenty-eighth to Ord, Birney, and Kautz, defined the mission as "to get possession of the City of Richmond. Failing that, to make such serious and determined demonstration to that end as shall draw reinforcements from the right of the enemy's line in sufficient numbers . . . to enable the Army of the Potomac to move upon the enemy's communications near Petersburg." The plan also detailed the routes of march and attack, estimated the position and numbers of the enemy (it was unusually accurate—a tribute to Butler's intelligence gathering), identified the enemy's sources of rein-forcement near Richmond, and explained "exactly what is to be done in Richmond."[17]

The movement would be a mammoth undertaking. On the morning of the twenty-ninth Butler would cross the James in two columns: seven brigades of Ord's corps via a new pontoon bridge to be laid near Aiken's Landing and, via Deep Bottom, ten brigades under David Birney—his own X Corps plus Paine's XVIII Corps division. Ord's 8,000-man wing would push northwest toward the entrenched camp at Chaffin's Bluff, the southern anchor of Richmond's three defense lines and the land protector of Confederate water batteries along the James. The more easterly column, nearly 16,000 strong, would return to New Market Heights to make the attack Birney had been forced to withhold on August 14. If it broke through, this column would shift in Ord's direction to help assault Richmond's intermediate line. Finally, while the infantry battered at Richmond's front door, most of Kautz's cavalry would cross the James in Birney's rear, gain the Darbytown Road, and dash around the upper flank of the distracted defenders. Butler demanded that his horsemen enter Richmond at all costs.

Kautz lauded Butler's planning, which "evinced great thought and much labor and unusual knowledge of the situation and what was essential to success. . . . It was the only instance, in the whole war, that I experienced, where the course for each officer was so clearly and minutely laid down." Moreover, Butler again demonstrated his organizational expertise, massing 26,200 troops at Bermuda Hundred and getting them to their assigned crossing sites so efficiently that the movements did not alert the enemy. By achieving surprise Butler ensured that a ratio of six attackers to one defender would prevail early in the offensive.[18]

Almost precisely on schedule, Ord's column began crossing early on September 29. Once on the Northside, Stannard's division advanced across bottomland broken by clumps of pines. "Just as the first streaks of dawn were seen in the East," wrote Edward Ripley, commanding a brigade farther to the rear, "the quick, spiteful flashing of Musketry told us we had wakened the enemy up." Stannard pressed forward, driving skirmishers through the pines toward the attackers' first major barrier— a complex of fortifications, the largest being Fort Harrison, a six-gun bastion atop high ground near where a wall of the entrenched camp at Chaffin's Bluff met the southwestern corner of Richmond's exterior line. Stannard quickly decided the fort must be taken if the XVIII Corps was to reach Richmond from that direction.[19]

The first sustained clash of the day, however, occurred on David Birney's front. Having delayed his departure from Petersburg until 3:00 P.M. on the twenty-eighth, the newest member of the Army of the James did not move toward Deep Bottom until four o'clock the following morning, some time after Ord began crossing. Birney's men tired greatly from their long hike to the pontoons. There was widespread straggling, especially in the division formerly commanded by the typhoid-stricken Turner and now led by Foster. In contrast to the white troops, General Paine's African-Americans were fresh and in good spirits. They held the post of honor at the head of the western prong of Birney's column.

Paine initiated the fighting. Advancing beyond the Deep Bottom works, his troops thrust the nearest Confederates as far as the Kingsland Road, that recent barrier to X Corps progress. Resistance stiffened at about 5:30 A.M. as Paine reached the enemy's main line below and along the New Market Road. As Foster's division formed in his rear and Terry's went into line farther to the right, Paine attacked the Rebel west flank with Duncan's and Holman's brigades, preceded by large units of skirmishers. Gray troops behind works on top of a ravine lashed the brigade with rifle and cannon fire. Paine promptly committed Draper and Holman, both of whose brigades forced the Confederate right to coil backward upon itself north of the New Market Road. Cheering blacks occupied the heights beyond as the enemy commander, Brigadier General John Gregg, pulled back to reinforce the more strategic position at Chaffin's Bluff.[20]

Gregg's troops were too late to prevent Ord from taking a large segment of the entrenched camp. After sweeping through the bottomlands toward Fort Harrison and its satellite works, Colonel Michael Donohoe's brigade of Stannard's division advanced in long skirmish lines across the open approach to the works, chasing would-be defenders from advance positions along the Varina Road. The Rebels retreated for more than two miles under the nervous gaze of Lieutenant General Richard S. Ewell, commander of the Department of Richmond. Soon only Fort Harrison appeared to stand between Ord's vanguard and the Rebel capital. It looked formidable enough, protected by a dry moat and ramparts eighteen feet high. But Harrison lacked interior defenses and, except for the moat, external barriers; worse, faulty design prevented its guns from reaching a sector at the base of the hill on which it sat. Then, too, the fort was held by a small and inexperienced force of artillerymen, many of whose guns were faulty or inoperable.[21]

Unaware of their opponents' weaknesses and determined to take the position regardless, Ord and Stannard hastily planned an attack. At about six o'clock, one of Stannard's three brigades advanced on the left of the Varina Road, and the others—Hiram Burnham's in the lead—took the right side. Preceded by Donohoe's skirmishers, the main body of the division crossed a farm field open on all sides to enemy fire. To complicate matters, the attackers had to halt periodically to remove fallen trees and other barriers. The only factor in their favor was that the pea green gunners inside Fort Harrison fired their few workable pieces too high to inflict much damage.

The Federals left the Varina Road where it angled north toward Richmond, waded a tributary of Three Mile Creek, and occupied the blind spot at the base of the fort. After catching their breath, they crossed the dry moat and worked their way toward the fort's left flank under a shower of rifle fire from neighboring works. Just before Gregg's reinforcements arrived, Stannard's advance echelon shot and slashed its way inside the bastion, killing several cannoneers and chasing away the others.

The attackers then raced down the hill and took adjacent batteries in flank and rear positions. In minutes, their defenders were fleeing, some toward Richmond, most heading for the entrenched camp farther west. As Union banners went up over three of those works, their captors attempted to turn Confederate cannon on the Rebel troops. While helping manhandle one of the guns, General Burnham received a fatal wound in the abdomen. One of his soldiers expressed heartfelt regret: "It did seem too bad to loose [sic] this brave, sensible old fellow."[22]

Burnham was not the only casualty. Soon after Fort Harrison fell, Ord was shot below his right knee. Hoping to exploit his column's momentum, the corps leader had led a part of Stannard's division toward Chaffin's Bluff. In his haste to seize those James River bridges by which Lee might reinforce Ewell, Ord had exposed himself. His unwilling trip to the rear would jeopardize Butler's offensive.[23]

Command of Ord's force passed to General Heckman. Following his capture at Drewry's Bluff and many weeks in prison camp, the German-American had been paroled, returned to Butler's army, and marked for promotion. During General Ames's absence (he was in Minnesota, visiting his parents), Heckman, by virtue of seniority, assumed command of Ord's 2nd Division for the thrust above the James. Heckman's military abilities, modest as they were, appear to have atrophied during his confinement. For one thing, when he replaced Ord, he failed to heed his superior's parting directions. Instead of leading his column through the woods lining the Varina Road, then westward on Stannard's right, Heckman lost his bearings and landed most of his men in a swamp. Two regiments under Colonel Ripley avoided the bog but, lacking guidance from Heckman, continued up the Varina Road toward the lower end of Richmond's exterior line instead of westward toward Fort Harrison.

The problem worsened when Heckman failed to intercept Gregg's Confederates, who had rushed west from New Market Heights directly across his path. Gregg then beat his adversaries to larger works along Richmond's intermediate line, including Fort Johnson on its southern flank and, farther north, Forts Gregg and Gilmer. Heckman also rejected Ord's plan to capture the bridges near Chaffin's Bluff and move north behind the wall of the Fort Harrison complex until he could roll up Dick Ewell's line from right to left. Ripley wrote that Heckman "seemed to have become crazed" when he took over the column; without Ord's supervision, he "was good for nothing."[24]

Learning that Ripley had breached the exterior line and occupied two abandoned batteries, Heckman had him lead his brigade against Forts Gregg and Gilmer. At the same time, he ordered Colonel Harrison S. Fairchild to attack Fort Johnson. By directing his subordinates to take all three works in front instead of by surprise from the rear, as Ord had intended, Heckman ensured failure. Artillery fire stalled Ripley's drive before it could hit home, whereupon the colonel took it upon himself to suspend operations. Fairchild's command reached its objective but at such a rapid gait that its men were too exhausted to hold anything they captured. Confederate counterattacks broke Fairchild's hold on Fort Johnson and forced his brigade to head south in some confusion.

By 10:00 A.M. Butler's west wing had stalled at the intermediate line; Heckman had been unable to break through at any point. At the same time, troops in the forts at the lower end of the entrenched camp had blocked Stannard's drive southward from Fort Harrison. To stiffen the defense, Confederate gunboats were blasting any Federals who tried to push toward the bridges near Chaffin's Bluff.

At this juncture, David Birney's column reached the scene of fighting along Heckman's front. At about half past eight the wing commander had started from New Market Heights at the head of Foster's division. He left Paine's, Terry's, and William Birney's troops inside the lines they had captured, enabling Kautz's troopers to start up the New Market Road toward Richmond. Birney's westward advance was slowed by retreating Rebels and, near Laurel Hill Church, by a cavalry brigade and artillery ordered up by Ewell. The hit-and-run tactics of this small force halted Foster's men for about ninety minutes until the Federals outflanked the Confederates and chased them along the New Market Road. At about 9:30 A.M. Birney called up Paine's division, followed by Terry's and William Birney's, deployed them in Foster's rear, and sent them northwestward. Close to noon the combined force reached the intermediate line along the New Market Road, where it prepared to attack—with or without Heckman's help—Forts Gregg and Gilmer.[25]

After a long personal reconnaissance in the manner of Baldy Smith, General Birney decided that Fort Gilmer was the primary target. Leaving his brother's troops, along with Terry's, to confront Fort Gregg, he sent Foster's division, backed by Paine's, around to the north side of Gilmer. At half past one Foster led his straggler-depleted division against the upper bastion, which mounted two sixty-four-pounder guns positioned to sweep a long, treacherous approach. The odds against the attackers were long enough, but they approached the impossible when Foster advanced in a single line, thirteen regiments long. Lacking adequate depth, the column was cleaved by artillery fire as it crossed three gorges. "Death fairly reveled in that third ravine," wrote a New York sergeant. "Shells hissed and exploded about our ears incessantly, and crushed heads and mangled bodies thickly strewed our pathway." Those who cleared the gullies and a cornfield beyond were cut down by canister and rifle fire. After several dozen had gone down, their comrades hustled back to the ravines, which became sanctuaries instead of barriers to advance.[26]

Foster rallied the survivors and added one of Paine's regiments. Such a small reinforcement was useless; minutes after the assault resumed, it collapsed again. Only Paine's outfit got as near as 100 yards to the fort. The white soldiers turned and ran for home before advancing half as far.

David Birney tried to salvage a rapidly deteriorating situation. Calling up his brother's division, he ordered an attack on Fort Gilmer from the east. The result was another botched performance, this time by William Birney, who attacked piecemeal and failed to use Colonel Plaisted's brigade, which had been attached to his command that morning.

Leading Birney's assault, the 9th U.S. Colored Troops hurled itself against the curtain connecting Forts Gregg and Gilmer, only to be tossed backward. Birney then sent the 8th USCT against Gregg and the 7th Regiment against Gilmer. It appears that he ordered each to attack in one four-company line, a ridiculous formation in the face of such heavy opposition. With great valor, part of the 7th braved the cannon fire and musketry to scale Gilmer's ramparts, but every attacker who showed his head above the parapet went hurtling through the open air with a rifle slug in his skull.[27]

After Birney's division retreated in bloody fragments, three separate actions closed out the day's fighting. Frantic to accomplish something, Heckman sent the 2nd Brigade, 2nd Division, XVIII Corps, under Colonel James W. Jourdan, northwest of Fort Harrison to try to take a small redoubt on the Mill Road. Despite a terrific cannonade, Jourdan's 54th Pennsylvania, backed by the 148th and 158th New York, forged bravely across naked ground until halted short of the road and forced to retire. The second combat ended more successfully for the Federals as the 3rd Brigade of Stannard's division, led by Edgar Cullen, assaulted an earthwork on the far Rebel right where the Chaffin's Bluff defenses crossed the Osborne Turnpike. Most of its garrison had fled, enabling Cullen's 58th and 188th Pennsylvania to seize Fort Hoke, several guns, and a few prisoners.[28]

The last operation, and the most promising of the three, extended into the thirtieth. Passing through David Birney's victorious ranks on the New Market Road at about seven o'clock that morning, General Kautz, with five regiments of riders and two batteries of horse artillery, trotted north across the crest of New Market Heights. Turning west onto the Darbytown Road at about nine o'clock, Kautz reached works two miles from Richmond along the upper reaches of the intermediate line. Though fewer than 100 Confederates held this position, Kautz approached with extreme caution. When the defenders opened fire, the lead unit, the 5th Pennsylvania, quickly retreated. Kautz then headed north in search of a clearer approach. By abandoning the Darbytown Road in violation of his orders, he frustrated Terry's effort to join him in attacking along that strategic thoroughfare.

This start set the tone for what followed. Over the next twenty hours Kautz made feeble attempts to find gaps in the intermediate line. At about 1:00 P.M. the cavalry attacked up the road to Charles City. Repulsed by a fairly large force, it looped north toward the Williamsburg Road, still seeking an open road to the capital.

After resting his men for four hours, Kautz attempted to turn westward along the Creighton Road. In gathering darkness his troopers approached some works, which they probed cautiously on foot. Two of the dismounted patrols lost their bearings, fired into each other by mistake—inflicting casualties and alerting the enemy—and then took Rebel musketry at close range. Disengaging yet again, the cavalry salved its self-inflicted wounds before following Kautz via Seven Pines, White's Tavern, and the battlefield of Fussell's Mill, to rejoin the infantry early the next morning along the Darbytown Road. Despite miles of riding, Kautz had contributed nothing to the campaign against Richmond.[29]

Long before Kautz returned, Birney and Heckman agreed they should hold the works they had seized and have their soldiers improve defenses around Fort Harrison. To clear fields of fire against anticipated counterattacks, Stannard's division razed several obstructions that faced westward, including the fort's barracks. The labor had one lasting effect: it tired the troops so much that by morning they were in no shape to attack Forts Gregg, Gilmer, Johnson, or any other point along the intermediate line. Ben Butler strongly recommended a new offensive, but Grant, who appears to have had a better picture of the condition of Butler's troops, rejected the proposal.[30]

By the morning of the thirtieth Robert E. Lee, concerned for the safety of his upper flank and for Richmond itself, had come up from Petersburg to supersede Ewell. With him came the infantry divisions of Robert Hoke and Major General Charles W. Field, the former with five brigades and the latter with three. About noon, after the gunboats in the James shelled the captured works, Hoke charged his enemy's southern flank at and below Fort Burnham (as its captors had rechristened Fort Harrison). At the same time, Field, farther to the rear, struck the opposite flank along the captured segment of the exterior line.

For three hours the Confederates failed in as many attempts to dislodge their foe, testimony to how well the Federals had improved their position. Many Rebels who were not killed or wounded were captured, including more than 200 in Brigadier General Thomas Clingman's brigade. Among the relatively few Union casualties was Stannard, shot off an observation post atop Fort Burnham. With his right arm shattered, Stannard spent the remainder of the war on inactive service. His loss would make itself felt in future crises; as Colonel Ripley put it, "he was an Army in himself in such supreme moments."[31]

By 3:00 P.M., having suffered more than 1,200 casualties to his enemy's 260, Lee suspended his counterattacks. Chagrined and dejected, he kept the survivors well out of rifle range for the balance of the day. That night a visitor at army headquarters found Lee "with a face on him as long as a gun barrel." Lee planned a fourth effort the next morning to retake Fort Burnham but abruptly canceled it. He contented himself with building up his position along the intermediate line and down the middle of the entrenched camp. He also digested reports of the Army of the Potomac's movement below Petersburg, begun early on the thirtieth. Forced to contend with offensives at both ends of his elongated line, Lee may have despaired of stopping either.[32]

While the Fort Burnham–Chaffin's Bluff sector saw little fighting on October 1—the antagonists concentrated on digging—Grant launched a final attempt to enter Richmond. He ordered David Birney to dispatch Terry, with two infantry brigades bolstered by artillery and preceded by half of Kautz's division, along the rain-swept Darbytown Road. To support this reconnaissance-in-force, aimed at locating a weak point in the line, the rest of Kautz's horsemen advanced up the Charles City Road, pressuring Lee's pickets.

At approximately three o'clock the troopers in Terry's front recoiled from rifle and cannon fire a few miles outside the capital. Relieving the cavalry, Terry opened a cannonade, deployed Joshua Howell's old brigade (now led by Colonel Pond, Howell having been killed two weeks earlier in a riding accident), and sent forward Hawley's brigade, now under Colonel Joseph C. Abbott.

Brandishing Spencer repeaters, Abbott's two New Hampshire and two Connecticut regiments crossed muddy fields and, with some difficulty, waded a swollen stream. Thirty minutes of travel brought them within view of the upper reaches of the intermediate line, the barrier that had resisted the attacks of Birney, Heckman, and Kautz over the past two days. With five well-defended redoubts facing him, Abbott halted abruptly and sent back for Terry's advice. The expeditionary leader, who had heard that the cavalry had been halted on the Charles City Road, disengaged from his unpromising position. Terry and Kautz returned to Birney's main body, having probed as near to Richmond as any force would venture until the final week of the war in Virginia.[33]

Thus ended Grant's and Butler's most ambitious offensive north of the James. The attackers had suffered in excess of 3,300 casualties on September 29–30 without seizing their primary objective. However, they had kept Lee from sending additional troops to the Shenandoah Valley and had placed Richmond in fear for its life. More significantly, Butler's army had clamped a grip on the Northside it would not relinquish. It had forced the Confederates to abandon their new line between Chaffin's Bluff and Fussell's Mill. These accomplishments ensured that Lee's upper flank would stretch ever closer to the breaking point. Meanwhile, Lee's right had been lengthened by the advance of Meade's V and IX Corps from Globe Tavern to Peebles' Farm and Poplar Spring Church, three miles southwest of Petersburg.[34]

These gains notwithstanding, the troops in blue might have achieved more through better preparation and execution. Despite the apparent thoroughness of Butler's plan, he had erred by putting twice as much weight behind Birney's column, which faced lighter opposition and less important objectives than Ord's wing. With his much smaller force, Ord had done well to capture Fort Harrison and its surrounding works, even with the element of surprise on his side. Much more would have been gained, however, had Ord not been wounded and had Heckman, his successor, pursued the plan to take the exterior and intermediate lines from the rear rather than charged into Rebel guns.

Neither had Birney performed flawlessly. The X Corps leader had failed to coordinate with Heckman the movements against Forts Gregg and Gilmer; he had not even coordinated his own attacks against Gilmer. Birney's staggered assaults increased his losses and ensured his ultimate repulse. Finally, Kautz's cavalry had failed miserably, though Butler's insistence that the horsemen enter Richmond at all hazards was as unreasonable as it was impracticable.

Grant's poor sense of timing may have contributed to Butler's inability to crack Richmond's second line of defense. Had the commanding general launched Meade's offensive at the same time as Butler's, Lee might have failed to defend either of his flanks adequately. As it was, not until he rushed north to block Birney's further progress did the Confederate commander learn of the Army of the Potomac's advance from Globe Tavern. Grant must have foreseen a shift of enemy forces to the Northside; for that reason, Butler's offensive, which preceded Meade's, looked like a diversion in favor of the Army of the Potomac. Yet Grant forever claimed that Butler's was the principal movement and Richmond the primary objective. If so, Grant's strategy seems curiously out of sequence.

———————

Quiet prevailed above the James for six days after Lee's unsuccessful counter-attacks. Both armies built defensive lines, consolidated positions gained, and salvaged what remained of positions lost. Butler's troops used the respite to extend their breastworks and entrenchments from below Fort Burnham across the New Market and Darbytown Roads. By October 6 those defenses ended just short of the road to Charles City. Other than spadework, a New Hampshireman recalled, "matters were apparently at a standstill. . . . We laid around in a rather loose manner, filling in the time by swapping camp rumors and speculating on the probability of being paid off."[35]

The army—its command section, at any rate—should have been con-templating a new offensive. Logic dictated that Lee would try again to loosen the Federals' grip on the threshold of Richmond. A strike at the Union right flank via the Darbytown Road should have appeared the most likely prospect, since that sector was guarded by only dismounted cavalry and a few units of horse artillery under Kautz. Cavalry had notoriously low staying power, even when on foot, and Kautz's position was not protected by a complete line of works like that of the infantry. Kautz repeatedly petitioned Butler for entrenching tools, only to be told that the X and XVIII Corps had greater need of them.

The cavalry's precarious position on the forward edge of Butler's main body troubled Kautz. Days of quiet along the lines only heightened his concern, for he suspected Lee was up to something. He was especially worried that if attacked and cut off from support, his artillery, unlimbered beside an almost impassable swamp, would be trapped. He communicated this concern to Butler, who ordered him to hold his ground. Kautz was obliged to do so with only 1,500 troopers; one of his regiments, the 1st District of Columbia, had been temporarily attached to the infantry.

Two refugees from Richmond informed Kautz on the evening of October 6 that Confederate infantry and cavalry were moving toward his upper flank. He alerted Butler but received neither advice nor assistance. For consolation, he had only the wisdom Butler had imparted the day before when Kautz asked what to do if attacked in heavy force. "Cavalry," he quoted Butler as replying, "had legs and could run away."[36]

At about seven o'clock on the morning of October 7 Kautz discovered a column of infantry under Field, supported by Hoke's division and preceded by the mounted brigade of Brigadier General Martin W. Gary, bearing down on him between the Darbytown and Charles City Roads. Field and Gary had used the entrenchments running south from Chaffin's Bluff to mask their approach while Hoke advanced along the west side of the trenches. The plan, devised by Lee, was to turn the Federal right, pry loose the occupiers of Fort Burnham, and retake that work.

Within minutes of contact, fighting was swirling along Kautz's line, with the 5th Pennsylvania and 3rd New York of Robert West's brigade taking the heaviest blows. West's tiny command, exploiting what protection its half-completed works could provide, held its ground south of the Darbytown Road as long as possible. Only when the enemy was 100 yards off did the Pennsylvanians and New Yorkers mount and fall back. As they fled they found that a detachment of Gary's command had turned their right flank to create havoc among their supply train. Although able to chase the Confederates away, Kautz withdrew in unseemly haste toward the X Corps' position on the New Market Road.

The retreat produced some embarrassing sights. From his vantage point below the New Market Road, an officer in the X Corps saw the horsemen stampede for the rear "as though the devil was after them; there was no organization; every man for himself and all making straight for Deep Bottom. Horses without riders, and horses with the saddles under their bellies were running about in great confusion." Another infantryman claimed that "such a conglomerated mess of hatless, shoeless and coatless horsemen was not often seen. Some even left their sabres and carbines behind."[37]

At the height of the retreat Kautz's worst fears materialized when his batteries bogged down in the swamp. The Rebels swarmed over the guns, capturing eight of them plus caissons, limbers, and dozens of cannoneers and their mounts. Still, most of the cavalry fled so quickly they eluded not only Field's infantry but also Gary's main body, which had advanced down the Charles City Road in an unsuccessful attempt to isolate Kautz. Because Hoke had gotten a late start from the Richmond defenses, he could not strike the cavalry's left at the same time that Field turned its right and Gary menaced its rear.

With Kautz's men in mid-retreat, David Birney led those X Corps units nearest the threatened sector toward the sound of the fighting. Though suffering so much from fever and debility that he could barely remain in the saddle, the corps commander personally deployed three brigades across the path of the oncoming Rebels. In a broken area in advance of his main line, he prepared an ambush with several companies of sharpshooters, each armed with a Spencer repeater.[38]

After an artillery barrage, Field's division charged the hastily formed Federals. Before the attackers got up a full head of steam, Birney's sharpshooters poured a devastating fire into them. Field's stunned men fell back to wait for Hoke's support. When he failed to show, Field withdrew a short distance, revived his advance, and overpowered Birney's marksmen. Charging in supposed triumph, the Confederates ran hard into Terry's densely packed ranks— Pond's brigade on the left, Abbott's in the center, and Plaisted's on the left, backed by Curtis's brigade of Foster's division.

This clash north of the New Market Road was described by one Federal as "the only stand up fight I witnessed during the war—neither side had any protection. It was stand up and take it and the best army won." In fact, both Pond and Abbott held shallow trenches, with a partial abatis in front. The Spencer repeaters appeared to have decided the outcome but only after enemy pressure had caused the 100th New York of Plaisted's brigade (whose term of service had expired the previous day) to run for the rear. Half an hour after the fighting began the Confederates withdrew, having suffered approximately 600 casualties, including the mortally wounded Gregg. A veteran from Maine claimed that "I never before had the privilege of helping whip the Rebels so handsomely."[39]

As the enemy departed, a portion of Foster's division pursued at a conservative pace. Behind the foot soldiers, Kautz's troopers moved just as cautiously back to the Darbytown Road, below which both arms of the service bivouacked. The Federals had taken 450 casualties, half of them in Kautz's division. The most significant loss was David Birney, who, by exerting himself, had shattered his already poor health. The next day he was reported to be bedridden and delirious. Rushed by train to his home in Philadelphia, where state elections were under way, Birney had himself carried to the polls, where he voted the straight Republican ticket. Back at home he lapsed into semiconsciousness. He lingered till the eighteenth, in his delirium shouting orders and encouragement to his troops. Friends preserved his last words: "Keep your eyes on that flag, boys!"[40]

※

On October 11–12 Kautz confirmed through reconnaissance that Field and Hoke had begun to build a line in advance of Richmond's intermediate line. The new defenses, small redoubts connected by rifle pits and covered by slashings and abatis, stretched north of Laurel Hill on the New Market Road toward the Charles City Road. The cavalry chief notified Butler, who relayed it to City Point. Late on the twelfth Grant instructed Butler to attack. Butler selected Terry's old division, now under Adelbert Ames; William Birney's USCT division; and the troopers who had stampeded the previous week. Reliable or not, Kautz's division was the army's only cavalry. The force was ordered to drive the redoubt builders and trench diggers closer to Richmond.[41]

Because of a flag-of-truce conference that lasted all day, the movement, with Terry commanding, did not get under way till the crisp morning of October 13. Ames's division led the way on the right of the Darbytown Road, with Birney's division on the left; Kautz's troopers trotted along the right flank, and three light batteries rumbled along in the rear. Impressed by the scale of the movement, the chaplain of the 10th Connecticut found the early stages of the operation "exhilarating and inspiriting." Other participants were less excited. "It was manifest," Kautz wrote afterward, "that the movement was doubtful of everything except a severe loss."[42]

On this occasion the cavalry leader was a seer. The high command was gambling that the Confederates had made little progress on their new line and that they held it with an understrength force. Neither assumption was true: the redoubts and entrenchments were formidable and defended by more troops than Terry had at hand. Instead of a demonstration in force, Grant and Butler ought to have gathered further intelligence.

As Kautz had anticipated, his division had a hard day. Swinging west between the Darbytown and Charles City Roads, the horsemen on the left quickly ran into stout opposition. The 7th South Carolina Cavalry of Gary's brigade delayed Colonel West's brigade for some hours, while farther south the Hampton (South Carolina) Legion, backed by the 24th Virginia Cavalry, held the ground along the Darbytown Road against Spear's dismounted brigade. Heavy skirmishing continued on West's and Spear's fronts for most of the day; no Union trooper reached the enemy line.[43]

Terry's infantry made no greater progress. By 10 A.M. his main body was forging west on either side of the Darbytown Road, Ames's division north of it, and Birney's men to the south. Curtis's brigade supported Birney's left flank, while Colonel John W. Moore's brigade linked Curtis to the entrenched Union line to the rear. After driving in some pickets, Birney encountered Field's division; spirited but indecisive fighting lasted until early afternoon. Meanwhile, Terry's main body was kept pinned down by Field's artillery, which virtually destroyed the woods in which the Federals had taken shelter. Torn between hugging what cover he could find and trying to silence the barrage, Terry made little headway against the enemy line; by midafternoon he had lost perhaps 100 men killed or wounded.

By about three o'clock the embattled Kautz was trying to help the infantry move off dead center. He had discovered what appeared to be a gap along the enemy left unprotected by slashing or abatis. If Terry could slip through that crease, he might flank the defenders and gain their rear. The expeditionary leader moved at once, via the north side of the Darbytown Road, to exploit the perceived weakness.[44]

But as the drive began, the Confederates took countermeasures. General Lee had arrived on the scene, and when he learned that the Federals were moving against Field's left, he ordered that sector strengthened. The brigades of Brigadier Generals George T. Anderson and Dudley M. DuBose and Colonel William F. Perry moved into position along the north side of the Darbytown Road, where they immediately entrenched. Bratton's brigade moved from the main line to the south side of the road, while the Hampton Legion and the 24th Virginia Cavalry shifted from Kautz's front to the Charles City Road. The only force now holding the Confederate defenses, Hoke's division, spread out to fill the gaps while continuing to oppose Birney at long range.

Although some of Terry's subordinates, including Colonel Pond, considered the crease in the Confederate line a mirage, the flanking movement proceeded. Pond led the attack along the Darbytown Road at about 4:00 P.M. with his own 39th Illinois and 62nd and 67th Ohio, plus the 10th Connecticut of Plaisted's brigade. To the rear, the rest of Pond's and Plaisted's troops, along with the brigade of Joseph Hawley, closely supported the offensive.[45]

Pond's suspicions were confirmed within minutes. His men faced not a weakened sector but entrenchments held by four infantry brigades supported by artillery. Cannon fire peeled human layers from both of Pond's flanks and musketry shredded his center. The Federals took almost 200 casualties before the survivors fled for their lives.

Realizing that he had blundered, Terry called off the offensive. For the rest of the afternoon he kept his troops under trees beyond the range of enemy fire. Terry would have been devastated had he known that he could have withdrawn, with the approval of the high command, before losing so many troops. Around noon, before being fully committed, he had apprised headquarters of his lack of progress and the apparent strength of the enemy's position. Butler had forwarded the dispatch to Grant, who replied, "I would not attack the enemy in his intrenchments. . . . To attack now we would lose more than the enemy, & only gain ground which we are not prepared to hold." This good advice, however, did not reach Terry until shortly before his seven o'clock withdrawal from the battlefield. By then his main force had been reduced by more than 400 casualties, plus Kautz's 41. Thus ended what a Maine soldier called as "thoughtless [a] waste of life" as the army had ever experienced.[46]

CHAPTER TWELVE

From the James to the Hudson

BY MID-OCTOBER, ACCORDING TO THE *ARMY AND NAVY JOURNAL*, "IT IS THE 'Army of the James,' as it lies strongly entrenched north of that river, that now chiefly absorbs public attention, while the achievements of the Army of the Potomac, southwest of Petersburgh, are usually looked upon as merely cooperative." If Butler's army indeed held center stage, it put on an uninspired act for two weeks after its disastrous offensive of the thirteenth, before capping the year with another failed effort to crack the Confederate defenses above the James River.[1]

Organizational and personnel matters occupied the army in the interim. Kautz's division, whose weakness had been glaringly revealed during the near-disaster of October 7, was strengthened with two regiments that had been attached to the infantry, the 1st New York Mounted Rifles and the recently remounted 1st Maryland Cavalry. Kautz then went on extended leave to recuperate from a recurrence of malaria and was temporarily replaced by Colonel West. Another whose command had just been strengthened— General Paine, whose 3rd Division, XVIII Corps, absorbed several black regiments recruited in Kentucky—took sick leave at this time, being succeeded by Colonel Holman.[2]

General Graham relinquished command of the Naval Brigade in mid-October to take charge of the Bermuda Hundred defenses. His new sphere encompassed not only a provisional division of infantry but also the heavy artillerists and siege train personnel of Colonel Abbot. At Grant's urging, Graham strengthened his works against an impending attack by Pickett. Graham did such a good job that the assault was called off. Finally, from the seventeenth to the twenty-sixth, the army began to weatherize its quarters. Pine cabins and stockaded tents sprang up everywhere as the first gusts of winter began to blow through the camps along the James.[3]

If Butler's troops believed active campaigning was done for the year, they soon learned differently. Butler issued orders on October 26—appending to them a copy of his September 29 instructions on "what to do when you get into Richmond"—that involved two-thirds of the army in a new attempt to outflank or breach the Rebel lines on the Northside.

The impetus had come from Meade. Acting on the erroneous premise that Lee's lines south of Petersburg were vulnerable, Meade had suggested to Grant an operation against the Southside Railroad, the last supply link between Petersburg and the Deep South. In approving the idea Grant also envisioned a diversionary movement against Lee's left north of the James. Butler was receptive but changed the plan into yet another assault on Richmond—this time, with himself in command.

The operation, designed to keep Field and Hoke from reinforcing the Southside defenses against Meade, presented attractive possibilities to Butler. With Lincoln all but assured of reelection, Butler could hardly have viewed the mission as a stepping stone to the White House. On the other hand, any glory he achieved on the threshold of Richmond would aid his political future.

Glory was not on the minds of his troops when word of the operation spread on the evening of the twenty-sixth. The recent failures on the Northside had left the army pessimistic, if not downright gloomy. That night, many soldiers wrote what they suspected would be their final letters home. Hawley, temporarily in charge of William Birney's division, informed his wife that great peril, perhaps doom, awaited the army. He was grateful that the work of readying his new command for the task left him "no time to think—only occasionally a moment to breathe 'Our Father in Heaven,' or 'God help us.'"[4]

On the chilly, rainy morning of October 27 Terry and Weitzel (the latter now commanding the XVIII Corps) roused their dispirited troops, and by 5:00 A.M. both columns were heading northwestward. Physically unwell and commanding from the front seat of a buggy, Terry led his 8,500 infantrymen and two batteries up the New Market Road, accompanied on horseback by Butler. At about the same time, Weitzel, having left 2,500 men to hold the lines evacuated by both columns, advanced up the Varina Road at the head of 7,500 foot soldiers and eight guns. In advance of both wings rode the recently strengthened cavalry under Colonel West.

Despite its early start, the expedition did not meet the timetable established by Grant, which presumed a rapid advance. Not until seven o'clock did the invaders cover the mile and a half that separated Butler's lines from Rebel outposts on the Darbytown Road. As it approached, Terry's column absorbed shelling from batteries hidden on either side of the road as well as from ahead, where Hoke's soldiers occupied a position in advance of their recently constructed defense line. Terry had to stop and deploy; he placed Foster's division below the road, Ames's above it, and Hawley's in the rear as support. The enemy suddenly appeared to fall back, whereupon the X Corps surged forward for about 300 yards until halted by increased fire.

Throwing out a large skirmish force, Terry spent the next three hours probing Hoke's lines. When resistance again appeared to slacken, the Federals resumed their advance, only to collide with their now-retreating skirmishers, pursued by a small but combative enemy force. It was the middle of the afternoon before Terry could thrust the gray troops inside their works.[5]

By 4:00 P.M. Terry's advance had bogged down short of Hoke's line. Butler decided his best hope lay with Weitzel's advance farther north. The army leader directed Terry to make a diversion. Against his better judgment but unwilling to create another confrontation with his superior, Terry sent the brigades of Newton Curtis and Louis Bell charging toward Hoke's defenses. Terry reported that they captured some advanced rifle pits before being "met with a severe fire of grape and case-shot. . . . After advancing to within about eight rods of the enemy's works it was found impracticable to proceed."

Weitzel needed even more support, for by now he was having at least as much difficulty with Field's division as Terry had with Hoke. In fact, Weitzel had it worse; he not only faced a larger opponent but also lacked Terry's familiarity with the terrain. After a long, frustrating march over soggy roads and through swampy woods, Weitzel's column reached the Williamsburg Road at about 7:00 A.M., upon which it was to move west. Weitzel did not even realize he had struck the road he was seeking until one of his officers, who had served in the area during the Peninsula Campaign of 1862, told him. Weitzel acknowledged his confusion and informed Butler that because he was "entirely lost from Terry," he doubted his ability to coordinate with the lower column. Thus far, the only fighting on Weitzel's front had been by the cavalry, which had clashed repeatedly with Gary's brigade near the intersection of the Charles City and Williamsburg Roads.[6]

As West's division pressed westward, driving Gary's troopers before it, Weitzel followed to just beyond White Oak Swamp, where he spied Field's line of defense. Like Terry, Weitzel halted, threw out skirmishers, and tapped at the enemy position. By midday the corps commander had become convinced ("as I still firmly believe," he asserted four days later) that only three guns and a small force of Gary's cavalry barred his path. In authorizing the army's movements, Grant had expressly forbidden a head-on assault against field works; Weitzel, however, believed that he was exempt from this prohibition. Thus he formed two attack columns, one on each side of the Williamsburg Road, bolstered them with artillery and dozens of dismounted carbineers from West's division, and attacked at about four o'clock.[7]

Like Terry on October 13, Weitzel was walking into a trap. Instead of a thinly held line, the Federals struck Field's strongest position. Having identified Terry's limited assault as a diversion for Weitzel, Lieutenant General James Longstreet, who had taken command of the combined Confederate forces, had shifted most of Hoke's division northward to hold Field's position. This enabled Field's main body to occupy prepared works straddling the Williamsburg Road. Weitzel had not only lost his sense of direction, he had failed to detect the enemy transfer. The lapse had disastrous effects.

North of the road, two brigades of Stannard's old division, now commanded by General Marston, charged the works held by Bratton's South Carolina brigade. On the south side Ripley's brigade of Heckman's division attacked the Texas brigade formerly led by John Gregg. In both sectors the Confederates sliced the attackers into fragments. Of the regiments that got as far as the works, six lost their colors and two, the 19th Wisconsin and the 118th New York, were captured nearly whole.[8]

While the white troops were meeting defeat on the Williamsburg Road, a portion of Holman's division (only one brigade of which was on hand) launched a secondary assault farther to the north near Fair Oaks. Sometime after three o'clock Holman's 1st and 22nd U.S. Colored Troops charged a thinly held line of works between the Williamsburg and Nine Mile Roads. The 22nd became disordered while maneuvering and broke apart under a cannonade. However, despite the wounding of Holman and his second in command, Colonel Kiddoo, the 1st overran the enemy position and captured two twelve-pounder Napoleons.

By perhaps 5:00 P.M. the victorious blacks had positioned themselves to sweep down on the rear of the troops thrashing Weitzel's column. The anticipated blow, which might have greatly altered the fighting along the Williamsburg Road, was deflected at the last minute when Gary's cavalry rushed up from the south and drove Holman's startled troops back down the Nine Mile Road. Before they could rally, Weitzel recalled them, having decided (perhaps too hastily) that their partial success had been gained "too late in the day to be of any service."[9]

Resigned to defeat and distressed by heavy casualties, a stricken Weitzel broke contact with the enemy. He kept his forces close in hand for the balance of the day, employing them only in long-range skirmishing. After dark he led the way back to the Charles City Road through mud, chill, and rain. He later described the march as "the most fatiguing and trying one that ever I have known troops to undertake."[10]

Next morning, cheered by fair weather and new hope, Weitzel deployed most of his infantry for a new offensive. He also dispatched the cavalry to demonstrate against Field's defenses, enabling some of Heckman's troops, who had been pinned down close to the Rebel line throughout the night, to disengage. But at 10:00 A.M., as Weitzel probed for an opportunity to strike Field, Butler ordered him to return to his starting point of the twenty-sixth. Butler had reluctantly concluded that today—like many other days—would not bring him victory.

Although disappointed, Weitzel complied, reaching his winter camp near Fort Burnham at six o'clock. By then his weary, miserable troops had had enough of campaigning in raw weather; as one noted in his diary, "The glory of this expedition is reduced to mud and water." A comrade, reflecting on the more than 1,600 casualties the army had suffered over the past two days and aware that Meade's operations below Petersburg had ended just as unhappily, cursed the "general stupidity which had characterized the movement."[11]

Back in dry clothing and lodgings, the Army of the James slowly adjusted its frame of mind. One factor that revived morale was the general belief (which proved to be true) that the army had fought its last battle of the year. However comforting that was, another truth troubled the more introspective members of Butler's command. Soon after setting out on the road to Richmond five months earlier, they had gotten to within seven miles of the capital before being turned back at Drewry's Bluff. Now, at year's end, they remained five miles from their objective. Those two miles had cost 15,000 officers and men killed, wounded, or missing—nearly half the original strength of the army.

⇒⊶⊷⊰

The men built winter quarters but were not allowed to remain snugly indoors throughout the cold weather. In November and December thousands were called to serve in far-off climes. A substantial portion of the X Corps went to the North Carolina coast. Another mission carried members of both corps to New York City.

By the late autumn of 1864 Wilmington, North Carolina, remained the only Confederate port of strategic value. It had vexed the Union since the war's earliest days. Hundreds of blockade runners out of Britain, Canada, the Bahamas, and Bermuda had docked there, bringing almost $30 million worth of goods into the Confederacy. As other Southern ports were closed, Wilmington's commerce grew; during one three-month period late in 1864, blockade runners carried into the city 8,652,000 pounds of meat, 1,933,000 pounds of saltpeter, 1,507,000 pounds of lead, 546,000 pairs of shoes, 520,000 pounds of coffee, 316,000 blankets, 69,000 rifles, 2,639 boxes of medicine, 97 crates of revolvers, 43 field guns, and great quantities of other food and munitions.[12]

The North Atlantic Blockading Squadron, which patroled off Wilmington, could not shut off this flow of goods. The city lay twenty-two miles from the ocean—too far for naval ordnance to reach—and its access to open water was via the narrow channels of the Cape Fear River, infested with shoals and shifting bars. Sleek, maneuverable blockade runners could negotiate the inlet easily, even by night, but large warships could not. To complicate Union naval surveillance, the runners could pass into the Cape Fear via a channel directly below the river's mouth. The local weather also favored the importers. As Union naval lieutenant (and future admiral) George Dewey remarked, "The runners could frequently slip by under cover of fog or when a gale was blowing."[13]

The U.S. government knew that this situation had prevailed for too long. Since late 1862 Navy Secretary Gideon Welles had struggled to mount an expedition against Wilmington, believing that closing the port was tantamount to "severing the jugular vein in the human system." His blockading officers agreed. A paymaster aboard a frigate within sight of the coast believed that "in taking Wilmington we do more to end the Rebellion than we could do in any other way. . . . A man, in my opinion, might live a lifetime and yet die dissatisfied if he did not see" the closing of the port.[14]

Neither Welles nor his most combative officer seriously believed the navy alone could board up Wilmington. Only a large amphibious expedition, supported by light-draught gunboats, could overcome the defenses at the mouth of the Cape Fear: Fort Caswell and smaller works along the western bar, which guarded the lower inlet; and Fort Fisher, a massive earthwork at the base of a marshy peninsula known as Confederate Point, almost twenty miles south of Wilmington, which covered New Inlet.

Fort Fisher was by far more formidable and commanded the direct route to Wilmington. Built in April 1861 to supplement ancient masonry fortifications, it had begun as a sandbag-reinforced redoubt 100 yards long whose six guns appeared incapable of turning back a modest landing party. Since mid-1862, with the support of his immediate superior, Major General William H. C. Whiting, Colonel William Lamb had put huge amounts of time, energy, and state funds into Fort Fisher. Lamb had created a work that foreign observers likened to the Malakoff Tower, the famed Russian fortress of the Crimean War.[15]

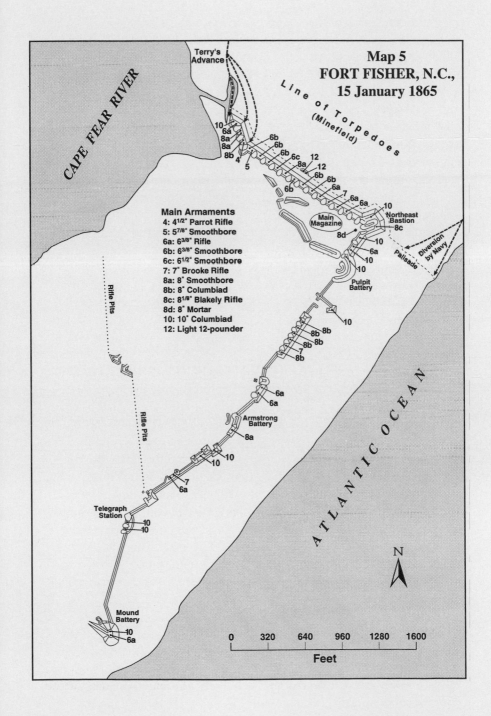

Map 5
FORT FISHER, N.C.,
15 January 1865

Terry's Advance

CAPE FEAR RIVER

Line of Torpedoes
(Minefield)

10
6a
8a
8a
8b
4
5

6b
6b
6b
6c   12
8a   12
6b
6b
6a

6b

7   6a
6a

10

Northeast
Bastion
8c

Diversion
by Navy

Main
Magazine

8d

Palisade

Main Armaments
4: 4¹/²" Parrot Rifle
5: 5⁷/⁸" Smoothbore
6a: 6³/⁸" Rifle
6b: 6³/⁸" Smoothbore
6c: 6¹/²" Smoothbore
7: 7" Brooke Rifle
8a: 8" Smoothbore
8b: 8" Columbiad
8c: 8¹/⁸" Blakely Rifle
8d: 8" Mortar
10: 10" Columbiad
12: Light 12-pounder

10
6a
10
10

Pulpit
Battery

10

8b
8b
8b
7
8b

Rifle Pits

6a
6a

Armstrong
Battery

8a

Rifle Pits

10
10

7
6a

Telegraph
Station
10
10

ATLANTIC OCEAN

N

Mound
Battery
10
6a

0   320   640   960   1280   1600
Feet

The fort had two main works, or faces, that met at a 90-degree angle near the ocean beach of Confederate Point. The land face, which ran for almost 700 yards across the peninsula, mounted twenty guns, most of them 6⅜-inch smoothbores and 10-inch Columbiad rifles. This face began about 100 feet from the Cape Fear with a half-bastion and extended along a heavy curtain to a full bastion on the ocean side about 300 feet from the shore. The wall of the land face stood 20 feet high, was pitched at a 45-degree angle to foil attackers, and was sodded with marsh grass. The parapets, 25 feet thick, shielded chambers containing cannon mounted *en barbette* or on specially made carriages.

Lamb explained the absence of casemated ordnance by noting that "casemates of timber and sand bags were a delusion . . . against heavy projectiles." To compensate for this potential deficiency, the guns along the land face were protected by massive traverses of sand. These interior walls, designed primarily to deflect enfilading fire, extended 12 feet above the parapet. The traverses contained powder magazines and bombproof rooms ventilated by air chambers and connected by passageways that gave access to the fort's 14,500-square-foot interior. The walls were sturdy enough to withstand direct hits from 15-inch naval guns and 150-pounder rifles.[16]

As further protection for the land face, Lamb had dug a 7-foot ditch in front of it, behind which stood a 9-foot-high palisade of sharpened logs with embrasures for sharpshooters. This permitted enfilading fire to be directed along a wide extent of the face. The most vulnerable point on the land face, a salient near the river edge of the palisade, was protected by natural and man-made barriers: a muddy slough that lined the river road leading into the fort and a one-gun battery commanding the bridge that crossed this swamp. As if these defenses were not enough, the land face was shielded by three detached works. Four miles north of the outer slope stood two redoubts—each mounting only one gun but able to accommodate numerous troops—known as the Flag-Pond and Half-Moon Batteries. Between these and the palisade, stretching 600 yards across Confederate Point, was a network of land mines that could be detonated from inside the fort.[17]

The sea face of Fort Fisher, which led south from the full bastion for almost 2,000 yards, was even more formidable. It mounted twenty-four heavy guns, including two monster pieces: a 170-pounder Blakely rifle and a 130-pounder Armstrong cannon, both of which had come through the blockade from England. From a crescent-shaped bombproof just below the bastion, a series of batteries extended toward the ocean channel, facing east. Like the land face, the sea face featured gun chambers protected against ricochet fire by earthen traverses. The line of works was also guarded by mines connected to a battery. At its southern base, where the channel ran close to the beach, the sea face boasted a Mound Battery, an artificial dune 60 feet high that had taken six months to construct with the aid of two inclined steam railways. From atop it two heavy guns could direct a plunging fire against troops attacking via the channel.

For more than a mile between the Mound Battery and the southern tip of Confederate Point ran a stretch of unprotected ground. Here a level sand plain, much of it submerged during high tide, stretched toward New Inlet. Three-quarters of a mile west of Mound Battery, however, sat an elliptical work, known as Battery Buchanan, whose four guns faced the inlet as well as the mouth of the Cape Fear, where they guarded a steamboat wharf. Battery Buchanan provided Lamb with a final refuge, a stronghold to which an overpowered garrison might retreat and await reinforcements by water.

The fort's garrison, though not huge, was large enough to make a retreat seem unlikely. Through the unstinting efforts of Lamb and Whiting, the defenders had grown from a few dozen in mid-1861 to almost 700 by early December 1864, and that number would double before year's end. North Carolina infantry held the land and sea faces, including Mound Battery, while Confederate sailors manned Battery Buchanan. If needed, reinforcements were close by. Four miles above Fort Fisher lay an entrenched camp at the summit of a dune known as Sugar Loaf. Stationed there were many of the 6,000 troops charged with guarding the Southern land approaches to Richmond, commanded by Jefferson Davis's erstwhile military adviser, General Braxton Bragg.

Despite its defenses, Fort Fisher was not impregnable. The lack of casemates threatened to reduce its staying power. Furthermore, as Lamb acknowledged, "There was no moat with scarp and counter-scarp, so essential for defense against storming parties, the shifting sands rendering its construction impossible with the material available." From Mound Battery to Battery Buchanan and from Buchanan north, only rifle pits protected the rear of the fort. Then, too, the electrical apparatus required to activate the land mines was so unreliable that they were nearly worthless. Even so, the "Confederate Gibraltar" appeared so inherently strong and the approaches to it sufficiently treacherous as to defy any attack, whether from land or water.[18]

The perception that Fisher was unassailable except at excessive cost explained why no operation against Wilmington reached fruition during the first three and a half years of the conflict. Despite the Navy Department's enthusiasm for such an undertaking, the War Department failed to consider an expedition against the city until late 1863. By that time the project had been assigned to Ben Butler as commander of the Department of Virginia and North Carolina.

Characteristically, Butler displayed none of the reticence of his predecessors. At least five times between December 1863 and September 1864 he and his lieutenants had made serious attempts to attack Fort Fisher and the city. The first was short-lived—called off, perhaps, by the attention Butler was forced to devote to Wistar's raid on Richmond and then to the Bermuda Hundred Campaign. The second attempt Butler entrusted to Brigadier General Innis N. Palmer, commanding the District of North Carolina, who in May 1864 assembled 5,000 infantry at New Bern for an amphibious expedition against Wilmington. That operation was canceled at the last minute when Palmer failed to secure sufficient transports.[19]

A month later Colonel Jourdan, commanding the Sub-District of Beaufort, navigated the North Carolina coast to within shelling distance of Fort Fisher. An accompanying naval force balked, however, when the colonel asked it to move in close enough to land 1,500 troops on Confederate Point. Naval opposition also scuttled the fourth attempt to close Wilmington early in August, when Admiral Lee convinced Grant that Butler's plan to isolate Wilmington by mining both channels of the Cape Fear would not succeed.

Butler, who appreciated the political as well as the military benefits of slamming shut the Confederacy's last door, never gave up on the project. When the mining operation became a dead issue, the departmental commander studied a plan developed by General Graham. It had originated with a civilian, an amateur strategist who called for two land columns and a seaborne expedition to bypass Fort Fisher and converge between it and Wilmington. Perhaps deterred by the intricate cooperative requirements, Butler rejected it.[20]

In September 1864 Grant took the Wilmington project out of Butler's hands. Heeding Washington's demands for a campaign in North Carolina and convinced that the operation would aid the siege of Petersburg by cutting Lee's supply lines to the south, the general in chief decided that a considerable portion of the Army of the James (commanded by someone other than Butler) should spearhead an amphibious attack against Wilmington. The War Department approved the operation but suggested an expeditionary leader whom Grant immediately vetoed, Quincy Gillmore. Grant fixed October 1 as the launching date, and two weeks before the operation was to begin, he sent Godfrey Weitzel, his first choice to command, to reconnoiter the city's defenses.

The late September offensive against Chaffin's Bluff and New Market Heights, which demanded the services of virtually everyone in Butler's command, delayed the expedition yet again. By then Grant had decided to attack Fort Fisher; he pledged to do so as soon as operations in Virginia

ceased for the winter. But he would not begin until he was certain that reinforcements sent by Lee to Bragg in response to Weitzel's survey had returned
to Virginia.[21]

The Navy entered into the planning enthusiastically. Realizing that the
cautious Admiral Lee was not the man for the job, Gideon Welles offered the
command to Admiral Farragut. When the hero of New Orleans and Mobile
Bay turned it down, pleading poor health, the mission devolved upon his foster
brother and former subordinate, acting Rear Admiral David Dixon Porter,
commander of the Mississippi Squadron. On September 22 the bearded,
leathery-faced Porter, at forty-one a veteran of thirty years' service afloat, left
the western theater for his new station. Upon arriving in Virginia he super-
seded Admiral Lee, then spent two weeks overseeing a buildup of frigates,
sloops, ironclads, and monitors in Hampton Roads.

Unaware that he was excluded from active involvement in the mission,
Butler continued to regard the project as a way to reap the glory denied him
in Virginia. Not surprisingly, he developed a novel approach to the task. He
had observed carefully in July the effects of blasting powder on Elliott's Salient.
The following month he had studied the results of the explosion at City Point.
And in mid-October he had read newspaper accounts of an accident in
England in which two military magazines and two ordnance barges had
exploded along the Thames River, detonating more than 100,000 pounds
of powder. The blast, which leveled dwellings and blew their inhabitants to
atoms, had been felt fifty miles away.[22]

Ever alert to the military applications of such phenomena, Butler launched
a theoretical inquiry into the effects of detonating large quantities of powder
aboard vessels grounded along a riverbank. As he later explained, "I believed
that possibly, by bringing within four or five hundred yards of Fort Fisher
a large mass of explosives, and firing the whole in every part at the same
moment—for it was the essence of the experiment to have the powder all
exploded at the same instant—the garrison would at least be so far paralyzed
as to enable, by a prompt landing of men, a seizure of the fort."[23]

In the last week of October, with quiet prevailing along his lines, Butler
returned to Fort Monroe. There he hoped to observe the navy buildup and to
delve more deeply into his scientific inquiry. Soon after reaching Hampton
Roads, however, he was ordered to Washington for a confidential assignment.
Over the next two weeks he would be involved in a much different, but no
less interesting, experiment.

Within three weeks of the fall of Atlanta Butler had taken his own advice, heading toward home as the presidential election neared. On September 24 he wrote to a Union Party official, regretting his inability to speak at a New York City rally in behalf of the Lincoln-Johnson ticket but promising to strive militarily toward the same end. Shortly afterward he wrote to Lincoln's friend and former war secretary, Simon Cameron, and hinted that he would formally endorse the president's reelection; the letter was subsequently published on the front page of the *New York Herald.* Late in October, following Union Party successes in the early state races in Pennsylvania, Ohio, and Indiana (races that told Butler "Mr. Lincoln is already re-elected"), the commander of the Army of the James made official his unambiguous support of his commander in chief. In a letter to his old supporter, Henry J. Raymond, now chairman of the Union Party's executive committee, the general urged patriotic Americans to sustain the administration at all costs, an effort that "will go very far toward [ending] all contest in the field."[24]

The letter, which was circulated throughout the North via newspaper, did not escape White House notice. Concluding that Butler was again worthy of his good will, Lincoln decided to tap Butler's administrative ability and experience in military government for a difficult assignment that appeared tailored to his gifts.

While the government considered the war all but won, it feared a last-ditch effort by Rebel fifth-columnists, perhaps by subverting the electoral process. If the enemy could throw the presidential election into turmoil, its results might be invalidated. In that event, even if the South's candidate, George B. McClellan, failed at the polls, a politician more conciliatory than Lincoln might emerge as a compromise congressional choice.

Many of Lincoln's closest advisers, including Secretary of War Stanton, believed that Confederate officials had devised an elaborate and carefully coordinated plan to disrupt the election by terrorizing Northern cities. During the summer and early fall Confederate agents and their allies in the North had spread destruction and panic in sections of the East and North-west; by late October reports circulated that saboteurs were prepared to strike on a larger scale at election time. Rumored targets included Chicago, Cleveland, Boston, Philadelphia, and especially New York. Rioters in Manhattan were reportedly prepared to seize City Hall, the Treasury office on Wall Street, and other government and financial institutions. Copperhead policemen supposedly would raid their own headquarters and block attempts to suppress the outbreak. Other rioters would burn the courthouse and other federal buildings and free political prisoners from Forts Hamilton and Lafayette in the harbor. Assaults were planned against polling places by mobs under such disaffected soldiers as Fitz John Porter, John H. H. Ward, and Abram Duryee, each a staunch ally of McClellan.[25]

While discounting the more exaggerated tales of terror, the Lincoln administration was genuinely concerned about the electoral atmosphere in New York. Long a center of Democratic politics and for a time in 1860–61 full of secessionist sympathy, the city was ruled by a Tammany Hall "sachem," Mayor C. Godfrey Gunther, a supporter of the state's antiwar governor, Horatio Seymour. The commander of the state militia, Major General Charles W. Sandford, a Seymour appointee, was a vocal opponent of the administration's military policies, as were many of his subordinates. Given the atmosphere of rumor and suspicion, Gunther and Sandford could have been willing tools of Confederate agents.

Lincoln and his advisers believed that most of the militia and city police force would uphold the government in a crisis. Even so, they remembered the July 1863 draft riots, which had threatened briefly to bring the war to a halt. Recalling the feeble efforts of the city's Democratic officials to suppress the four days of violence and bloodletting, the White House decided that a man capable of maintaining law and order against all odds must govern Manhattan during the election. In view of his recent, if belated, attempts to seek the administration's forgiveness, Ben Butler qualified nicely for the job. He was called to Washington, where on November 2 he conferred with Lincoln and Stanton at the White House. When he learned the nature of his assignment, he was eager to take it on.[26]

As early as October 29 Stanton had telegraphed City Point, requesting that Grant detach an infantry brigade from the Army of the Potomac for peace-keeping duties in New York. Three days later, the secretary decided that even more regiments were needed. Butler was temporarily attached to Major General John Dix's Department of the East, his jurisdiction confined to "the troops in the Harbor and City of New York sent up from Virginia." Though he later chafed at this restriction, Butler accepted it readily enough, and late on November 1 he went by train from Washington to his new station.[27]

As he left the capital, Butler wired General Terry, who was commanding the army in his absence, to dispatch several infantry and artillery units to New York. Butler estimated that 5,000 troops, chosen for their reliability and past conduct, could quell a mob by their show of force. Thus, on the third and fourth, eight infantry regiments of the X Corps and four of the XVIII Corps left Virginia, with the initial contingent reaching Manhattan on November 6, one day behind the Army of the Potomac's complement.

Earlier, Butler had booked a floor at the Hoffman House, off Madison Square, where he established a telegraph link with police precincts and polling places. From his suite he conferred with General Dix, who shared Governor Seymour's and Mayor Gunther's skepticism over election day violence. Butler came away from the meeting concerned that Dix wished to restrict his jurisdiction to areas outside Manhattan. Thus he sought and received War Department assurance that he exercised authority over troops sent to the city "to meet existing emergencies."[28]

Over the next several days Butler and Dix planned how to dispose of these troops. At Dix's insistence and with War Office approval, Butler agreed to send 3,000 to upstate cities considered ripe for sabotage and mob violence. He dispatched the 11th and 14th U.S. Infantry to Buffalo, where they came under the authority of another general on special assignment, John J. Peck, once a district commander under Butler. Butler also sent part of the 12th Infantry to Peck while directing the balance of the regiment to Elmira, another scene of preelection unrest.

Butler then detached two of his own regiments, the 81st and 98th New York, to guard the Watervliet Arsenal near Albany, a likely target of conspirators seeking weapons. He stationed two other regiments beyond his authority by attaching them to Dix's headquarters at Fort Hamilton. These dispositions left 2,000 foot soldiers and cannoneers in New York City, a force that Dix (who wanted to avoid the impression that the army intended to overawe the electorate) considered more than ample for crisis duty.[29]

Butler was not so confident. Early on November 5 he issued General Order No. 1, in which he declared that the army sought only "to protect public property, to prevent and punish incursions into our borders [from Canada, long a theater of Confederate espionage], and to insure calm and quiet." As for claims that the soldiers would inhibit voters, "nothing could be further from the truth. . . . The armies of the United States are 'ministers of good and not of evil.' They are safeguards of constitutional liberty, which is freedom to do right, not wrong."[30]

More than a few New Yorkers interpreted Butler's admonition to "do right" as "to vote the Union Party ticket." Seymour, Gunther, Sandford, and other Democrats were incensed by what they regarded as a power play. They were particularly aroused by Butler's attempt to take charge of the militia, as well as the Federal troops, in the city. Sandford heatedly challenged Butler's authority to do so. So did his subordinate at Buffalo, Brigadier General John A. Green, Jr., who implied that he would use force to keep Butler from meddling in militia affairs. Butler bristled at such strong talk; when he heard a rumor that Green had quietly removed arms from the state arsenal, he asked Washington to help him bind the militia to his will. Although sharing some of Butler's concerns, Lincoln and Stanton directed him to avoid a constitutional confrontation.[31]

Butler was more circumspect in deploying the troops who remained in Manhattan. He stationed a few near polling places, police precincts, fire-houses, and government buildings. Most he consigned to less conspicuous positions aboard transports, ferries, revenue cutters, and tugs anchored along the Manhattan waterfront. From such locations, the temporary seamen could guard potential targets of rioters: banking houses, the stock exchange, the Treasury office, the Customs House, the telegraph cable to New Jersey, and slums such as "Mackerelville" and the Battery, home to the city's rowdiest elements.

Kept aboard cramped and poorly ventilated vessels for several days without sufficient heat, rations, or sanitary facilities, the troops from the Army of the James grew restive and surly. "We have never endured more hardships before the enemy," complained one regimental commander. Left to brood over their unhappy situation, many soldiers resolved to take out their discontent on any rioters they encountered. If sent into the streets against "the unruly element," a New Hampshireman decided, "there would be shooting to kill and lots of it."[32]

The soldiers had no opportunity to release such hostility. Despite rumors of violence, November 8 passed peacefully. Small disturbances common to any city on such an occasion broke out, when high spirits mingled with distilled spirits, but only once did Butler react to a "demonstration of disloyal character," and he had the navy attend to it. High Bridge, linking Manhattan to the Bronx, was rumored to be the target of an anti-Lincoln mob. Butler asked Admiral Hiram Paulding, commanding the Brooklyn Naval Yard, to send a gunboat up the Harlem River. Anchoring off the bridge, the warship trained its seven guns on the near shore, which remained quiet for the rest of the day.[33]

As the afternoon wore on, Manhattan held a placid expression; at one point, Butler telegraphed Washington from "the quietest city ever seen." Nor did large disturbances break out across the river or to the north. The wave of terror that had threatened the East and Northwest seeped away, leaving isolated eddies of disorder.[34]

Reports of New York's tranquility magnified the joy that swept the Lincoln camp by day's end. Published returns indicated that the metropolis had joined outstate districts (as well most cities, towns, and villages throughout the North) in reelecting Lincoln. Statewide, Lincoln squeaked out a 6,000-vote victory over McClellan. The local effects of the Republican triumph helped nudge Seymour, Lincoln's least favorite governor, out of office in favor of a staunch unionist, Reuben E. Fenton.

Butler's soldiers had done their part to keep Lincoln in the Executive Mansion, validating their commander's reputation for turning out the vote.

In none of the regiments that voted in the field did McClellan outpoll the president. In fact, in New York as well as in other Democratic strongholds, the soldiers' votes provided Lincoln with his margin of victory. To widen the margin as much as possible, Butler ensured that the New Yorkers in his expeditionary force delivered their ballots to state election agents. To circumvent a law that prohibited a New Yorker from voting if he was in the state on election day but not in his local district, Butler sent ships filled with upstate regiments to vote in New Jersey when their presence was not required elsewhere.[35]

For all these efforts, Butler received numerous letters, telegrams, and personal expressions of gratitude. Thanks came from the White House and Congress, state officials, and hundreds of private individuals. Applauding the calming effect of his unobtrusive yet ubiquitous presence in the city, New York newspapers touted Butler for political office; a prevalent rumor, probably started by some enterprising editor, was that the general would soon succeed Stanton. On November 14, the day most of Butler's troops left the city for Virginia, civic leaders threw a banquet for him at the Fifth Avenue Hotel. One of the many guests, the Reverend Henry Ward Beecher, proposed him for the presidency in 1868.[36]

What, specifically, had Butler and his men accomplished? They may have preempted outbreaks of civil disobedience. Credible reports supported the government's belief that potentially violent antiwar and anti-Union demonstrations had been planned for election day, although it is doubtful that any such disturbances would have posed insurmountable problems for the Metropolitan Police. The presence of troops did, in fact, postpone a major campaign to terrorize the city. A small but active band of Confederate saboteurs had planned to spread panic throughout the city on the eighth. Unknown to Butler, the enemy agents had occupied rooms one floor above him at his hotel.

Surrounded by soldiers, the saboteurs deferred their effort until two weeks after Butler left the city. On November 25, too late to cow would-be voters, the Rebels doused strategic districts of lower Manhattan with an incendiary liquid called Greek Fire, inflicting more than half a million dollars' worth of damage and earning worldwide publicity. Before the police could sniff out their trail, the agents fled to Canada.[37]

To a certain extent, the presence of the Army of the James in New York served a less tangible purpose. As representatives of armies opposing rebellion from the Atlantic coast to the Trans-Mississippi, they had reminded the hectic, business-as-usual Northerners of the war's reality. The soldiers had likewise alerted voters to the presence of terrorists and fifth columnists who hoped, by subverting the electoral process, to gain a victory denied them in combat.

Thus, Butler and his troops may have helped influence the electorate to settle the issue not at the bargaining table but on the battlefield.

—➤●◄—

After a stopover in Washington on the way south, Butler reached Bermuda Hundred on the seventeenth, four days after the return of the Army of the James's contingent from New York. The next morning he returned to the front and relieved Alfred Terry.

He had arrived in time to supervise the retaking of a sector of the peninsula defenses. At eight o'clock the previous evening, two of Pickett's brigades had assailed the center of the line, converging on two salients, Batteries Carpenter and Dutton, which had none of the natural cover of the other defenses. Gaining footholds in front of both forts, the attackers took more than 100 prisoners, many of them raw recruits but also some of the veteran 12th New Hampshire. "The few that escaped," claimed one attacker, left behind "guns, haversacks, overcoats, blankets, oil-cloths, & etc. They might have inflicted considerable injury on us if they had stood manfully in their rifle pits . . . but they seemed to be perfectly confused and panic stricken."[38]

Alarmed by the weakness of the salients and the lack of Union tenacity, Butler promptly counterattacked. Under a covering fire from batteries all along the line, the Federals slowly evicted the enemy. By midday every square yard of ground lost to Pickett had been recovered.

One result of this minor disaster was Butler's decision to expedite long-term efforts to bolster his army with veteran black troops. Many who had fled from Pickett's evening attack were members of large but inexperienced ninety-day regiments from Pennsylvania, recently arrived at Bermuda Hundred and grouped with the New Hampshiremen into a provisional brigade under Colonel (later Brigadier General) Joseph H. Potter. Aware that many months of training were needed to bring the Pennsylvanians up to par with the rest of his command, Butler offered to trade them to Meade in exchange for an equal number of black troops.

Although a bit surprised, Grant agreed almost at once. Within a week the Pennsylvanians had been replaced at Bermuda Hundred with the entire complement of blacks from the Army of the Potomac. To enhance racial pride and military cohesiveness, Butler combined the newly arrived troops with the black soldiers he had commanded for the past year; the result was the XXV Corps, the only army corps in American history to be composed solely of African-American regiments. To command, he selected his old protégé, Godfrey Weitzel, overriding Weitzel's concern that he was being advanced beyond his ability. To lead the army's white units, now known as the XXIV Corps, Butler went with the obvious choice, Edward Ord. The move pleased Ord, who disliked and mistrusted black troops and doubtless was glad to be rid of them.[39]

The Rebel attack of November 17 was the last sustained action of the year along the army's front on either side of the James. On the twenty-third the first snow fell. The numbing temperatures appeared to signal a lengthy stretch in winter quarters for Federals and Confederates alike.

Quarters were mostly bleak and cheerless, although the unexpected arrival of good things from home temporarily relieved the gloom. Thanksgiving Day, November 24, saw little respite from normal military activity, but the following day—twenty-four hours late but in plenty of time to delight the recipients—holiday delicacies from soldiers' benefit societies across the North inundated the Army of the James. For two days the troops feasted on great amounts of turkey, goose, capon, duck, mince pie, cake, fruit salad, and preserves. The fare, much of it prepared at Delmonico's Restaurant in New York, was such that after eating, a New York veteran readjusted his belt and wrote to his brother that "we have been living like fighting cocks." A comrade from New Hampshire observed solemnly that "the men appreciated the donation, and did it ample justice."[40]

The holiday atmosphere did not endure. On the day that Butler's army gorged itself, Grant, who had taken leave to visit his family in New Jersey and to confer with superiors in Washington, returned to the front with a plan of campaign. A reporter covering the army soon found a "note of warlike preparation . . . everywhere" along the lines. The activity turned out to be the by-product of a recent decision by Grant, Stanton, and Welles to resume preparations to attack Wilmington. The many ideas Butler had concocted for operating against Fort Fisher were going to be tested during one of the most ambitious amphibious operations in American history.[41]

CHAPTER THIRTEEN

Closing the Last Door

BY THE END OF NOVEMBER BUTLER WAS SPENDING AN INCREASING amount of time planning how to blast his way inside Fort Fisher. During his recent visits to Washington he had outlined his pet project to officials of the War and Navy Departments as well as to Lincoln. At first, neither the president nor his service secretaries indicated much enthusiasm, though Welles had reached the point where he would consider virtually any scheme that would expedite an army-navy effort against Wilmington. At Welles's initiative, engineering and ordnance experts convened in the capital to study Butler's proposal for a powder-laden vessel to be launched against Fort Fisher.

Their findings did not bode well for the project. Brigadier General Richard Delafield, chief of the army's engineer corps, opined that a powder boat, even if grounded within a few hundred yards of the earthwork, would achieve "no useful result." Major James G. Benton of the Washington Arsenal considered any attempt to launch such a boat under the fort's guns too chancy to be worth the investment in resources, manpower, and time.[1]

The project might have died were it not for Assistant Navy Secretary Gustavus Vasa Fox, a forceful New Englander who had been a schoolmate of Butler's. Fox, who had authority over the advisory panel, rejected its findings, reconvened the body, and persuaded its members to approve the outfitting of a powder boat. By the time Fox was through, even the crotchety Delafield was seeking permission to observe what he now called an "interesting and important operation." Before November was out Welles and Stanton also went on record in support of the mission.[2]

If Fox sold Butler's plan to the government, Admiral Porter brought it to fruition. Despite his later avowals that he never seriously expected the venture to succeed, from the day he learned that Welles had approved it Porter supported it enthusiastically. By early December the squadron commander had procured the 295-ton steamer *Louisiana,* a mail packet on the Fort Monroe–Norfolk run that had sunk three weeks earlier but had been raised intact. Aboard this seaworthy but expendable vessel the Navy Department agreed to pack 150 tons of powder, an amount the army promised to match. In the end, however, only 215 tons were hauled aboard her, packed in barrels throughout the ship.

The powder was to be detonated by a Gomez fuse, a rubber tube lined with fulminating powder capable of burning so rapidly that one mile of tubing could be ignited in four seconds flat. Dozens of Gomez fuses, which Porter likened to "a huge tape-worm [running] through piles of powder-bags," would ensure that the ship's contents would explode at virtually the same instant. Sparks to ignite the fuses would come from three musket tubes fitted with percussion caps, the caps to be crushed by a grapeshot dropped from a trigger arm activated by a clockwork mechanism.[3]

Porter's enthusiasm for Butler's plan joined the officers in an association that, had it endured, would have facilitated the mission. The pair had clashed over various issues during their joint participation in the New Orleans expedition; more recently, attempts by Porter's subordinates to interfere in the possibly illicit trade conducted by friends of Butler had caused friction between the officers. Now Porter was agreeably surprised to find that Butler appeared to have "learned the courtesies due from one service to the other, and I never anticipated having any difficulty with him in the future."[4]

As preparations intensified in December, however, the new relationship threatened to come apart. The admiral began to chafe at the general's penchant for secrecy. Porter also began to ridicule Butler's relish for technology. When the Yankee tinkerer hinted that the powder boat was only one trick he might play on the defenders of Wilmington, Porter suggested to his officers that Butler "intends to introduce rattlesnakes into Fort Fisher on the sly." He used the same disparagement to curry favor with Grant, whom Porter knew to think little of the powder boat. Before long Porter was trying to undercut Butler's role in the operation. The admiral informed Grant that Butler would probably outmaneuver Weitzel and take command of the expedition, a power play that might lead to disaster. Porter did not think much of Weitzel (his opinion dated from the New Orleans campaign, when Porter came to view his army colleague as weak-kneed and incompetent), but at least Weitzel was a professional soldier with extensive field experience. Butler was not.[5]

Porter's concern about Butler leading the expedition was validated on December 6, with the powder vessel nearly outfitted and 6,500 soldiers poised to board transports anchored off Bermuda Hundred. On that day Grant issued orders intended for Weitzel, which Butler, as Weitzel's superior, withheld. In fact, Butler never informed Weitzel that he was Grant's choice to command the expedition. Butler appeared late on the sixth at City Point to announce that he would accompany the troops to Wilmington. Grant was astonished but did not forbid him to go; he felt he could not do so without committing "a moral affront." Grant later informed Stanton that "I never dreamed of Butler going," but since "the operations [were] taking place within the geographical limits of his department," Butler had a right to command.[6]

While Butler's announcement may have strained his relations with Grant, the major general's relationship with Porter deteriorated to the point that the two could not even agree on a launching date. Since late November Grant had been advising both to proceed as soon as possible, taking advantage of Braxton Bragg's transfer of troops from Wilmington to Savannah, Georgia, where William T. Sherman's armies were heading. By the first week in December Grant explained that "Sherman may now be expected to strike the sea coast any day, leaving Bragg free to return [to Wilmington]. I think it advisable for you to notify Admiral Porter and get off . . . with or without your powder boat."[7]

Butler would never have left the boat behind, but the delay was not so much his fault as it was Porter's and Grant's. On December 7 there finally were enough transports at Bermuda Hundred to permit Butler's troops to board. That day Grant ordered Butler to load additional entrenching tools (if the army could not take Fort Fisher by storm, it was to lay siege to it), adding to the delay. Even when the implements were on board and Butler's vessels sailed to Fort Monroe, Porter was still loading his wooden warships and examining the seaworthiness of his ironclads. Despite repeated inquiries from Butler, Porter could not say when he would be ready to sail.

On the morning of December 10 Butler prepared to leave Fort Monroe with or without the navy, when a gale struck Hampton Roads, trapping the transports in the anchorage. For two days it rained and blew, making life miserable for the landlubbers packed aboard the swaying, bobbing vessels. Not until early on the twelfth did the weather abate, just in time for an eleventh-hour complication to delay the embarkation further. Finally ready to sail, Porter asked Butler to remain in port for thirty-six hours to give his warships and the powder boat time to recoal at Beaufort, North Carolina. According to the admiral, Butler agreed to the arrangement because he too wanted to resupply at Beaufort; the ten days of rations issued to his troops on the seventh would run out long before they reached Wilmington. Butler forever maintained, however, that Porter insisted on an army-navy rendezvous not at Beaufort—where Butler had no intention of going—but at a point twenty-five miles off Fort Fisher, far enough to sea to spare the armada any damage when the powder boat was detonated. Butler claimed he agreed to meet Porter at that point after grouping his transports at Masonboro Inlet. As one participant later put it, "The two arms of the service were at sixes and sevens on the eve of battle."[8]

While neither commander accepted blame for the mix-up, both appear to have been at fault. After the mission Porter acknowledged having told Butler that his wooden warships would take station twenty-five miles off Fort Fisher, though he insisted Butler knew that Porter, his ironclads, and the powder boat would first resupply at Beaufort. Butler later confessed that Porter told him he was heading for the supply base, but the general seems to have gotten the impression that the stopover would be only a few hours and that the fleet would reach Fort Fisher before the army.[9]

The greater fault may have been Butler's. As commander of the landing that the navy must support, he bore primary responsibility for keeping communication open. Butler's assertions to the contrary notwithstanding, no evidence indicates that he so much as informed Porter of the route he intended to take to North Carolina. For his part, Porter provided the army leader with maps of his course as well as copies of his predeparture orders to his fleet.

Inexcusably poor communication persisted up to December 13, when the army and navy got under way at last. Porter informed Butler early that afternoon that he would sail in a few hours. Without replying, Butler steamed out of Hampton Roads at about 3:00 P.M., before the navy could start. Concerned that the long delay had alerted enemy observers, the general took his transports on a feint up Chesapeake Bay, then sixty miles along the Potomac River to Matthias Point. The diversion fooled not only the enemy but also his own soldiers, who believed they were bound for a winter campaign in the Shenandoah Valley, and Butler's naval friends as well. By the time the troopships returned to Hampton Roads on the morning of the fourteenth, Porter's sixty-nine-ship fleet was long gone. The navy was en route to Beaufort, its commodore believing he was trailing the army rather than preceding it. Here was a bizarre beginning to a costly, labor-intensive, and strategically important campaign.[10]

⇒●⇐

Thanks to a calm sea and mild weather, Butler's trip down the coast from Cape Henry was rapid and uneventful. The flotilla's progress left the general in an unusually lofty mood, considering that the expedition boded fair to make or break his career.

He remained confident that he had the advantage of surprise; he felt certain his run up the Potomac had fooled the enemy. Beyond that, he had implicit faith in the powder boat, which also would be helped by the element of surprise. Not even his lack of contact with the navy dampened his spirits; he believed he had made his intentions known to Porter, whom he expected to find waiting for him off Fort Fisher.

His confidence was only slightly shaken the following afternoon when his transports reached Masonboro Inlet, where they were to group before descending the coast to Wilmington. While the large, clumsy vessels maneuvered toward the rendezvous, Butler in his swift flagship, the *Ben DeFord,* churned southward until he reached the station of the blockading squadron off Wilmington. In response to Butler's inquiry, the squadron commander reported no sign of Porter. A mildly concerned Butler returned to his troopships and led some of them to the point, twenty-five miles out to sea, where he expected to meet the admiral. There he found only a few of Porter's larger vessels. The captain of one warship told Butler that as far as he knew, Porter was at Beaufort.[11]

Not knowing what else to do, Butler marked time and, on the fifteenth sailed about in lazy circles in weather he described as "never more zephyr-like." The next day, with no sign of Porter, he sent Weitzel and Colonel Cyrus B. Comstock, an engineer who was Grant's representative on the mission, to reconnoiter New Inlet. Twenty-four hours later, Butler had the pair repeat the errand with General Ames, who would command the landing force. By the eighteenth, with Porter and most of his fleet still absent, Butler's placid mood began to fade along with the good weather and the advantage of surprise. Where was the navy?

Butler's volatile attitude mirrored that of his troops. The first couple of days at anchor passed quickly and pleasantly. By day the men amused themselves by improvising fishing tackle and hauling up codfish (which they called "Lincoln trout") and herring ("Lincoln sardines"). By night they enjoyed music and dancing. "We have a violin," a New Yorker wrote his family, "good singers and contrabands [runaway slaves] without number whose performances in the Terpsichorean line will make you laugh yourself into an apoplexy."[12]

By the third day out the soldiers had grown more than a little restive. Accommodations were cramped, food and water were running low, and fishing had lost its appeal. On the seventeenth a black sergeant complained: "When will this tiresome floating about end[?] Here we are kept without one thing to relieve the monotony & sameness." One of his officers reflected that "either we are not to land here or the expedition is commanded by a lunatic."[13]

Some of Butler's subordinates wondered whether they could land at all. Aboard the *Herman Livingston,* General Paine noted on the eighteenth, "We are lying . . . out of sight of land, but we have drifted once or twice at night in sight of shore, so I presume the rebs know we are here." If incautious seamanship imperiled military secrecy, so did news reports of the expedition. As early as December 16 the *New York Times* leaked some facts about the mission. The following day the *Herald* provided vital details, including the destination. By the nineteenth papers in several Eastern cities were printing full accounts of the campaign and disclosing, among other things, the names of Porter's vessels, the number of guns they mounted, and the admiral's sailing orders.

When the stories broke Grant railed at the "impudence of the public press," which had forced cancellation of earlier efforts against Wilmington. An equally furious Stanton launched an investigation that implicated a number of journalists, several of whom were jailed and tried by military tribunal. By then the damage was done. On December 21 Richmond newspapers were reprinting the Northern accounts and General Lee was forwarding them to Wilmington. In response he detached the North Carolinians of Robert F. Hoke and sent them to the targeted city. Reaching Sugar Loaf by train on the twenty-second, Hoke added his 6,500 men to the few thousand troops under Bragg, many of whom, in confirmation of Grant's fears, had recently returned to North Carolina following their failure to waylay Sherman.[14]

Although unaware of this chain of events, Butler was in a black mood when, late on December 20, Porter's ironclads and the bulk of his wooden ships appeared off Fort Fisher. Porter's excuses—insurmountable delays in resupplying the fleet, bad weather at Beaufort, the need to rearrange the disordered cargo of the powder boat, and the time needed to disguise the boat to resemble a blockade runner—appeared to mollify the general. Butler turned angry, however, when he learned that Porter had directed Commander A. C. Rhind, in charge of the *Louisiana,* to set the clocks and fuses and place the vessel in position to be detonated. This unilateral action suggested that the navy meant to steal credit for the weapon's success. Moreover, the surf was rising, heralding bad weather. A storm would prevent troops from landing quickly enough to exploit the effects of the powder boat. A furious Butler demanded that the *Louisiana* be recalled; Porter reluctantly agreed.[15]

The impending storm, added to the depletion of his food and water, forced Butler to postpone the landing indefinitely. At Porter's suggestion, he directed the troopships to head for Beaufort, there to ride out the weather. The navy, whose crews were used to rough seas, would hold its station until Butler's return. Leaving behind Ames's flagship, the *Baltic*, which alone had enough fuel and provisions to remain off Wilmington, Butler led the rest of his fleet to the comparative safety of the Union-occupied port. They arrived just before the storm reached full fury.[16]

The gale lashed the Carolina coast for three days. Porter's warships, although stabilized by long anchors, bobbed crazily. The troopships at Beaufort had almost as rough a time, rolling, pitching, and shuddering as breakers crashed against them. Once numbed by boredom, the passengers were now overcome by terror. Those who did not pray for salvation, as one passenger wrote, heaped "curses and invectives bitter and long" on the officers responsible for their plight. Above and below decks, pandemonium ruled. A soldier on the *General Lyon* described his ship as "swerving upward as the billow struck her bows, her deck . . . dangerously inclined." He added, with bitter amusement, that "the unfamiliar infantry lost its legs at every bound, clinging to stanchions and ropes'-ends for dear life." He found disheveled troops down in the hold as well as "knapsacks, muskets, blankets, and the seasick, praying negro-soldiers, all rolling together in a wild mixture." Aboard the *Weybosset,* officers' horses broke free and "floundered together amid the rubbish, from one side of the vessel to another, mangling and mutilating each other most frightfully." Many animals had to be shot and thrown overboard.[17]

By the twenty-second the storm had abated without loss of human life. Quartermaster personnel, still unsteady on their feet, began to take on rations and equipment. Coal barges refueled the transports while fresh water was run in by rail from a depot fifteen miles away. The work was completed late on the twenty-third, whereupon the vessels weighed anchor for Fort Fisher.

By then many of those crammed into the ships' holds had little stomach for risking their lives on the beaches. One noncommissioned officer whose letters home had been notable for their restraint vented his anger and frustration: "Day after day we have been tossed drearily on the waves off the bleak coast, out of sight of land, living on raw pork and hardtack, and crowded almost without breathing room into [this] filthy old transport. . . . Had our soldiers been so roughly treated by the rebels, there would be no end to cries of 'shame' and the accusation of 'barbarity' from the enlightened press. Probably a more mismanaged expedition never left our ports."[18]

The extent of the mismanagement was yet to be revealed. That evening Butler sent one of his aides on ahead to the rendezvous to inform Porter that the army would arrive the next day, the twenty-fourth, ready to land on Confederate Point on Christmas morning. The following morning, before Butler could leave Beaufort at the head of his fleet, the staff officer returned with word that Porter had sent the powder boat into action. Enraged, Butler started for Porter's new station, twelve miles off New Inlet, as fast as the *Ben DeFord* could travel.

Later the admiral defended his actions by claiming an understanding with Butler that "I should select the first good night, where the beach was favorable for [a] landing." In fact, no understanding had been reached. Porter also tried to excuse himself on the grounds that Ames and his 1,200 soldiers remained with the navy—plenty of men to exploit the powder boat's impact. With Butler and most of the other troops miles away, however, this excuse rings hollow. It seems evident, as Butler claimed, that Porter intended to upstage the landlubbers and reap what benefits he could from the *Louisiana.*

In the end, neither army nor navy profited from the powder boat, which proved a pitiful failure. Towed in toward shore just shy of midnight on December 23, she hove to within sight of Fort Fisher's signal beacons. At that point Commander Rhind activated the clocks and implemented several backup procedures, even starting a fire below deck. He then maneuvered the burning ship toward the fort's dim outline. Once the *Louisiana* moved off under steam, Rhind rowed furiously toward her escort ship, the *Wilderness,* which in minutes carried him beyond danger.

According to Rhind's calculations, the powder boat got within 300 yards of the northwest angle of the fort before grounding on a shoal. When one adds the 300 yards that separated the shore and the fort, the vessel lay too far away to do maximum damage. Furthermore, the cargo did not detonate as planned. The clocks should have touched off the powder at 1:20 A.M., but twenty minutes passed before it exploded; by then, the boat was engulfed in flames. Nor did the powder go up all at once. One observer recorded, "A huge column of fire rushed straight upward, four loud explosions followed at intervals of about half a second, and all was darkness." Watching from the deck of the *Wilderness,* Rhind exclaimed, "There's a fizzle!"[19]

Once it became obvious that the blast had not even singed the grass along the sea face of Fort Fisher, the navy tried to distance itself from the fiasco. Porter and his officers declared they had always doubted the practicality of the experiment, which only "quasi-scientific" men had expected to succeed. But one of Porter's subordinates later admitted, "We all believed in it, from the admiral down; but when it proved so laughable a failure we . . . laid its paternity upon General Butler."[20]

Butler would have none of it. Then and thereafter, he asserted that the seamen who had outfitted and positioned the craft had botched the job. He doubted that the trigger mechanism had been activated, that enough powder had been stored above the waterline to prevent the surf from muffling the blast, and that the fire had been started in the proper place. Later Rhind acknowledged that because the Gomez fuses had been improperly placed, they failed to reach the mass of powder below deck, preventing an instantaneous explosion. Butler rightly identified another failure: Rhind's inability to ground the *Louisiana* close enough to land, where the explosion might have shaken the earth under the fort.[21]

Even after considering every possible factor in the "fizzle," neither army nor navy could understand how the effects had been so slight. Weeks later, when interviewing captured members of Fort Fisher's garrison, Union officers sought to determine what had gone wrong. The defenders, they learned, could not even identify the source of the explosion and believed it to be the result of a blockade runner or signal gun blowing up. Incredulous interrogators pressed one callow Confederate: had not the effect of the detonation been severe? "Oh, yes, it was *very severe,*" the youngster exclaimed. "It woke up everybody in the fort!"[22]

———————

What followed the powder boat's failure smacked of anticlimax and clumsy improvisation. Butler appears to have counted so much on the experiment's effectiveness that when a reconnaissance revealed the fort to be intact, he went about the rest of his mission as though resigned to defeat.

The navy, however, bent all efforts to do its part. At 11:30 A.M. on the twenty-fourth, nearly five hours before Butler and Porter met again, the warships, arranged in two lines, began to pound away at Fort Fisher. When firing stopped at half past five, Porter declared that the earthwork had been beaten down, its guns dismounted, its works dismantled, and its garrison demoralized beyond restoration. The admiral claimed that Butler's people could have captured the place without breaking a sweat.

Butler stoutly maintained that there was a vast difference between "a silent fort and a silenced one." It was true that Colonel Lamb's cannon had returned fire only intermittently and that the fort's sea face was torn up. But the general doubted that the fort was his for the taking, and rightly so.[23]

The Confederates had held off in order to save their ammunition until the Yankees landed. The garrison realized what Porter did not: at best, the warships—the nearest of which lay almost a mile from the garrison—could inflict only superficial damage from such distance. Lamb estimated that at least a third of the shells had fallen into the Cape Fear River or surrounding marshes. Far from being terrorized, the Rebels stayed snug in their bombproofs until after the barrage, ready to emerge when the land attack began.

Following the bombardment, Butler sent Weitzel and Comstock to confer with Porter aboard the *Malvern*. They worked out plans for a Christmas afternoon landing north of the fort. Porter agreed to furnish 150 landing craft and 200 crewmen to support the operation, whose success he continued to regard as assured. At 7:00 A.M. on the twenty-fifth many of his warships resumed the shelling, hoping to prevent the garrison (now under the direct command of General Whiting) from repairing any damage. The five-hour barrage strengthened Porter's conviction that the fort was defenseless and may already have been evacuated. He boasted to Butler, "There is not a Rebel within five miles of the fort."[24]

The landing called for Weitzel to place a 500-man force from Ames's division on the beach near the Half-Moon and Flag-Pond Batteries. According to Butler, Weitzel was to "ascertain its true condition . . . so that if it were found practicable to assault all the troops could be landed." To support this endeavor, Weitzel asked Admiral Porter to send a section of his flotilla into New Inlet below the fort and neutralize a fleet of Rebel gunboats reportedly prowling the Cape Fear. Porter demurred, citing a shortage of light-draught ships as well as the presence of mines in New Inlet. Butler would later charge that the admiral could have carried out the mission and that the mines were imaginary. In the end, Porter's unwillingness to run the inlet (which Welles had urged him to do) did not hinder the troop landing, for the enemy gunboats offered no opposition. Still, the maneuver would have brought Porter's vessels closer to the fort and made their shelling more accurate.[25]

Shortly before noon Captain Oliver S. Glisson, commanding the eighteen ships in Porter's first line of attack, informed the *Malvern* that the detached forts north of the main earthwork had been silenced; the single twenty-pounder in the Half-Moon Battery had burst in an effort to maintain counterfire. Minutes after this news went out to the army, landing craft carrying Weitzel and 500 members of Newton Curtis's brigade cast off under a covering fire from Glisson's gunboats. Although the surf was rough, the boats promptly reached shore about a half mile above the silenced batteries. Shaking out a skirmish line, Weitzel moved south, slowly and cautiously.

The Flag-Pond Battery proved to be an easy prize. Demoralized by Porter's shelling, its sixty-seven defenders raised a surrender flag while Curtis's men were several hundred yards off. Before the army could get to them, a landing party from one of Glisson's gunboats rushed up the beach and captured the entire force. Again, the navy appeared determined to seize whatever glory it could.[26]

Curtis's troops, seeking a prize of their own, advanced along the beach toward the Half-Moon Battery. Before reaching it the 117th New York captured a Confederate major who turned out to be the battery's commander. Prodding the officer, hands above his head, toward his fieldwork, the Federals bagged his command without firing a shot. In minutes seven officers and 218 enlisted members of the 3rd North Carolina Junior Reserves—teenagers below the normal enlistment age—were marching dejectedly toward their captors' rowboats.

From the Half-Moon Battery, Weitzel and Curtis advanced gingerly toward Fort Fisher. The garrison offered no resistance, although several soldiers fell victim to overshots by Porter's gunboats. Despite this hazard, by late afternoon the Federals were within fifty yards of the land face. As darkness came the commanders scanned the deserted parapets of the earthwork. While they mulled over their next moves, one of Curtis's more impetuous officers, Lieutenant William H. Walling of the 142nd New York, dashed from behind a dune, braved the minefield, crawled through a hole cut in the palisade by a naval shell, and snatched up a Confederate flag that had been shot off the parapet. The feat would win the young subaltern a Medal of Honor.[27]

Observing Walling's easy entry into the fort, Curtis concluded that an assault could succeed. He relayed his opinion to Ames, who toward sunset landed on Confederate Point with the advance of his 2,300-man force. Impressed by his subordinate's assessment, Ames readied a full-scale attack—only to be overruled by Weitzel. Having examined Fort Fisher's intact parapets, bastions, and traverses, Weitzel disagreed with Curtis. Despite Porter's shelling, seventeen guns apparently remained in operating condition along the land face alone. Thus Weitzel hustled back to the landing site, where he found Butler maneuvering toward shore aboard an army gunboat. He rowed out and informed his superior that "it would be murder to order an attack on that work with that force." Believing Confederate Point impregnable, Weitzel urged an immediate withdrawal. Later he claimed he would have suppressed that suggestion had he known of Grant's prohibition against retreating once a landing had been made.[28]

Distressed by Weitzel's observations and advice, Butler made a hurried reconnaissance of the fort. Observing no substantial damage to the earthwork and having learned from Curtis's captives that Hoke's division had reinforced Sugar Loaf within rifle range of the Union rear, Butler suspended the offensive and ordered everyone to return to sea. Against the strident objections of Curtis and the milder protests of Ames, the reembarkation commenced at once.

Conducted by early evening in an extremely rough surf, the withdrawal was not only hazardous but deadly. Waves capsized several of the smaller craft, drowning two Federals and one of their prisoners. After an hour or so, the ocean grew so turbulent that no more boats could be launched. The 800 or so troops still on the beach were forced to remain there, huddling under Fort Fisher's guns, throughout the night. Alert to their plight, Porter's warships kept up such fire that the garrison could not come out to capture the stranded men. Because the sea remained high and rough for three days, the last unfortunate was not removed from the beach until midafternoon of the twenty-eighth.[29]

Porter could not understand why the army had aborted its offensive. According to Porter, Butler informed him the next morning that his orders from Grant had not contemplated a siege and thus left him free to withdraw if, in Butler's judgment, an attack was not practical. The admiral reacted with disgust, especially after learning that Butler was preparing to return to Virginia while hundreds of his men remained stranded. Porter vowed to remain on station, maintaining an intermittent fire, until further notice from the Navy Department. As Butler departed for home, the admiral fired a parting shot: "I wish some more of your gallant fellows had followed the officer who took the flag from the parapet. . . . I think they would have found it an easier conquest than is supposed."[30]

Ignoring the jeers, most of Butler's transports were under way by 2:00 P.M. on the twenty-sixth, and at eight o'clock the following evening they docked at Fort Monroe. Butler immediately wired news of his return, informing City Point that against heavy odds, he had done his best to accomplish his mission, only to be defeated by bad weather, a treacherous sea, and inaccurate naval gunnery. He played up his many captives and played down his casualties, most of which he attributed to Porter's errant shelling.

Though doubtless disappointed, Grant did not immediately respond. A week later he went to Fort Monroe for a conference. Butler may have told him on this occasion what he later imparted to a government panel investigating the expedition: although his orders appeared to compel him to besiege the fort if unable to capture it, the proximity of Bragg and Hoke rendered that course impossible. Furthermore, Grant's instructions required him to dig in only "if I had effected a landing." A landing, however, "required something more than to land 2,500 men, out of six thousand five hundred, on a beach with nothing but forty rounds in their cartridge-boxes, and where their supplies would be driven off [by] the first storm."[31]

Butler's dogged search for loopholes appears to have forestalled any disapproval Grant might have been tempted to lodge at that time. Butler later claimed that the lieutenant general "never made any criticisms of any description to me except upon the action of the navy." This may have been true, for Grant realized that many of the delays in launching the expedition, which had permitted Bragg's reinforcement, had been Porter's fault. Grant's emmissary, Colonel Comstock, blamed Porter for other sins, including misuse of the powder boat. For a time, the prevailing view at army head-quarters, as General Rawlins wrote to his wife, was that "the tardiness of the navy" had scuttled the expedition.[32]

Naturally, when Butler's version of events made the newspapers, Porter objected. In fact, even before criticism of the navy began to circulate, the admiral opened fire. He informed Welles on the twenty-ninth that his fleet remained off Fort Fisher, which "is ours at any moment when we can get a moderate and proper kind of force to go into the works. . . . I feel ashamed that men calling themselves soldiers should have left this place so inglori-ously." He professed to have become inured to disappointing campaigns "where so many incompetent men in the Army are placed in charge of important trusts." The admiral inserted these same criticisms, in less heated language, into his campaign report, which was published in its entirety in the December 30 *New York Herald*.[33]

After studying Porter's report and upon learning that Welles vouched for the admiral, Grant appears to have changed his mind, at least to a degree, about where the blame should rest. By then, too, he had discovered that Butler's critics were not confined to the navy. Soon after returning to Virginia, a furious Colonel Curtis had sought out Grant to complain of Butler's crim-inal blundering on Christmas Day. The brigade commander buttressed his charges with testimony from several subordinates, including Lieutenant Walling. Grant was also influenced by news accounts that appeared during the first half of January. Written by reporters who had accompanied the expedi-tion, many of the stories criticized Butler for turning tail and running.

The views of other critics never came to Grant's attention. One USCT enlisted man pronounced himself and his comrades "grievously disgruntled" over the retreat and the man who had ordered it. A white sergeant wrote his brother that "curses enough have been heaped on Butler's head to sink him in the deepest hold of the bottomless pit. . . . Everybody is disgusted. Officers and men expressed that the fort was ours and that no one but Butler prevented them from taking it. . . . The officers raved and the men swore, but back they had to come."[34]

Public discontent spread quickly. Butler's political foes began to fill legislative chambers and Congress with cries for his removal or court-martial. On the last day of the year Welles reported that everyone he met in Washington considered Butler to be incompetent, cowardly, or both. As 1865 dawned the rank and file of the Army of the James believed their commander was on the way out.[35]

The reaction against Butler appears unwarranted. Despite the accusations of Porter, Curtis, and others who had considered Fort Fisher to be silenced, it had not been pounded into submission. All but two of the cannon along the land face remained operable, and despite the mangled palisade, most of the earthworks were intact. The navy's cannonade had inflicted only 38 casualties among the garrison. "A few guns, a few carriages, a patching up of sods," a Confederate officer wrote after the abortive assault, "and Fort Fisher will not show signs that it was attacked." In February Butler elicited testimony of this sort from General Whiting, then lying mortally wounded in a Federal prison. After Porter's bombardment, Whiting stated, the fort remained "very strong, the garrison in good spirits and ready." The fire it might have directed against any attackers would have been heavy.[36]

The navy was primarily to blame. Porter had failed to bring the full weight of his firepower to bear on the fort. During his Christmas Day bombardment he had not employed every warship, and many of those he did use fired smaller, less destructive rounds than their guns could handle. Many shells were timed to explode in the air instead of after lodging in the walls or floor of the fort, so they did minimal damage to parapets, traverses, and bombproofs. Porter's greatest failing was stationing his gunboats so far from the sea face that they could neither obtain optimum range nor closely support the movements of the army.[37]

These facts were unknown to, or ignored by, those who howled for Butler's scalp. By early January public pressure was leading Lincoln, Stanton, Welles, and Grant to a common realization: Butler must go. On the fourth Grant asked Stanton to endorse his decision to relieve Butler from command. "I do this with reluctance," the commanding general said, "but the good of the service requires it." Two days later Stanton arrived at Fort Monroe for a strategy session, during which he approved Grant's course, adding that Butler ought not to be reassigned to active duty.[38]

Butler, back at his headquarters at Bermuda Hundred, was handed the unhappy but not unexpected notice by Colonel Babcock of Grant's staff at noon on January 6. He was instructed to turn over command to Ord and to return to Massachusetts to await orders. With his customary dispatch and thoroughness, Butler disseminated the news of his dismissal, bade farewell to his staff, and briefed Ord on the army's condition.[39]

The news elicited predictable responses. The *New York Tribune*, ever his staunch supporter, declared him the scapegoat for the mistakes of Grant and Porter, though he remained "the ablest and least understood man that the war has brought forward." Long-critical journals such as the *New York World* portrayed Butler as flagrantly incompetent and richly deserving of his fate. More objective eulogists portrayed him as a man of many strengths and outsize flaws, like a tragic character in Greek drama. The common soldiers were similarly divided, though many felt that with the final campaign almost at hand, such a change was probably for the best.[40]

Before most of the postmortems were in, Butler delivered a farewell address to his troops ("To have commanded such an army is glory. No one could yield it without regret"), and then he was gone. Fully a week earlier, however, he had added an exclamation point to his military career.

To assuage the disappointment caused by his failure at Wilmington, Butler threw himself into the completion of the Dutch Gap Canal upon returning to Virginia. For nearly five months hundreds of soldiers and civilians had worked day and night on the project, which their leader believed was destined for an honored place in the annals of military engineering. Against natural and man-made obstacles, under his supervision the canal had moved slowly toward conclusion. By the last day of 1864 all that remained was to blow out the bulkheads on either end of Farrar's Island.

To mark the occasion and to honor the man whose vision and persistence had brought it about, Butler invited political officials, military men, and reporters to witness the New Year's Day opening of the waterway. The ceremonies promised to be "the grandest . . . ever witnessed at the opening of any public enterprise for internal improvement." A semidistinguished crowd gathered for the controlled detonation (Grant and Meade were conspicuously absent), and precisely on schedule at 3:45 P.M. on January 1 the bulkheads exploded. Tons of earth shot skyward, only to fall back into place, damming the river as before. By the time the debris was removed, the war would be over.[41]

The exploded bulkhead of the Dutch Gap Canal, early 1865. U.S. ARMY
MILITARY HISTORY INSTITUTE.

Porter remained off Wilmington because he suspected that sooner or later
the army would make another attempt against Fort Fisher. He was prescient: on December 29 Lincoln ordered his Grant to launch a second
expedition. Late the following day Grant notified Porter that a new movement under someone other than Butler would get under way as soon as
possible. The lieutenant general had already ordered his quartermasters to
reassemble the troopships that had returned from the first voyage and to
procure additional craft. Receiving the news on New Year's Day, Porter
thanked God that "we are not to leave here with so easy a victory at
hand."[42]

From the outset the second expedition proceeded more smoothly than
its predecessor. The principal difference was that the army contingent was
commanded by Alfred Terry, who possessed the tenacity, coolheadedness, and
combativeness that Butler appeared to lack. Grant and Stanton passed over
General Ord, whom they wished to remain in Virginia, and Weitzel, who
not only bore the taint of failure but also was about to take an extended leave.
Although Terry was a citizen-soldier like Butler, he had extensive experience
in amphibious warfare and enjoyed the confidence of his troops as well as of
the War Department. Grant summoned him to City Point for a conference
on January 2, but not for another four days did the Connecticut general
learn that he would command the mission to Wilmington. Until then Terry

had accepted Grant's cover story that he and several thousand troops were being sent to reinforce Sherman in Georgia.[43]

In addition to a more qualified commander and more sustained deception, the return trip benefited from a greater number of troops and a wider variety of armaments. Grant assigned Terry fully 8,000 men—those who had gone south in December plus Hawley's infantry brigade, led on this mission by Joseph Abbott. The foot soldiers were accompanied by two light batteries as well as by a segment of the Petersburg siege train, which since the failure at the crater had been stored at Broadway Landing. It was an added reminder that when he landed outside Wilmington, Terry would have to dig in and hold on.

Unlike Butler's expedition, Terry's was not crippled by delay and indecision. On January 4 the troops who had returned from North Carolina only days before again crowded aboard transports at Bermuda Hundred. At first the men groused, but they found their new accommodations to be an improvement. "We have more room," wrote a noncommissioned officer, "and better ventilation."[44]

Perhaps the most critical difference was that the second time out, army and navy were determined to give and receive maximum support. No one had to be reminded of the stakes. As Gustavus Fox wrote to Grant on the fourth, "The country will not forgive us for another failure at Wilmington."[45]

The expedition left Fort Monroe on the morning of the sixth. The foot soldiers and artillerists aboard Terry's nineteen transports were initially in good spirits, thankful they had been spared the monotonous, unhealthy delays of the first mission and eager to redeem themselves for the Christmas Day fiasco. Then, off Cape Hatteras, a strong wind jounced the passengers into fits of seasickness—an unhappy parallel with the first journey. By the morning of the eighth the storm had abated, and men who had been laid low for two days roused themselves for the work ahead. Later that day the ships arrived at the rendezvous twenty-five miles off Beaufort. Leaving the flotilla in charge of General Paine, Terry was rowed into the harbor for his introductory conference with Porter.

The commanders greeted each other warily. Butler had warned Terry of the admiral's ego, his competitiveness, and his ability to charm the army into doing his bidding. For his part, Porter found his colleague "rather cold and formal" and possessing the same exaggerated concern for secrecy that had alienated Butler's associates: "He did not meet me at once, with the frankness of a true soldier."

Despite Porter's misgivings, the interview went well. Before it ended, the admiral had sharply revised his first impression: Terry was "a good soldier and a man of talent besides. . . . He had a good formed head full of sense," and he exuded sincerity and cordiality. Soon Porter was writing to Welles that "there is a perfect understanding between General Terry and myself." At the same time, the general's younger brother and adjutant general, Captain Adrian Terry, observed, "No disagreement or discord occurred[,] both the Admiral and Alfred being willing to yield everything that would prevent the most perfect harmony of action."[46]

During this initial conference general and admiral agreed on a strategy for taking Fort Fisher. When Porter acquainted his colleague with the history of the first expedition, Terry understood that he would have to land, as Butler did, north of the earthwork. He must entrench and prevent Bragg and Hoke from advancing beyond Sugar Loaf to shove him off the beach, and he must closely coordinate his attack on Fort Fisher's land face with Porter's gunners. In a spirit of cooperation, Terry accepted the admiral's offer to add a contingent of sailors and marines to the assault, which Butler would have interpreted as naval grandstanding. To cover the landing, Porter offered to move part of his fleet as close to the fort as the surf would permit, something he had not done for Butler.[47]

On the morning of January 12 Terry's transports, convoyed by forty-eight of Porter's ships, moved south on a calm sea under a cloudless sky. Arriving at Confederate Point after dark, Terry arranged to land the next morning. True to his word, Porter provided the most responsive support any ground commander could desire. His first-division ships, four miles above the fort, shielded the transports as they unloaded, while some of Porter's ironclads anchored less than 1,000 yards from the sea face, against which they opened fire with devastating effect. Sand and timber flew as round after round slammed into, rather than sailed over, the earthwork.

Under the pounding, no defender dared show his head outside a bomb-proof, enabling Terry to get his men ashore quickly and safely. Terry reported that by three o'clock in the afternoon almost 8,000 soldiers had landed, along with "six days' supply of hard bread in bulk, 300,000 additional rounds of small-arms ammunition, and a sufficient number of intrenching tools."[48]

Once on shore, the troops buckled down to work. Abbott's brigade guarded the extra provisions and munitions. Curtis's brigade, again acting as the vanguard of Ames's division, pushed to within 600 yards of the land face, passing the deserted Flag-Pond and Half-Moon Batteries. Simultaneously, Paine's USCTs, backed by the white brigades of Galusha Pennypacker and Louis Bell, cast about for a suitable location in which to entrench, blocking any attempt by the Rebels at Sugar Loaf to threaten the offensive. Not until after midnight, however, did the combined force begin building a line of works across the neck of the peninsula about two miles above the fort. By that evening, Terry's ten-gun complement of light artillery had landed behind this line, which consisted of "a good breast-work, reaching from the river to the sea . . . partially covered by abatis."[49]

Already Terry had accomplished what Butler had not: he had secured a foothold from which to besiege the Wilmington defenses. To that end Abbott's siege train—mostly thirty-pounder Parrott rifles and Coehorn mortars— prepared to land early on the fifteenth. But by then Terry and his subordinates had determined that an assault was preferable to investment, if only because siege warfare required the kind of regular supply lines difficult to maintain on an open beach. As a result, the siege train remained aboard ship.[50]

At 9:00 A.M. on the fifteenth, during final preparations for attack, Porter's ironclads ceased the desultory cannonade they had kept up for several hours and began to rake the fort at close range. At the same time, the navy deposited on the beach, about three miles above the fort, 1,600 sailors and 400 marines under Lieutenant Commander K. Randolph Breese.

The potential of the landing party was dubious; most of the seamen carried pistols and cutlasses instead of rifles. But there was no doubt as to the effectiveness of the cannonade; by the time it ceased, around noon, large sections of the earthwork had been blown away, and every gun along the land face except one eight-inch Columbiad had been put out of commission. The close-in tactics had succeeded.[51]

About 3:30 P.M., as the whistles of Porter's fleet signaled an advance, the guns shifted their fire from the northern approaches to the fort, and the army swept forward—Curtis's brigade toward the northwest angle and Porter's sailors and marines toward the center and left of the land face. Alerted by the whistles and the new gunnery pattern, Lamb's garrison left its bomb-proofs and rushed to the parapets. Attention was immediately drawn to the naval column, with devastating effect. As seamen toppled under a fusillade, Breese's column came to a confused halt near where the sea face met the land face. Within minutes the would-be attackers had suffered 300 casualties. Survivors not pinned too close to the fort to retreat raced up the beach in utter rout.[52]

Cheering their success, the garrison was eager to turn on Terry's people. But as they did so, the Rebels were horrified to see the Stars and Stripes moving along the ramparts. Foolhardy though it had been, the navy's assault had held the garrison's attention long enough to permit Terry to gain a lodgement.

The infantry had struck in a single column, with Curtis's brigade in front preceded by a force of 100 sharpshooters and a team carrying explosives to blow the palisade apart. As Curtis attacked, Pennypacker's brigade moved forward to the right and rear while Bell's brigade remained farther back, crowding the bank of the Cape Fear. The explosives were not needed; not only had Porter's guns destroyed the palisade, but the cables to the minefield had been cut as well. Curtis's troops crossed the approach to the land face without halting.[53]

As they charged through the remains of the stockade, Curtis's men absorbed fire from a few Rebels on the ramparts. The attackers kept moving toward Fisher's sally port until the single operable cannon opened on them, forcing them to veer westward. Their new heading carried them toward the part of the parapet nearest the Cape Fear. Scrambling up the grass-covered glacis, flag bearers in front planted their national and regimental colors atop the first traverse.

Belatedly reaching the threatened point, hundreds of defenders mixed with the Federals in some of the most frantic hand-to-hand fighting of the war. Curtis was shot four times, one wound costing him an eye. For gallantry in leading the first wave, the colonel would win a brevet brigadier general-ship and a Medal of Honor.

Although Lamb tried to bar the way, not enough defenders were initially on hand to keep the Yankees out. The balance of Curtis's brigade poured across the parapet and through the embrasures, passing numerous dismounted cannon en route to the fort's interior. In the gun chamber beyond the first traverse, they finally met stiff opposition, forcing Ames to call up his second brigade. The larger part of Pennypacker's command piled in behind Curtis's while the rest ducked into a covered way that fronted the river, emerging into a field next to the open rear of the earthwork.

While the smaller force tried to secure its position, Pennypacker led his main body across the second parapet, slowly driving the garrison into the third gun chamber. Like his predecessor, the nineteen-year-old Pennypacker suffered for being in front. A defender nearly blew away his right thigh. Other Confederates killed Pennypacker's ranking subordinate, Colonel John W. Moore of the 203rd Pennsylvania, as well as Moore's executive officer, Lieutenant Colonel Jonas Lyman.[54]

A third brigade leader fell after Pennypacker's advance bogged down atop the third traverse. To regain the initiative Ames sent Bell's brigade into the fort via the river road. Ames watched approvingly as the New Hampshireman led his men up the earthen walls along the northwestern corner of the land face, then into the third and fourth gun chambers. For a time Bell threatened to sweep away the last resistance. Then the giant Columbiad in the northeast bastion teamed with some reversed barbette guns along the sea face to concentrate fire on the attackers, spattering traverses and gun chambers with human fragments. When Bell toppled, his troops fell back to rally inside a captured salient. Babbling in pain and delirium, Bell was carried to a safe spot where he spent his final hour counting imaginary assailants. A surgeon recalled that "the numbers ran in unbroken succession into the thousands . . . till he died."[55]

With Bell's brigade repulsed and Curtis's and Pennypacker's men exhausted, the Federal attack appeared to sputter. At that critical moment, Porter's fleet came to the rescue. Apprised by semaphore that a crisis loomed, the admiral had his ironclads sweep the eastern flank of the land face. The precise barrage drove the defenders from one gun emplacement to the next and enabled the Federals, shielded against stray shells by the traverses, to resume their advance.

Of equal benefit to the attackers, the warships prevented reinforcements from reaching Lamb. About noon Bragg had dispatched by river part of Hoke's division—the brigade of Hagood Johnson, which eight months earlier had helped the Army of the James inaugurate the Bermuda Hundred campaign—to the landing above Battery Buchanan. Barely 350 Rebels reached shore before Porter's fleet scorched the ground between Fort Fisher and the battery, keeping Hagood's men from where they were desperately needed. Terry signaled Porter to "fire away; your shells are doing good execution and our men are in no danger from them." The navy continued its shelling, with increasing effect. Soon Lamb had lost possession of most of the land face.[56]

At half past six, with the outcome still in doubt, the shelling tapered off. It had grown so dark that the navy could not fire for fear of injuring Ames's soldiers. Terry then called up his reserves in an effort to take the northeast bastion, where resistance remained strong. Because Paine's troops alone had been able to hold back Bragg and Hoke, repulsing a feeble attack against their line at about 4:00 P.M., Terry felt able to commit Abbott's brigade.

Relieving the white soldiers with the seamen who had survived Breese's assault, Terry personally led them toward the fort, supported closely by Paine's 27th U.S. Colored Troops. The reserves entered the fort and struck the rear of the gun chambers from which Lamb's troops continued to resist. Flanking the northeast angle, Abbott's men slowly pried the Rebels loose from their last refuge and thrust them down the length of the sea face toward Mound Battery. Sometime before ten o'clock opposition melted away and the Stars and Stripes waved along the length and breadth of the fort.[57]

Their morale shattered by the pounding of Porter's ships and the momentum of Abbott's brigade, the sailors and soldiers in Mound Battery and Battery Buchanan disabled their guns before escaping across the Cape Fear in the few available boats. Lamb's survivors could not hope to carry on the contest from their detached defenses. Once they realized the futility of further resistance, what remained of the garrison huddled on the moon-washed beach, ready to surrender. In their midst, lying on litters, were the wounded Lamb and the dying General Whiting, the most distinguished of the almost 700 casualties the defenders had suffered that day.

Once he rounded up the last of the Rebels inside the fort, Terry led Abbott's brigade, supported in the rear by the 27th USCT, toward Battery Buchanan. Terry expected "every moment to receive a shower of grape and musketry from this last refuge of the rebels." He instead came upon several hundred gray-clad fugitives, "utterly cast down and helpless." Upon Terry's approach, Whiting raised himself and handed over his sword. He asked that the survivors be accorded the rights of prisoners of war but added, "I care not what becomes of myself." As Terry's brother recorded, "Alfred assured him of kind treatment for himself and his command and then, mounting one of the horses which had been brought down . . . rode back at full speed to send the joyful news to General Grant."[58]

The news provoked rejoicing from one end of the Union to the other and blanketed the Confederacy in gloom. Terry and Porter had effectively blocked enemy access to the Cape Fear while cutting off less strategic defensive works. Their respective garrisons blew up Fort Caswell the following day and abandoned Smith's Island. Thus, despite Bragg's continued presence at Sugar Loaf, the fall of Wilmington became a matter of time. In mid-February, Terry's reinforced command marched into the city, bands blaring, even as Bragg's defenders hastened out the other end. By then, as General Ames told his family, "the Confederacy is going with a crash."[59]

Terry's victory was costly—651 killed or wounded after six hours of unrelenting combat. Success had been gained largely through the close support of the navy, whose shelling was much more effective than it had been on Christmas Day. Even so, desperate hand-to-hand fighting had gained the victory. Neither service could have conquered Fort Fisher on its own, but army-navy cooperation had been an unbeatable combination.

This much said, it is entirely possible that Lamb and his defenders could have turned back the second expedition as they had the first. Their only chance, however, had been lost by the time Terry's soldiers set foot on the beach late on the thirteenth. Two days later Lamb repeatedly begged Bragg to drive off the enemy, but by then it was too late: Paine's and Abbott's commands had secured a foothold, strengthened by navy firepower. Lamb made surrender inevitable by lying low until Terry's assault on the fifteenth. Believing his earthwork to be impregnable, the colonel chose to fight inside it instead of at the only point where an amphibious force could be repulsed—its landing site.

Despite the navy's critical role, credit for Fort Fisher's demise would go primarily to Terry and his detachment of the Army of the James. He and his troops received the thanks of Congress for the seizure of the most formidable fixed work in all the South. The victory made Terry a major general of volunteers and a brigadier general in the regular service. For a time he became the most celebrated soldier in the Union, surpassing Sherman, Sheridan, and even Grant. In the public arena Terry easily supplanted Butler, who, on the day news of Fort Fisher's capture reached Washington, was insisting to a congressional committee that he had been sent to North Carolina on an impossible mission.[60]

CHAPTER FOURTEEN

Winter of Content

THE ARMY THAT EDWARD ORD INHERITED FROM BEN BUTLER EARLY IN January 1865 had undergone considerable change over the previous two months. For one thing, the command was smaller by several thousand troops. Terry's infantry and light artillery remained in North Carolina until the close of the war, though Abbott's siege train returned to Virginia, in increments, between late January and early March. Reinforcements, including several white regiments transferred from the Army of West Virginia and the last of the African-American outfits to come over from the Army of the Potomac, helped offset Terry's loss. The additions and subtractions left the all-white XXIV Corps with 18,000 troops in three divisions. The two divisions of Colored Troops in Weitzel's XXV Corps numbered 12,300 officers and men.

When Ord replaced Butler, he was expected to stamp his imprint on the army without delay, starting with a new headquarters staff. By mid-January, according to the pro-Butler departmental newspaper *New Regime,* Ord was discarding Butler appointees with unseemly dispatch. In fact, he retained many, including Captain Michie as chief engineer, Captain Charles E. Walbridge as chief quartermaster, Lieutenant Colonel Richard H. Jackson as inspector general and chief of artillery, and Captain Phineas A. Davis, Butler's favorite aide-de-camp.[1]

The most prominent member of Butler's military family to stay on was John Turner, who in early December had become chief of staff of the army following a near-fatal bout with malaria. Toward the end of the winter, however, when Turner reported his health fully restored, Ord returned him to the field as commander of the 2nd Division, XXIV Corps, composed largely of the units transferred from West Virginia. Another former division leader who had taken a staff assignment, Robert Foster, was also restored to field duty when Ord named him to command Terry's old 1st Division, XXIV Corps.[2]

Shortly after Ord took charge, new commanders joined the army and old ones returned after long absences. Two returnees stirred contrasting emotions in Butler's successor. Ord regarded Charles Devens, Jr., who had been confined to bed for months with inflammatory rheumatism, as a capable leader; thus he felt comfortable with Devens's replacing George Stannard at the head of the 3rd Division, XXIV Corps. Ord was much less enthusiastic about the unrepentant confrontationalist, Edward Wild, back with the army after seven months' exile. Wild's banishment had followed a series of outrageous acts that included the ritualistic flogging of one slaveholder and the cold-blooded murder of a second who had cursed the abolitionist for trespassing on his estate. Against his better judgment Ord yielded to political imperatives and permitted Wild to assume the command Butler had held open for him: the 3rd Division, XXV Corps.

From the start the Ord-Wild relationship was stormy. Ord frequently berated his subordinate for the poor discipline of his command, while Wild branded Ord a racist who "has expressed the meanest opinions [of], and done the meanest things to, and for, the negroes." Wild's criticism was echoed by his fellow division commander in the XXV Corps, William Birney, who claimed that Ord "spelt 'negro' with two G's." Ord trusted neither officer and kept them on a short leash. Moreover, he assigned to them subordinates loyal to him only, including a couple of old regulars, Colonels Henry G. Thomas and Charles S. Russell, who led Wild's brigades, and three gifted volunteer officers, Colonels James Shaw, Jr., Ulysses Doubleday, and Edward Martindale, brigade leaders under Birney.[3]

As for the new faces among the hierarchy, Ord was not keen on Brigadier General Edward Ferrero, the Spanish-born New Yorker who had led the black troops of the Army of the Potomac until his composure (and career) were shattered at the crater. Having witnessed Ferrero's sorry performance there, and aware of rumors that he was a drinker and a gambler, Ord remained wary of him. Refusing to give Ferrero a field command, he installed him in a new position, commander of the Bermuda Hundred defenses. After a few months Ord grew dissatisified with Ferrero's service and replaced him with Major General George L. Hartsuff, a competent West Pointer and former corps leader who had seen relatively little field service since taking a disabling wound at Antietam in September 1862.

Three other newcomers won Ord's confidence and respect. Colonel Thomas Maley Harris, temporary commander of the "Wild Cat Division" from the Army of West Virginia, was a former physician prominent among civilian-soldiers elevated to command. Ord thought so highly of the colonel that he successfully lobbied the War Department for his promotion to brigadier general, without which the West Virginian would have been mustered out of the service along with his regiment. Ord was likewise impressed by Harris's command, agreeing with Colonel Ripley that the Wild Cats were "a rough crowd," lacking in polish and discipline but who "fight well, march well, and are intensely loyal" to the Union.[4]

Another general new to the army had been handpicked by Ord to rejuvenate the cavalry. Ord had never liked August Kautz, whom he considered lazy and inefficient. Ironically, Kautz's "distinguished services" had recently won him the brevet of major general of volunteers; an even greater irony was that the honor dated from October 7, 1864, the day Kautz's command had been routed on the Darbytown Road east of Richmond.

Ord's estimation of Kautz had steadily declined since early December. On the tenth Ord had praised the cavalry's combative response to a sortie north of the James by two Confederate divisions under James Longstreet. Attacking along the Darbytown Road, the Confederates carried the entrenched position of Colonel Andrew W. Evans, commanding Kautz's new third brigade, but farther north on the Charles City and Williamsburg Roads, the brigades of Colonels West and Spear repulsed more numerous attackers.

Ord's regard for the horse soldiers plummeted when a second advance by Longstreet less than a week later resulted in the capture of a position erroneously vacated by Evans's brigade. When Evans's men attempted to regain the ground, many were captured. The unpleasant outcome upset Ord considerably. At the close of the fight he ordered Kautz to inspect his picket line—all twelve miles of it—and to report its strength and dispositions to army headquarters. The cavalry leader did so but for weeks afterward grumbled about his superior's "exceptional orders" and "eccentric character."[5]

The friction increased early in the new year. On January 9 Ord conducted an unannounced inspection of the cavalry's lines on the Northside. Afterward he decided that "two-thirds of the [division's] horses should be condemned, and four-fifths of the men should be dismounted and transferred to the infantry." Kautz thought he was being facetious, "but he soon gave me to understand that he really meant what he said." The army leader later complained that Kautz's regiments were poorly organized, lacked good leaders, and were inappropriately utilized. The harried cavalryman meekly replied that his command would perform any duty Ord asked of it.[6]

Ord seemed to pick on the cavalry at every opportunity. Late in January he criticized Evans's brigade for not braving ice and snow to verify a report (later determined to be false) of a Rebel buildup near White Oak Swamp. A few days later the army leader blasted Kautz for not sending Evans's command into Richmond in response to an incredible rumor that every enemy picket between the Chickahominy River and the capital had been withdrawn.

In succeeding weeks the generals quarreled over the quality of the cavalry's picket duty in the army's rear, over Kautz's desire that civilian scouts attached to his headquarters be paid in army funds, and over Kautz's request to take leave to visit his family in Ohio and his publisher in Philadelphia (he had compiled a book of military customs, a project Ord did not consider fit for a field commander). When Ord refused him leave, Kautz went over his superior's head and gained Grant's permission. Ord was so incensed that when Kautz rejoined the army on March 20, he found he had been relieved of command.

Kautz tried to make the best of the situation. When he found he could not regain his old position, he accepted the only command Ord offered him: Wild's USCT division. Like Ord, Kautz was something of a negrophobe; he took the command because he wanted to be in on the kill when the army moved against Petersburg and Richmond and because ending the conflict on inactive duty might deny him a desirable postwar assignment.[7]

Brigadier General Ranald S. Mackenzie.
LIBRARY OF CONGRESS.

Even Kautz acknowledged that his successor, although lacking in cavalry experience, was a most promising youngster. Twenty-four-year-old Ranald Slidell Mackenzie, a New Yorker of Southern ancestry, a graduate of the West Point class of 1862, had risen from second lieutenant of topographical engineers to command a brigade of heavy artillery serving as infantry in the Army of the Potomac. He had repeatedly distinguished himself at Petersburg and later in the Shenandoah Valley, where he had become a brigadier general of volunteers. The young commander overflowed with energy and enthusiasm. He took hold of his new command, remounting and resupplying it, weeding out incompetents, promoting deserving officers and men. He also worked to convince all under him that despite their limited numbers, they could leave their mark on the spring campaign.[8]

Perhaps the most substantial contribution Ord made in personnel was his acquisition, in mid-January, of Major General John Gibbon to command the XXIV Corps. Long a mainstay of the II Corps, Army of the Potomac, and a distinguished West Pointer, Gibbon was an artillery expert who had become adept at handling infantry and would have been a corps leader long before had old friendships and army politics not barred his path. The tall, steely-eyed North Carolinian, a general since May 1862, had tasted glory while directing one of his army's elite units, the Iron Brigade, at Second Bull Run and Antietam. Since Fredericksburg he had been a division leader, while occasionally, as at Gettysburg (where he held the army's center against Pickett's Charge), he had ably exercised corps command.

When his immediate superior, Winfield Scott Hancock, had been invalided out of the army late in 1864, Gibbon was expected to gain corps command at last. Instead, he was shunted aside when Meade appointed his chief of staff and close friend, Major General Andrew A. Humphreys, to the post. Disappointed and resentful, Gibbon remained with his division but cast about for other opportunities. When command of the XXIV Corps opened up, he accepted it enthusiastically. The previous autumn Gibbon had led the XVIII Corps for almost three weeks while Ord convalesced from his Fort Harrison wound. Gibbon had enjoyed the experience; now he looked forward to serving with the Army of the James permanently.[9]

Ord, who was eager to apply to his own concepts of organization and discipline, wished to reform what he considered Butler's lax habits and low standards. He believed he had to tighten some screws and turn up the steam if the Army of the James was to perform to his satisfaction.

Ord began by instituting a demanding regimen of drill, target practice, and fatigue duty to promote physical fitness and raise morale throughout the ranks. For this to work, the army had to be kept near full strength throughout the winter. In the middle of January Ord severely restricted leaves for officers and men—a policy that Kautz defied, to his sorrow. When he found that officers had become accustomed to sleeping until nine or ten o'clock, Ord scheduled reveille at 5:00 A.M. sharp and saw to it that every man not excused from duty answered roll call. Some groused, but most appreciated the benefits of the new system. A Connecticut artilleryman noted that five o'clock was "an uncomfortable hour to get up in mid-winter to face icy winds and chilling rain, but . . . the older comrades in the Battery knew that the new recruits wanted a great deal of attention in the matter of drill," a shortcoming the extra work hours overcame.

Reinstating another practice that had lapsed under Butler, Ord decreed that regimental and brigade drill would be held "every fair afternoon excepting Saturday." Regiments that had not been subjected to tactical instruction for two years or more were soon drilling four hours every day across frozen earth. Ord was also fond of reviews and parades, which he saw not only as morale builders but also as evaluators of his army's conditioning. He may have gone overboard, however, for in late February a West Virginia surgeon diagnosed Ord as suffering from "review on the brain."[10]

To foster esprit de corps and to reduce a soldier's tendency to grow slovenly in camp, Ord instituted an army-wide inspection competition. With Gibbon's support, the regiments of the XXIV Corps vied for honors in neatness, soldierly deportment, and the condition of their arms and equipment. Winners received two weeks' freedom from fatigue and picket duty, which encouraged avid competition. Though it produced valuable results in the short run, the practice stirred resentment among the losers, who complained that rival outfits gained unfair advantage through the issuance of new uniforms and accoutrements. A New Hampshireman grumbled that the competition "resulted in more harm than good to the service." Fourteen years after the war, the historian of the 34th Massachusetts continued to rail against the "frequent and rigid inspections" the army underwent, sometimes in ankle-deep snow. Bowing to such criticisms, Ord ended the experiment less than a month after instituting it.[11]

Other winter-quarters reforms yielded benefits without causing hard feelings. Late in January Ord established a commission to monitor the army's rations. The program imposed uniform procedures on the storage and issuance of rations and produced a greater abundance of hard bread and salt beef. By the end of January a member of a heavy artillery regiment from Pennsylvania, given to complaining about the scarcity of rations in winter camp, declared that at last "we get plenty" of everything to eat. In February Ord reduced the licensing fees and property taxes imposed on sutlers, enabling the civilian merchants to offer less expensive wares.[12]

In February and March Ord inspected the army's camps along the length of its line. He scrutinized living conditions and sanitary facilities. Most troops he found to be "in the best of health and spirits," but he tongue-lashed at least two regimental commanders whose camps failed to meet his standards of neatness and hygiene.

To further promote the army's welfare, Ord unstintingly supported the relief agencies that served his troops, not only the Sanitary and Christian Commissions but also the Bureau of Negro Affairs, forerunner of the postwar Freedmen's Bureau. Ord established an especially beneficial relationship with Edward F. Williams, chief Christian Commission agent with the Army of the James. In mid-February Williams boasted seven Commission stations operating along the army's lines, proportionally more than served the Army of the Potomac. As a major gesture toward the Bureau of Negro Affairs, that month Ord agreed to issue army rations to employees who taught and counseled the black troops and their dependents. His program may have been politically motivated or inspired by personal conviction. Though he did not regard African-Americans as the intellectual equivalent of whites, Ord appears to have considered them worthy of government supervision and care.[13]

Ord's efforts did not go unnoticed or unappreciated. The *Army and Navy Journal* praised him for his innovative approach to discipline and efficiency. It especially lauded him for establishing evening classes for supplemental training of regimental officers. A more sweeping tribute was paid by a correspondent of the *Philadelphia Press* (a black reporter, no less), who celebrated Ord's "manifest fitness . . . to command this army," which under his supervision "continues in its present position, rendering a more effective service to the cause of the Union" than any other fighting force.[14]

If many of Ord's reforms received public acclaim, one that he implemented to the economic benefit of the government received little notice: he revamped the policies governing trade inside the Department of Virginia and North Carolina. This effort began as the result of a telegram from Grant on January 16, relaying reports from Washington of smuggling within Ord's realm. Supposedly, Northern traders were hauling $100,000 worth of cotton and tobacco out of Virginia and North Carolina every day in exchange for greenbacks and gold that helped sustain the Confederate war effort. Butler had not cooperated with earlier attempts to ferret out corruption; now Grant wished Ord to investigate the situation vigorously.[15]

Ord recommended a military inquiry. To staff it he suggested his adjutant general, Major Theodore Read, and General Potter, the new chief of staff of the XXIV Corps. For chairman he proposed Brigadier General George H. Gordon, a supernumerary officer with experience in directing military investigations. Ord cautioned Grant, however, that such a tribunal would generate political controversy, especially if it cast guilt (as he suspected it would) over Butler and his former subordinates.

Grant established the commission, but the investigation failed to meet Ord's expectations. Butler's name cropped up frequently during the month long hearings Gordon held at Norfolk, scene of many of the alleged crimes. The hearings produced 1,100 pages of testimony from a small army of witnesses—military and civilian, unionist and secessionist. The panel confirmed that an illicit trade had existed in the department well before Butler's November 1863 arrival at Fort Monroe but that it had grown dramatically during his tenure.

At intervals during Butler's thirteen-month reign, especially during late 1864, few or no restrictions had been imposed on trade through Norfolk from the North. Millions of dollars in goods—some that directly supported military operations—had been purchased by enemy quartermaster and commissary agents farther south. Because of their sometimes flagrant disregard of Treasury Department policies, Butler and his district commander at Norfolk, General Shepley, were harshly criticized by Gordon's commission. But in the end—to the chagrin of both Gordon and Ord— neither Butler nor Shepley could be definitively linked to any illegalities.[16]

One result of the Gordon commission—and Ord's support of it—was tighter control over interdepartmental commerce. On January 23 Ord suspended local trade permits other than those held by Treasury agents supervising the confiscation of enemy goods and property. Ord also saw to it that trading stations on the fringes of his department, where contraband had been exchanged for Northern currency, were permanently closed. Ord replaced Shepley with Gordon early in February, ignoring Shepley's protest that the act lent credence to the unproven charges against him.

Ord imposed strict enforcement. At his direction, infantry and cavalry units raided trading stations that refused to shut down. In March the 3rd New York Cavalry burned fifty bales of contraband cotton at the trading station near Murfree's Depot, just above the North Carolina line. A few days later the regiment destroyed a ferry on the Blackwater River carrying contraband toward a rendezvous with Yankee traders.[17]

The most ambitious effort against smugglers was made that month, when Ord detached a full brigade of infantry under Colonel Samuel H. Roberts and sent it up the James, Potomac, and Rappahannock Rivers to the country around Fredericksburg. Roberts's men discovered a huge cache of contraband tobacco, corn, and bacon that Confederate authorities had confiscated from farmers on the Northern Neck to trade for Yankee medicine and munitions. Roberts confiscated close to $1 million in goods, which he shipped to Fort Monroe.[18]

The winter of 1864–65—the first that most of Ord's soldiers spent as members of the Army of the James—passed with exasperating slowness. Even so, it was not an especially trying time. The veterans knew how to build, heat, and waterproof their lodgings. A member of the 142nd New York, encamped near Chaffin's Bluff, wrote to his wife that he and three comrades shared a cozy cabin: "We hav[e] a good fire-plase in it and two bunks. . . . We sleep warme and nice." A private in the 118th New York asserted that such was the case with the army as a whole: "We have good Comfortable Quarters, both men & officers, good log houses Covered with Tents . . . which makes [a] very pleasant place to live in." A member of the 12th West Virginia at Bermuda Hundred declared that he and everyone he knew "live happily as Kings."[19]

But hardships and unhealthful conditions had to be endured. The winter was one of the coldest in local memory. Men who had not properly chinked their log huts or stockaded their tents had a difficult time withstanding frosty days and frigid nights. Even those who enjoyed basically comfortable surroundings suffered from the confinement. As General Hawley observed, tent and cabin living "is a very dirty life; the pine wood fills our huts with sooty smoke & every thing is grimy & dirty."[20]

The hardships of winter camp were aggravated by a heavy work schedule, the result of Ord's insistence that the men stay busy and keep fit. The army seemed always to be digging trenches, felling trees for fuel, corduroying roads, or standing guard. A member of a heavy artillery outfit at Bermuda Hundred, who generally found life in winter camp enjoyable, observed that there "is only one thing to prevent our taking real comfort here and that is the amount of duty we have to perform. We have only been here 14 days and during that time I have been on picket 3 times, on fatigue 2, and am to go on picket again tonight." Picket duty was especially onerous for soldiers stationed near enemy lines, as no campfires were allowed even on the rawest nights. Those who broke the rule had to walk an additional twenty-four hours on the picket line for each offense.[21]

Despite the hardships, morale remained high. The men had few battle-field successes to show for their months of service, but they sensed that their fortunes would improve with the weather. The historian of the 12th New Hampshire recalled that even at the height of the cold season and "though their duties were many and burdensome . . . the men bore it all with submissive patience, for they fully believed that the time was short" before victory came. A Massachusetts officer agreed that "though the labors of the army were very onerous, yet its health remained good and its spirit rose to the height of the greatest achievements."[22]

A number of factors kept the army in a good mood. The general perception was that victory and peace were at hand. Throughout the winter Grant, Meade, and Ord maintained continuous pressure on Lee's lines, stretching the Confederate flanks above and below Petersburg. Despite the constant provocation, enemy retaliation was often feeble or spasmodic, as though the Army of Northern Virginia had resigned itself to defeat. An officer in the 4th U.S. Colored Troops informed his father early in January that the Confederates were falling to pieces before his eyes: "Their weakness is so apparent that all along our front where two months ago their forces seemed very formidable, little or no regard is paid to them except . . . to call forth our contempt."[23]

The deserters who streamed inside the army's lines throughout the winter testified to this deterioration. By late February at least 75 and as many as 300 Rebels were deserting every day along Ord's front, including the remnants of once-mighty regiments. During a truce party a Confederate officer jested to his Union counterpart that so many in his brigade had crossed the line that a general was being sent over to command them.

Another stimulus to morale was the news of Union successes in other theaters, including Major General George H. Thomas's mid-December victory at Nashville and Sherman's capture of Savannah at the close of his March to the Sea. In January word came of Terry's triumph outside Wilmington, for which the Army of the James could take credit. Five weeks later everyone celebrated the evacuation of Charleston, South Carolina, scene of the war's opening salvos. As on previous occasions, signal guns boomed and men "sang, ran, jumped, laughed, shouted, threw up their hats." Late in March a new round of celebrating greeted the news that Sheridan's army—then en route to the Petersburg front—had stamped out Confederate resistance in the Shenandoah Valley.[24]

In early February a triumph achieved not on a battlefield but in Congress was a cause for rejoicing in many corners of the army. In testimony to the antislavery impulse of the Army of the James, word that the House of Representatives had passed the Thirteenth Amendment touched off a demonstration that rivaled those that had greeted the successes of Sherman, Thomas, and Sheridan. The ban on slavery apparently was celebrated without parallel in any other Union command. An Ohio infantryman outside Richmond recalled, "You could hear the cheers and shouts of men rolling along, and echoing and re-echoing, until it seemed as though the whole army was uniting in one grand effort to all cheer at once, and mingled with it all was the tremendous roar of artillery from the forts and artillery parks off to our left [at Bermuda Hundred] and the gunboats and mortars on the river in our rear."[25]

Given the hopelessness of the enemy's position, efforts at crafting a peace short of a final bloodletting were inevitable. Because much of it was played out within its area of operations, the Army of the James gave particular attention to the one-man peace mission launched in January by a former Missouri congressman, Francis Preston Blair. The command also monitored the progress of an outgrowth of Blair's mission, a conference between Lincoln and three Confederate peace commissioners, held in Hampton Roads in early February. The failure of this meeting brought great disappointment to the soldiers who hoped that peace might be achieved beyond "the medium of the rifle, the cannon, and the saber." Reviewing the blasted hopes of his comrades, Kautz decided the army had been naive to suppose the Rebels would lay down their arms anywhere except on the battlefield: "We shall be compelled to make another campaign, before they will break up and go home."[26]

In all the army, no one was more disheartened by the collapse of the peace talks than Edward Ord. A conservative Democrat with border state roots and close friends on the other side, he longed to halt the killing. He did not believe the powers in Washington shared his sense of mission; Lincoln, Stanton, Secretary of State William Seward, and other high officials did "not feel their responsibilities" as peacemakers strongly enough. As far back as July 1864 Ord had written despairingly to his wife about the "great wrongs being committed" on and off the battlefield and of the insatiable "taste for blood, more blood" exhibited on both sides. In his desire to "quit this murderous business," he had vowed to try to halt it "even at the risk of falling under the ban of the men who rule and allow it." He may have expressed these feelings to Lincoln when the president visited army headquarters on February 4, shortly before returning to Washington following the failure of the peace conference.[27]

Ord acted on his sentiments three weeks later. On the afternoon of February 25, with Gibbon and members of the headquarters staff, he trotted out the New Market Road under a flag of truce to talk with General Longstreet, a friend from West Point days. Ostensibly seeking to curtail increasing fraternization between the armies, Ord used the meeting to broach the subject of an armistice. He proposed that leading officers take initial steps toward a cease-fire. In place of a meeting between mutually distrustful politicians, he advocated a Grant-Lee interview aimed at reaching a negotiated peace, an agreement the commanders might impose upon the civilian authorities and the general population as a fait accompli.

Longstreet was receptive and conveyed Ord's idea to Lee, who relayed it to Jefferson Davis. Supposing that Ord's initiative had the tacit support of Grant and perhaps Lincoln as well, the Confederate president endorsed a high-level military conference. Three days later Ord and Longstreet met for a second time and discussed the best way to set up the crucial meeting. According to Longstreet, Ord assured him that Grant had ample authority and only awaited an expression of Confederate interest. Accordingly, Longstreet informed Lee that "General Grant will take up the matter [of an armistice] without requiring any principle as a basis further than the general principle of desiring to make peace upon terms that are equally honorable to both sides."[28]

In truth, Ord had reached no understanding with Grant; it appears doubtful that he even informed the commanding general of his peace mission. The first clear indication that Grant had of Ord's unauthorized contacts with the enemy was Lee's March 2 invitation to work out a military convention with his Union counterpart. Shortly afterward, if not before, Grant discovered the full extent of Ord's politically dangerous involvement.

Wary of his course, the lieutenant general forwarded Lee's note to an abashed Stanton, who discussed it with the president and other cabinet members. Lincoln dictated a reply the following day that went out over Stanton's signature: Grant was to "have no conference with General Lee, unless it be for the capitulation of General Lee's army." On the fourth Grant dismissed Ord's peace overture, informing Lee that the commander of the Army of the James "could only have meant that I would not refuse an interview on any subject on which I have a right to act, which, of course, would be such as are purely of a military character."[29]

Thus ended an unprecedented initiative to halt the war through covert military negotiations. Ord's motives may have been noble; he seems to have believed that the president would be pleased to consider a peace overture were his hand forced by high-ranking officers. Still, the army leader clearly overstepped his authority by proposing what amounted to a separate peace and promoting it secretively. That Ord's involvement in such an undertaking did not cost him his command was testimony to his stature and to Washington's need of him in the coming campaign—one he had tried to render unnecessary.

With hopes of peace dashed, the army tried to nerve itself for the task ahead, which could prove rougher and longer than anyone imagined. General Hawley feared that the Rebels "will fight like the devils in hell this long time yet." A New York cavalry officer believed "the enemy are whipped nicely, yet they . . . seem determined to hold out" until the bitter, bloody end. "They will have every man in . . . the grate struggle [that] is to come," observed a Maine private. Ord himself noted that although "everything signifies the failure of their rebellion," additional months and even years of war were possible. He also feared that the Confederates might yet gain diplomatic recognition and military assistance from Europe, salvaging an eleventh-hour triumph.[30]

Though life in winter camp was generally placid, it was enlivened by enough combat to suggest that at least some of Lee's underclothed, underfed troops still packed a punch. Throughout the winter Pickett and others attacked the works at Bermuda Hundred taking whatever advantage that stealth and surprise could give. Other Rebel forces made intermittent efforts against Dutch Gap, especially Fort Brady, a heavy redoubt on the north side of the James upriver from Farrar's Island.

A few small-scale assaults produced outsize results. A midnight attack in early February against a fort on the New Market Road just west of Fort Burnham routed elements of the XXV Corps and the cavalry. Army mules broke out of a corral and stampeded alongside the fugitives, sending up an unearthly braying that lasted for hours. Embarrassed reinforcements retook the position only to find that the chaos had been created by no more than a dozen Confederate horsemen "who at that unseasonable hour dashed within our lines and then dashed out again." A New York officer observed that "the event was long after known in camp as 'The Mule Serenade.'"[31]

The most ambitious offensive of the winter pitted the Army of the James against the Confederate navy. On the evening of January 23 a Rebel fleet of three ironclad rams, four wooden gunboats, and four torpedo boats, with a mounting of twenty-five guns, steamed down from Drewry's Bluff toward Trent's Reach. The objective was to cut the pontoon spans linking Bermuda Hundred with the Northside, divide Ord's command, and penetrate as far as City Point, where the Rebels could shell Grant's headquarters.

The few Union gunboats remaining in the James after Porter's departure did not offer much resistance, leaving the army to halt the flotilla. When the ships came abreast of Fort Brady, the land artillery and sharpshooters pounded them. The barrage, which one USCT officer called the "grandest thing a mortal can ever see," caused two ironclads to ground on the shoals of Trent's Reach, blocking the other ships. When shells shattered two of the torpedo boats, the rest of the fleet quickly retreated.

It had been, as an Ohio soldier remarked, "a close call for the Army of the James," not only because of the flotilla's near success but also because Rebel infantry had massed near Fort Burnham, ready to attack should the fleet pass Trent's Reach. Had the ships cut Ord's army in two, at least half of it might have been forced to surrender. As General Hawley later informed his wife, the troops north of the James maintained only five days' rations; they would have starved if cut off from City Point and Bermuda Hundred for long. The worst had not happened, Hawley added, only because "God helped us."[32]

Unwilling to rely on divine intervention, the army improved its river obstructions, mined the James, and erected additional batteries near City Point. Such precautions forestalled what a New Hampshire veteran called a "last spasmodic effort to break the cordon of death that encircled" Lee's army.[33]

Late in March springlike weather returned to the James River country. Ice melted and muddy roads began to solidify. The change of seasons reminded everyone that, as the *Army and Navy Journal* noted on the twenty-fifth, "the critical moment approaches."

In preparation for active operations, Ord reduced the army's baggage, transferring surplus stores to Norfolk. He moved patients from field hospitals to the general hospitals at the City Point and Hampton Roads. The few soldiers who had secured furloughs were returning to the ranks. By the middle of the month rumors of an imminent movement circulated among the ranks. The troops appeared ready for action. Thanks to Ord's fitness regimen and make-work programs, the army was physically prepared for marching, fighting, and roughing it. The command's mental strength was such that it would endure severe hardships and make the most strenuous efforts to end the war quickly.

By the third week in March a newspaper correspondent at Ord's headquarters was observing that "a great many mysterious maneuvers are being made along these lines, which, if they puzzle the rebels as much as they do us, will make the strategy of General Grant complete." One such movement, up the York and Pamunkey Rivers, returned Roberts's brigade to the Northern Neck, this time on a partially successful hunt for the partisans of Lieutenant Colonel John Singleton Mosby. Meanwhile, detachments of Turner's infantry and Mackenzie's cavalry were sent to the banks of the Chickahominy to escort the troopers of Phil Sheridan, returning to Meade's army after their triumphant campaign in the Shenandoah.[34]

By the time Turner and Mackenzie rejoined the army, everyone had "put the war paint on" and was awaiting word to move out. Grant briefed Ord on the twenty-sixth, following a troop review by Lincoln, congressmen, cabinet members, and Admiral Porter, recently returned from Fort Fisher. Drawn up two days earlier, Grant's plan called for Sheridan, with the cavalry that had served him in the Valley, to sweep west of Petersburg, collapsing Lee's right flank. If "Little Phil" succeeded, Meade would attack the city from several points. During the winter the Army of the Potomac had extended its position as far west as the Vaughan Road's crossing of Hatcher's Run, nearly within reach of Lee's last line of supply, the Southside Railroad.[35]

The Army of the James had a major role in Grant's plans for Richmond and Petersburg. Ord was to keep in place outside the capital about a third of his command—enough troops to occupy the city should it weaken or be evacuated. The bulk of the army would accompany him south of the Appomattox to move against Petersburg. Despite the size of the column, the shift had to be made quickly enough to prevent Richmond from discerning Grant's strategy. Once concentrated about Petersburg, Ord's main body would relieve Meade's II and V Corps for operations closer to Sheridan's front that included a decisive thrust toward the Southside. Other segments would help Meade attack the works south of Petersburg.

Grant wished Ord to lead his troops to Petersburg personally. The force left near Richmond as well as that at Bermuda Hundred under General Hartsuff would come under the command of Godfrey Weitzel. Grant specified that Weitzel "will keep vigilant watch upon his front and if it is found at all practicable to break through at any point he will do so. A success north of the James should be followed up with great promptness." Grant added, however, that an assault "will not be feasible unless it is found that the enemy has detached largely" in response to Ord's departure.[36]

Grant was placing a heavy burden on Ord. Not only must he transfer two-thirds of his army to a new front forty miles away and do so as quietly as possible, he would have less than two days to prepare for the journey. Grant wished the operation to begin after dark on the twenty-seventh.

To ready his troops, a few days before his strategy session with Grant, Ord had withdrawn Foster's and Turner's divisions of the XXIV and Birney's division of the XXV Corps from the front line and massed them beyond range of Rebel artillery. To cover their vacated positions, he extended Kautz's and Devens's lines. When the shifting ended, Kautz's line ran north from Dutch Gap to above Fort Burnham. Devens extended the perimeter to the Charles City Road and southeastward toward the James.[37]

Mackenzie's cavalry, another command that Ord pulled to the rear in the last days of March, had anchored Devens's right flank; the evacuated position was soon held only by detachments of the 20th New York Cavalry and 1st New York Mounted Rifles, supported by the 4th and 5th Massachusetts and

2nd Colored Cavalry Regiments. Once occupied by more than 32,000 troops, the front entrusted to Weitzel was now held by fewer than 12,000. Weitzel was painfully aware of the trouble he would face should the enemy learn of Ord's departure and attack the units that remained.

Well prepared, Ord issued marching orders on the morning of the twenty-seventh. Turner's division would cross the pontoons that evening at Deep Bottom, preceded by artillery and a seventy-five-wagon train carrying sixty rounds of ammunition and eight days' rations per man. After Turner cleared the bridgehead, Birney's men, more artillery, and Foster's division would cross at Deep Bottom. The elongated line would pass in rear of the Bermuda Hundred defenses before splitting into two columns to cross the Appomattox at Broadway Landing and Point of Rocks. Mackenzie's main body would remain on the Northside for a full twenty-four hours after the infantry and artillery moved out. The horsemen would then take a more westerly route to Petersburg via the floating bridge near Aiken's Landing.[38]

Ord's initial destination was the Weldon Railroad near Globe Tavern and Fort Dushane, six miles from the center of Petersburg. From there, Army of the Potomac officers would guide the infantry to the camps of the II and V Corps near Hatcher's Run. Mackenzie's cavalry would go wherever Sheridan, under whose authority it would operate, thought it belonged.

Ord's dispositions did not find universal favor in the ranks. Many officers and some enlisted men under Kautz and Devens did not like serving far from what promised to be the main arena. "We, of course, do not feel . . . well at being left," Edward Ripley, one of Devens's brigade commanders, told his mother. Ripley doubted that Weitzel "is expected to do much more than lay here to threaten Richmond" while Grant, Ord, and Meade reaped the glory in the final campaign. Some of those selected to march to Petersburg also had complaints. Birney grumbled when he learned that his division would come under Gibbon's authority. He feared that Gibbon, who like Ord was skeptical of black troops' ability, would relegate the division to a rear-echelon role. Birney decided that "it was clearly not intended that the colored troops should win any glory in the last events of the war."[39]

Content or not, the marching men got under way as scheduled in the early, wet hours of the twenty-eighth. They left tents standing, campfires burning, and bands playing in an effort to make the enemy think nothing had changed. A diarist in one of Devens's regiments marveled at this deception: "Mounted buglers dash from Hdqrs. to Hdqrs. sounding call after call, while drum corps run from regiment to regiment and play the same farce. The bands play at their respective stations; their audience a few men, a few mules, a few grinning darkeys, and a wide, barren waste of deserted camps."[40]

Thanks to such ploys, the transfer of three divisions from one end of the siege lines to the other went quickly and smoothly. Despite the weather and the considerable number of men who had never made a forced march, the long, winding column made its way over the James and along the rear of the Bermuda Hundred lines, breaking for rest at frequent intervals. Only in the late stages of the journey, conducted through territory south of the Appomattox unfamiliar even to veterans, did the delays that Ord feared crop up, mostly caused by the steady rain and muddy roads. A member of Foster's division recalled that "the soft roads, cut up by artillery wheels and wagon trains, stretched here and there into wide morasses of knee-deep mire, into which we would plunge unexpectedly, to wallow through as best we could. [The route] led through woods, and in the darkness those deviating from the road ran against trees."[41]

Some soldiers made light of the ordeal. "When are the gunboats coming up?" men asked as they sloshed through the mud. The Israelites had followed Moses to the promised land; the soldiers were following Abraham, their commander in chief. Some called for a more appropriate patriarch: "Noah," they exclaimed, must "be sent to save the army!"[42]

Just before dawn the rain ceased and the grumbling diminished. The march continued at the steady pace the high command desired. Throughout the twenty-eighth the "Flying Column" passed through Army of the Potomac territory, crossing the Petersburg & City Point Railroad before swinging westward across the Weldon line, passing the trenches of Major General John G. Parke's IX Corps on the southeastern rim of Meade's siege lines. At about 8:00 A.M. on March 29 the column route-stepped past the camps of Wright's VI Corps south of Petersburg. Just shy of noon, after almost thirty-six hours on the road, Ord's vanguard approached the east side of Hatcher's Run. There it moved up to relieve elements of Humphreys's II and Warren's V Corps.[43]

The new arrivals were gratified by the ground they had covered and their adherence to the timetable. They had encountered obstacles, but like the many hardships, privations, and disappointments they had faced during the past year and longer, they had surmounted them in good style and humor. They were now in a position to contribute in a meaningful way to the closing campaign of the war in the East.

CHAPTER FIFTEEN

Final Triumph

BY THE EVENING OF MARCH 29 THE TROOPS OF ORD AND GIBBON HAD TAKEN position on the upper bank of Hatcher's Run, facing north. Foster's division held the most vulnerable sector, occupying the old II Corps trenches opposite Petersburg's outer defense line. Turner's division had gone into line in Foster's left rear, its left flank connecting with the right of Humphreys's new position farther west. Birney's division had been placed in the rear as an all-purpose reserve. Birney's position probably confirmed his suspicion of a plot to deny his troops a major role in the work ahead.

Skirmishing occupied the command throughout the day. This was fortunate, as Ord wished his footsore men to have a rest. The hiatus was brief, for at 5:30 P.M. Grant's headquarters directed Ord to shift northward at daylight as far as the Armstrong house, about a mile above where the Vaughan Road crossed Hatcher's Run. Ord was to probe the nearest works upon arrival; if he found them lightly held, he was to "try to make a hole" and push on until someone made him stop.

Ord not only carried out this plan but improved on it. In the early hours of the thirtieth he moved Foster to within sight of the Armstrong house and its adjoining gristmill. At that point the crackle of musketry told Ord he had gone as far as he dared. As Foster dug in, Turner's men crossed and then recrossed the run to align themselves more closely not only with Foster but with the II Corps as well. No further marching was required; the men remained in their new works, awaiting Grant's word to move against the outer defenses of Petersburg.[1]

The enemy, however, struck first. Early on the last day of the month, Rebels dug in north of the Armstrong house opened with artillery, concentrating on Turner's left and the adjoining flank of the II Corps. The Confederates then launched a limited assault. Barely had the attackers started south, however, when Turner and Humphreys, supported by Birney, repulsed them. The quick retreat was another sign that a once-formidable adversary had lost its power. Even the Rebel yell—for so many years a fearsome noise—sounded halfhearted. Perhaps the last clash would be quick and easy. Perhaps the war was already won.[2]

That night a storm of manmade thunder broke over Petersburg. Meade's artillery opened a furious barrage in preparation for an attack all along the line; the cannonade continued long into the morning of April 1. As though enraged by this display of malice, the troops opposite Ord launched another sortie at dawn, driving in Foster's and Turner's pickets before bogging down—literally—a few hundred yards from their works. Emboldened by their recent success, both divisions counterattacked over the swampy ground. In contrast to the Rebel effort, theirs was vigorous and sustained; Foster alone inflicted 100 casualties. Properly chastised, the enemy remained quiescent for the balance of the day, enduring Meade's shelling with sullen patience.[3]

Ord was briefed late that afternoon on the pending offensive, which Grant had fixed for daybreak on the second. The white troops were to push toward the left after an anticipated breakthrough by the VI Corps. To exploit the breach, Foster and Turner were to make for the Boydton Plank Road, which crossed Hatcher's Run about two miles northwest of Armstrong's Mill. They should follow that thoroughfare as far as the western extremity of Lee's line.

Ord's path would not be free of obstacles. Along the upper reaches of the plank road was a series of redoubts, the most formidable being Forts Gregg and Whitworth, which guarded, in effect, the back door to Petersburg. Known to be held in force, the redoubts had to be taken for Grant's strategy to succeed. This fact, however, had a less than chilling effect on Ord; late in the day his officers found him awash in confidence. At one point he boasted to Lieutenant Colonel Horace Porter of Grant's staff that his troops would slice through Lee's defenses "as a hot knife goes into butter."[4]

On the north side of the James the army's rear echelon was less optimistic. Kautz had predicted to Weitzel on March 26 that "our command would march into Richmond in less than ten days without a fight." Weitzel had been incredulous; he insisted that the troops remaining outside Richmond would be in grave danger once Longstreet realized that 20,000 fewer troops held the works in his front. Not even Ord's parting suggestion that Richmond would soon be evacuated eased Weitzel's mind. A New Hampshire officer remarked that as soon as Ord and Gibbon headed south, Weitzel was "all up and down the lines and everywhere at once, seeming to neither eat, drink, or sleep" and acting like a man "gone stark mad."[5]

Weitzel's overly dramatic behavior amused a number of observers. Some officers and men began to ridicule him; others questioned his fitness to command such an important operation. Major George Bruce, Devens's chief of staff, compared Weitzel to an old woman alone in a house whose every creak conjured up intruders. As the aide pointed out, even in their reduced state, the army's defenses were so formidable that their loss seemed highly unlikely.[6]

If pressed, even Weitzel would have had trouble explaining from which direction an attack would come. Between March 27 and April 1 his men observed no threatening movements either on the Northside or along Bermuda Hundred Neck. In fact, every day brought new evidence that Longstreet had shifted troops from Weitzel's front. Regardless, Weitzel remained convinced that once they learned of Ord's departure, the Rebels would attack out of the Richmond lines. His only hope was that Lee and Longstreet would not discover his weakness until Grant could assault Petersburg.

On the twenty-eighth Grant himself informed Weitzel that whether due to Ord's departure or coincidence, as much as a full Rebel corps had left Richmond for Petersburg. Grant did not have the numbers, but he doubted that more than two understrength divisions remained north of the James. Weitzel refused to be comforted. Fearful that Grant's message presaged an order to probe the lines opposite him, the corps leader replied that several thousand Confederates continued to confront him, enough to make their works impregnable. To suggest otherwise was to commit himself to an advance over a minefield against some of the most elaborate defenses in North America. He preferred to make do with long-range skirmishing and intermittent barrages and to indulge the theatrical instincts of his buglers and bandsmen.

If the troops under Devens and Kautz remained immobile, they also remained alert. One XXIV Corps picket remarked, "We have been flattering ourselves that we were vigilant. . . . The pressure of strict watching last night, to-day, and to-night along these lines, excels anything we have experienced since we have been in the army." To increase his men's watchfulness, Weitzel offered rewards to pickets who brought in deserters and prisoners. He detailed additional observers to his signal towers and had horsemen constantly "feeling for and hunting up the enemy on the right and front and gathering information."[7]

Weitzel's anxiety should have subsided late on the thirty-first, when Devens made an extended reconnaissance of the Darbytown Road and found no unusual activity. Instead of acknowledging relief, Weitzel double-checked his preparations for repelling an attack.

On the evening of April 1 the troops outside Richmond witnessed the unearthly effects of Meade's barrage. Even at that distance the din seemed to be coming from Weitzel's backyard. A USCT officer stared southward with mouth agape: "It was as if demons incarnate were holding a jubilee. As far as the eye could reach there was one blaze of fiery shot."[8]

Only when the shelling went unanswered from Richmond did Weitzel begin to hope that some of his opponents had slipped away. His optimism was short-lived, however. On the afternoon of the second he conducted a little experiment on the durability of the works facing him. He placed two cannon near his headquarters east of the Varina Road and pointed them at a double line of abatis he had rigged up to resemble the defenses across the way, held by Richard Ewell. The cannon blasted away with chain shot, bar shot, and other breaching ammunition. General Shepley, who despite his corruption-tainted career at Norfolk had been appointed Weitzel's chief of staff (the two had been close since serving together at New Orleans), remarked that "the experiments were not successful; chain-shot and Parrott shell and every other missile passed through the interlaced branches of the abatis, and left no visible break or opening." Shepley added that Weitzel "retired at night-fall, with the conviction that artillery was useless to help us in making the breaches."[9]

It had been an especially bad day for Weitzel, mainly because of an order that morning from Grant. Weitzel was to attack the lines at dawn on the third in an effort to occupy Longstreet and Ewell during the assault on Petersburg. The corps commander moaned to his staff that they had little chance of surviving a strike at the Richmond defenses: "The whole thing was a gigantic forlorn hope."[10]

Weitzel's assault was to be preceded by a demonstration at Bermuda Hundred on the second. Like his colleague to the north, George Hartsuff was not keen on leaving his well-protected enclave. Like Weitzel, Hartsuff had been advised by Grant's headquarters that many, if not most, of the Rebels opposite him had been drawn to Petersburg to augment Lee. Also like Weitzel, Hartsuff would have preferred some proof that this was so. On April 1 he shelled selected points along Pickett's line, hoping to judge by the response how many troops he faced. The results were dismayingly inconclusive: retaliation was moderate, which might only mean that Pickett was husbanding ammunition for an offensive of his own.

Hartsuff had no choice but to prepare for the dreaded advance. Late on the first he relayed Grant's order to Ferrero, who commanded the garrison at Bermuda Hundred, and Ferrero passed it on to the leader of his 2nd Brigade, Colonel George C. Kibbe. Kibbe briefed Major James B. Campbell, commander of the 10th New York Heavy Artillery, whose men would spearhead the demonstration, scheduled for 4:30 A.M. on the second. Campbell's outfit had been converted to infantry only a few months before and had no experience in charging fortifications. Like Weitzel's advance, Hartsuff's effort might prove suicidal. But as everyone at Bermuda Hundred realized, there was no help for it.[11]

∗

Mackenzie's troopers hated being tied to the pace of heavily laden supply wagons, but their movement to Petersburg was a tribute to their leader. After escorting the wagons to a supply depot along the Weldon Railroad at midday on March 30, the horsemen rested and ate in the rear of Ord's main body along Hatcher's Run.

At first Mackenzie wondered if he would accompany his army's infantry on its advance against Petersburg. Then, at 9:45 P.M. on the thirty-first, Grant directed Ord to send the cavalry westward to join Sheridan. It would augment three other divisions, two of which had served "Little Phil" in the Valley under Brigadier General Wesley Merritt. The third command, which had remained at Petersburg throughout the siege, had been Gregg's; now it was led by Major General George Crook. Grant's order was atypically urgent: "I want Mackenzie to go to-night," he told Ord. "It may be too late to-morrow morning."[12]

The events that spawned this order had begun two days earlier, when Sheridan and his 13,000 horsemen had ridden to Dinwiddie Court House, 12 miles southwest of Petersburg and 4½ miles southeast of a strategic crossroads known as Five Forks. At the crossroads Lee was trying to shore up his far right with five brigades of infantry and a large force of cavalry under Pickett. As Grant had predicted to Hartsuff, the Gettysburg hero had slipped across the Appomattox with many of the troops who had been guarding Bermuda Hundred Neck.

In some ways Pickett's new position was more important than the one he had held above the river, and his opponents knew it. Grant wished Sheridan to smash Pickett's line and occupy Five Forks, gaining Lee's rear and access to his last lines of supply. Sheridan had gotten off to a promising start by taking Dinwiddie Court House on March 29 and advancing northward to threaten Pickett's position. A probing action that day was followed by an advance two days later by all three of the divisions with Sheridan. All in all, the cavalry gave a good account of itself during the fighting near Dinwiddie, but in the end the much larger Confederate force—19,000 strong, thanks to recent reinforcements—had forced Sheridan to withdraw.[13]

Little Phil was far from finished. He planned to renew the fight as soon as possible, this time on more even terms. Grant saw to it that Sheridan would get the support of not only Mackenzie but also Warren's V Corps. Sheridan's offensive was set for the morning of the first; for this reason Grant had urged Ord to hasten his cavalry westward.

Mackenzie complied. His command rode throughout the night of the thirty-first and well into morning. Overtaking Warren's slow-footed infantry on the road to Dinwiddie, the troopers reached Sheridan's field headquarters just before dawn. Though pleased by Mackenzie's celerity, Sheridan critized Warren's advance. Long after 5:00 A.M., when Sheridan had intended to strike, the infantry was still a mile or more away. In fact, Warren moved so deliberately and conspicuously that Pickett had time to fall back into the Five Forks defenses. His infantry brigades held the main line, with cavalry on both flanks and in the rear. The tiny mounted brigade of Brigadier General William P. Roberts tried to connect Pickett's left with Lee's defenses at Petersburg.[14]

Disgusted by Warren's dawdling, Sheridan decided to begin the contest without him. Soon after dawn on the first he ordered Mackenzie to move north from Dinwiddie via the Crump Road as far as the White Oak Swamp Road, an extension of Pickett's main line; at that point the cavalry was to veer westward toward the Confederate left. Meanwhile, Merritt, with the divisions of Brigadier Generals Thomas C. Devin and George Armstrong Custer, would move against the enemy right and Crook's horsemen the center.

Though Sheridan's main force moved out promptly at six, Mackenzie lagged behind, awaiting the arrival of Warren, whose infantry would also operate against the enemy left. Warren's lead division under Brigadier General Charles Griffin did not near Mackenzie's position on the Crump Road until 7:00 A.M., when Mackenzie pulled off the road in favor of the foot soldiers. As Warren's troops shuffled past, the cavalry, having risen so early to no purpose, glared at them. In turn, the men of the V Corps looked dubiously at these horsemen. Aware of the cavalry's checkered past, Griffin advised one of his brigade commanders: "Don't be too sure about [support from] Mackenzie; keep a sharp look-out for your own right."[15]

Additional delays, not all of them Warren's fault, held up the combined offensive until after 1:00 P.M. Even then the attack lacked the full participation of the V Corps, which continued to advance so slowly that its main body did not hit the Confederates until long after Sheridan initiated the fighting. Along the Rebel right and center, the carbineers of Devin, Custer, and Crook charged Pickett's breastworks. On the left, Mackenzie, whose vanguard had passed to the north flank of the V Corps, piled into Roberts's brigade. After several minutes of formless fighting with swords and pistols, resistance suddenly broke under the pressure of a saber charge by the 11th Pennsylvania, at the head of which Colonel Spear fell severely wounded. Within minutes Roberts's men were scattering across the fields, and the road to White Oak Swamp lay open. Without hesitating, Mackenzie forged westward toward Pickett's main force.

The mounted column soon came within rifle range of the Rebel infantry, which was making a desperate defense. Already, however, Pickett's line was weakening under the hammering of Sheridan's squadrons and horse artillery batteries. Mackenzie hoped to increase the pressure intolerably. By dislodging the Confederate cavalry, he had effectively isolated Pickett from Lee's army at Petersburg. If he could drive farther into the Confederate left, the Five Forks line would become untenable.

Mackenzie dismounted most of his command, keeping only the 1st Maryland in the saddle to guard the western end of the road. Here the young brigadier displayed a tactical preference that contrasted with his predecessor's penchant for fighting in the saddle no matter what. Just as Mackenzie poised to strike Pickett's infantry on his own, he saw the head of Warren's corps engulf Pickett's line farther to the west. Having taken an oblique path to the northwest, the V Corps surged over the breastworks, forcing the Confederates to retreat.[16]

Mackenzie was about to add his weight to the infantry effort when Sheridan directed him to hit the Confederate rear as Warren and the rest of Sheridan's cavalry attacked Pickett's front. Hastily remounting, the troopers of the Army of the James soon were north of Five Forks, building breastworks between Pickett's position and Hatcher's Run.

In this sector Mackenzie's men rendered their most valuable service of the day, cutting loose with their repeating carbines and dislodging sections of the enemy line. Mackenzie found his adversaries "giving way without much resistance." As a finishing blow he had the 1st Maryland, supported by the 5th Pennsylvania, charge the length of the Rebel rear. Harried beyond endurance, scores of Confederates threw up their hands.

While Mackenzie's men herded the captives to the rear, Merritt's divisions breached Pickett's right flank. But as the victorious troopers prepared to link with their friends in the Army of the James, Rooney Lee's cavalry interposed. Standing firm, Robert E. Lee's son shored up the crumbling flank long enough for hundreds of foot troops to escape through woods north and west of Five Forks.

As though annoyed by the last-ditch heroics, Sheridan rode along the line, seeking Warren's help in overcoming this final spasm of resistance. Unable to locate the infantry commander, who had left his field headquarters to oversee operations in a remote sector, Little Phil exploded. Even as shouts of triumph went up along the line, Sheridan exercised authority given to him by Grant: when he found Warren, he relieved him of command and sent him back to Petersburg in disgrace. The humiliated officer eventually was assigned a rather nebulous command under Hartsuff at Bermuda Hundred.

Thus the day ended on an unhappy note for the V Corps, Army of the Potomac. In sharp contrast, the morale of the Army of the James's cavalry had never been so high. Having accomplished more than anyone under Sheridan or Warren could have expected—its trophies including upward of 5,000 prisoners and an open road to Petersburg—the cavalry had gained in a few hours of fighting under Mackenzie more success than it had achieved in a year of service under Kautz.[17]

By four o'clock on the morning of April 2 Meade's artillery outside Petersburg had fallen silent. Soon afterward, the VI and IX Corps attacked the city from southeast, south, and southwest. The sound of musketry thundered along Hatcher's Run, but another two hours passed before Ord's soldiers could release pent-up tension by charging toward the nearest stretch of Rebel defenses.

Ord committed all of Foster's units and most of Turner's; only Birney's division was left in the rear to provide support. The attackers drove forward so furiously that they were in the enemy's trenches almost before they realized it, the defenders having fled for their lives. By sunrise Ord's command had penetrated picket lines, overrun rifle pits, and scaled abatis and slashings. As Grant later wrote, "The outer works of Petersburg were in the hands of the National troops, never to be wrenched from them."[18]

By 8:00 A.M., as the Army of the James dug in, reversing the works it had seized, it learned that wider and deeper penetrations had occurred on the VI and IX Corps' front. Many of Wright's men had turned westward and were mingled with Ord's troops, with whom they shared confiscated breastworks. Gibbon, who had immediate command of the effort against the outer defenses, suggested that the VI Corps cooperate with Foster's and Turner's divisions in moving up the Boydton Plank Road. Wright assented, placing several brigades in column on Gibbon's right and forming the bulk of his corps into a strike force along the western flank. Soon the mixed force was abandoning the outer works and tramping northeastward, weapons ready.

In about thirty minutes the VI and XXIV Corps were within sight of the forts that guarded Petersburg's inner line. Halting just beyond artillery range, Gibbon readied his assault. Foster would strike Fort Gregg diagonally to the northwest while Harris's brigade, with the rest of Turner's division in its rear, would attack westward against Fort Whitworth. On either side of the assault columns, Wright provided support by moving up sharpshooters; in the rear, Birney did the same.[19]

Foster's and Harris's objectives lay along the west side of a little creek on high ground that permitted a plunging fire of artillery. Fort Gregg was the stronger work; its garrison was heavier—300 members of the 12th and 16th Mississippi infantry regiments—and it was anchored by several guns. An enclosed redoubt whose position commanded Fort Whitworth as well as smaller works, Fort Gregg boasted parapets eleven feet high and a surrounding ditch fourteen feet wide and at least ten feet deep. In contrast, Fort Whitworth, 100 yards to the northwest, was held by far fewer troops and mounted only three cannon; it was vulnerable from the rear due to an uncompleted parapet and ditch. Another weakness was the lack of a connecting curtain to shield efforts by one redoubt to reinforce the other.

Following a barrage intended to weaken both forts, Foster's division was sent in against Fort Gregg at one o'clock in the afternoon, with Colonel Thomas O. Osborn's brigade on the right and the brigades of Colonels George Dandy and Harrison Fairchild on the left. With a cheer, Foster's men ran toward the redoubt's ditch against a barrage of shot and shell, to which the gunners in Fort Whitworth added enfilading fire. Throwing down ladders and logs, men in front scrambled across the moat, secured a foothold at the base of the redoubt, and started up the glacis. They did not get far; one participant recalled that "the steepness and slippery nature of the sides of the fort . . . rendered futile all our efforts to scale them." Blasted from many angles, the attackers tried repeatedly to reach the top until "nearly frantic" from wasted energy. The survivors fled across the moat, past dozens of dead and wounded.[20]

No sooner had the first wave met defeat than a second went rolling north. A Maine soldier watched from the rear as "the little fort was enveloped in a surging mass of assailants. They filled the ditches, and eagerly sought for a footway by which to reach the stubborn defenders, who fought with magnificent desperation." Again desperation triumphed; again survivors retreated.[21]

A third time the division went forward, causing comrades to gasp in admiration of its spirit, if not its luck. This effort ended like the others, though a handful of attackers managed to scale the incline and top the parapet, only to be impaled on Rebel bayonets or shot down at close range. Other assailants staked a stand of colors on the forward slope, but it was soon shredded by rifle fire.[22]

A fourth assault, with some of Turner's and Birney's troops going in with Foster's, carried the position. Pulling themselves up by grasping rifles embedded in the glacis, enough assailants gained the parapet to hold it against several counterattacks. Most of those who reached the top passed beyond the redoubt to strike its garrison in the rear. From there the Federals gained entrance, and the men of Dandy's brigade competed with the Colored Troops in clearing the works.

When the half hour of shooting, stabbing, and clubbing had ceased, survivors stood among piles of corpses that included fifty-seven defenders. One victor compared the fort "to nothing but a slaughter-pen. The blue and gray were there promiscuously heaped together." Another Federal recalled wading through "a pool of blood, a sight which can never be shut from memory."[23]

Within minutes Harris's West Virginians, who had been huddling behind some farm buildings under a cannonade from Fort Whitworth, rushed the smaller redoubt. Aided by artillery fire from II and VI Corps batteries, they ran across 150 yards of shell-swept ground. Even before they reached Whitworth's uncompleted parapet, the cannonade ceased. Scaling the forward slope and entering the work, the attackers discovered that the Confederates had fled to avoid the fate of Gregg's men. The Wild Cat Brigade then occupied both redoubts, freeing Foster's division for duty closer to Petersburg.

The assault on Fort Gregg had cost Gibbon 10 officers and 112 men killed, plus 27 officers and 565 men wounded, an appalling toll for thirty minutes of fighting. In addition to the Confederate dead inside Fort Gregg plus perhaps 12 others killed before and after the assault, Gibbon claimed to have taken 200 prisoners. According to one witness, some barely escaped death at the hands of captors enraged by their furious resistance.[24]

The toll not only in Ord's sector but also along the length of Meade's line shocked the Union command. Grant had intended to follow initial success with an all-out effort to occupy Petersburg by nightfall. Foreseeing the casualties that such a push would entail, he decided that Meade should resume his bombardment from a closer position. If Lee did not evacuate, Grant would then launch a new offensive at 6:00 A.M. on the third. His armies had been waiting to enter Petersburg for more than nine months; they could wait another day.[25]

Early on April 2 Grant again urged Weitzel at Bermuda Hundred to attack westward, followed the next day by an advance on Richmond. At three o'clock that morning Hartsuff's batteries began to blast the works recently occupied by Pickett's division and now held by troops of unknown identity. The ninety-minute barrage went virtually unanswered; one observer recalled that two shells sailed inside the Union lines.

About half past four, with dawn breaking, Colonel Kibbe's demibrigade went forward as scheduled. For a time the advance met no opposition. But when the Federals struck a picket line a few hundred yards out, the Confederate batteries opened up. Having withheld their fire despite extreme provocation, the Rebels unleashed a barrage that for a time trapped the attackers between the lines. Finally Hartsuff's guns produced a covering fire that enabled Kibbe's men to return to their works, minus eighty casualties.

Clearly the enemy held the lines along Bermuda Hundred neck in force. Hartsuff wired the news to Weitzel, who passed it on to City Point with a hint of I told you so. Shortly after noon, however, army headquarters sent word that Hartsuff should attack again in response to recent unmistakable signs that the Confederates were crossing the Appomattox to reinforce Petersburg. Their departure, Grant informed Weitzel, "will evidently leave your front very thin by night." Aghast at such an order, especially considering the cannonade on Hartsuff's front, Weitzel was further distressed by Grant's reminder that at dawn Devens and Kautz should advance toward Richmond.[26]

Nevertheless, each hour brought Weitzel hopeful signs. Throughout the second his signalmen reported troops passing down the turnpike to Petersburg. A message came in that a Rebel cavalry post on the Darbytown Road had been abandoned. Soldiers just released from Belle Isle and Libby Prisons reported that General Ewell's garrison expected to evacuate Richmond.

When he learned of Ord's and Meade's success outside Petersburg, Weitzel wondered whether the evacuation rumors were true. Even so, he was hugely relieved to learn from Grant, just before midnight, that no advance should be made against Richmond until further notice. Grant added that even if Richmond was not evacuated, Weitzel need not move against the city until the Army of the Potomac could support him. Standing beside his superior as he read the message, General Shepley saw Weitzel's face brighten for the first time in a week as "the heavy weight of this responsibility lifted from him."[27]

Although a crisis had passed, the Federals outside Richmond were even more vigilant that evening than in days past. They strained tired eyes to pick up signs of unusual activity across the lines. To keep his troops alert, Weitzel had each regimental band "run at full blast until midnight."[28]

He needed not have bothered, for few of his soldiers slept after two o'clock that morning, when Richmond exploded with an unearthly roar. Seconds later pickets were gaping at a horizon ablaze with flame. The men were kept awake by subsequent detonations that rocked the city for hours, spreading uncontrollable fires.

The capital's evacuation was a fact. Late the previous night Ewell's men had filed through the city streets, heading westward. As they departed, a rear guard set fire to government storehouses to prevent them from falling into Yankee hands. Wind spread the flames in every direction, engulfing arsenals and ordnance depots. The resulting explosions and fire would ultimately destroy $30 million in public and private property.

With the capital evacuated, Weitzel hoped he might occupy it without loss. Shortly before 5:00 A.M. General Devens sent a picket unit creeping toward the nearest fortifications, which proved to be empty. A member of the division later wrote to his wife, "You should have heard the shout from our men!"[29]

Volunteers went forward to clear away land mines. Most were easily located; the defenders had departed so hastily they had not removed the stakes that marked them.

Dawn arrived and made the flames from the city seem all the more lurid. Many soldiers believed the fire lighted their way to "the promised land." One

The ruins of Richmond, April 1865. LIBRARY OF CONGRESS.

remarked that "we marched on eager to see this place . . . the goal of a good many thousand brave men who have given up their lives and were not permitted to see it." Rather than apocalyptic, some sights were mundane to the extreme. Major Bruce's ruminations were interrupted on the outskirts of the city by "a farmer ploughing in a field while cinders from the burning capital were falling at his feet."[30]

With the prize so near at last, a race sprang up for the honor of being the first to enter. Although destined to stir much dispute, the contest appears to have been won by Major William J. Ladd, a boyish member of Devens's staff who was on the forward picket line when dawn broke. Heedless of the danger, Ladd spurred his horse up the New Market Road and entered Richmond at about 5:30 A.M. He rode to the naval yard, where through daring or lunacy he climbed the rigging of a burning ship to seize its flag minutes before the its magazine exploded. Wrapping the souvenir about his shoulders, Ladd returned nonchalantly to his lines.[31]

The first unit to reach Richmond was thirty pickets from the 13th New Hampshire under Lieutenant Royal B. Prescott. One of the forces that had probed the capital's outer defenses the previous several days, Prescott's band came up to the intermediate works, just beyond the junction of the New Market Road and the Osborne Turnpike, at 6:30 A.M. There it met a carriage carrying Mayor Joseph Mayo, who was seeking someone to whom to surrender and to secure a pledge of tolerance and forbearance in dealing with the population. Prescott considered himself too junior to grant so important a request, so he referred the mayor to Weitzel, then cantering up the New Market Road amid his staff. So that not even his commander could beat him into Richmond, Prescott then doubled-quicked his unit into the capital shortly before 7:15.

Because he halted to confer with Mayo, Weitzel realized he would be delayed in entering the city. He dispatched one of his aides, Major Thomas Thatcher Graves, and two companies of the 4th Massachusetts Cavalry to reach the capital by the shortest route and claim it for the U.S. Army. The horsemen clattered into the city between 7:15 and 7:30 and made for City Hall, where Graves planted the first Union colors, his regimental guidons. Not long after, Lieutenant Jonathan DePeyster, another member of Weitzel's staff, unfurled the first full-size banner atop the capitol.[32]

In advancing up the New Market Road, the troopers overtook long columns of infantry streaming toward Richmond; the cavalry detachment ran several soldiers off the road, oblivious to their cries and curses. Soon after the horsemen passed, a race developed between the white troops of Devens's division on the New Market Road and Kautz's black soldiers, advancing up the Osborne Turnpike. Because of a head start, the black soldiers reached the junction before Devens's men. Not surprisingly, they were angry and disappointed when, at Devens's order, they were moved off the road to permit the white troops to reach the city ahead of them.

For a time the African-Americans stared sullenly at their white comrades. They regained their spirits, however, when Kautz led them at the double-quick up both sides of the pike. This ensured that they would outdistance the whites, who maintained route step. Even so, shortly before eight o'clock, when they reached the outskirts of the city, the USCT were halted at Weitzel's order so that Devens's troops would enter first. Military tradition held that the first troops to enter a captured city secured and policed it; mid-nineteenth-century sensibilities would not permit black troops to fill that role.[33]

The first brigade to march into Richmond was that of Brevet Brigadier General Ripley, who would be provost marshal. Ripley learned of his good fortune some miles south of the city; he giddily rode the rest of the way. As he recalled years afterward in purple prose that fit the occasion:

> I rode backward and forward along the column, exchanging congratulations with the officers, and looking down into the flashing eyes and quivering faces of the men. . . . It was hardly needed, so eager and furious was the march and so well closed up the ranks from the anxiety of the rear regiments to grasp the long-fought-for prize as soon as the head of the column, but as I drifted back and forth along the flank, and occasionally sat still in my saddle to enjoy the sight of that long column rushing by, I sang out, as of old . . . 'No straggling in the ranks of the First Brigade to-day! Close up! Close up!'[34]

With its bands blaring and thumping, Ripley's command entered Richmond via the suburb of Rocketts, swung up Main Street to 27th Street, crossed over to Franklin Street, then on to Governor Street, and swarmed into Capitol Square. As his main body continued to file through, past sullen whites and the joyous faces of blacks, Ripley appropriated City Hall for his headquarters, from which he reigned as the "Duke of Richmond."[35]

Ripley's early duties included guarding strategic points to quell looting and vandalism that arose after Ewell's evacuation. His men put out the fires and sought to calm the skittish. Providing for them was an even more formidable task. Ripley was staggered by the sight of ragged, destitute women and emaciated children. One occupier wrote: "Of all the sights I ever saw, Richmond, on the 3d of April, was the hardest. The people were literally starving. The market looked as if it had not had a pound of meat in it for years." A New York officer observed that "all was so pitiful that it dampened the thrill of victory."[36]

When he finally entered the city and made his office in the Confederate White House, Weitzel observed that the people were "perfect pictures of utter despair. It was a sight that would have melted a heart of stone." He quickly ordered army commissary and quartermaster wagons into the city, providing not only for the troops but also for a population that could no longer sustain itself.[37]

It took weeks to eradicate the misery, but the military governor of Richmond made a good start. Working closely with staff, city fathers, and representatives of the Sanitary and Christian Commissions, Weitzel formed relief committees that produced immediate benefits. Within four days Edward Williams of the Christian Commission alone distributed almost 9,000 rations to Richmonders, plus blankets, medicines, religious material, and health-care articles.[38]

Not every sight saddened observers. After Devens's men had passed through, Kautz's African-Americans made a triumphal entrance, creating a scene laden with military, political, and social significance. A *Chicago Tribune* correspondent who watched them march through the streets rejoiced that "the survivors of those who fell in the disastrous assault of the 'crater' at Petersburg have had the post of honor in the final consummation." Even Devens, who had cleared the New Market Road of black troops, brushed away tears as Kautz's men paraded past. It was, he told an aide, "a great sight for us to behold—the deliverance of a race."[39]

After Charles F. Adams, Jr., and his regiment of black cavalry rode through the city, the colonel wrote proudly of the event in a letter to his father, the United States ambassador to the Court of St. James. In reply, the elder Adams stressed the appropriateness of a fourth-generation representative of one of America's first families setting "foot in the capital of the Ancient Dominion . . . at the head of a corps which prefigured the downfall of the policy which had ruled in that capital." For four years his son's generation had been paying "the bitter penalty for . . . the shortcomings of the original founders of the Union."[40]

As the occupying army settled in for an indefinite stay, Weitzel dashed off telegrams detailing the city's occupation. Because Grant was far from a communications relay, the news did not reach him until two o'clock the following morning. It traveled more quickly to Washington, where it touched off raucous demonstrations. Church bells there and in hundreds of cities and towns across the Union pealed in celebration. Guns were fired in commemorative salvos, men and women shouted and cheered, and children set off fireworks. Years of dashed hopes, unfulfilled pledges, and unanswered prayers were swept away by the joyous din.[41]

Early on the third, Hartsuff sent skirmishers toward defenses that had been heavily manned for the past ten months, locking the Army of the James inside Bermuda Hundred. The works were empty.

At first he did not know how to react. He conferred with Ferrero and other subordinates and sought the advice of the recently arrived Gouverneur Warren. Out of these meetings came Hartsuff's decision to send Ferrero, with several hundred men, as far west as they could go, possibly to the railroad and turnpike. The journey, the first over that ground since June, was uneventful. Nearing the railroad about noon, Ferrero encountered not Pickett's men but members of the Army of the Potomac just up from Petersburg, with word that the Rebels had pulled out of that city as they had the lines opposite Hartsuff.

Ferrero's happy men turned toward Richmond but got only as far as Chester Station before they met scores of enemy stragglers, who told of Weitzel occupying the capital. Taking the fugitives in tow, Ferrero burned a train found to contain rations for Lee's army. Knowing no other course, he backtracked to Bermuda Hundred to update Hartsuff. The army's deliberate return to its bottle seemed like a prisoner afraid to leave a familiar cell.

Hartsuff knew that for him and his men the war was over. The next day Grant ordered him down to Petersburg to help oversee its occupation, which reunited the general with his old command, the IX Corps. That afternoon Hartsuff left behind a peninsula one reporter described as "very listless and half empty." After nearly a year of violent activity, the fields and woods of Bermuda Hundred lay wrapped in the stillness of peace.[42]

As Grant had hoped, Meade's and Ord's success along Petersburg's outer works on April 2 forced Lee to evacuate both the city and the capital it had long supported. He placed his troops on the roads leading to Amelia Court House, Jetersville, and Lynchburg.

The sector held by the Army of the James was slow to get definitive word of the move. By 4:00 A.M. on April 3, when Ord reported to Grant's headquarters that every work within supporting range of Forts Gregg and Whitworth had been abandoned, Grant had already launched a full-scale pursuit.[43]

The Army of the Potomac, principally Humphreys's II Corps and the V Corps, now under Griffin, headed northwestward, preceded by Sheridan with Merritt's, Crook's, and Mackenzie's cavalry. At first Ord was held back to let Meade's vanguard take the lead. Then he was told to move south to keep Lee from uniting with forces opposing Sherman in North Carolina. Ord formed a long column and moved it out the Cox Road, directly above the Southside Railroad and parallel to Meade's line of march.

For the balance of that day and well into the fourth, the Army of the James headed west as quickly as possible, hoping to bring Lee to bay short of a final bloodbath. Turner had the lead, with Foster immediately behind and Birney conspicuously in the rear. The black soldiers divided their time between marching and repairing sections of the Southside Railroad that the Federals had wrecked during the winter, now useful to them as a line of supply. The work was especially onerous because Birney's troops had to re-lay one side of the tracks, reducing the five-foot gauge to accommodate the smaller gauge of the U.S. Military Railroad trains. By nightfall, with Birney lagging, Turner and Foster were three miles beyond Sutherland's Station, having gone fifteen miles since 8:00 A.M. The pace had left the soldiers "completely worn out," and most fell quickly to sleep.[44]

The following day, as the pursuit continued, the Army of the James covered fifteen miles. That evening Ord's column shuddered to a halt near Wilson's Station, two-thirds of the way between Petersburg and Burkeville Junction. At Burkeville—one of Kautz's old haunts—the Richmond & Danville intersected the Southside. Ord realized that if Lee got to the depot first, he might ride the R&D into North Carolina. The junction was strategic as long as the Army of Northern Virginia ran free. Thus far only Sheridan had made contact with the Confederates, who had recrossed the Appomattox east of Amelia Court House to remain above and ahead of the pursuers.

April 5 was even harder on the army. The pace increased in response to Grant's worry that Lee might evade Meade. After 11:00 P.M., when Ord drew up outside Burkeville, having made twenty-two miles along a rough and dusty road, Meade nearly forfeited a chance to overtake Lee. Believing his enemy would linger the next day at Amelia Court House to scare up food, Meade obtained permission to lead his army up the R&D come morning. In case Meade had guessed wrong and Lee kept moving west, Ord's troops were to continue in that direction, with Sheridan's horsemen in the lead, hoping to overtake the fugitives near Farmville.

The gamble backfired. When the head of Meade's army came within sight of Amelia Court House after daybreak on April 6, it discovered the Confederates, hungry but mobile, steadily trudging westward. Meade had to take a position well to the rear, conceding his opponent a greater lead than before.

Some in the Army of the Potomac feared the Rebels might parlay that advantage into a flanking movement south.[45]

By the time it retook the road shortly after dawn on the sixth, the Army of the James had marched more than fifty miles in three days. Instead of sleeping, the men had spent several hours erecting breastworks at Burkeville in case Lee attacked. Birney was engaged in an even harder march, straining to catch up with the comrades who had left him behind, desperate to get in on the climactic confrontation.[46]

The army was as footsore as it had ever been, but Grant wanted more speed. Anxious to get across Lee's path near Farmville, he had Ord cull from Turner's division 500 members of the 54th Pennsylvania and 123rd Ohio. Escorted by 80 troopers of the only cavalry unit attached to the pursuit column, the 4th Massachusetts, and placed under the latter's commander, Colonel Francis Washburn, the foot soldiers left Burkeville before dawn on the sixth. They were to beat the Rebels to Farmville, seven miles to the northwest, and burn High Bridge over the Appomattox, which should have halted Lee's retreat. Washburn promised Ord he would succeed or die trying.

A few hours after the detachment left, Ord discovered that the head of Lee's column was much closer to Farmville than he had suspected—close enough to cut off and crush the expeditionary force. Hoping to recall Washburn, he dispatched several riders under his chief of staff, Major Read. If Read determined that the High Bridge operation was still feasible, however, he was to have Washburn tend to that first.[47]

Read reached Farmville late in the morning, where he found Washburn confronting a redoubt that defended the sixty-foot-high bridge. When Washburn assured the staff officer he could still complete his errand, Read permitted him to try. But just as infantry and dismounted cavalry flanked the redoubt and prepared to seize it, horsemen from Lee's advance guard swept in from the east and slammed into Washburn's force. A firefight ensued, with the Federals slowly gaining the upper hand.

Additional Rebel cavalry, the main body of Major General Thomas L. Rosser's division, reached the scene just before the Federals could extricate themselves. Rosser attacked Washburn's infantry support as well as the 4th Massachusetts, overwhelming and scattering both forces. In the melee Washburn was shot three times, fell from his horse, and lost consciousness, then took a saber slash in the face as he lay on the ground. A Union trooper charged that the assailants "murdered Colonel Washburn long after the fight," although the officer did not succumb to his wounds until the twenty-second. Read, while trying to rally cavalry and infantry, also took a mortal wound. The survivors ran for their lives, many hiding in woodlots where Ord's column found them wandering about in a daze, overcome by nervous exhaustion.[48]

Although Washburn's and Read's effort had been dramatic ("it resounded," as one unit historian put it, "with echoes of medieval combat"), it had been defeated by Ord's flawed tactics. A slow-moving infantry force ought not to have set the pace for a mission that required speed. Had Washburn's regiment alone ridden to High Bridge, it might have destroyed the trestle before Lee's advance arrived.

Postwar writers imparted strategic significance to the fight at High Bridge by arguing that it made Lee believe he confronted a much larger force than he had supposed. Yet Lee's decision to halt for the rest of the day at Rice's Station, near Farmville, which enabled Meade's pursuers to make up lost ground, was not the product of Washburn's defense. Lee's plan for the sixth, which he drew up earlier in the day, called for at least a part of his army to lay over at Rice's Station in an imperative (but ultimately futile) attempt to secure supplies via the railroad.[49]

⎯⎯⎯►●◄⎯⎯⎯

After Five Forks Mackenzie's cavalry had handled a variety of assignments. On April 2 the little division rode with Sheridan's main force to Sutherland's Station, but the next day it was detached to escort hundreds of prisoners from Petersburg to the custody of Meade's provost marshals south of the city. On the fourth Mackenzie linked again with the divisions of Devin, Custer, and Crook to begin the pursuit of Lee. By hard riding in the lead of Sheridan's column, Mackenzie closed in on his target late in the afternoon, skirmishing for hours with the Rebel rear guard near Amelia Court House but failing to halt the retreat.

The cavalry of the Army of the James again parted company with Sheridan on the fifth as he rode off with Custer and Devin in a more aggressive effort to head off Lee. Along with George Crook's troopers, Mackenzie remained in Lee's rear, trying to slow and distract him while Sheridan sought to capture his supply trains near Jetersville. By making demonstrations that forced the Confederates to halt and give battle, only to see the horsemen draw out of range, Mackenzie delayed the fugitives, aiding Sheridan's strategy.

Suspecting, like Meade, that Lee intended to take the Richmond & Danville into North Carolina, Mackenzie on the sixth rode south toward Jetersville, only to learn that the Rebels had left the railroad and were headed west with Meade's army in remote pursuit. Inexplicably, Sheridan ordered Mackenzie to rejoin part of Ord's army at Burkeville. Mackenzie idled at the depot for most of the day before being ordered to Sheridan's new location, Prospect Station on the Southside Railroad. Reaching Sheridan's side early on April 8, Mackenzie accompanied Crook toward Appomattox Court House.

Late that day, upon nearing the courthouse village, Mackenzie's troopers realized that by hard riding—and thanks to Lee's stopover at Rice's Station—they and the rest of the cavalry had gotten ahead of their quarry. Sheridan's reunited command turned north that evening to block Lee's path and force his weary, hungry troops to give battle along the road to Lynchburg. As Mackenzie saw it, there was one sticking point: for the cavalry to halt so large a force, it had to have help from Meade or Ord. As of midday on April 8 both armies remained miles to the east.[50]

⫸⬦⬤⬦⫷

During the fighting at High Bridge, Ord moved his column out of Burkeville and headed for Farmville. Late on the sixth, short of its destination, Ord's advance encountered a Confederate force laying over at Rice's Station. The Rebels were well entrenched; darkness fell before the Army of the James could dislodge them.

Ord had no chance to uproot them the next morning. Dawn revealed that Lee had resumed his westward journey in search of a safe haven. The Confederates were now moving in two columns; the previous day the remnants of the corps of William Mahone and Lieutenant General John Brown Gordon had crossed the Appomattox on the bridge that Rosser's cavalry had secured. However, the rear guard botched an attempt to burn the span, permitting Meade to maintain pressure. Meanwhile, what remained of Longstreet's corps straggled over the Appomattox near Farmville. On the far bank, the men wolfed down their first issue of rations in five days.

Ord's objective was now to overtake Longstreet's column. With his command at full force—Birney's troops had rejoined him after a killing march from Sutherland's Station—the army leader strained throughout the seventh to bring his weight to bear on Longstreet's rear. His men struck the tag end of the Rebel column outside Farmville and refused to be shaken loose. Throughout the day they killed or captured hundreds of the enemy, demolished dozens of supply wagons, and seized several pieces of artillery. Ord's prisoners, many of whom had given themselves up willingly, wore the pallor of the living dead. In contrast, the pursuers never felt stronger or more eager to fight. As Grant noted, by the afternoon of the seventh "straggling had entirely ceased, and every man was now a rival for the front."[51]

At 3:00 A.M. on the eighth, a few hours after Grant sent a surrender demand through the lines, the Army of the James retook the road after a few hours' rest. Ord picked up the pace, marching almost without a halt for more than twenty hours. By day's end, through almost superhuman effort, the army had come thirty-eight miles from Farmville. "The march," one participant later claimed, "certainly has no parallel in the history of the Rebellion, or any war in Europe."[52]

As if that trek had not been brutal enough, Ord allowed the men barely three hours' sleep before resuming in the direction of Appomattox at three o'clock in the morning of April 9, Palm Sunday. Three hours of marching brought Foster's division, at the head of the column, to the outskirts of the county seat, where it heard skirmishing slowly rising in volume. The slapping sound of carbines raised the prospect that Sheridan's cavalry was engaging Lee's vanguard.

At a signal soldiers dropped out of line, ostensibly to eat their first breakfast in several days. Most were so weary, however, that they fell asleep as soon as they sank to the ground. When the carbine fire increased sharply, napping and eating halted. Hustled back into column, the men allowed themselves to be guided across open fields sloping down to a tree-fringed valley. Bleary-eyed veterans cursed their commander's lack of common decency. Then, suddenly, the mood changed drastically, fatigue and disgruntlement melting away. Officers had galloped up with word that Sheridan had indeed crossed Lee's path on the Lynchburg Road. It lay just across the valley, over the next rise. If the army could get there before the cavalry was swept away, Sheridan's roadblock would hold. Boxed in, Lee would have to surrender.

The news so galvanized the troops that they seemed not to mind Ord's command to double-quick the distance. Men who had been dead on their feet were suddenly racing across the fields, no longer in formation but in groups large and small. As they rushed toward the ridge, Ord spurred past on his charger, waving his hat and shouting: "I promise you, boys, this will be the last day's march you'll have to endure!"[53]

———⟶•⟵———

Soon after gaining the Lynchburg Road about a mile and a half southwest of Appomattox, Sheridan's troopers had been confronted by a formidable-looking column of infantry advancing rapidly from the east. The enemy force continued to grow, overflowing the road on both sides. Glancing to the north, the Federals spied a body of Confederate horsemen advancing against their left flank.

To counter the threat, Sheridan ordered Crook—to whose division Mackenzie was now attached—to dismount the cavalry of the Army of the James. Mackenzie whipped his men into skirmish lines facing north. The move was made so quickly that the troopers lacked the time to nail down their position. Their commanders realized the fact; as Mackenzie later wrote in his report, "I was ordered by General Crook, through one of his staff, to withdraw slowly when it became necessary . . . [which] would be, he stated, very soon."[54]

It came sooner than either officer expected. Mackenzie had barely taken position when the Confederate horsemen attacked. The force split the skirmish line, isolating half of it from Sheridan's main body. As ordered, the embattled troopers withdrew grudgingly toward their mounts, which, through some error, had been held far behind the firing line. The time lost to remounting and galloping back to the front permitted the Rebels to capture one of Mackenzie's artillery pieces. Crook helped Mackenzie stop the Confederate drive but failed to recover the cannon.

The halt proved to be temporary. Desperate to burst through the road-block before enemy infantry arrived, the Confederates surged westward and threatened to overwhelm the Union horsemen. Under this pressure the troopers gave ground slowly at first, then rapidly and in some disorder. As they were forced back, they glanced over their shoulders, looking for infantry support. Their withdrawal, and the opening of the road to Lynchburg, could be no more than minutes away. General Merritt likened the situation to "opposing the force of a cyclone with a wall of straw."[55]

About 9:00 A.M., with Sheridan's line beginning to collapse, Osborn's brigade of Foster's division topped the last rise and scrambled into position behind the cavalry, building a bulwark south of the road behind which the troopers could rally. Minutes later Dandy's brigade hastened to Osborn's left, astride and above the road. Then the brigade of Harrison Fairchild, backed by a battery of light artillery, extended Dandy's line farther to the north. As they came under musketry, the newcomers began to fashion breastworks and scoop out rifle pits.

Aware that deliverance was at hand, Sheridan's men, cheering as they fell back, formed in the infantry's rear. Many stared in amazement at the almost maniacal enthusiasm with which the infantry took position on both sides of the road. "Here, for the first time during the war," marveled one cavalry officer, "I saw men straggling ahead of their colors to get into a fight!"[56]

By the time the last trooper took shelter in its rear, Foster's division was virtually all in place. Perceiving one last chance to dislodge its foe, Lee's vanguard moved to strike both Union flanks before they could be anchored. Minutes before the blows could land, however, Turner's division came hurtling up from the south. Although hustled into formation without time to dig in, Turner eased the threat to Foster's right flank.

North of the road, the head of Birney's column, at last reaching the scene, tried to deflect the blow aimed at Foster's left. Although happy to be a part of the climactic struggle, the USCT command was in something of a foul mood. The previous day, in confirmation of his worst fears, Birney had been forced to halve his force and attach one brigade to each of Ord's white divisions. For reasons that remain unclear (probably because Birney protested the arrangement), Ord had relieved him and ordered him back to Petersburg.[57]

Although the effect of this episode cannot be determined, one of Birney's erstwhile brigades broke during the assault on the Union left, though it was bolstered by a fast-firing battery. Before the flank could cave in, Turner sent another black brigade to relieve the first; linking with remnants of the unit that had given way, the new arrivals repulsed the assault and shored up the position.

Slowly at first, then with growing haste, the Confederates withdrew along both sides of the road. As they retired, Union artillery got the range of the guns that had broken the Colored Troops and put them out of commission. That essentially ended the contest, but at first only the Federals appeared to realize it. Ord reappeared, riding the length of the rear and shouting, "Your legs have done it, my men!"[58]

Within minutes the Confederates saw the truth. At first many believed they had dislodged the cavalry, clearing a path to Lynchburg. Some had begun to shout the Rebel yell one more time. Now Ord's infantry snuffed out any hope of continued resistance. Looking on in satisfaction, one Federal noted that the enemy suddenly "recoiled and shrank back as if paralyzed!"[59]

CHAPTER SIXTEEN

Postwar Service

A FEW HOURS AFTER ORD AND SHERIDAN CUT OFF HIS RETREAT, LEE SURREN-dered to Grant in a home on the outskirts of the courthouse village. Ord was the only member of the Army of the James to observe the event, along with numerous members of Grant's staff and several high-ranking officers of the Army of the Potomac. Afterward Ord, mindful of the historic importance of the ceremony, located the owner of the home and paid Wilmer McLean $40 for the marble-top parlor table on which Lee had penned his acceptance of Grant's terms.[1]

Almost immediately after leaving the house, Ord turned his command over to Gibbon. The next morning he joined Grant on his trip to Richmond. Two days later Ord stepped from the train in the occupied capital.

Gibbon and most of his officers and men remained around Appomattox for another week. Grant ordered the army to help Meade carry out the surrender terms and attend to the Confederates' needs.

The army of the James did so with energetic dedication. Colonel Michael P. Small, Gibbon's commissary chief, supplied the famished Confederates with 25,000 rations. Small did his job so well that some members of his command complained he was depriving them of bread, coffee, and meat. More sensitive comrades applauded his humanitarian impulse. Surveying the "confused mass" of "half-starved" Rebels camped near the courthouse, one Massachusetts officer described it as "a scene to melt the bravest heart."[2]

As the Rebels ate, Mackenzie gathered up the Confederates' few resources and entrusted them to Gibbon's acting quartermaster, Captain Abram B. Lawrence. Within three days of Lee's surrender Lawrence confiscated 15,900 small arms, 147 cannon, great quantities of ammunition, infantry and cavalry equipment, battery and supply wagons, and hundreds of horses and mules.[3]

The day after the surrender the 4th Massachusetts Cavalry escorted Lee and five members of his staff on the long, sad journey to Richmond. The five-day horseback trip was solemn in the extreme; instead of being elated over the enemy's downfall, the Federals felt borne down by Lee's profound melancholy. At journey's end Lee was teary-eyed as he thanked the escort commander for his kindness. Though he kept his composure, the Union officer was unable to repress "a deep sympathy for the broken-down old man."[4]

Two days after Lee departed Appomattox, his army laid down its battle flags and remaining weapons in an elaborate ceremony staged in fields outside the village, an event planned by Gibbon and two of Meade's subordinates. On the twelfth Gibbon helped guide the fragments of the once-invincible Army of Northern Virginia into assigned positions. Later he and his staff conveyed to Secretary Stanton in Washington the seventy-seven banners surrendered that afternoon under a gray sky.[5]

After the surrender rituals Lee's troops (all of whom had been paroled, many via the pen of officers of the Army of the James) began to make their way home. At the same time, many of Gibbon's troops also dispersed. The African-Americans of Birney's division, now commanded by the army's former artillery chief, Brigadier General Richard H. Jackson, started back to Richmond. Detachments of Mackenzie's cavalry rode to Staunton, Charlottesville, and other points to confiscate munitions and stamp out pockets of resistance.[6]

Late on the twelfth the rest of the cavalry, followed by John Turner's infantry division with Gibbon in command, moved westward to receive the surrender of the Lynchburg supply base. En route the army mingled with numerous homeward-bound Confederates, who, while understandably downcast, displayed a spirit of resignation that boded well for the suddenly reunited nation. One Ohio veteran remarked: "At night the rebels camped with us, ate with us, slept with us, and told camp stories with us. With scarce an exception they were glad the war was over, and they on their way to their homes. There was not half the rancorous feeling among them that we found among the citizens who had not been in the army."[7]

After pacifying the Lynchburg area, confiscating or destroying military stores, and liberating former slaves, most of Gibbon's troops retraced their path to Appomattox on the fifteenth. There they prepared to embark on their long journey to Richmond and Petersburg. Before they could leave, however, they received news of Lincoln's assassination. At first stunned, the army swiftly plunged into mourning. One soldier informed his mother, "I don't think I ever herd any news that made me feal so bad as when I herd of Old

Abe being murderd." Years later another veteran wrote, "The revulsion of feeling and the terrible depression it [the news] caused among the soldiers has never been, and can never be, described."[8]

Perhaps inevitably, grief turned to anger, bitterness, and a desire for revenge. The troops unleashed their fury on any Southerner, soldier or civilian, who lingered near Appomattox. A New York officer advised the locals to give the Federals a wide berth for several days, "for the soldiers would have but little mercy on any of them, even the non-combatants." This held true in Richmond and Petersburg as well. Outside Petersburg a Pennsylvania heavy artillerist remarked that "revenge is the cry with all" in his regiment. Inside the former Confederate capital a Massachusetts infantryman saw his fears confirmed when comrades "pounced with the ferocity of wild beasts upon every rebel soldier they could lay their hands upon, beating and driving them from the streets, the poor fellows all the while in ignorance of the cause of their bad treatment. They, however, soon learned to what it was due, and for the next day or two kept out of sight, as it was absolutely unsafe for them to be seen."[9]

To divert the men's attention and siphon off their aggression, Gibbon started them east earlier than planned, on the morning of the seventeenth. The march lasted a week, interrupted by stops at Burkeville, Prospect Station, Farmville, and other points along the railroad. The layovers were needed: with the thrill of the chase gone, the road felt hard indeed.

The ground over which the soldiers trudged was familiar enough, but the sights were startlingly different from those two weeks earlier. The farms and fields—recently deserted and barren, scorched earth all around—were being worked by men in gray or mufti. One route-stepping veteran marveled that "those who had met us in battle were busy repairing the damage wrought by war; in fields over which armies had trod, plows were turning up the soil for spring crops." Years seemed to have passed since they had chased Lee toward his day of reckoning, as if war had never visited this region. An officer in the 11th Pennsylvania Cavalry found himself in a countryside he had visited on three raids the previous spring and summer, but one barely familiar: "At Flat Creek Bridge and Chula Station . . . no longer were the bridges watched with zealous eyes. No longer were men marching to death. No longer did foes vie for supremacy." He could scacely believe the war that had ruled his life for the past four years had become history.[10]

<hr />

Gibbon's column made a triumphal entry into Richmond late on the twenty-fourth. Saluted by the brass bands and honor guard of Devens's division, the newcomers trooped through the city and across the James to Manchester. There they went into fixed camp for the first time since leaving the Northside for Petersburg in the waning days of March.

The XXIV Corps had Richmond to itself, for Birney's old division had been at Petersburg since its return the week before. When Ord reached Richmond on the twelfth, he had sent Weitzel's black soldiers there, too. Some of their officers considered the transfer further proof of the army leader's prejudice. General Wild claimed that upon meeting him in the capital, Ord snapped: "You must get these damned niggers of yours out of Richmond as fast as you can!"[11]

Ord later explained that the presence of black troops in Richmond would stir resentment, complicating occupation rule. Other departmental officials claimed that the blacks had been evicted because their officers were incompetent, their discipline was poor, they had committed crimes against the populace including "atrocious rape," and they were exerting a bad influence on black civilians. To be sure, some African-American units had a history of rowdiness: Ord arrested Colonel Adams in response to citizen complaints that his troopers were thieves. Even so, it would appear that Ord rid the city of Colored Troops to defuse a racial situation that troubled him rather than to halt a crime wave.[12]

A secondary motive may have been Ord's low opinion of Weitzel, Shepley, Kautz, and Wild. His return to Richmond enabled him to relieve Weitzel as a matter of course. He also replaced Shepley, whom Weitzel had named military governor of the city, with Devens, who gave way on the twenty-first to Brigadier General Frederick T. Dent, Grant's brother-in-law and aide. Within three weeks of reaching the capital, Ord got rid of Kautz, whom the War Department would select, along with Generals Foster and Harris, for the tribunal that would try the Lincoln assassination conspirators. Ord did not wait nearly so long to dispose of the contentious Wild. One day after detraining at Richmond, he summarily relieved the abolitionist from duty. By the twentieth, after unsuccessfully appealing his removal to Grant, Wild was on a train for Massachusetts.[13]

Early on April 13, in compliance with Ord's wishes, Weitzel led his troops from Richmond to camps southeast of Petersburg recently occupied by the VI Corps. The blacks' new home received mixed reviews. Kautz liked the log huts erected by Wright's troops, but Weitzel found his camp near Poplar Grove Church filthy and noisome, its only water source a polluted stream. Eventually Ord permitted him to move west of Petersburg. On the twentieth Kautz's division made camp along the Cox Road, with Jackson's division farther south near the Boydton Plank Road.

In their new location the black troops took up many of the duties they had turned over to their white comrades at Richmond. They policed the countryside, arresting lawbreakers and vagrants; they guarded public and, in some cases, private property; they rebuilt fences, regraded roads, and relaid railroad track; they returned property the army had confiscated during the siege; and they hauled food and supplies into devastated Petersburg.[14]

For a time it appeared that the blacks' stay in Virginia would be brief. At an early date Ord cautioned Weitzel to hold his troops ready to move to North Carolina with the VI Corps and Sheridan's cavalry to help Sherman subdue General Joseph E. Johnston's dwindling but defiant army. In the third week of April Sheridan's troopers started south, but on the twenty-sixth, before Weitzel's men could break camp, Johnston surrendered.

For a time rumor also had the XXV Corps leaving for numerous distant locales. Every report was unfounded. Perhaps, Weitzel thought, his troops would remain at Petersburg until they were mustered out.[15]

>>●<<

Until June Ord oversaw the military occupation of Virginia. From Richmond he tried to revive the state's economy, especially local commerce. In time, however, he fell victim to Unionists who accused him of being too cordial with ex-Confederates. Ord's seemingly benevolent attitude toward his defeated countrymen (or, as one critic put it, his tendency to "show all smiles to violent and wealthy Traitors") cost him the support of the War Department. When Ord provided forage, subsistence, and transportation to paroled Confederates, even his old patron Grant rebuked him for misusing government resources. The commanding general sternly declared, "We cannot undertake to bear all the hardships brought on individuals by their treason and rebellion."[16]

Within two weeks of Appomattox Ord's decreasing stature in Washington sealed his demotion; on April 22 he was replaced at Richmond by former army chief of staff Henry Halleck, head of the new Military Division of the James. Halleck was determined to do the bidding of a War Department and Congress unsympathetic toward Virginians striving to rise above defeat. At Stanton's behest he laid a heavy hand on local whites, restricting their freedom, limiting their livelihood, and reminding them that they must bow to the government if they wished to regain their rights and privileges. Halleck effectively instituted Reconstruction in the upper South.

By late spring the Army of the Potomac appeared to be nearing wholesale mustering out. The Army of the James, however, seemed destined to remain on active duty indefinitely. When Halleck divided the Department of Virginia into eleven occupation districts and subdistricts, each embracing from one to nine counties, he assigned only four to commanders and units of the Army of the Potomac. Most he entrusted to elements of the Army of the James led by Hartsuff (District of the Nottoway), Gordon (District of Eastern Virginia), Ferrero (Sub-District of the Roanoke), Colonel Ludlow (Sub-District of the Rappahannock), Colonel Voris (Sub-District of the South Anna), and Colonel Gilbert H. McKibbin (Sub-District of the Blackwater).[17]

Halleck assigned these commanders and their troops (most districts were occupied by a dozen or more regiments) a variety of duties. They guarded government and private property and policed their realm. They established training camps, storage depots, and farms in each county to feed the troops and needy citizens. They recruited free blacks as military laborers and built barracks for them and camps for their dependents. They staffed the Labor Districts established to adjudicate employer-employee disputes and regulate contracts between ex-slaves and their former masters. In Richmond, Petersburg, and other cities they cleared rubble and restored transportation and communications. In Norfolk and Portsmouth they helped resume North-South trade.

Though Halleck closely supervised some of his district commanders, others, especially those far from Richmond and Petersburg, enjoyed near autonomy. At the same time, these subordinates had to fend for themselves when promised support was slow to arrive. Voris, for instance, found that after establishing his headquarters at Beaver Dam Station on the Virginia Central Railroad early in May, he had to wait three weeks for Halleck to send supplies "to contribute to the wants of the destitute poor of my district." Even at that late date Voris had received "no instructions except such general ideas as I have had from conversation with yourself . . . and would like to be directed by such orders as are given to commanding officers regarding the distribution [of relief] contemplated by the government."[18]

Largely by trial and error, Voris labored to satisfy the public needs. He traveled almost constantly over the 200 miles of middle Virginia that he ruled, conversing with residents and calling town meetings. His biographer noted that at these gatherings Voris informed the people "as to their new duties and responsibilities, urging justice, equal rights, and freedom for all, and forbearance, fair dealing and honesty of purpose upon all."

Voris's efforts appear to have succeeded. Once the sharpest echoes of the war began to fade, he persuaded planters, poor whites, longtime freedmen, and lifelong slaves to work, more or less in harmony, toward common prosperity.

To his relief he found that his region, which had been spared the worst of the war's devastation, supported enough of a crop "to keep the people from suffering, if it can be properly distributed, and necessity will develop effort on the part of the needy and force distribution on the part of those having supplies."

Voris was also gratified that the blacks in his district did not loll about, sponging off the Army, as some of his occupation colleagues had predicted: "The freedmen are making very creditable efforts to aid in the production of a new crop—Vagrancy has not manifested itself as a vice among them." His resources were taxed more by the disabled white veterans, widows, and orphans of the North Anna country, whom he helped as best he could. Though perhaps not typical of most occupation zones, where sustenance was scarce, the condition of Voris's region appears to have been in common with other rural districts in the military division.[19]

Halleck's reign, like Ord's, was brief. He strove not only to restore prosperity but also to reinstate self-rule as quickly as his civilian overlords would allow. He federalized some police forces to serve with Army provost units. He helped restore rail and canal service between Richmond and the Deep South. He even promoted Southern history by establishing an archive of Confederate military and political records.[20]

Ultimately, however, Halleck encountered trouble on both local and national levels. He invariably insisted that Virginians swear allegiance to the Union in order to regain many civil rights—engaging in business, entering a profession, transporting goods, even marrying. His iron rule antagonized many clergymen, magistrates, editors, and other pillars of the community. When he intervened in local government by invalidating municipal elections in Norfolk won by ex-Confederate officers, then imposing martial law on the city, the publicity made even Stanton wince. Midway through June General Terry was recalled from North Carolina and two weeks later replaced Halleck.[21]

If Virginians were upset by Halleck's rule, Terry was even harder to bear. The hero of Fort Fisher tightened up martial law policies and restricted trade in Richmond and Norfolk to businesses operated by avowed Unionists or people who had repudiated secessionist loyalties. He reaffirmed the repeal of codes by which whites sought to control ex-slaves. In closing the book on these enactments, Terry declared, "People of color will henceforth enjoy the same personal liberty that other citizens and inhabitants enjoy."[22]

Early in July Terry invoked confiscations throughout his reconstituted Department of Virginia. Treasury agents seized property owned by Richmond's Tredegar Iron Works as well as other businesses and banks in Richmond,

Norfolk, and Portsmouth. Owners had to pay rent on land whose ultimate disposition would be decided in the federal courts. Terry also oversaw the appropriation of private homes for use by the new Freedmen's Bureau. Early in August the departmental commander began to auction off other property—wagons, farm implements, dray animals—seized under this program.

The new regime followed the old in its close monitoring of local elections, voiding results as it saw fit. In July Terry's ranking subordinate, General Turner, who had recently been appointed to command the District of Henrico, overturned elections in Richmond that, like those at Norfolk, had returned prominent ex-Confederates to office. Not for several months did Terry and Turner again permit Richmonders to vote—and then only after leading secessionists had been stricken from the ballot. When the city's press raised an outcry, Terry shut down one newspaper for printing "disloyal utterances" and threatened others with similar punishment.

As if these acts were insufficient, Terry fueled resentment by well-publicized efforts to reduce government relief to poor whites. To the last, he maintained a paternalistic attitude toward blacks, a course that in the summer of 1866 gained him the post of assistant commissioner of the Freedmen's Bureau in Virginia. In all likelihood it was this studied benevolence toward African-Americans that prompted the War Department to sustain Terry's regime while failing to support Halleck's and Ord's.[23]

For a time during the late spring and early summer of 1865, members of the Army of the James wondered if they would ever return to their families. Many considered themselves betrayed when, early in May, most of the regiments in the Army of the Potomac paraded through Petersburg and from there into civilian life. Later that month, Sherman's troops, just up from the Carolinas, passed through southeastern Virginia, bound for a "grand review" in Washington and then a mustering out. By this time the troops of the Department of Virginia were "[al]most crazy" to go home, but they remained on occupation duty without prospect of discharge.[24]

Seeking to appease the disgruntled troops, Halleck suggested to the War Department that the XXIV Corps be inactivated, a prerequisite to the whole-sale mustering out of its units. Despite issuing such a decree on August 1, however, Stanton authorized Halleck to discharge only the white regiments whose enlistments would expire before the close of September. This led to the departure of nearly forty regiments and batteries, but some sixty others remained on duty.

By late summer soldiers ineligible for immediate discharge were becoming restive. The average enlisted man had signed on for three years or until the end of hostilities, whichever came first. Early in May Lincoln's successor, Andrew Johnson, had proclaimed that armed resistance to federal authority in the former Confederacy "may be regarded as virtually at an end." If so, what right did the government have to keep men under arms? Some regiments presented their grievances to district commanders; other units talked of mutiny. Not enough men rebelled, however, to soften government recalcitrance.[25]

Summer became autumn, chilly winds gusted through the streets of Richmond and across the meadows of rural Virginia, and the men of the Army of the James kept at their posts, walking guard, performing fatigue duty, feeding indigent Rebels, and arbitrating disputes between former slaves and their masters. By late October twenty regiments of infantry and cavalry remained on active service. A member of one of these outfits, the 11th Maine, began to despair of seeing relatives and friends. As he wrote to his brother, "Last April I expected to be out of the service before the middle of June. In June I set August for the month, and in August I called it October. But there seems to be no more prospect than there was last April."[26]

Slowly, almost imperceptibly, as the regular service took on the burden of occupation duty, the volunteer army dwindled to skeleton strength. Most of the remaining white outfits finally headed home during the early part of the winter. By mid-January 1866 only five regiments remained on station in Terry's bailiwick; even the private who had readjusted his timetable again and again had gone home to Maine. Even so, not until February 6 did the last unit of white troops in the Department of Virginia, the 96th New York Infantry, a veteran of every engagement from Bermuda Hundred to the Appomattox Campaign, entrain for the North. Its departure left only Weitzel's black soldiers on duty.[27]

⟶⊷⊶⟵

The ultimate disposition of the XXV Corps was decided shortly after the command was transferred from Richmond to Petersburg. Early in May 1865 rumors of its dispatching to various points crystallized into a report that it was bound for Texas. This time the grapevine got it right: by May 24 transports had begun to carry Weitzel's troops to Fort Monroe. Throughout June they were conveyed around the tip of Florida to Mobile Bay and thence to the Rio Grande country. The vanguard reached the Brownsville–Brazos de Santiago region in midmonth following lengthy delays in Alabama; two weeks later other brigades landed farther up the coast at Corpus Christi and Indianola.[28]

The blacks had come not merely to prod unreconstructed Texans into the Union fold. They had become instruments of U.S. diplomacy in a long-deferred confrontation with the French troops that had invaded Mexico under Emperor Ferdinand Maximilian. The French had imposed a puppet government on that country in flagrant violation of the Monroe Doctrine, secure in the knowledge that a distracted United States could protest only vocally. Grant, for one, considered the intervention "a direct act of war against the United States" and a challenge not to be ignored. With the tacit support of his civilian superiors, Grant mounted an expedition under Phil Sheridan, composed of not only the XXV Corps but also more than 50,000 white troops formerly stationed at Mobile, Alabama; Little Rock, Arkansas; and Nashville, Tennessee.[29]

Assigned to the sector commanded by Major General Frederick Steele, the black troops spent seventeen months of desultory service along the border. During that period Sheridan's generals maneuvered for position against the French troops of Marshal Achille Bazaine, covertly supported republican forces under Benito Juárez, and negotiated for the return of war materiel given Maximilian by renegade Confederates under General Edmund Kirby Smith. Sheridan strove in vain to secure authority to cross the Rio Grande and restore the Juárez government. When Maximilian returned some of the stores he had unlawfully received, service on the border settled into a pattern of unwarlike routine.

Weitzel's troops saw no combat in Texas. They lay in camp atop the sand hills above the river so long that they found "soldiering had lost its interest." When not lying about, they performed the duties of garrison life while also helping Sheridan build an eighteen-mile-long railroad from Brazos de Santiago to Clarksville. While thus engaged, the men endured a rich variety of discomforts: 100-degree heat, almost impenetrable dust storms, snakes, scorpions, tarantulas, lizards, and the sand fly, a creature one USCT officer described as "a compound of all the disagreeable qualities of mosquitos, fleas, lice, gnats and bedbugs."[30]

Numerous officers reached their limit and resigned. Able-bodied enlisted men, of course, could not opt out of the service. Though many of the rank and file had no homes to return to in the North—at least no permanent residences—most longed for a more pleasant environment. But those who hoped for an early return to Virginia were disappointed.

In January 1866 the XXV Corps, a unique military organization and a racial experiment of largely unfulfilled promise, formally passed out of existence. Most of its troops, however, remained in Texas, assigned to Sheridan's Military Division of the Gulf. Not for another ten months—until shortly before Maximilian's government collapsed, an outcome at least partly attributable to pressure exerted by Sheridan—could the black soldiers leave for points north, where they received their final pay and discharge. Many doubtless shared the sentiment of General Weitzel, who considered his relief from duty on the Rio Grande the happiest hour of his military career.[31]

The veterans of the Army of the James attempted to keep it alive in memory through regimental reunions, political rallies, and patriotic assemblages. In May 1868 prominent officers, including Benjamin F. Butler, established the Society of the Army of the James "to perpetuate the kind social relations formerly existing among the officers of the 10th, 18th, 24th, and 25th Army Corps." The quasipolitical nature of the organization was reflected in its first triennial reunion, held in Chicago during the week in which the Republican Party gathered there to nominate Grant as its presidential candidate. For unknown reasons the society folded shortly after its third reunion at New York in October 1874. Thereafter the veterans tried to keep the spirit of the army alive through membership in such organizations as the Grand Army of the Republic, the Society of the Army of the Potomac, and various regimental and battery survivors' associations.[32]

By the 1930s most of these groups had passed from the scene, but the veterans and the memories they shared lingered on. The Army of the James may be said to have passed away on July 20, 1945, when its last survivor, Horace W. Simpson, a veteran of the 23rd Illinois Infantry, died at Faulkton, South Dakota, at the age of ninety-seven.[33]

The Army of the James has come down through history as a hard-luck army, an army of incompetents, or both. To be sure, it lost nearly every engagement it fought. When it did not fail outright, it could not reap the fruits of victory; its capture of Fort Harrison in September 1864, for instance, put enough pressure on the Richmond defenses to have made them untenable; still, they held for another six months and then collapsed only as a result of the fall of Petersburg. The army's two major victories were qualified. It managed to capture Fort Fisher in January 1865 as much through the support of David Porter's fleet and the unwillingness of Braxton Bragg to relieve the besieged garrison as through the power and valor of its troops. And although the army cut off Robert E. Lee's retreat from Petersburg and Richmond, forcing his surrender, the Army of Northern Virginia had been rendered gaunt and weak by heavy attrition, relentless marching, scant rations, and defeatism.

If historians are correct in describing the Army of the James as an army of losers, they have failed to examine the sources of its failure and frustration, most of which lay outside its ranks. Although the army's first and preeminent commander, Ben Butler, was no military genius, he displayed more competence than most critics then or since have granted him. He was, after all, a talented administrator, and his ability to conceptualize and convey the essence of military operations—evidenced by his twenty-page plan for capturing Richmond's exterior defenses in September 1864—was impressive. Butler's primary deficiency was his unwillingness to supervise the tactics of his subordinates, possibly from a fear of physical harm on the front lines. Still, it was primarily the inadequacy of Quincy A. Gillmore and William Farrar Smith that brought disaster to the army during its early, critical period in the field, thus denying it opportunities to capture Richmond in May 1864 and Petersburg early the following month. Their inability to cooperate, plus their distrust of and lack of respect for Butler, virtually guaranteed the army's failure to realize Grant's strategic objectives.

Then, too, those objectives and the way Grant explained them to Butler handicapped the army from the outset. The conditions and restrictions Grant imposed on the army during the Bermuda Hundred campaign caused Butler to strain unnaturally to coordinate his movements with the Army of the Potomac's. This unrealistic effort was further hampered by the War Department's contradictory reports of Meade's dispositions and intentions, which prompted Butler to curtail promising advances against both Richmond and Petersburg. The upshot was a tragic blend of miscommunication, misjudged intentions, and lost opportunities. Similar opportunities to capture Petersburg, to sever Lee's army from its support base in the Deep South, and perhaps to end the conflict in one sweeping movement were squandered on June 9 through Gillmore's incompetence and six days later through Smith's professional, physical, and emotional incapacity. Afterward fortune never smiled so sweetly on the Army of the James.

Even after Smith and Gillmore left the army, it experienced more than its share of frustration, demoralization, and defeat. As before, much of its travail was not of its making. Its brightest prospect to take Petersburg after mid-June—the brilliant plan wrecked by the disaster at the crater—failed through the blundering of Ambrose E. Burnside and his subordinates. Other ranking officers of the Army of the Potomac, as well as Grant himself, were largely to blame for tactical blunders during the Richmond offensives of late July, mid-August, and late September, all of which began with promise and ended in defeat. Even so, the Army of the James served proudly and effectively on the north side of its namesake river, especially during Robert S. Foster's seizure and defense of Deep Bottom and in the attacks on Forts Harrison and Gilmer, which came so close to breaking Lee's hold on his capital.

The army's two major efforts against Richmond in October 1864 came to grief more from faulty intelligence and Confederate reliance on interior lines than from any glaring deficiency of Butler or his troops. Even Butler's abject failure during the initial Fort Fisher campaign was not entirely his own. The lack of close support from the navy conspired with Butler's irresolution to doom the effort to close the Confederacy's last major seaport. During the second expedition to North Carolina, when Admiral Porter made amends for his earlier inadequacy, he divided with Butler's successor, Alfred Terry, credit for one of the most successful amphibious operations in U.S. history. Afterward the main body of the Army of the James, under Ord, rose above its record of hardship and hard luck by occupying evacuated Richmond and overtaking Lee's fugitives on the road to Appomattox. These acts of redemption and vindication awakened the army from its long nightmare.

Despite its often tragicomic nature, the Army of the James enjoyed opportunities to make a significant, even crucial, contribution to the war in the East. In May 1864 it could have seized Richmond, whose defenses were insufficiently manned until about the tenth. Thus, during its first five days in Southside Virginia, Butler's army might have attacked and held the place against all comers. A more carefully chosen route toward the capital, circumventing the heavy works at Drewry's Bluff, would have given the army easy access to its eastern or western environs. From there it could have neutralized Fort Darling and burned bridges across the James before either Lee or Beauregard could arrive to stop it. This would have doomed the most important piece of real estate in the South. By 1864 the Confederacy's true strength was in its field armies, but Richmond continued to symbolize its political integrity; the capital's loss would have denied Confederate claims of nationhood, spreading demoralization and disaffection.

After Beauregard and his supports reached the capital during the second week in May, the Army of the James had no realistic hope of taking the city. It nevertheless attempted to exploit opportunities to capture equally important Petersburg on May 9 and 28 and June 9 and 15. With most of its garrison transferred to Richmond, Petersburg lay open until the Army of Northern Virginia came down to secure it on June 18. Its fall would have forced the troops of Lee and Beauregard to wander westward in search of supplies, as their link with the Confederate interior would be irreparably broken. If Richmond's fall would have stripped the Confederacy of its political legitimacy, the loss of Petersburg would have dealt the Southern nation a devasting physical blow.

Not every operational failure of the Army of the James was due to circumstances beyond its control. One significant factor was the army's small size, which limited its staying power. Its operational elements—two infantry corps, one of which had only part of its original order of battle, plus a chronically undermanned cavalry division—were too small to guarantee success against every opponent the army encountered on the road to Richmond and Petersburg. Moreover, the army's hasty formation and its varied composition required months of campaigning to overcome. Its early service revealed the difficulty of cooperation. Not until the summer of 1864 did the corps form a team, in which commanders easily combined elements when warranted.

The army's racial mixture may also have limited its effectiveness. Although Butler's black troops showed themselves to be fit for combat as early as May 1864, white comrades required months to accept them as military equals. Only after the attacks on New Market Heights and Fort Gilmer did the whites acknowledge the steadfastness, intelligence, and courage of the black soldiers. Ironically, the army achieved its greatest tactical success after segregation, the formation of an all-black corps. During the Appomattox Campaign, a negrophobe, General Ord, relegated the African-Americans to the rear, which many USCT officers and men justifiably took as an insult.

Factors of size, composition, and race, however, counted for less in the long run than the shortcomings of the army's ruling elite. Butler appears to have waged every campaign with an eye on public office, trying to gauge the political advantage of every military movement. Given the loose rein he exercised over his senior commanders, Gillmore, Smith, and Kautz were too often permitted to hamper the army through timidity and vacillation, a reluctance to commit troops, and a penchant for relying on their own erratic judgment. Though all three were well-educated professionals, they appear to have been more suited to administrative or engineering duties than to the demands of field command. Too often each demonstrated faulty tactics, inadequate planning, and downright incompetence.

In some respects the amateurs performed better than the professional soldiers of this army. For every erratic politician-general such as Charles Heckman and Isaac Wistar and every malcontent like Edward Wild, the army enjoyed the talents of able civilian appointees such as Alfred Terry, Galusha Pennypacker, Robert Foster, Joseph Hawley, Hiram Burnham, Thomas Harris, N. Martin Curtis, and Gilman Marston. The influence of other competent citizen-soldiers such as Edward Hinks, Charles Devens,

David Birney, and George Stannard proved to be less enduring because of wounds or chronic illnesses.

Under such commanders, supported by the great number of non-professional soldiers in the lower ranks, the army persevered, endured, and eventually overcame. Officers and men encountered more than their fair share of adversity and had few victories to sustain them. Still, most served gamely and effectively to the last, refusing to quit short of that final triumph to which their fortitude and fidelity entitled them.

NOTES

ABBREVIATIONS USED IN NOTES

BB   *Autobiography and Personal Reminiscences of Major-General Benj. F. Butler: Butler's Book* (Boston: A. M. Thayer & Company, 1892)

BFB   Benjamin F. Butler

BL   *Battles and Leaders of the Civil War,* ed. Robert Underwood Johnson and Clarence Clough Buel, 4 vols. (New York: Century Company, 1887–88)

CWTI   *Civil War Times Illustrated*

DVNC   Department of Virginia and North Carolina, Letters Sent and Received, 1863–65

GP   General's Papers

GRSWR   Generals' Reports of Service, War of the Rebellion

JCCW   Joint Committee on the Conduct of the War, 3 vols. in 8 (Washington: Government Printing Office, 1863–68)

LC   Library of Congress, Washington

MOLLUS   Military Order of the Loyal Legion of the United States

NA   National Archives, Washington

OR   *The War of the Rebellion: A Compilation of the Official Records of the Union and Confederate Armies,* 4 series, 70 vols. in 128 (Washington: GPO, 1880–1901)

ORN   *Official Records of the Union and Confederate Navies in the War of the Rebellion,* 2 series, 30 vols. (Washington: GPO, 1894–1922)

PMHSM   *Papers of the Military Historical Society of Massachusetts,* 14 vols. (Boston, 1895–1918)

POCB   *Private and Official Correspondence of Gen. Benjamin F. Butler during the Period of the Civil War,* comp. Jessie Ames Marshall, 6 vols. (Norwood, Mass.: Plimpton Press, 1917)

RG–, E–   Record Group–, Entry–

CHAPTER 1

1. *BB*, 374–77; *OR*, I, 15: 650; William E. S. Whitman and Charles H. True, *Maine in the War for the Union: A History of the Part Borne by Maine Troops in the Suppression of the American Rebellion* (Lewiston, Maine, 1865), 385–86.

2. Ezra J. Warner, *Generals in Blue: Lives of the Union Commanders* (Baton Rouge: Louisiana State University Press, 1964), 60–61; Theodore Lyman, *Meade's Headquarters, 1863–1865: Letters of Colonel Theodore Lyman from the Wilderness to Appomattox,* ed. George R. Agassiz (Boston: Atlantic Monthly Press, 1922), 192.

3. George M. Wolfson, "Butler's Relations with Grant and the Army of the James in 1864," *South Atlantic Quarterly,* 10 (October 1911): 289; Harold B. Raymond, "Ben Butler: A Reappraisal," *Colby Library Quarterly* 6 (September 1964): 458–59; William Dana Orcutt, "Ben Butler and the 'Stolen Spoons,'" *North American Review,* 207 (January 1918): 66–80.

4. William Farrar Smith memoirs, appendix, 43, Smith Papers, Vermont Historical Society, Montpelier; Cyrus B. Comstock diary, April 1, 1865, LC.

5. Peyton McCrary, *Abraham Lincoln and Reconstruction: The Louisiana Experiment* (Princeton, N.J.: Princeton University Press, 1978), 86–89; Joseph T. Glatthaar, *Forged in Battle: The Civil War Alliance of Black Soldiers and White Officers* (New York: Free Press, 1990), 4, 7–10, 67, 176.

6. Arnold A. Rand memoirs, 38, Massachusetts MOLLUS Collection, U.S. Army Military History Institute, Carlisle Barracks, Pa.; George A. Bruce, "General Butler's Bermuda [Hundred] Campaign," *PMHSM* 9: 307; *New York Tribune,* May 9, 1864; August V. Kautz, "How I Won My First Brevet," *Sketches of War History,* 1861–1865 (Ohio MOLLUS) 4: 374.

7. Bruce, "Butler's Bermuda Campaign," 307; Lyman, *Meade's Headquarters,* 192; George Stowits, *History of the One Hundredth Regiment of New York State Volunteers* (Buffalo, New York: Matthews & Warren, 1870), 245; James Parton, *General Butler in New Orleans: History of the Administration of the Department of the Gulf in the Year 1862* (Boston: Ticknor & Fields, 1866), 627.

8. Joseph R. Hawley to Gideon Welles, August 2, 1864, Welles Papers, LC.

9. Parton, *Butler in New Orleans,* 614; Wickham Hoffman, *Camp, Court and Siege: A Narrative of Personal Adventure and Observation during Two Wars* (New York: Harper & Brothers, 1877), 14–15; BFB, *Character and Results of the War* (Philadelphia, 1863), 1–29.

10. *OR*, I, 5: 755; 11, pt. 3: 207, 211–13, 333, 379, 381–83; 27, pt. 3: 827; Frederick H. Dyer, *A Compendium of the War of the Rebellion* (Des Moines, Iowa: Dyer Publishing Company, 1908), 298–300, 330–34, 390.

11. *OR*, I, 18: 268–80, 301–22, 558, 562, 565, 570, 575, 637, 662, 676–77, 686, 690–95, 735–36; 27, pt. 1: 17–20; pt. 2: 817–59; Edwin B. Coddington, *The Gettysburg Campaign: A Study in Command* (New York: Charles Scribner's Sons, 1968), 100–102, 627n.

12. *OR*, I, 27, pt. 3: 723; *New York Times,* November 3, 1863; *New York Tribune,* November 9, 1863.

13. Louis Taylor Merrill, "General Benjamin F. Butler in the Presidential Campaign of 1864," *Mississippi Valley Historical Review* 33 (March 1947): 540–45; Adam Gurowski, *Diary,* 3 vols. (Boston, New York, and Washington: 1862–66), 2: 187; 3: 86.

14. *OR*, I, 29, pt. 2: 397, 447, 494–95.

15. *New York Tribune,* November 3, 1863; *New York Herald,* November 9, 1863.

16. *Richmond Examiner,* November 7, 1863.

17. *New York Herald,* November 11, 1863.
18. *OR,* I, 29, pt. 2: 524, 618–21; Charles K. Graham to Edward W. Smith, January 25, 1865, Graham's GP, RG-94, E-159, NA.
19. *History of the Eleventh Pennsylvania Volunteer Cavalry* (Philadelphia: Franklin Printing Company, 1902), 165; Francis A. Lord, "Killed (Not in Action)," *CWTI* 8 (October 1969): 32; *Philadelphia Daily Evening Bulletin,* June 16, 1864; *OR,* I, 42, pt. 2: 464–65.
20. Martin P. Kennard, *Address of Martin P. Kennard . . . on . . . the Late Brig.-Gen'l Edward Augustus Wild* (Brookline, Mass.: Printed for the Town, 1894), 1–13; Edward G. Longacre, "Brave Radical Wild," *CWTI* 19 (June 1980): 8–19; Edward Wall, "The First Assault on Petersburg," *Proceedings of the New Jersey Historical Society* n.s. 3 (October 1918): 201–2; Thomas L. Livermore, *Days and Events, 1860–1866* (Boston: Houghton Mifflin Company, 1920), 356; Isaac J. Wistar, *Autobiography of Isaac Jones Wistar, 1827–1905: Half a Century in War and Peace* (Philadelphia: Wistar Institute of Anatomy and Biology, 1937), 417–25, 446.
21. *OR,* I, 29, pt. 2: 524, 571, 576–77; 33: 482; Charles H. Bartlett, *Oration . . . on Gen. Gilman Marston . . .* (Manchester, N.H.: John B. Clarke, 1891), 6–22.
22. *New York Herald,* November 26, December 2, 1863; BFB to Isaac J. Wistar, November 27, 1863; to John Murray Forbes, December 18,1863; both, DVNC, RG-393, E-5046, vol. 3, NA; Edward A. Pollard, *Observations in the North: Eight Months in Prison and on Parole* (Richmond: E. W. Ayres, 1865), 101–3; Henry L. Swint, ed., *"Dear Ones at Home": Letters from Contraband Camps* (Nashville: Vanderbilt University Press, 1966), 100.
23. *Ibid.,* 107, 110; BFB to "Captain Wilder," November 26, 1863, DVNC, RG-393, E-5046, vol. 3, NA; Wistar, *Autobiography,* 417, 438–39; George H. Gordon, *A War Diary of Events in the War of the Great Rebellion, 1863–1865* (Boston: James R. Osgood & Company, 1882), 360–61.
24. *OR,* I, 51, pt. 1: 1282–84.
25. Gurowski, *Diary,* 3: 86.
26. BFB to George W. Getty, November 27, December 22, 1863; to J. M. Bell, December 23, 1863; all, DVNC, RG-393, E-5046, vol. 3, NA; *OR,* I, 29, pt. 1: 653–55; *BB,* 617–18.
27. Francis H. Peirpoint, *Letter of Governor Peirpoint . . . on the Subject of Abuse of Military Power in the Command of General Butler in Virginia and North Carolina* (Washington: McGill & Witherow, 1864), 36–37.
28. *OR,* I, 29, pt. 1: 911–17; pt. 2: 595–96; John G. Barrett, *The Civil War in North Carolina* (Chapel Hill, N.C.: University of North Carolina Press, 1963), 177–80; Richard S. West, Jr., *Lincoln's Scapegoat General: A Life of Benjamin F. Butler, 1818–1893* (Boston: Houghton Mifflin Company, 1965), 222–25; Thomas J. Wertenbaker, *Norfolk: Historic Southern Port* (Durham, N.C.: Duke University Press, 1962), 225.
29. *OR,* II, 6: 776–77.
30. BFB to William J. Manden and Pender Weeks, January 26, 1864; to James M. Hinton, January 27, 1864; to John J. Peck, February 27, 1864; all, DVNC, RG-393, E-5046, vol. 4, NA; Edward A. Wild to G. H. Willis, January 14, 1864, Willis Collection, Mugar Memorial Library, Boston University, Boston.
31. *OR,* I, 29, pt. 1: 562, 974–77, 991–92; 33: 26–28, 225–27, 246–47, 360; 51, pt. 1: 1148–52; *BB,* 618; BFB to Gilman Marston, January 6, 1864, DVNC, RG-393, E-5046, vol. 4, NA; Martin A. Haynes, *History of the Second Regiment New Hampshire Volunteers: Its Camps, Marches and Battles* (Manchester, N.H.: Charles F. Livingston, 1865), 161; *New York Tribune,* February 3, 1864.
32. *OR,* I, 33: 146–48.

33. *Ibid.*, 143–50, 502, 512–13, 519, 521–22, 532, 552–54, 1074, 1081, 1131; 51, pt. 1: 1143; *Richmond Enquirer,* 8, February 9, 1864; *BB,* 619–21; BFB to anon., January 8, 1879, Butler Papers, LC; Wistar, *Autobiography,* 426–30; *New York Times,* February 10, 1864; *New York Tribune,* February 14, 1864; *Army and Navy Journal,* February 13, 1864; *Eleventh Pennsylvania Cavalry,* 173.

34. *OR,* I, 33: 144–45; Abraham Lincoln, *The Collected Works of Abraham Lincoln,* ed. Roy P. Basler, 8 vols. (New Brunswick, N.J.: Rutgers University Press, 1953), 7: 59; Copy of Special Order #—, Headquarters DVNC, February 8, 1864, Butler Papers, LC.

35. BFB to Office of the Guard, Fort Monroe, Va., February 9, 1864, *ibid.; Army and Navy Journal,* February 27, 1864; *The New Regime: Official Journal of the Department* [of Virginia and North Carolina], March 16, 1864; *BB,* 620; BFB to Joseph Holt, February 17, 1864, DVNC, RG-393, E-5046, vol. 4, NA.

CHAPTER 2

1. Rand memoirs, 6–9, Massachusetts MOLLUS Collection; Edward K. Wightman to Frederick B. Wightman, August 30, 1864, Wightman Papers, Robert W. Woodruff Library, Emory University, Atlanta; *JCCW,* 1865, pt. 2: 45–46; *New York Times,* September 4, 1864; Henry N. Hudson, *A Chaplain's Campaign with Gen. Butler* (New York, 1865), 16–17; BFB and John I. Davenport, *Official Documents Relating to a "Chaplain's Campaign (Not) with General Butler," but in New York* (Lowell, Mass.: Charles Hunt, 1865), 4–5.

2. Wertenbaker, *Norfolk,* 227; West, *Lincoln's Scapegoat General,* 270–72; *New Regime,* July 2, 1864; Francis H. Peirpoint to the General Assembly of Virginia, December 6, 1864, Butler Papers, LC; John McMurray, *Recollections of a Colored Troop* (n.p., 1916), 15; Frank Moore, ed., *The Rebellion Record: A Diary of American Events,* 12 vols. (New York, 1861–68), 8: 337–38; BFB to "Capt. Sawtelle," December 2, 1863, DVNC, RG-393, E-5046, vol. 4, NA.

3. BFB to James Barnes, January 2, 1864, *ibid.;* Moore, *Rebellion Record,* 8: 28; *BB,* 848; *New Regime,* September 20, November 24, 1864.

4. BFB to J. M. Bell, December 23, 1863, DVNC, RG-393, E-5046, vol. 3; I. B. Hutchins to BFB, July 10, 1864, DVNC, RG-393, E-5063, box 5; both, NA; BFB to H. Risley, F. B. Voegele Collection, Rutherford B. Hayes Library, Fremont, Ohio; *POCB,* 4: 523; George F. Shepley to Edward O. C. Ord, February 16, 1865; Edward O. C. Ord to George F. Shepley, February 19, 1865; both, Shepley Papers, Maine Historical Society, Portland.

5. Robert S. Holzman, *Stormy Ben Butler* (New York: Macmillan Company, 1954), 94–95, 145–46; Hans L. Trefousse, *Ben Butler: The South Called Him BEAST!* (New York: Twayne Publishers, 1957), 134; Ludwell H. Johnson, "The Butler Expedition of 1861–1862: The Profitable Side of War," *Civil War History* 11 (September 1965): 229–36; Ludwell H. Johnson, "Northern Profit and Profiteers: The Cotton Rings of 1864–1865," *Civil War History* 12 (June 1966): 105; Sylvanus Cadwallader memoirs, 561, Illinois State Historical Library, Springfield, Ill.; Gordon, *War Diary,* 377–81; *The Record of Benjamin F. Butler, Compiled from the Original Sources* (Boston, 1883), 14–17, 24–29, 48–49.

6. *ORN,* I, 10: 163; Gideon Welles, *Diary of Gideon Welles, Secretary of the Navy under Lincoln and Johnson,* ed. Howard K. Beale, 3 vols. (New York: W. W. Norton & Company, Inc., 1960), 2: 56, 81; Peirpoint, *Letter of Governor Peirpoint,* 10, 13,

23–24, 26–28, 31–32, 39–40; *New Regime,* August 2, 1864; Sylvanus Cadwallader memoirs, 561–62.

7. BFB to E. H. Goodman, January 4, 1864, DVNC, RG-393, E-5046, vol. 4, NA; *New York Herald,* 14, May 27, 1864.

8. Edward P. Smith, *Incidents of the United States Christian Commission* (Philadelphia: J.B. Lippincott & Company, 1871), 297; Lemuel Moss, *Annals of the United States Christian Commission* (Philadelphia: J.B. Lippincott & Company, 1868), 415, 436–38, 448–49, 452–53; Edward F. Williams diary, February 11, 1865; Edward F. Williams to "Brother Whitney," October 21, 1864; both, Williams Papers, Amistad Research Center, Dillard University, New Orleans; Samuel H. Merrill, *The Campaigns of the First Maine and First District of Columbia Cavalry* (Portland, Maine: Bailey & Noyes, 1866), 259.

9. *POCB,* 4: 135; Bernard A. Weisberger, *Reporters for the Union* (Boston: Little, Brown & Company, 1953), 203–5; William H. Steiner to Frederic Hudson, April 21, 1864, James Gordon Bennett Papers, LC.

10. Weisberger, *Reporters for the Union,* 159–61, 262–64; Joseph R. Hawley to Gideon Welles, August 2, 1864, Welles Papers.

11. Sylvanus Cadwallader, *Three Years with Grant, as Recalled by War Correspondent Sylvanus Cadwallader,* ed. Benjamin P. Thomas (New York: Alfred A. Knopf, 1955), 236, 277.

12. *POCB,* 4: 94; BFB to "Commander Boutelle," December 19, 1863; Copy of Statement of "Cary," July 22, 1864; Rufus B. Long to BFB, July 26, 1864; Henry Finegass to John Clark, July 30, 1864; all, Butler Papers, LC; "A Visit to General Butler and the Army of the James," *Fraser's Magazine* 71 (April 1865): 445–48; *OR,* I, 33: 520.

13. Lester L. Swift, ed., "Recollections of a Signal Officer," *Civil War History* 9 (March 1963): 46–47; J. Willard Brown, *The Signal Corps, U.S.A., in the War of the Rebellion* (Boston: Wilkins & Company, 1896), 425.

14. *New York Herald,* May 29, August 11, 1864; Henry E. Taintor to his father, June 12, 1864, Taintor Papers, William R. Perkins Library, Duke University, Durham, N.C.; *OR,* I, 40, pt. 3: 487; 42, pt. 2: 744; Joseph J. Scroggs diary, August 4, 1864, *CWTI* Collection, U.S. Army Military History Institute.

15. Cyrus B. Comstock diary, November 25, 1864, LC; P. Halsted to BFB, October 19, 1864; BFB to D. C. G. Field, April 5, 1864; both, Butler Papers, LC; *OR,* I, 42, pt. 3: 117; Lyman, *Meade's Headquarters,* 282–84.

16. John S. C. Abbott, "The Military Hospitals at Fortress Monroe," *Harper's New Monthly Magazine* 29 (August 1864): 306–10; James E. Glazier to Editor, *Boston Journal,* December 27, 1864, Butler Papers, LC.

17. Abbott, "Hospitals at Fortress Monroe," 306–22; George Lawall to his mother, July 26, 1864, Lawall Papers, U.S. Army Military History Institute; Hilon A. Parker to his father, August 23, 1864, Parker Papers, William L. Clements Library, University of Michigan, Ann Arbor, Mich.; BFB to Edwin M. Stanton, January 26, 1864, DVNC, RG-393, E-5046, vol. 4, NA; *New York Herald,* 3, May 27, 1864; James Horrocks, *"My Dear Parents": The Civil War as Seen by an English Union Soldier,* ed. A. S. Lewis (New York: Harcourt Brace Jovanovich, 1982), 94; *New York Times,* May 22, 1864.

18. Carrington MacFarlane, *Reminiscences of an Army Surgeon* (Oswego, N.Y.: Lake City Print Shop, 1912), 52–54; George Worthington Adams, *Doctors in Blue: The Medical History of the Union Army in the Civil War* (New York: Henry Schuman, 1952), 70, 103; *OR,* I, 36, pt. 3: 41–42; *New York Tribune,* June 29, 1864;

S. Millett Thompson, *Thirteenth Regiment of New Hampshire Volunteer Infantry in the War of the Rebellion, 1861–65: A Diary Covering Three Years and a Day* (Boston: Houghton Mifflin & Company, 1888), 522; *New York Herald*, November 4, 1864; Clara Barton to Annie Barton, September 14, 1864, Ira Barton Moore Collection, American Antiquarian Society, Worcester, Mass.

19. Edward Bates, *The Diary of Edward Bates, 1859–1866*, ed. Howard K. Beale (Washington: Government Printing Office, 1933), 276–77.

20. Merrill, "Butler in the Campaign of 1864," 546–48; William Roscoe Thayer, ed., "Lincoln and Some Union Generals: From the Unpublished Diaries of John Hay," *Harper's Monthly Magazine* 130 (December 1914): 100.

21. Erwin S. Bradley, *Simon Cameron, Lincoln's Secretary of War: A Political Biography* (Philadelphia: University of Pennsylvania Press, 1966), 236, 239–40; A. K. McClure, *Abraham Lincoln and Men of War-Times* (Philadelphia: Times Publishing Company, 1892), 118–19.

22. BFB, "Vice-Presidential Politics in '64," *North American Review* 141 (October 1885): 332–33.

23. Lincoln, *Collected Works*, 7: 207 and n.

24. Merrill, "Butler in the Campaign of 1864," 546, 551; BFB, "Vice-Presidential Politics," 331–32.

25. *OR*, I, 33: 394–95, 649; Ulysses S. Grant, *Personal Memoirs of U. S. Grant*, 2 vols. (New York: Charles L. Webster & Company, 1885–86), 2: 114–16.

26. *OR*, I, 51, pt. 1: 1287–88; *New York Tribune*, May 9, 1864; *New Regime*, April 2, 1864; John A. Rawlins to his wife, April 2, 1864, James Harrison Wilson Papers, LC; Cyrus B. Comstock diary, 1, April 2, 1864, LC.

27. Warner, *Generals in Blue*, 462–63; James Harrison Wilson, *Life and Services of William Farrar Smith* (Wilmington, Del.: John M. Rogers Press, 1904), 13–83; Lyman, *Meade's Headquarters*, 140, 148; William Farrar Smith to James Harrison Wilson, August 4, 1864, Wilson Papers.

28. Grant, *Memoirs*, 2: 132–33.

29. *Ibid.*, 132, 148; *OR*, I, 33: 861; John A. Rawlins to his wife, April 2, 1864, Wilson Papers.

30. *Army and Navy Journal*, January 2, 1864; *OR*, I, 21: 812–13.

31. Samuel P. Heintzelman diary, February 17, 1864; Samuel P. Heintzelman "Journal," February 10, May 9, 1864; Samuel P. Heintzelman to BFB, February 17, 1864; all, Heintzelman Papers, LC; *OR*, I, 51, pt. 1: 1287–88.

32. William Farrar Smith, "Butler's Attack on Drewry's Bluff," *BL*, 4: 206 and n., 207.

33. *Ibid.*, 207; William Farrar Smith memoirs, appendix, 40; William Farrar Smith to "Mr. Shattuck," n.d.; both, Smith Papers; William Farrar Smith to James Harrison Wilson, March 16, 1864, Wilson Papers.

34. Grant, *Memoirs*, 2: 148.

35. John A. Rawlins to his wife, April 13, 1864, Wilson Papers.

36. *OR*, I, 33: 885–86.

37. *Ibid.*, 904–5.

38. BFB to Ulysses S. Grant, April 8, 1864, Butler Papers, LC; *POCB*, 4: 508–9; Warner, *Generals in Blue*, 47, 55–56; John L. Cunningham, *Three Years with the Adirondack Regiment, 118th New York Volunteer Infantry* (Norwood, Mass.: Plimpton Press, 1920), 148; Charles W. Washburn memoirs, 86, American Antiquarian Society.

39. Warner, *Generals in Blue*, 257–58; August V. Kautz to "My Dear Mrs. Savage," May 1, 1864, Kautz Papers, Illinois State Historical Library.

40. Warner, *Generals in Blue*, 529–30, 548–49; *OR*, I, 36, pt. 2: 777–78; David Dixon Porter "Journals," 841, Porter Papers, LC.

41. *OR*, I, 29, pt. 2: 886–87, 896, 905, 939, 946–47; 33: 804; *POCB*, 4: 110; Alfred H. Terry to Edward W. Smith, April 13, 1864, Terry Papers, Connecticut Historical Society, Hartford; Joseph R. Hawley to William Faxon, April 25, 1864; to his wife, May 1, 1864; both, Hawley Papers; Swift, "Recollections of a Signal Officer," 46.

42. Warner, *Generals in Blue*, 176; *POCB*, 4: 108; Joseph R. Hawley to his wife, August 9, 1865, Hawley Papers; Alfred H. Terry to Polly Terry, January 31, 1864, Terry Family Collection, Sterling Library, Yale University, New Haven, Conn.; *New York Times*, April 9, 1888.

43. *POCB*, 4: 137.

CHAPTER 3

1. *POCB*, 4: 159; *OR*, I, 42, pt. 3: 567–69.

2. Dyer, *Compendium of the War of the Rebellion*, 394–96; *OR*, I, 14: 380.

3. Charles A. Carleton, comp., *Report of the Proceedings of the Society of the Army of the James*, 3 vols. (New York: G. W. Carleton & Company, 1869–74), 3: 81.

4. E. Milby Burton, *The Siege of Charleston, 1861–1865* (Columbia, S.C.: University of South Carolina Press, 1970), 153–71; John E. Johns, *Florida during the Civil War* (Gainesville, Fla.: University of Florida Press, 1963), 190–99; Vaughn D. Bornet, ed., "A Connecticut Yankee after Olustee," *Florida Historical Quarterly* 27 (April 1949): 385, 388, 391–93; Samuel Jones, "The Battle of Olustee, or Ocean Pond, Florida," *BL*, 4: 76–79; James M. Nichols, *Perry's Saints, or the Fighting Parson's Regiment* [48th New York Infantry] *in the War of the Rebellion* (Boston: D. Lothrop & Company, 1886), 210; Abraham J. Palmer, *The History of the Forty-eighth Regiment New York State Volunteers in the War for the Union, 1861–1865* (New York: Charles T. Dillingham, 1885), 144.

5. M. R. Morgan, "From City Point to Appomattox with General Grant," *Journal of the Military Service Institution of the United States* 41 (July–August 1907): 242; William A. Russ, Jr., ed., "Some Letters Reflecting the Civil War Experiences of Company D, 76th Regiment P.V.I. [Pennsylvania Volunteer Infantry]." *Susquehanna University Studies* 5 (May 1956): 299.

6. "The Armies of the United States in the Civil War," *Photographic History of the Civil War*, ed. Francis Trevelyan Miller, 10 vols. (New York: Review of Reviews Company, 1911), 10: 178, 180; *OR*, I, 18: 288, 385; Wistar, *Autobiography*, 444.

7. *Ibid.*, 440; *POCB*, 4: 130; Haynes, *Second New Hampshire*, 160; Albert H. C. Jewett, *A Boy Goes to War* (Bloomington, Ill., 1944), 60–61.

8. Solon A. Carter, "Fourteen Months' Service with Colored Troops," *Civil War Papers* (Massachusetts MOLLUS) 1: 159; *Philadelphia Press*, July 6, 1864; James Marion Tucker, "Kautz Raiding around Petersburg," *Glimpses of the Nation's Struggle* (Minnesota MOLLUS), 5: 124; James Harrison Wilson, "The Cavalry of the Army of the Potomac," *PMHSM*, 13: 59; Edward H. Ripley, *Vermont General: The Unusual War Experiences of Edward Hastings Ripley, 1862–1865*, ed. Otto Eisenschiml (New York: Devin-Adair Company, 1960), 263–64; BFB to Andrew G. Curtin, April 7, 1864, DVNC, RG-393, E-5046, vol. 4, NA.

9. GRSWR, 10: 206, RG-94, E-160, NA.

10. Washington: Davis, *Camp-Fire Chats of the Civil War* (Chicago: Sidney C. Miller & Company, 1887), 284–85; *OR*, I, 40, pt. 2: 459, 489.

11. Ella Lonn, *Foreigners in the Union Army and Navy* (Baton Rouge, La.: Louisiana State University Press, 1951), 94, 96–98, 217–18, 227–28, 257; William L. Burton, *Melting*

Pot Soldiers: The Union's Ethnic Regiments (Ames, Iowa: Iowa State University
Press, 1988), 135–37; Simon Wolf, *The American Jew as Patriot, Soldier and
Citizen* (Philadelphia: Levytype Company, 1895), 136–54, 238–39.

12. Edward G. Longacre, "Black Troops in the Army of the James, 1863–65," *Military
Affairs* 45 (February 1981): 1–8.

13. W. A. Nichols to BFB, March 1, 1864, DVNC, RG-393, E-5063, vol. 5, NA; *OR*,
III, 3: 1139–44; Moore, *Rebellion Record*, 8: 261–64; *New Regime*, March 2,
1864.

14. "Visit to General Butler," 443–44; BFB to Henry Wilson, March 4, 1864; to Edwin
M. Stanton, July 31, 1864; both, DVNC, RG-393, E-5064, vol. 4; Edward
A. Wild to Robert S. Davis, June 29, 1864; Wild's GP, RG-94, E-159;
GRSWR, 10: 390–91, RG-94, E-160; all, NA.

15. Swint, *"Dear Ones at Home,"* 122–23; *POCB*, 4: 428.

16. Smith, *Christian Commission*, 358; Andrew B. Cross to Edward F. Williams,
December 6, 1864, Williams Papers; *Record of the Services of the Seventh
Regiment, U.S. Colored Troops* (Providence: E. L. Freeman & Company, 1878),
86–87.

17. Smith, *Christian Commission*, 357–58; BFB to William P. Webster, March 12,
1864, DVNC, RG-393, E-5046, vol. 4, NA.

18. *OR*, III, 3: 1144; Moore, *Rebellion Record*, 8: 264; McMurray, *Colored Troop*, 63;
E. Henry Powell, *The Colored Soldier in the War of the Rebellion* (Burlington,
Vt., 1893), 6.

19. *Daily Richmond Examiner*, October 20 and 28, 1864; *New York Times*, October 23,
1864; John Beauchamp Jones, *A Rebel War Clerk's Diary at the Confederate
States Capital*, ed. Howard Swiggett, 2 vols. (New York: Old Hickory Book-
shop, 1935), 2: 308–9; Richard J. Sommers, "The Dutch Gap Affair: Military
Atrocities and the Rights of Negro Soldiers," *Civil War History* 21 (March 1975).

20. *OR*, III, 3: 1139–44; Moore, *Rebellion Record*, 8: 261–64; *JCCW*, 1865, pt. 2: 47;
New York Herald, August 4, 1864.

21. *OR*, I, 42, pt. 2: 411, 600, 610–11; III, 3: 1139–41; Moore, *Rebellion Record*,
8: 262; *New York Times*, September 13, 1864.

22. *POCB*, 5: 345–46; BGB to William P. Webster, March 12, 1864, DVNC, RG-393,
E-5046, vol. 4, NA; Raymond, "Ben Butler: A Reappraisal," 466.

23. *Seventh U.S. Colored Troops*, 87–89; James Shaw, Jr., *Our Last Campaign and Subsequent Service in Texas: Personal Narratives of Events in the War of the Rebellion*
(Providence: Snow & Farnham Company, 1905), 33; John Coughlin to
Edward O. C. Ord, February 13, 1865, Ord Papers, Bancroft Library, University
of California, Berkeley, Calif.

24. *OR*, III, 3: 1142–44; Moore, *Rebellion Record*, 8: 263–64; Gordon, *War Diary*,
360–61; BFB to Isaac J. Wistar, November 27, 1863, DVNC, RG-393,
E-5046, vol. 3, NA.

25. John H. Burrill to his parents, November 7, 1863, *CWTI* Collection, U.S. Army
Military History Institute.

26. William A. Walker to James P. Walker, January 16, 1864, James Perkins Walker
Collection, Firestone Library, Princeton University, Princeton, N.J.; Russ,
"Company D, 76th Regiment P.V.I.," 293.

27. Washington: Vosburgh to "Ella," 18, August 22, 1864, Nina Ness Collection, Bentley
Historical Library, University of Michigan, Ann Arbor, Mich.; Thompson,
Thirteenth New Hampshire, 382.

28. Francis C. Choate to William Farrar Smith, June 27, 1864, Smith Papers.

29. Charles Francis Adams et al., *A Cycle of Adams Letters, 1861–1865,* ed. Worthington Chauncey Ford, 2 vols. (Boston: Houghton Mifflin Company, 1920), 2: 195, 216–17; Charles P. Bowditch, "War Letters of Charles P. Bowditch," *Massachusetts Historical Society Proceedings* 57 (June 1924): 474; Albert Rogall diary, December 29, 1864, Ohio Historical Society, Columbus, Ohio.

30. George E. Sutherland, "The Negro in the Late War," *War Papers* (Wisconsin MOLLUS), 1: 175, 180; *Seventh U.S. Colored Troops,* 89; Shaw, *Our Last Campaign,* 33; William A. Walker to James P. Walker, January 16, 1864, James Perkins Walker Collection; Adams et al., *Cycle of Adams Letters,* 2: 216.

31. Christian Fleetwood to James Hall, June 8, 1865, Carter G. Woodson Collection, LC; Smith, *Christian Commission,* 364.

32. Swint, *"Dear Ones at Home",* 123.

33. Edward A. Wild to Godfrey Weitzel, May 8, 1865, Massachusetts MOLLUS Collection, U.S. Army Military History Institute.

34. William Birney to Salmon P. Chase, April 25, 1864, Chase Papers, Historical Society of Pennsylvania, Philadelphia; Henry T. Knox to Atherton H. Stevens, December 18, 1864, Stevens Papers, Massachusetts Historical Society; Joseph J. Scroggs diary, March 30, 1864, *CWTI* Collection.

35. *The Medal of Honor of the United States Army* (Washington: Government Printing Office, 1948), 150–202; *POCB,* 5: 192; *BB,* 742–43; Dudley Taylor Cornish, *The Sable Arm: Negro Troops in the Union Army, 1861–1865* (New York: Longmans, Green & Company, 1956), 266.

36. *OR,* I, 33: 1053–55; Warner, *Generals in Blue,* 229–30; E. E. Hale to Sarah Butler, May 29, 1864, Butler Papers, LC; Livermore, *Days and Events,* 358–59.

37. *OR,* I, 33: 1053–54, 1057–58.

38. *Ibid.,* 1055–56; Warner, *Generals in Blue,* 497; Alfred P. Rockwell, "The Tenth Army Corps in Virginia, May 1864," *PMHSM,* 9: 269; Joseph R. Hawley to Gideon Welles, December 16, 1864, Hawley Papers, LC; Charles M. Clark, *The History of the Thirty-ninth Regiment Illinois Volunteer Veteran Infantry (Yates Phalanx)* (Chicago, 1889), 202; Daniel Eldredge, *The Third New Hampshire and All About It* (Boston: E. B. Stillings & Company, 1893), 534.

39. John W. Turner to his father, April 13, June 27, 1864, Turner Papers, U.S. Army Military History Institute.

40. *OR,* I, 33: 1056; I, 36, pt. 3: 111; *New York Herald,* June 14, 1864; Edward K. Wightman to "Dear Rod," June 30, 1864, Wightman Papers; A. Gilchrist to John W. Turner, July 3, 1864, Turner's GP, RG-94, E-159, NA; Palmer, *Forty-eighth New York,* 172; Nichols, *Perry's Saints,* 268, 271.

41. *OR,* I, 33: 1056; E. J. Cleveland, Jr., ed., "The Siege of Petersburg: As Seen through the Eyes of a New Jersey Soldier," *Proceedings of the New Jersey Historical Society* 66 (July 1948): 189, 191; H. C. Lockwood, "A Man from Maine: A True History of the Army at Fort Fisher," *Maine Bugle* 1 (January 1894): 40.

42. *OR,* I, 33: 1009; 36, pt. 2: 471, 519, 588, 779, 803, 834.

43. *New York Herald,* May 8, 1864.

44. Rowland M. Hall to his father, April 30, 1864, Hall Papers, North Carolina State Department of Cultural Resources, Raleigh, N.C.

45. John M. Spear to anon., May 2, 1864, Spear Papers, Massachusetts Historical Society, Boston; W. P. Derby, *Bearing Arms in the Twenty-seventh Massachusetts Regiment of Volunteer Infantry during the Civil War, 1861–1865* (Boston: Wright & Potter,

1883), 288; William Farrar Smith, *From Chattanooga to Petersburg under Generals Grant and Butler: A Contribution to the History of the War, and a Personal Vindication* (Boston: Houghton, Mifflin & Company, 1893), 17–18.

46. *BB,* 629, 638.

47. *Ibid.,* 628, 656; BFB to W. P. Derby, June 28, 1882, Butler Papers, LC.

48. William Farrar Smith memoirs, 86, Smith Papers; John Russell Young, *Around the World with General Grant,* 2 vols. (New York: American News Company, 1879), 2: 304.

49. William Farrar Smith to William B. Franklin, April 28, 1864, Franklin Papers, LC.

CHAPTER 4

1. Charles W. Washburn memoirs, 87–88, American Antiquarian Society; *New York Herald,* May 23, 1864; Dudley Taylor Cornish and Virginia Jeans Laas, *Lincoln's Lee: The Life of Samuel Phillips Lee, United States Navy, 1812–1897* (Lawrence, Kans.: University Press of Kansas, 1986), 130.

2. Andrew A. Humphreys, *The Virginia Campaign of '64 and '65: The Army of the Potomac and the Army of the James* (New York: Charles Scribner's Sons, 1883), 140.

3. BFB to S. Phillips Lee, April 25, 1864, Butler Papers, LC; *BB,* 638; Welles, *Diary of Gideon Welles,* 2: 19.

4. Smith, "Butler's Attack on Drewry's Bluff," 207; J. A. Mowris, *A History of the One Hundred and Seventeenth Regiment N.Y. Volunteers* (Hartford, Conn.: Case, Lockwood & Company, 1866), 103; B. S. DeForest, *Random Sketches and Wandering Thoughts . . . with a Historical Sketch of the Second Oswego Regiment, Eighty-first New York State V. I.* [Volunteer Infantry] (Albany, N.Y., 1866), 145–46; *New York Times,* May 8, 1864.

5. *OR,* I, 33: 795; 35, pt. 2: 79; 36, pt. 2: 25, 326–27, 345, 391–93; William Glenn Robertson, *Back Door to Richmond: The Bermuda Hundred Campaign, April–June 1864* (Newark, Del.: University of Delaware Press, 1987), 35, 55–56; Quincy A. Gillmore to BFB, 22, 24, April 29, 1864, Butler Papers, LC; to BFB, May 6, 1864, DVNC, RG-393, E-5063, box 5, NA; *BB,* 639, 642; *POCB,* 4: 161–63, 165.

6. *OR,* I, 36, pt. 2: 392.

7. *Ibid.,* 33: 1030–31; 36, pt. 2: 327, 349; BFB to Ulysses S. Grant, May 1, 1864, Butler Papers, LC; *BB,* 638; *New York Times,* May 8, 1864; Rockwell, "Tenth Army Corps in Virginia," 273; "Notes on the May [1864] Campaign on the James River," *United States Service Magazine* 3 (January 1865): 23–24.

8. *OR,* I, 36, pt. 1: 20; pt. 2: 10–11, 327, 430, 524; *BB,* 640, 645; *New York Herald,* May 9–10, 1864; Frederick W. Browne, *My Service in the U.S. Colored Cavalry* (Cincinnati, 1908), 3–4.

9. *OR,* I, 33: 795; 36, pt. 2: 171.

10. GRSWR, 10: 199, RG-94, E-160, NA; August V. Kautz, "Operations South of the James River: I. First Attempts to Capture Petersburg," *BL,* 4: 533.

11. *POCB,* 4: 161; *OR,* I, 36, pt. 2: 171–72, 176, 179, 181, 184, 188–89, 394, 431; August V. Kautz memoirs, 69–70, U.S. Army Military History Institute; *New York Herald,* May 14, 1864; *Eleventh Pennsylvania Cavalry,* 107–8; Horace W. Bolton, *Personal Reminiscences of the Late War* (Chicago, 1892), 75–76; Henry Lyle to his mother, May 3, 1864, Norman Daniels Collection, U.S. Army Military History Institute.

12. *OR,* I, 36, pt. 2: 172, 176, 179, 181–82, 184–85, 187, 189–90, 262–64, 624–25, 647, 972; 51, pt. 2: 899–901, 903, 906–7; *New York Herald,* May 14, 1864;

Philadelphia Press, May 25, 1864; Kautz, "First Attempts to Capture Petersburg," 533–34; August V. Kautz diary, May 6–10, 1864, Kautz Papers, LC; GRSWR, 10: 199–200, RG-94, E-160, NA.

13. *OR,* I, 36, pt. 2: 239, 246, 520, 941–42, 946, 950, 957–59, 964; 51, pt. 2: 886, 888–91, 894–95, 897, 904; Alfred Roman, *The Military Operations of General Beauregard in the War Between the States, 1861–1865,* 2 vols. (New York: Harper & Brothers, 1884), 2: 193–200.

14. *ORN,* I, 10: 4–5; Sylvester B. Partridge, "With the Signal Corps from Fortress Monroe to Richmond, May, 1864–April, 1865," *War Papers* (Maine MOLLUS), 3: 85–86; Edward Simonton, "The Campaign up the James River to Petersburg," *Glimpses of the Nation's Struggle* (Minnesota MOLLUS), 5: 481–82.

15. *OR,* I, 36, pt. 2: 21–22, 165, 430, 432; Joseph J. Scroggs diary, May 5–7, 1864, *CWTI* Collection; Christian Fleetwood diary, May 5, 1864, Fleetwood Papers, LC; A. H. Stein, *History of the Thirty-seventh Regt. U.S.C.* [United States Colored] *Infantry* (Philadelphia: King & Baird, 1866), 15.

16. Washington: Vosburgh to "Ella," May 7, 1864, Nina Ness Collection.

17. *POCB,* 4: 163, 165, 430; *BB,* 640; *OR,* I, 36, pt. 2: 430, 471–73.

18. Bruce, "Butler's Bermuda Campaign," 311–12; Derby, *Twenty-seventh Massachusetts,* 288; *BB,* 640–42.

19. *OR,* I, 36, pt. 2: 22, 32, 265, 431–32, 471, 473–74, 476, 524, 559; Cornish and Laas, *Lincoln's Lee,* 131; Humphreys, *Virginia Campaign of '64 and '65,* 140–41; *ORN,* I, 10: 9–15; *New York Herald,* May 23, 1864; J. Thomas Scharf, *History of the Confederate States Navy* (New York: Rogers & Sherwood, 1887), 731; Milton F. Perry, *Infernal Machines: The Story of Confederate Submarine and Mine Warfare* (Baton Rouge, La.: Louisiana State University Press, 1965), 111–13.

20. *OR,* I, 36, pt. 2: 559.

21. *Ibid.,* 475; Robertson, *Back Door to Richmond,* 72.

22. *OR,* I, 36, pt. 2: 475, 518, 521; *POCB,* 4: 171; *BB,* 644; Joseph R. Hawley to his wife, June 27, 1864, Hawley Papers.

23. *OR,* I, 36, pt. 2: 107–8, 154, 156–57, 239–40, 251, 255–56, 475; 51, pt. 1: 231; pt. 2: 898; *POCB,* 4: 167–69; *BB,* 643; William Farrar Smith to J. Wilson Shaffer, May 6, 1864; to BFB, 6, May 7, 1864; all, DVNC, RG-393, E-5063, box 5, NA; GRSWR, 9: 601, RG-94, E-160, NA; Robertson, *Back Door to Richmond,* 76–79; Edmund J. Cleveland, Jr., ed., "The Campaign of Promise and Disappointment," *Proceedings of the New Jersey Historical Society* 67 (October 1949): 309–12; Harvey Clark, *My Experience with Burnside's Expedition and 18th Army Corps* (Gardner, Mass., 1914), 57; Hermann Everts, *A Complete and Comprehensive History of the Ninth Regiment New Jersey Vols. Infantry, from Its First Organization to Its Final Muster Out* (Newark, N.J.: A. Stephen Holbrook, 1865), 104; David L. Day, *My Diary of Rambles with the 25th Mass. Volunteer Infantry . . . Army of the James* (Milford, Mass.: King & Billings, 1884), 138.

24. *OR,* I, 36, pt. 2: 35, 73–75, 87, 101–4, 111, 124–25, 132–33, 136–38, 146, 154–55, 170, 240–42, 245–46, 251–52, 517, 519–23, 558, 965, 972; 51, pt. 1: 222, 231–32; pt. 2: 899–901; William Farrar Smith to BFB, May 7, 1864, DVNC, RG-393, E-5063, box 5, NA; *POCB,* 4: 169; *BB,* 643; *New York Herald,* May 10, 1864; James H. Clark, *The Iron Hearted Regiment: Being an Account of the Battles, Marches and Gallant Deeds Performed by the 115th Regiment N.Y. Vols.* (Albany, N.Y.: J. Munsell, 1865), 105–8; MacFarlane, *Reminiscences of an Army Surgeon,* 52–53.

25. *OR,* I, 36, pt. 2: 74, 85, 87, 112, 124, 517, 972; *BB,* 643; Bruce, "Butler's Bermuda Campaign," 320; Wistar, *Autobiography,* 445; Angus James Johnston, II, *Virginia*

Railroads in the Civil War (Chapel Hill, N.C.: University of North Carolina Press, 1961), 198; William A. Willoughby to his wife, May 10–11, 1864, Willoughby Papers, American Antiquarian Society.

26. *OR*, I, 36, pt. 2: 74–75, 84–85, 102, 108, 111, 118, 124–25, 133, 136–38, 155, 171, 241, 245, 251–53; Johnson Hagood, *Memoirs of the War of Secession* (Columbia, S.C.: State Company, 1910), 223–27; Bruce, "Butler's Bermuda Campaign," 321.

27. *OR*, I, 36, pt. 2: 471, 517–18, 521; *POCB*, 4: 168–71; *BB*, 643; Wolfson, "Butler's Relations with Grant," 382.

28. *BB*, 645; *POCB*, 4: 175; Humphreys, *Virginia Campaign of '64 and '65,* 145; "Notes on the May Campaign," 28; Arthur Herbert, "The Seventeenth Virginia Infantry at Flat Creek and Drewry's Bluff," *Southern Historical Society Papers* 12 (1884): 290; Roman, *Military Operations of Beauregard,* 2: 108–9; Douglas Southall Freeman, *Lee's Lieutenants: A Study in Command,* 2 vols. (New York: Charles Scribner's Sons, 1942–44), 3: 463–66, 471; *OR*, I, 36, pt. 2: 34, 555–59, 977–80; 51, pt. 2: 901–4, 906–9, 915–16.

29. *Ibid.*, 36, pt. 2: 555–59.

30. *Ibid.*, 45, 50, 59, 66, 69, 75–77, 80, 91, 96–97, 99, 106–7, 126, 148–49, 155, 589, 592; 51, pt. 2: 908; *New York Herald,* May 14, 1864.

31. Bruce, "Butler's Bermuda Campaign," 327; Robertson, *Back Door to Richmond,* 111.

32. *OR*, I, 36, pt. 2: 34–35, 46, 66, 91, 96–97, 106–7, 126–27, 133–34, 137–38, 146, 149, 155–56; 51, pt. 1: 1224, 1231–32, 1238–39.

33. James A. Emmerton, *A Record of the Twenty-third Regiment Mass. Vol. Infantry in the War of the Rebellion, 1861–1865* (Boston: William Ware & Company, 1886), 179.

34. *OR*, I, 36, pt. 2: 34–35, 46, 66, 91, 96–97, 106–7, 126–27, 133–34, 137–39, 146, 149, 155–56, 243–44, 250, 588–92, 975, 978–81; 51, pt. 1: 226, 1224, 1231–32, 1238–39; pt. 2: 908; *New York Herald,* May 14, 1864; *POCB*, 4: 177–82, 187–88; *BB*, 645; Edward K. Wightman to Frederick B. Wightman, May 11, 1864, Wightman Papers; DeForest, *Random Sketches and Wandering Thoughts,* 147–48; William Kreutzer, *Notes and Observations Made during Four Years of Service with the Ninety-eighth N.Y. Volunteers, in the War of 1861* (Philadelphia: Grant, Fairies & Rodgers, 1878), 187–89; Everts, *Ninth New Jersey,* 105–6; Alfred H. Terry to Edward W. Smith, May 11, 1864, Terry Papers, Connecticut Historical Society; William A. Walker diary, May 9, 1864, James Perkins Walker Collection.

35. *OR*, I, 36, pt. 2: 22–23, 28–29, 147, 165–66, 243, 593–94; 51, pt. 1: 226, 228–29; pt. 2: 906; Christian Fleetwood diary, May 9, 1864, Fleetwood Papers; Joseph J. Scroggs diary, May 9, 1864, *CWTI* Collection; Livermore, *Days and Events,* 338–42.

36. *OR*, I, 36, pt. 2: 35–36, 165–66, 587, 590, 624–25; *POCB*, 4: 181–84, 193; *BB*, 645–48; BFB to W. P. Derby, June 26, 1882, Butler Papers, LC.

37. *BB*, 645–47.

38. *OR*, I, 36, pt. 2: 35–36, 590, 593–94, 624.

39. BFB to "Generals," May 9, 1864; Quincy A. Gillmore to BFB, May 9, 1864 (two letters); all, Butler Papers, LC; Wolfson, "Butler's Relations with Grant," 382–84; A. W. Bartlett, *History of the Twelfth Regiment New Hampshire Volunteers in the War of the Rebellion* (Concord, N.H.: Ira C. Evans, 1897), 188.

40. *OR*, I, 36, pt. 2: 35; *BB*, 647–48.

41. *OR*, I, 36, pt. 2: 623–24.

42. *Ibid.*, 45–47, 149; 51, pt. 1: 221, 1224–25; I, 36, pt. 2: 36, 46–47, 58–59, 61, 66, 70–71, 92–93, 104–7, 109–11, 149–50, 214–17, 220–21, 223–24, 230–36, 250, 618, 620–23, 984–85; 51, pt. 1: 221, 226, 1224–25, 1232–34, 1239–40;

New York Herald, May 14, 1864; *New Regime,* May 19, 1864; Hermon Clarke, *Back Home in Oneida: Hermon Clarke and His Letters,* ed. Harry F. Jackson and Thomas F. O'Donnell (Syracuse, N.Y.: Syracuse University Press, 1965), 132; Arthur E. Clark diary, May 10, 1864, Minnesota Historical Society, Saint Paul, Minn.; Martin Eddy to his brother, May 11, 1864, William R. Perkins Library, Duke University.

43. *OR,* I, 36, pt. 2: 36, 47, 58–59, 61, 66, 69–71, 80, 96, 106–7, 134, 137, 139, 156, 199, 256–57, 618, 620–24, 986, 991–92; 51, pt. 1: 1232–33; *New York Herald,* May 14, 1864; Herbert M. Schiller, *The Bermuda Hundred Campaign: "Operations on the South Side of the James River, Virginia—May, 1864"* (Dayton, Ohio: Morningside House, Inc., 1988), 165, 194–95, 206–9.

44. *OR,* I, 36, pt. 2: 688–91, 985, 991, 994–96; 51, pt. 1: 222–23, 226–27, 229, 231; William Farrar Smith to BFB, May 14, 1864, Smith Papers; Joseph J. Scroggs diary, May 10, 1864, *CWTI* Collection.

CHAPTER 5

1. *OR,* I, 36, pt. 2: 26, 36, 41, 50, 60, 67, 72, 78, 81, 85, 94, 97–98, 113–14, 127, 134, 137, 139, 141, 151, 157, 163, 689, 745, 807, 988; pt. 3: 76; 51, pt. 1: 1241; Edward K. Wightman to Frederick B. Wightman, May 17, 1864, Wightman Papers; William A. Walker diary, May 12, 1864, James Perkins Walker Collection; Clark, *Thirty-ninth Illinois,* 179; Nichols, *Perry's Saints,* 207; Richard W. Musgrove, *Autobiography of Capt. Richard W. Musgrove* (Bristol, N.H., 1921), 138; Herbert E. Valentine, *Story of Co. F, 23d Massachusetts Volunteers in the War for the Union, 1861–1865* (Boston: W. B. Clarke & Company, 1896), 111.

2. *OR,* I, 36, pt. 2: 113, 647–51; BFB to W. P. Derby, June 26, 1882; J. Wilson Shaffer to William Farrar Smith, May 11, 1864; both, Butler Papers, LC; *POCB,* 4: 194–95; *BB,* 650.

3. William M. Robinson, Jr., "Drewry's Bluff: Naval Defense of Richmond, 1862," *Civil War History* 7 (June 1961): 172–75; Cornish and Laas, *Lincoln's Lee,* 131–32; *OR,* I, 36, pt. 2: 745, 807; pt. 3: 76.

4. *POCB,* 4: 197, 228; August V. Kautz diary, May 12, 1864, Kautz Papers, LC.

5. *OR,* I, 36, pt. 2: 173–74, 177–78, 180, 183, 185–86, 190, 803, 1000–1001, 1003–4; 51, pt. 2: 926, 931–33; Kautz, "First Attempts to Capture Petersburg," 534; Bolton, *Personal Reminiscences,* 77–78; *Philadelphia Inquirer,* May 14, 1864; *New York Herald,* May 25, 1864; Edward Wall, "Raids in Southeastern Virginia Fifty Year[s] Ago," *Proceedings of the New Jersey Historical Society* n.s. 3 (July 1918): 147–51; Herbert, "Seventeenth Virginia Infantry," 292; Edward G. Longacre, ed., "'Would to God That War Was Rendered Impossible': Letters of Captain Rowland M. Hall, April–July 1864," *Virginia Magazine of History and Biography* 89 (October 1981): 455–56.

6. *OR,* I, 36, pt. 2: 174, 178, 180–81, 183–84, 186, 190, 266–27, 1006, 1014–15, 1018–19; August V. Kautz diary, May 15–17, 1864, Kautz Papers, LC; *Eleventh Pennsylvania Cavalry,* 111–15, 118–19; GRSWR, 10: 200–201, RG-94, E-160, NA.

7. *OR,* I, 36, pt. 2: 175; Wall, "Raids in Southeastern Virginia," 156–57; Johnston, *Virginia Railroads in the Civil War,* 202–4; Kautz, "First Attempts to Capture Petersburg," 534; Robertson, *Back Door to Richmond,* 167–68.

8. *OR,* I, 36, pt. 2: 11, 36, 41, 94, 113–14, 123, 127, 129, 131, 134, 139, 151, 157, 688–93; 51, pt. 1: 223, 226; pt. 2: 924–25; *POCB,* 4: 195–97; Rockwell, "Tenth Army Corps

in Virginia," 287–88; "Notes on the May Campaign," 245; Charles A. Currier memoirs, 99a, Massachusetts MOLLUS Collection; Edward K. Wightman to Frederick B. Wightman, May 17, 1864, Wightman Papers.

9. Smith, "Butler's Attack on Drewry's Bluff," 209; *Rebellion Record,* 11: 495–96; Nichols, *Perry's Saints,* 207; Joseph W. Hughes memoirs, 6, Harrisburg Civil War Round Table Collection, U.S. Army Military History Institute.

10. *OR,* I, 36, pt. 2: 36–37, 41–42, 50–51, 60, 67, 72, 78, 81, 85–86, 94, 100, 103, 114–15, 123, 127, 134, 139, 141–42, 151, 163–64, 740–43, 771–72; 51, pt. 1: 223, 228–29, 231–32, 1241–42; *POCB,* 4: 199–202; *BB,* 651; Smith, "Butler's Attack on Drewry's Bluff," 209; "Notes on the May Campaign," 245; Elias A. Bryant, *The Diary of Elias A. Bryant . . . as Written by Him While in His More Than Three Years' Service in the U.S. Army in the Civil War* (Concord, N.H.: Rumford Press, n.d.), 146–48; Horrocks, *"My Dear Parents,"* 79; William L. Haskin, comp., *The History of the First Regiment of* [United States] *Artillery from Its Organization in 1821, to January 1st, 1876* (Portland, Maine: B. Thurston & Company, 1879), 411–17; Alfred S. Roe, *The Twenty-fourth Regiment Massachusetts Volunteers, 1861–1866: "New England Guard Regiment"* (Worcester: Blanchard Press, 1907), 281.

11. *OR,* I, 36, pt. 2: 37, 42, 52, 60, 72, 78–79, 81–82, 86, 90, 94, 97, 115, 121, 127, 131, 134, 137, 139, 142, 146, 148, 151, 158–59, 164, 771, 773–75, 806; 51, pt. 1: 223, 229, 1242–43; pt. 2: 930–31; William Farrar Smith to BFB, May 14, 1864 (two letters), Butler Papers, LC; *New York Herald,* May 17, 1864; DeForest, *Random Sketches and Wandering Thoughts,* 149; Clark, *Iron Hearted Regiment,* 112–15; *POCB,* 4: 204–9; *BB,* 651–53; Joseph R. Hawley to his wife, May 17, 1864, Hawley Papers; David F. Dobie to "My Dear Friend Hattie," May 17, 1864, Dobie Papers, Virginia State Library, Richmond.

12. Hudson, *Chaplain's Campaign,* 47–48; BFB to Quincy A. Gillmore, May 26, 1864; Quincy A. Gillmore to BFB, May 26, 1864; both, Butler Papers, LC; Swift, "Recollections of a Signal Officer," 49.

13. *OR,* I, 36, pt. 2, pp. 115–16, 776–77, 804–5; William Farrar Smith memoirs, appendix, 44, Smith Papers.

14. *Ibid.;* Charles A. Clark to William Farrar Smith, April 5, 1902; Maurice S. Lamprey diary, May 15, 1864; all, Smith Papers; Robertson, *Back Door to Richmond,* 170.

15. Smith, *From Chattanooga to Petersburg,* 151; Smith, "Butler's Attack on Drewry's Bluff," 212.

16. *OR,* I, 36, pt. 2: 50, 113, 115, 195, 648, 692–93, 744–45; *New York Herald,* May 10, 1864; William Farrar Smith to "Mr. Shattuck," October 4, 1892, Smith Papers; Smith, *From Chattanooga to Petersburg,* 164; Bruce, "Butler's Bermuda Campaign," 129–30; Wistar, *Autobiography,* 451; Everts, *Ninth New Jersey,* 108; GRSWR, 9: 603, RG-94, E-160, NA.

17. *OR,* I, 36, pt. 2: 150, 152; *BB,* 658; Smith, *From Chattanooga to Petersburg,* 163–64; Smith, "Butler's Attack on Drewry's Bluff," 210 and n; William Farrar Smith to "Mr. Shattuck," 1, October 4, 1892, Smith Papers; Derby, *Twenty-seventh Massachusetts,* 287, 289–90.

18. *OR,* I, 36, pt. 2: 116, 129, 131, 143–44, 151; *BB,* 663; James Madison Drake, *The History of the Ninth New Jersey Veteran Volunteers* (Elizabeth, N.J.: *Journal* Printing House, 1889), 188–91, 201, 353; Emmerton, *Twenty-third Mass.,* 182–83; Derby, *Twenty-seventh Massachusetts,* 267–68; J. Waldo Denny, *Wearing the Blue in the Twenty-fifth Mass. Volunteer Infantry* (Worcester, Mass.: Putnam & Davis, 1879), 289; Valentine, *Co. F, 23d Massachusetts,* 112–13; Harvey Clark, *My Experience,* 61.

19. Clark, *Thirty-ninth Illinois,* 179.

20. *BB,* 652–57; *POCB,* 4: 207, 209, 214, 217, 222, 225.

21. *OR,* I, 36, pt. 2: 771; BFB to W. P. Derby, June 26, 1882; BFB to anon., c. January 8, 1879; both, Butler Papers, LC.

22. *OR,* I, 36, pt. 2: 1002; 51, pt. 2: 927–28, 931; Roman, *Military Operations of Beauregard,* 2: 200; P. G. T. Beauregard, "The Defense of Drewry's Bluff," *BL,* 4: 197; "Notes on the May Campaign," 28.

23. *OR,* I, 36, pt. 2: 199, 201, 988, 1004–5, 1024–25; 51, pt. 2: 933–34; Roman, *Military Operations of Beauregard,* 2: 201–5, 211–16; Freeman, *Lee's Lieutenants,* 3: 471, 478–86, 493–94; Beauregard, "Defense of Drewry's Bluff," 197–201.

24. *Ibid.,* 197–203.

25. Amos E. Stearns, *Narrative of Amos E. Stearns, Member Co. A, 25th Regt., Mass. Vols* (Worcester, Mass.: Franklin P. Rice, 1886), 9–10; John M. Spear to anon., May 20, 1864, Spear Papers.

26. *OR,* I, 36, pt. 2: 135, 152, 196–97, 201; 51, pt. 2: 938; *New York Herald,* May 19, 1864; Bruce, "Butler's Bermuda Campaign," 333; "Notes on the May Campaign," 247; Humphreys, *Virginia Campaign of '64 and '65,* 152; William A. Willoughby to his wife, May 16, 1864, Willoughby Papers; Haskin, *First Artillery,* 423–25.

27. *OR,* I, 36, pt. 2: 112, 116–17, 123, 126, 128–32, 135, 137, 139, 142–44, 150–52, 157–58, 162–64, 195–97, 201, 212, 834–35, 1014; Smith, *From Chattanooga to Petersburg,* 163; Wistar, *Autobiography,* 451–52; *BB,* 663–64; Bruce, "Butler's Bermuda Campaign," 333–35; Samuel H. Putnam, *The Story of Company A, Twenty-fifth Regiment Mass. Vols., in the War of the Rebellion* (Worcester, Mass.: Putnam, Davis & Company, 1886), 278; Emmerton, *Twenty-third Mass.,* 185; Derby, *Twenty-seventh Massachusetts,* 284; Kreutzer, *Notes and Observations,* 191–92; Alfred O. Chamberlin to his parents, May 18, 1864, Chamberlin Papers, William R. Perkins Library, Duke University, Durham, N.C.; William A. Walker diary, May 16, 1864; William A. Walker to James P. Walker, May 18, 1864; both, James Perkins Walker Collection.

28. *OR,* I, 36, pt. 2: 37–39, 42–43, 48–49, 53–54, 62–63, 68, 72–73, 79–80, 83–84, 86, 94–95, 97–98, 100–101, 103, 197, 202–3, 212, 237–38, 247–49, 253–54, 834–37; 51, pt. 1: 223–24, 226–27, 230, 232, 1243–45; BFB to William Farrar Smith, May 16, 1864; William Farrar Smith memoirs, appendix, 45; both, Smith Papers; Smith, "Butler's Attack on Drewry's Bluff," 210–12; Wistar, *Autobiography,* 452–54; GRSWR, 11: 590–92, RG-94, E-160, NA; Edward K. Wightman to Frederick B. Wightman, May 17 and 31, 1864, 1 [2], June 4 and 11, 1864, Wightman Papers.

29. *OR,* I, 36, pt. 2: 37–40, 834–36; 51, pt. 1: 1163–65, 1168–69; *POCB,* 4: 220–24, 442–43; *BB,* 664; *New York Times,* May 20, 1864; Hudson, *Chaplain's Campaign,* 49; GRSWR, 11: 592–98, RG-94, E-160, NA.

30. *OR,* I, 36, pt. 2: 116–17, 122, 151–52, 202, 213; BFB to W. P. Derby, June 26, 1882, Butler Papers, LC; Wistar, *Autobiography,* 454–56; Smith, "Butler's Attack on Drewry's Bluff," 211; Bruce, "Butler's Bermuda Campaign," 335–45.

31. *OR,* I, 36, pt. 2: 12, 18, 23, 40, 43–44, 48–49, 54, 63, 68, 73, 79–80, 84, 86, 95, 97–98, 101, 117, 128, 130, 132, 135, 137, 140, 142–44, 148, 152–53, 163, 171, 198, 204–5, 836–37; 51, pt. 1: 1245.

32. Humphreys, *Virginia Campaign of '64 and '65,* 53–57; "Notes on the May Campaign," 249; Bartlett, *Twelfth New Hampshire,* 194–95; DeForest, *Random Sketches and Wandering Thoughts,* 151–52; Charles K. Cadwell, *The Old Sixth* [Connecticut] *Regiment: Its War Record,* 1861–5 (New Haven, Conn.: Tuttle, Morehouse & Taylor,

1875), 91–92; Ferdinand Davis memoirs, 108, Bentley Historical Library, University of Michigan, Ann Arbor, Mich.; Lemuel E. Newcomb to his father, May 18, 1864, Newcomb Papers, C. H. Green Library, Stanford University, Palo Alto, Calif.; Henry Snow to his mother, May 17, 1864; to "Dear Friend," May 23, 1864; both, Snow Papers, Connecticut Historical Society.

33. *OR,* I, 36, pt. 2: 36, 108–9, 199–200, 203–5, 210–11, 256–61, 773, 776, 806, 837–38, 1002, 1004–9; 51, pt. 2: 931, 934–35, 939; *POCB,* 4: 210–13; Beauregard, "Defense of Drewry's Bluff," 203–4; Roman, *Military Operations of Beauregard,* 2: 208–10, 217–20; Clark, *Iron Hearted Regiment,* 118–19; Humphreys, *Virginia Campaign of '64 and '65,* 155–57; Hal Bridges, *Lee's Maverick General: Daniel Harvey Hill* (New York: McGraw-Hill Book Company, Inc., 1961), 263.

34. Thompson, *Thirteenth New Hampshire,* 335; Drake, *Ninth New Jersey,* 180.

CHAPTER 6

1. *OR,* I, 36, pt. 2: 40, 43–44, 54, 95, 135, 859–62; 51, pt. 1: 1245; *BB,* 664.

2. Livermore, *Days and Events,* 342; Joseph R. Hawley to his wife, May 17, 1864, Hawley Papers; David F. Dobie to "My Dear Friend Hattie," May 17, 1864, Dobie Papers.

3. Elbridge J. Copp, *Reminiscences of the War of the Rebellion, 1861–1865* (Nashua, N.H.: *Telegraph* Publishing Company, 1911), 352; Clarke, *Back Home in Oneida,* 138; William A. Walker diary, May 16, 1864, James Perkins Walker Collection; Joseph R. Hawley to his wife, May 21, 1864, Hawley Papers.

4. *New York Herald,* May 22, 1864; *New York Times,* May 25, 1864; William H. Steiner to Frederic Hudson, May 22, 1864, James Gordon Bennett Papers.

5. *OR,* I, 36, pt. 2: 11–12; *POCB,* 4: 228–29.

6. Beauregard, "Defense of Drewry's Bluff," 204; Lemuel E. Newcomb to his father, May 18, 1864, Newcomb Papers.

7. *POCB,* 4: 235–36.

8. Horace Porter, *Campaigning with Grant,* ed. Wayne C. Temple (Bloomington, Ind.: Indiana University Press, 1961), 124.

9. *BB,* 664; William A. Walker diary, May 21, 1864, James Perkins Walker Collection; Warner, *Generals in Blue,* 313.

10. *Ibid.,* 471; BFB to Edwin M. Stanton, April 29, 1864, Butler Papers, LC; Denny, *Twenty-fifth Mass.,* 357; Derby, *Twenty-seventh Massachusetts,* 344; Joseph R. Hawley to his wife, August 9, 1864, Hawley Papers.

11. Thomas L. Livermore, *Numbers and Losses in the Civil War in America, 1861–65* (Boston: Houghton, Mifflin & Company, 1900), 113–14; *OR,* I, 36, pt. 2: 13–18, 205; Rockwell, "Tenth Army Corps in Virginia," 298–99; Robertson, *Back Door to Richmond,* 217–18.

12. *New York Times,* May 21, 1864; Thomas St. George to "Dear Friend Kittie," May 18, 1864, Kate Camenga Collection, William R. Perkins Library, Duke University; Isaiah Price, *History of the Ninety-seventh Regiment, Pennsylvania Volunteer Infantry, During the War of the Rebellion, 1861–65* (Philadelphia, 1875), 414; *OR,* I, 36, pt. 2: 900–902.

13. *OR,* I, 36, pt. 2: 899–901; *POCB,* 4: 232–34; Hagood, *Memoirs,* 250.

14. *OR,* I, 36, pt. 2: 1021–25; Roman, *Military Operations of Beauregard,* 2: 214–15.

15. *OR,* I, 51, pt. 2: 951–52; Beauregard, "Defense of Drewry's Bluff," 204–5; David E. Johnston, *Four Years a Soldier* (Princeton, W.Va., 1887), 324–25; Robertson, *Back Door to Richmond,* 220–21.

16. William H. Huntington diary, May 19, 1864, Connecticut Historical Society; Thomas St. George to "Dear Friend Kittie," May 18, 1864, Kate Camenga Collection.

17. *OR,* I, 36, pt. 3: 34; Quincy A. Gillmore to BFB, May 20, 1864, Butler Papers, LC; *POCB,* 4: 238–39; *BB,* 665.

18. *OR,* I, 36, pt. 3: 36; Smith, *From Chattanooga to Petersburg,* 143–48; *POCB,* 4: 239; *BB,* 665–66; William Farrar Smith memoirs, 86, Smith Papers.

19. Price, *Ninety-seventh Pennsylvania,* 278–79, 414; "Notes on the May Campaign," 251; Edward K. Wightman to Frederick B. Wightman, May 23, 1864, Wightman Papers.

20. Bryant, *Diary,* 156–57.

21. *OR,* I, 36, pt. 3: 28–29; 51, pt. 1: 1235, 1237–38; Alfred H. Terry to Headquarters, X Corps, May 21, 1864, Terry Papers, Connecticut Historical Society; Joshua B. Howell diary, May 20, 1864, Savitz Learning Center, Rowan College Library, Glassboro, N.J.; Joseph R. Hawley to his wife, May 21 and 26, 1864, Hawley Papers; Maurice S. Lamprey diary, May 20, 1864, William Farrar Smith Papers; *BB,* 665n.; *Philadelphia Press,* June 9, 1864; "Notes on the May Campaign," 253–54.

22. *OR,* I, 36, pt. 3: 71; Clark, *Iron Hearted Regiment,* 123; Cleveland, "Campaign of Promise and Disappointment," 325; Edward K. Wightman to Frederick B. Wightman, May 23, 1864, Wightman Papers.

23. Robertson, *Back Door to Richmond,* 222; *OR,* I, 36, pt. 2: 167, 904; Livermore, *Days and Events,* 345; Benjamin W. Ludlow to Salmon P. Chase, May 18, 1864, Chase Papers, LC.

24. *OR,* I, 36, pt. 2: 167; pt. 3: 72, 75; *POCB,* 4: 247–48; Edward W. Hinks to BFB, May 28, 1864; Joseph B. Kiddoo to BFB, May 22, 1864; both, DVNC, RG-393, E-5063, box 5, NA.

25. *OR,* I, 36, pt. 2: 270–72; pt. 3: 180–82; *ORN,* I, 10: 88–91; Simonton, "Up the James River," 482–83, 487; *BB,* 670.

26. Lyman A. Smith, *Memorial of Adjt. M. W. Smith: A Tribute to a Beloved Son and Brother* (Newark, N.J., 1864), 41–42.

27. *OR,* I, 36, pt. 2: 269–72; pt. 3: 181–82; Simonton, "Up the James River," 482–83; *BB,* 669–70; Kennard, *Edward Augustus Wild,* 14; Moore, *Rebellion Record,* 11: 504.

28. *OR,* I, 36, pt. 3: 176; *POCB,* 4: 258–59.

29. *OR,* I, 36, pt. 1: 21; pt. 3: 234–35, 243–44, 278; William Farrar Smith to "Mr. Shattuck," October 4, 1892, Smith Papers; *BB,* 671–72; *POCB,* 4: 246–47, 279–80; Christian Fleetwood diary, May 28, 1864, Fleetwood Papers; Henry W. Halleck to M. C. Meigs and John G. Barnard, May 21, 1864, Butler Papers, LC.

30. M. C. Meigs diary, May 22–23, 1864, Meigs Papers, LC; Edward Everett Hale to Mrs. Sarah Butler, May 23, 1864; Michael P. Small to anon., May 23, 1864; both, Butler Papers, LC; *OR,* I, 36, pt. 3: 140–41; *POCB,* 4: 255–56.

31. *OR,* I, 36, pt. 3: 177–78; *POCB,* 4: 257–58.

32. Grant, *Memoirs,* 2: 151–52.

33. *OR,* I, 36, pt. 3: 145, 176–77.

34. *Ibid.,* 234; *POCB,* 4: 268; William Farrar Smith memoirs, 50, Smith Papers.

35. *OR,* I, 36, pt. 3: 235–36, 239, 319, 429–30; William Farrar Smith, "The Eighteenth Corps at Cold Harbor," *BL* 4: 222; August V. Kautz diary, May 26–27, 1864, Kautz Papers, LC; Henry Snow to his mother, May 28, 1864, Snow Papers; Cunningham, *Adirondack Regiment,* 126; *The Story of the Twenty-first Regiment, Connecticut Volunteer Infantry* (Middletown, Conn.: Stewart Printing Company, 1900), 441–42.

36. Price, *Ninety-seventh Pennsylvania,* 285–87; Bartlett, *Twelfth New Hampshire,* 198–99; S. Thompson, *Thirteenth New Hampshire,* 336; *OR,* I, 36, pt. 1: 998.

37. *Ibid.*, 998–99; Hyde, *One Hundred and Twelfth N.Y.*, 80; Andrew Byrne diary, May 30, 1864, Connecticut Historical Society.

38. *OR*, I, 36, pt. 1: 998–99; pt. 3: 285; William H. Steiner to Frederic Hudson, May 28, 1864, James Gordon Bennett Papers; Price, *Ninety-seventh Pennsylvania*, 287–88; Smith, "Eighteenth Corps at Cold Harbor," 222–23.

39. *Ibid.*, 222; *OR*, I, 36, pt. 1: 999; Emmerton, *Twenty-third Mass.*, 204; Thompson, *Thirteenth New Hampshire*, 338.

40. Smith, "Eighteenth Corps at Cold Harbor," 223; Kreutzer, *Notes and Observations*, 197; *OR*, I, 36, pt. 1: 999.

41. *Ibid.*, 999; pt. 3: 466.

42. *Ibid.*, pt. 1: 999–1000; Smith, "Eighteenth Corps at Cold Harbor," 223.

43. *OR*, I, 36, pt. 1: 996–97, 1000, 1005–6, 1012, 1018–20.

44. *Ibid.*, pt. 3: 507; 51, pt. 1: 1248–49, 1253, 1266; Smith, "Eighteenth Corps at Cold Harbor," 223–24; Hyde, *One Hundred and Twelfth N.Y.*, 82–83; *Philadelphia Press*, June 9, 1864.

45. *OR*, I, 36, pt. 1: 1018; Kreutzer, *Notes and Observations*, 200–201; Nichols, *Perry's Saints*, 226–31; *Twenty-first Connecticut*, 232–33; Charles A. Currier Memoirs, 103a–103b, Massachusetts MOLLUS Collection.

46. *OR*, I, 36, pt. 1: 1000–1001; pt. 3: 467–68.

47. *Ibid.*, pt. 1: 1001; pt. 3: 468; Smith, "Eighteenth Corps at Cold Harbor," 224.

48. Price, *Ninety-seventh Pennsylvania*, 287; Bryant, *Diary*, 160; Edmund J. Cleveland, Jr., ed., "The Second Battle of Cold Harbor: As Seen through the Eyes of a New Jersey Soldier," *Proceedings of the New Jersey Historical Society* 66 (January 1948): 30; Edward K. Wightman to Frederick B. Wightman, June 7, 1864, Wightman Papers; *Twenty-first Connecticut*, 236.

49. *OR*, I, 36, pt. 1: 1003–4; pt. 3: 504–5; Smith, "Eighteenth Corps at Cold Harbor," 224–25.

50. *Ibid.*, 225, 230; "The Opposing Forces at Cold Harbor," *BL*, 4: 185–87; *OR*, I, 36, pt. 1: 1002–3, 1006, 1012–17; pt. 3: 553; 51, pt. 1: 1254–55, 1261–65; Haynes, *Second New Hampshire*, 234; Bartlett, *Twelfth New Hampshire*, 202; Putnam, *Company A, Twenty-fifth Mass*, 286–88; Smith, "Eighteenth Corps at Cold Harbor," 225–26; Andrew Byrne diary, June 3, 1864.

51. Smith, *From Chattanooga to Petersburg*, 22; *OR*, I, 36, pt. 1: 1003–4; pt. 3: 553; 51, pt. 1: 1254; Smith, "Eighteenth Corps at Cold Harbor," 226–27; *New York Times*, June 7, 1864.

52. *OR*, I, 36, pt. 1: 1005; Smith, "Eighteenth Corps at Cold Harbor," 227–28.

53. *New York Times*, June 12, 1864; "Opposing Forces at Cold Harbor," 187; William Farrar Smith memoirs, appendix, 32, Smith Papers.

CHAPTER 7

1. *POCB*, 4: 275.

2. *Ibid.*, 276–77.

3. Merrill, "Butler in the Campaign of 1864," 554; *POCB*, 4: 289, 292.

4. *Ibid.*, 290–91.

5. *New York Herald*, May 31, 1864; Roe, *Twenty-fourth Massachusetts*, 308; Longacre, "'Would to God That War Was Rendered Impossible,'" 458; August V. Kautz diary, May 28, 1864, Kautz Papers, LC.

6. *OR*, I, 36, pt. 3: 370, 415, 420–23; *New York Times*, June 3, 1864; *New York Herald*, June 3, 1864; *POCB*, 4: 290; Christian Fleetwood diary, May 31, 1864, Fleetwood Papers.

7. August V. Kautz diary, June 1, 1864, Kautz Papers, LC; *OR*, I, 36, pt. 3: 475; Joseph R. Hawley to his wife, June 1, 1864, Hawley Papers; Stowits, *One Hundredth New York*, 264; Luther S. Dickey, *History of the Eighty-fifth Regiment Pennsylvania Volunteer Infantry, 1861–1865* (New York: J. C. & W. E. Powers, 1915), 327.

8. *OR*, I, 36, pt. 3: 515–20; 51, pt. 1: 1235–36; Alfred H. Terry to Headquarters, X Corps, June 3, 1864, Terry Papers, Connecticut Historical Society; Clark, *Thirty-ninth Illinois*, 200–202.

9. *OR*, I, 36, pt. 3: 515–20; *New York Times*, June 5, 1864; *New York Herald*, June 5–6, 1864; Jerome Tourtellotte, comp., *A History of Company K of the Seventh Connecticut Volunteer Infantry in the Civil War* (n.p., 1910), 128.

10. *POCB*, 4: 300; William A. Willoughby diary, June 3–6, 1864, Willoughby Papers.

11. Merrill, "Butler in the Campaign of 1864," 554–55; *POCB*, 4: 304, 313; August V. Kautz diary, June 7, 1864, Kautz Papers, LC.

12. *OR*, I, 36, pt. 3, p. 662, 694; August V. Kautz diary, June 7–8, 1864, Kautz Papers, LC.

13. *Ibid.*, June 8, 1864.

14. *OR*, I, 36, pt. 2: 275–76; *BB*, 672, 677.

15. *OR*, I, 36, pt. 2: 275–77, 287; *BB*, 677; Livermore, *Days and Events*, 353; Kautz, "First Attempts to Capture Petersburg," 534; *Philadelphia Inquirer*, June 13, 1864; August V. Kautz diary, 8, June 9, 1864, Kautz Papers, LC.

16. *OR*, I, 36, pt. 2: 277, 287–88, 292; pt. 3: 705; *POCB*, 4: 325, 347–48; William Glenn Robertson, "Cockades under Fire: The Battle for Petersburg, June 9, 1864," 55, 58, M.A. thesis, University of Virginia, 1968.

17. *OR*, I, 36, pt. 2: 277–78, 288, 292–93, 298–99, 308, 310–11; pt. 3: 707–8; August V. Kautz memoirs, 74.

18. *OR*, I, 36, pt. 2: 277–78.

19. *Ibid.*, 278, 288; pt. 3: 718.

20. *Ibid.*, pt. 2: 277–78, 288, 292–93, 299, 302–6, 308, 306, 310, 314; pt. 3: 719; *BB*, 677; Edward W. Smith to Quincy A. Gillmore, June 16, 1864, Gillmore's GP, RG-94, E-159, NA; Swift, "Recollections of a Signal Officer," 51; August V. Kautz diary, June 9–10, 1864, Kautz Papers, LC.

21. *OR*, I, 36, pt. 2: 288, 295, 306–7; Livermore, *Days and Events*, 353; *POCB*, 4: 334–35, 339–41, 351; Robertson, "Cockades under Fire," 108–12; Edward W. Hinks to Quincy A. Gillmore, June 18, 1864; both, Gillmore's General's Papers, RG-94, E-159, NA; James M. Barnard to Quincy A. Gillmore, June 11, 1864; Quincy A. Gillmore to Edward W. Hinks, June 18, 1864; both, Hinks Papers, Mugar Memorial Library, Boston University, Boston, Mass.

22. *OR*, I, 36, pt. 2: 289, 294–302, 306–7; pt. 3: 719; Livermore, *Days and Events*, 353; James M. Bernard to Quincy A. Gillmore, June 11, 1864, Gillmore's GP, RG-94, E-159, NA.

23. *OR*, I, 36, pt. 2: 276–77, 289, 295, 307; *POCB*, 4: 331, 351–52; *BB*, 678; Joseph R. Hawley to Gideon Welles, June 19, 1864, Hawley Papers; Stephen Walkley, *History of the Seventh Connecticut Volunteer Infantry* (Southington, Conn., 1905), 145; Ferdinand Davis memoirs, 110.

24. *OR*, I, 36, pt. 2: 308; August V. Kautz diary, June 8–9, 1864, Kautz Papers, LC; Wall, "Raids in Southeastern Virginia," 156, 159; Kautz, "First Attempts to Capture Petersburg," 534; GRSWR, 10: 201, RG-94, E-160, NA; Samuel P. Spear to Quincy A. Gillmore, June 18, 1864, Gillmore's GP, RG-94, E-159, NA.

25. *OR*, I, 36, pt. 2: 311, 314–15, 317–18; August V. Kautz memoirs, 74; R. E. Colston, "Operations South of the James River: II. Repelling the First Assault on Petersburg," *BL*, 4: 536.

26. Kautz, "First Attempts to Capture Petersburg," 534; *OR*, I, 36, pt. 2: 308–15, 317–18; 51, pt. 1: 1271; *BB*, 678–79; Colston, "Repelling the First Assault on Petersburg," 536–37; GRSWR, 10: 201, RG-94, E-160, NA; August V. Kautz diary, June 9, 1864, Kautz Papers, LC; *New York Times*, June 15, 1864; *Eleventh Pennsylvania Cavalry*, 121; Merrill, *First Maine and First District of Columbia Cavalry*, 256–58; *Petersburg Express*, June 10, 1864; Roman, *Military Operations of Beauregard*, 2: 224–25.

27. Joseph R. Hawley to Gideon Welles, June 19, 1864, Hawley Papers; Wolfson, "Butler's Relations with Grant," 387; Robertson, "Cockades under Fire," 220, 234.

28. Livermore, *Days and Events*, 354; Joseph R. Hawley to his wife, June 27, 1864, Hawley Papers.

29. August V. Kautz diary, June 10, 1864, Kautz Papers, LC.

30. Cyrus B. Comstock diary, June 9, 1864, LC.

31. *OR*, I, 36, pt. 2: 287–88.

32. *Ibid.*, 274–83, 289; *POCB*, 4: 330, 333.

33. *OR*, I, 36, pt. 2: 283–87, 290–91.

34. *POCB*, 4: 357–58.

35. *Eleventh Pennsylvania Cavalry*, 122; Porter, *Campaigning with Grant*, 187–99; Livermore, *Days and Events*, 354–55; *OR*, I, 36, pt. 3: 754–55.

36. Merrill, "Butler in the Campaign of 1864," 554–55; James G. Blaine, *Twenty Years of Congress: From Lincoln to Garfield*, 2 vols. (Norwich, Conn.: Henry Bill Publishing Company, 1884–86), 1: 522; *POCB*, 4: 337.

37. Cleveland, "Second Battle of Cold Harbor," 31; Charles A. Currier memoirs, 105, Massachusetts MOLLUS Collection; Andrew Byrne diary, June 4–7, 1864.

38. *New York Tribune*, June 15, 1864; Charles Mead to anon., June 8, 1864, Nina Ness Collection; Henry Snow to his mother, June 20, 1864, Snow Papers.

39. Nicholas Bowen diary, June 5, 1864; William Farrar Smith memoirs, appendix, 9; both, Smith Papers; James Harrison Wilson, *The Life of John A. Rawlins . . . Major General of Volunteers, and Secretary of War* (New York: Neale Publishing Company, 1916), 228.

40. Porter, *Campaigning with Grant*, 187–88; Cleveland, "Second Battle of Cold Harbor," 37.

41. Charles A. Currier memoirs, 108, Massachusetts MOLLUS Collection; William S. Hubbell to anon., June 12, 1864, William Farrar Smith Papers.

42. George H. Buck, *A Brief Sketch of the Service of Co. G, 40th Massachusetts Volunteer Infantry, 1862–1865* (Chelsea, Mass.: Charles H. Pike & Company, 1910), 12–13.

43. *OR*, I, 36, pt. 3: 766–67; 51, pt. 1: 1262; Porter, *Campaigning with Grant*, 194; William S. Hubbell, "Recollections of the March from Cold Harbor to the White House, June 12th, 1864"; William Farrar Smith memoirs, appendix, 7, 11; both, Smith Papers; Smith, *From Chattanooga to Petersburg*, 22–23, 123.

CHAPTER 8

1. Smith, *From Chattanooga to Petersburg*, 22–23, 91–92; William Farrar Smith, "The Movement against Petersburg, June, 1864," *PMHSM*, 5: 80, 103–4, 112–15.

2. August V. Kautz diary, June 1, 1864, Kautz Papers, LC; William T. H. Brooks to William Farrar Smith, March 3, 1866, Smith Papers; *OR,* I, 40, pt. 1: 721; 51, pt. 1: 1268–70; Smith, *From Chattanooga to Petersburg,* 23, 70–71.

3. *OR,* I, 40, pt. 1: 721; George A. Bruce, "Petersburg, June 15—Fort Harrison, September 29 [1864]: A Comparison," *PMHSM,* 14: 86; McMurray, *Recollections of a Colored Troop,* 33–34.

4. *Eleventh Pennsylvania Cavalry,* 123; Livermore, *Days and Events,* 355–57; *OR,* I, 40, pt. 2: 104–5, 141, 721; 51, pt. 1: 265–66; *POCB,* 4: 385; Bowditch, "War Letters," 480.

5. *OR,* I, 40, pt. 1: 724; 51, pt. 1: 264, 266; Carter, "Fourteen Months' Service with Colored Troops," 163–65.

6. Clarke, *Back Home in Oneida,* 142; Moore, *Rebellion Record,* 11: 580; William Farrar Smith memoirs, appendix, 13; William Farrar Smith to James F. Rhodes, October 30, 1900; both, Smith Papers.

7. Moore, *Rebellion Record,* 8: 261–64; *New Regime,* March 2, 1864.

8. P. G. T. Beauregard, "Four Days of Battle at Petersburg," *BL,* 4: 540–41; Freeman, *Lee's Lieutenants,* 3: 529–32; Henry A. Wise, "The Career of Wise's Brigade, 1861–5," *Southern Historical Society Papers* 25 (1897): 13.

9. William T. H. Brooks to William Farrar Smith, March 3, 1866, Smith Papers; Livermore, *Days and Events,* 369.

10. John H. Martindale to William Farrar Smith, December 11, 1865; Nicholas Bowen diary, June 15, 1864; William Farrar Smith to "Mr. Shattuck," September 2, 1892; all, Smith Papers; Smith, *From Chattanooga to Petersburg,* 26, 79, 82; Smith, "Movement against Petersburg," 90, 95.

11. Smith, *From Chattanooga to Petersburg,* 79, 83; Bruce, "Petersburg—Fort Harrison," 109; G. W. Kelley to William Farrar Smith, July 2, 1898, Smith Papers.

12. Smith, "Movement against Petersburg," 96–97; Charles A. Clark to William Farrar Smith, April 6, 1902, Smith Papers; *Aaron Fletcher Stevens, August 9, 1819, May 10, 1887* (Nashua, N.H., 1901), 54–55; Cunningham, *Adirondack Regiment,* 132.

13. William S. Hubbell to his parents, June 18, 1864, William Farrar Smith Papers; Smith, *From Chattanooga to Petersburg,* 24; Thompson, *Thirteenth New Hampshire,* 387–88, 390.

14. *OR,* I, 40, pt. 1: 700; 51, pt. 1: 1247; Price, *Ninety-seventh Pennsylvania,* 291; Edward K. Wightman to Frederick B. Wightman, June 16 and 18, 1864; to Tom Kennedy, June 22, 1864; all, Wightman Papers.

15. Samuel A. Duncan to William Farrar Smith, April 11, 1866, Smith Papers; *OR,* I, 40, pt. 1: 722, 725; 51, pt. 1: 267–68; Smith, *From Chattanooga to Petersburg,* 26.

16. Thomas L. Livermore, "The Failure to Take Petersburg, June 15, 1864," *PMHSM,* 5: 59–60; McMurray, *Recollections of a Colored Troop,* 38.

17. Smith, *From Chattanooga to Petersburg,* 84; Bowditch, "War Letters," 481; *OR,* I, 40, pt. 1: 728–30; 51, pt. 1: 1256, 1262–63, 1268–70; Wall, "First Assault on Petersburg," 201–2; Livermore, *Days and Events,* 356; August V. Kautz diary, June 15, 1864, Kautz Papers, LC.

18. Edward K. Wightman to Frederick B. Wightman, June 16, 1864, Wightman Papers.

19. Smith, *From Chattanooga to Petersburg,* 85–86; *BB,* 689–93; *OR,* I, 40, pt. 2: 83; *POCB,* 4: 380.

20. Beauregard, "Four Days of Battle," 541; P. G. T. Beauregard, "Defence of Petersburg in June, 1864: Letter of General Beauregard," *Transactions of the Southern Historical Society* 1 (1874): 135; William Farrar Smith memoirs, appendix, 18–19; Maurice S. Lamprey diary, June 15, 1864; William Farrar Smith to James F. Rhodes, October 30, 1900; all, Smith Papers.

21. Smith, *From Chattanooga to Petersburg*, 24–25; William Farrar Smith to James F. Rhodes, October 30, 1900; Samuel A. Duncan to William Farrar Smith, April 17, 1866; both, Smith Papers; *OR*, I, 40, pt. 2: 59–60, 75.

22. *Ibid.*, 83; Smith, "Movement against Petersburg," 79, 93–94, 96; William Farrar Smith memoirs, appendix, 18–19, Smith Papers; Frank E. Peabody, "Crossing of the James and First Assault upon Petersburg, June 12–15, 1864," *PMHSM*, 5: 143–44; Smith, *From Chattanooga to Petersburg*, 25, 93, 101, 108–10; *OR*, I, 40, pt. 1: 305.

23. Frank Wilkeson, *Recollections of a Private Soldier in the Army of the Potomac* (New York: G. P. Putnam's Sons, 1887), 162.

24. H. W. Beecher, *History of the First Light Battery, Connecticut Volunteers, 1861–1865*, 2 vols. (New York: A. T. De La Mare Printing Company, 1901), 2: 484; *POCB*, 4: 383; Walkley, *Seventh Connecticut*, 208.

25. *OR*, I, 40, pt. 1: 683.

26. Alfred H. Terry to Adelbert Ames, June 16, 1864, Joseph R. Hawley Papers; *BB*, 688; *POCB*, 4: 384; Walkley, *Seventh Connecticut*, 209–10.

27. *POCB*, 4: 384–85, 387.

28. *OR*, I, 40, pt. 1: 683–84; pt. 2: 111; *New York Times*, June 21, 1864; Martin A. Haynes, *A History of the Second Regiment, New Hampshire Volunteer Infantry, in the War of the Rebellion* (Lakeport, N.H., 1896), 247–48.

29. *OR*, I, 40, pt. 2: 98–99, 101, 106–7, 110–11; *POCB*, 4: 388–89, 395; *New York Times*, June 21, 1864; Joseph R. Hawley to Gideon Welles, June 19, 1864, Hawley Papers.

30. *OR*, I, 40, pt. 1: 684, 686, 690; pt. 2: 101; *POCB*, 4: 395; Clark, *Thirty-ninth Illinois*, 204, 349; Eldredge, *Third New Hampshire*, 275, 498.

31. Walter Harrison, *Pickett's Men: A Fragment of War History* (New York: D. Van Nostrand, 1870), 129–30; Francis W. Dawson, *Reminiscences of Confederate Service, 1861–1865* (Charleston, S.C.: *News and Courier* Book Presses, 1882), 117–18.

32. *OR*, I, 40, pt. 1: 684, 686; Dickey, *Eighty-fifth Pennsylvania*, 329; Joshua B. Howell diary, June 16, 1864; Joseph R. Hawley to Gideon Welles, June 19, 1864, Hawley Papers.

33. Beecher, *First Light Battery, Connecticut*, 2: 487–88; *OR*, I, 40, pt. 1: 684, 687–88, 690; Sylvester M. Sherman, *History of the 133d Regiment O.V.I.* [Ohio Volunteer Infantry] (Columbus, Ohio: Champlin Printing Company, 1896), 76–79; Robert Brady, *The Story of One Regiment: The Eleventh Maine Infantry Volunteers in the War of the Rebellion* (New York: J. J. Little & Company, 1896), 35; Henry F. Little, *The Seventh Regiment, New Hampshire Volunteers in the War of the Rebellion* (Concord, N.H.: Ira C. Evans, 1896), 268, 275.

34. *OR*, I, 40, pt. 1: 714; pt. 2: 90, 112; 51, pt. 2: 1078; John C. Ropes, "The Failure to Take Petersburg on June 16–18, 1864," *PMHSM*, 5: 160–61; Beauregard, "Four Days of Battle," 541.

35. Price, *Ninety-seventh Pennsylvania*, 292–93; George W. Ward, *History of the Second Pennsylvania Veteran Heavy Artillery* (Philadelphia, 1904), 94.

36. *OR*, I, 40, pt. 1: 715; pt. 2: 113–14; Hyde, *One Hundred and Twelfth N.Y.*, 87.

37. Thompson, *Thirteenth New Hampshire*, 405; Kreutzer, *Notes and Observations*, 213.

38. *OR*, I, 40, pt. 2: 118, 140–41, 144, 662–63; 51, pt. 2: 1078; *Petersburg Express*, June 18, 1864; Ropes, "Failure to Take Petersburg," 166–67; E. P. Alexander, "The Movement against Petersburg," *Scribner's Magazine* 41 (February 1907): 184; Bruce Catton, *Grant Takes Command* (Boston: Little, Brown & Company, 1969), 292–93; McMurray, *Recollections of a Colored Troop*, 40; Beauregard, "Four Days of Battle," 540–41.

39. *OR,* I, 40, pt. 2: 100, 130, 140–41, 149; Francis A. Osborn, "Bermuda Hundred, June 16–17, 1864," *PMHSM,* 5: 202; George T. Stevens, *Three Years in the Sixth Corps* (New York: D. Van Nostrand, 1870), 364–65.

40. *New York Herald,* June 24, 1864; Clark, *Thirty-ninth Illinois,* 205; John M. Spear diary, June 17, 1864, Spear Papers; Roe, *Twenty-fourth Massachusetts,* 315; *OR,* I, 40, pt. 2: 130, 143, 152.

41. *OR,* I, 40, pt. 2: 130–31, 143; *POCB,* 4: 402–3, 405; Smith, *From Chattanooga to Petersburg,* 104–5.

42. *OR,* I, 40, pt. 2: 151; Joseph R. Hawley to Gideon Welles, June 19, 1864, Hawley Papers.

43. *OR,* I, 40, pt. 2: 188–89.

44. *Ibid.,* 197, 199–200.

45. *Ibid.,* 176, 203; 51, pt. 1: 1257.

46. *Ibid.,* 40, pt. 2: 204–5; 51, pt. 1: 268, 1257–58, 1263; Clark, *My Experience with 18th Army Corps,* 72–73; Derby, *Twenty-seventh Massachusetts,* 338.

47. *OR,* I, 40, pt. 1: 205–6; 51, pt. 1: 1258.

48. Beauregard, "Four Days of Battle," 543–44; Livermore, *Days and Events,* 362.

CHAPTER 9

1. *OR,* I, 40, pt. 1: 169; pt. 2: 157, 232–33.

2. Calvin D. Cowles, comp., *Atlas to Accompany the Official Records of the Union and Confederate Armies* (Washington: Government Printing Office, 1891–95), Plate LXV, Map 6; Plate LXVII, Map 7.

3. *OR,* I, 40, pt. 1: 677; pt. 2: 209, 222, 227, 262; *POCB,* 4: 417.

4. GRSWR, 8: 611–13, RG-94, E-160, NA: *OR,* I, 40, pt. 1: 677; pt. 2: 264; Stowits, *One Hundredth New York,* 272–73.

5. Richard J. Sommers, *Richmond Redeemed: The Siege at Petersburg* (Garden City, N.Y.: Doubleday & Company, Inc., 1981), 6, 14; Moore, *Rebellion Record,* 11: 575–76; James M. Granger, *MOLLUS, Minnesota Commandery: Companion Warren Granger* (Hartford, Conn.: Case, Lockwood & Brainard Company, 1895), 28–29; Edward L. Cook to his parents, June 22, 1864, Cook Papers, University of California at Santa Barbara Library, Santa Barbara, Calif.; John M. Spear diary, June 27, 1864, Spear Papers.

6. *OR,* I, 40, pt. 1: 678, 711–12, 718, 739; pt. 2: 228, 233, 258, 261, 264–66, 368; 51, pt. 1: 1250; *POCB,* 4: 422–23, 425; Smith, *From Chattanooga to Petersburg,* 158–60; Valentine, *Co. F, 23rd Massachusetts,* 128; Harvey Clark, *My Experience,* 74; Kreutzer, *Notes and Observations,* 215; George Wheeler diary, June 21, 1864, Nebraska State Historical Society, Lincoln; Louis Bell to George Bell, August 12, 1864, Samuel and S. Dana Bell Collection, New Hampshire Historical Society, Concord.

7. *OR,* I, 40, pt. 2: 299–300.

8. *Ibid.,* 300; Smith, *From Chattanooga to Petersburg,* 158, 160–62.

9. *OR,* I, 40, pt. 2: 300–301.

10. *POCB,* 4: 421.

11. Kautz, "First Attempts to Capture Petersburg," 535; GRSWR, 10: 202, RG-94, E-160, NA.

12. Stephen Z. Starr, *The Union Cavalry in the Civil War,* 3 vols. (Baton Rouge, La.: Louisiana State University Press, 1979–85), 2: 127–37; August V. Kautz memoirs, 78; *OR,* I, 40, pt. 2: 286.

13. *Ibid.*, pt. 1: 730–31, 742; pt. 2: 320; Kautz, "First Attempts to Capture Petersburg," 535; August V. Kautz memoirs, 79; William C. Archibald, *Home-Making and Its Philosophy* (Boston, 1910), 236.

14. James Harrison Wilson, *Under the Old Flag: Recollections of Military Operations in the War for the Union*, 2 vols. (New York: D. Appleton & Company, 1912), 1: 460; George L. Cruikshank, *Back in the Sixties: Reminiscences of the Service of Co. A, 11th Pennsylvania* [Cavalry] *Regiment* (Fort Dodge, Iowa: *Times* Printing House, 1893), 70; *Eleventh Pennsylvania Cavalry,* 127–28; *OR,* I, 40, pt. 1: 621, 626, 645, 731, 733.

15. *Ibid.*, 731, 733–34, 739–40; pt. 2: 683, 690, 694; August V. Kautz diary, June 24–25, 1864, Kautz Papers, LC; Kautz, "First Attempts to Capture Petersburg," 535; "The Gallant Defence of Staunton River Bridge," *Southern Historical Society Papers* 37 (1909): 323–24; *Daily Richmond Enquirer,* June 30, 1864; *Petersburg Express,* June 30, 1864.

16. *OR,* I, 40, pt. 1: 731, 734, 740; August V. Kautz memoirs, 80; GRSWR, 10: 202, RG-94, E-160, NA; August V. Kautz diary, June 25, 1864, Kautz Papers, LC; Stephen Z. Starr, ed., "The Wilson [and Kautz] Raid, June, 1864: A Trooper's Reminiscences," *Civil War History* 21 (September 1975): 227–28; Longacre, "'Would to God That War Was Rendered Impossible,'" 460–61.

17. Merrill, *First Maine and First District of Columbia Cavalry,* 264; *Daily Richmond Examiner,* July 5, 1864.

18. August V. Kautz diary, June 28, 1864, Kautz Papers, LC; August V. Kautz memoirs, 80–81; *Eleventh Pennsylvania Cavalry,* 131; *OR,* I, 40, pt. 1: 731–32, 734–35, 740; pt. 2: 702; *Petersburg Express,* July 1, 1864.

19. *OR,* I, 40, pt. 1: 325–27, 366–69, 382–83, 735, 737; pt. 2: 685; August V. Kautz memoirs, 81; Thomas W. Hyde, *Following the Greek Cross; or, Memories of the Sixth Army Corps* (Boston: Houghton, Mifflin & Company, 1894), 217–18; Stevens, *Three Years in the Sixth Corps,* 370–71; *New York Tribune,* July 6, 1864.

20. *OR,* I, 40, pt. 1: 623, 636, 654, 728, 732, 735, 740–41; Wilson, *Under the Old Flag,* 1: 470; August V. Kautz diary, June 29–30, 1864, Kautz Papers, LC; Bolton, *Personal Reminiscences,* 85; Longacre, "'Would to God That War Was Rendered Impossible,'" 462; Robert W. Hatton, ed., "Just a Little Bit of the Civil War, as Seen by W. J. Smith, Company M, 2nd O.V. [Ohio Volunteer] Cavalry," *Ohio History* 84 (Summer 1975): 118–29.

21. *Eleventh Pennsylvania Cavalry,* 134.

22. *OR,* I, 40, pt. 1: 68, 113, 232, 238, 733; pt. 2: 632, 701–2; pt. 3: 15–16, 35–36, 80, 113; August V. Kautz diary, July 9, 1864, Kautz Papers, LC; *Daily Richmond Enquirer,* July 1, 1864; *Richmond Examiner,* June 27 and July 1, 2, 5, 1864; Wilson, *Under the Old Flag,* 1: 528–30; August V. Kautz memoirs, 81–82; Johnston, *Virginia Railroads in the Civil War,* 214–15.

23. *OR,* I, 40, pt. 1: 655, 658, 671–72; pt. 2: 320, 328, 614, 617; pt. 3: 19, 85–86; Henry S. Graves to his wife, July 18, 1864, Betty Beeby Collection, Western Michigan University Archives, Kalamazoo, Mich.; Henry Snow to his mother, July 27, 1864, Snow Papers.

24. *Philadelphia Inquirer,* June 24, 1864; *OR,* I, 42, pt. 2: 849, 895; Cleveland, "Siege of Petersburg," 83; Hyde, *One Hundred and Twelfth N.Y.,* 89; Mowris, *One Hundred and Seventeenth N.Y.,* 118; Kreutzer, *Notes and Observations,* 216–17.

25. *OR,* I, 40, pt. 1: 710–11, 716, 718; 51, pt. 1: 1250; DeForest, *Random Sketches and Wandering Thoughts,* 245–46.

26. *OR,* I, 40, pt. 1: 697; pt. 2: 325, 400–401, 421, 426, 428–29; Smith, *Memorial of Adjt.*

M. W. Smith, 44; Cleveland, "Siege of Petersburg," 84; *POCB,* 4: 447–48; Bryant, *Diary,* 165; Clark, *Iron Hearted Regiment,* 138–39.

27. *OR,* I, 40, pt. 1: 697–98, 703–4; pt. 2: 539; 51, pt. 1: 1189; Harrison S. Fairchild to Adelbert Ames, July 1, 1864, DVNC, RG-393, E-5063, box 5, NA; Bryant, *Diary,* 166–67; *New York Herald,* July 3–4, 1864; Price, *Ninety-seventh Pennsylvania,* 301–2; Hyde, *One Hundred and Twelfth N.Y.,* 91.

28. *New York Times,* June 28, 1864; Charles W. Washburn memoirs, 95, 114; William H. Newcomb to his father, June 28, 1864, Lemuel E. Newcomb Papers.

29. John W. Turner to his father, June 27, 1864, Turner Papers.

30. William A. Willoughby diary, June 29, 1864, Willoughby Papers; Dickey, *Eighty-fifth Pennsylvania,* 347; Eldredge, *Third New Hampshire,* 510.

31. Nicholas Bowen diary, June 24, 1864; F. C. Choate to "Major Russell," June 27, 1864; both, William Farrar Smith Papers. *OR,* I, 40, pt. 2: 202 and n., 203, 459–60, 372; *POCB,* 4: 450–52.

32. William Farrar Smith to his wife, June 29, 1864, Smith Papers.

33. Smith, *From Chattanooga to Petersburg,* 52–53, 174–79; William Farrar Smith memoirs, appendix, 27–29, Smith Papers.

34. Smith, *From Chattanooga to Petersburg,* 54.

35. *BB,* 698.

36. George J. Stannard to Solomon Foot, July 15, 1864, Andre deCoppet Collection, Firestone Library, Princeton University, Princeton, N.J.; Isaac J. Wistar to William Farrar Smith, January 23, 1893, Smith Papers; Smith, *From Chattanooga to Petersburg,* 191–94.

37. *OR,* I, 40, pt. 2: 558–59, 598; pt. 3: 32; *POCB,* 4: 457–58, 470–71; William D. Mallam, "The Grant-Butler Relationship," *Mississippi Valley Historical Review* 41 (September 1954): 261–62; Stephen E. Ambrose, *Halleck, Lincoln's Chief of Staff* (Baton Rouge, La.: Louisiana State University Press, 1962), 172.

38. *OR,* I, 40, pt. 3: 122; Smith, *From Chattanooga to Petersburg,* 43–44, 52–56; William Farrar Smith memoirs, appendix, 29–30; James Harrison Wilson to William Farrar Smith, July 9, 1864; both, Smith Papers.

39. J. Wilson Shaffer to BFB, July 10, 1864, Butler Papers, LC; *BB,* 695–96; *POCB,* 4: 481–82; Catton, *Grant Takes Command,* 329; Smith, *From Chattanooga to Petersburg,* 50–53; *OR,* I, 40, pt. 3: 113–14.

40. *Ibid.,* pt. 2: 558–59.

41. *Ibid.,* 595; pt. 3: 19–20; William Farrar Smith memoirs, appendix, 29–30; William Farrar Smith, "A Chapter on Petersburg," 51; both, Smith Papers.

42. *OR,* I, 40, pt. 2: 558–59; Wolfson, "Butler's Relations with Grant," 392–93; William Farrar Smith to "Mr. Shattuck," July 29, August 9, and December 17, 1892, and January 5, 1893; William Farrar Smith memoirs, appendix, 30–34; all, Smith Papers.

43. William Farrar Smith to Ulysses S. Grant, July 2, 1864; Smith, "A Chapter on Petersburg," 51; both, Smith Papers; Ulysses S. Grant to William Farrar Smith, July 2 and 8, 1864, Smith's GP, RG-94, E-159, NA; OR, I, 40, pt. 2: 594; pt. 3: 334; John A. Rawlins to his wife, July 19, 1864, James Harrison Wilson Papers.

44. William Farrar Smith memoirs, appendix, 35–36; William Farrar Smith to "Mr. Shattuck," January 5, 1893; Charles A. Dana to William Farrar Smith, January 30, 1893; all, Smith Papers; William Farrar Smith to George Suckley, August 2, 1864, Dreer Collection, Historical Society of Pennsylvania.

45. William Dupew, Jr., to William Farrar Smith, August 2, 1864; William Farrar Smith, "The Foote [Foot] Letter," 31; both, Smith Papers.

CHAPTER 10

1. Hilon A. Parker to his father, July 17, 1864, Parker Papers; Charles A. Currier memoirs, 113–15, Massachusetts MOLLUS Collection.

2. Henry S. Graves to his wife, July 2, 1864, Betty Beeby Collection; William A. Willoughby to his wife, May 22, 1864, Willoughby Papers; Kreutzer, *Notes and Observations*, 260.

3. *OR*, I, 40, pt. 2: 324, 326–27, 673–74; Samuel H. Brink diary, July 16, 1864, Brink Papers, Henry W. Seymour Library, Knox College, Galesburg, Ill.; Brady, *Story of One Regiment*, 221.

4. *OR*, I, 40, pt. 1: 267 and n., 692–96; pt. 3: 206, 379–80, 420, 434, 497; Orton S. Clark, *The One Hundred and Sixteenth Regiment of New York State Volunteers* (Buffalo: Matthews & Warren, 1868), 188–91; *History of the Second Battalion Duryee Zouaves* (New York: Peter DeBaun & Company, 1904), 26; William F. Tiemann, comp., *The 159th Regiment Infantry, New-York State Volunteers in the War of the Rebellion, 1862–1865* (Brooklyn, 1891), 86–88; *A Memorial of the Great Rebellion: Being a History of the Fourteenth Regiment New-Hampshire Volunteers* (Boston: Rand, Avery & Company, 1882), 174–75; *New York Times*, July 27, 1864; Beecher, *First Light Battery, Connecticut*, 2: 517–21.

5. *OR*, I, 40, pt. 3: 451, 484, 488, 491, 709–10, 712; Samuel C. Jones, *Reminiscences of the Twenty-second Iowa Volunteer Infantry* (Iowa City, Iowa, 1907), 74–75; Richard B. Irwin, *History of the Nineteenth Army Corps* (New York: G. P. Putnam's Sons, 1892), 355; Edward L. Molineux diary, July 25–29, 1864, in possession of Mr. Will Molineux, Williamsburg, Va.; Jubal A. Early, "Early's March to Washington in 1864," *BL*, 4: 492–99; *POCB*, 4: 541, 548, 565.

6. *Ibid.*, 544–45; *OR*, I, 40, pt. 3: 401, 435; *New York Times*, August 1, 1864; August V. Kautz diary, July 26–27, 1864, Kautz Papers, LC; August V. Kautz memoirs, 83.

7. *OR*, I, 40, pt. 1: 744; pt. 3: 573–74; *POCB*, 4: 544–45; August V. Kautz diary, July 27, 1864, Kautz Papers, LC; Merrill, *First Maine and First District of Columbia Cavalry*, 271–72; Archibald, *Home-Making and Its Philosophy*, 242.

8. *OR*, I, 40, pt. 1: 308–12, 367, 383; pt. 3: 619–20; August V. Kautz diary, July 28, 1864, Kautz Papers, LC; *Eleventh Pennsylvania Cavalry*, 136–37.

9. *OR*, I, 40, pt. 1: 692–93; pt. 3: 546, 584–85, 588; Beecher, *First Light Battery, Connecticut*, 2: 522–26; Stowits, *One Hundredth New York*, 278–79.

10. *OR*, I, 40, pt. 1: 744; pt. 3: 589, 619–21, 630–34, 674; *POCB*, 4: 563–64; *Eleventh Pennsylvania Cavalry*, 137; August V. Kautz diary, July 29–30, 1864, Kautz Papers, LC; Merrill, *First Maine and First District of Columbia Cavalry*, 272–73.

11. Warner, *Generals in Blue*, 349–50; *OR*, I, 40, pt. 3: 122, 144.

12. *Ibid.*, pp. 56, 139, 272, 328, 376; William T. H. Brooks to adjutant general, U.S. Army, July 1864; to Godfrey Weitzel, July 7, 1864; both, Brooks's GP, RG-94, E-159, NA; Edward O. C. Ord to his wife, July 21, 1864, Ord Papers, C. H. Green Library, Stanford University, Stanford, Calif.

13. Stephen M. Weld, "The Petersburg Mine," *PMHSM* 5: 205–19; William H. Powell, "The Battle of the Petersburg Crater," *BL*, 4: 545–50; Joseph Gould, *The Story of the Forty-eighth . . . Regiment Pennsylvania Veteran Volunteer Infantry* (Philadelphia, 1908), 215; Henry Pleasants, Jr., and George M. Straley, *Inferno at Petersburg* (Philadelphia: Chilton Book Company, 1961), 46–51.

14. *OR*, I, 40, pt. 3: 631–34, 698–99, 706, 719; *New York Times*, August 1, 1864; Ulysses S. Grant to BFB, May 2, 1864, Butler Papers, LC; William A. Coan to Edward O. C. Ord, August 5, 1864, Ord Papers, Bancroft Library; Charles Hadsall diary,

July 29, 1864, Nebraska State Historical Society; MacFarlane, *Reminiscences of an Army Surgeon,* 59; Joseph J. Scroggs diary, July 30, 1864, *CWTI* Collection; *Twenty-first Connecticut,* 270.

15. Joseph J. Scroggs diary, July 30, 1864, *CWTI* Collection; Powell, "Petersburg Crater," 550–53; *JCCW,* 1865, pt. 1: 101, 119; *OR,* I, 40, pt. 1: 698–99, 706–7, 719; pt. 3: 685; John W. Turner to Edward O. C. Ord, July 30, 1864, Ord Papers, Bancroft Library.

16. Lyman, *Meade's Headquarters,* 201; Livermore, *Days and Events,* 384–85; Augustus Woodbury, *Major General Ambrose E. Burnside and the Ninth Army Corps* (Providence: Sidney S. Rider & Brother, 1867), 435; *OR,* I, 40, pt. 1: 707–8.

17. *JCCW,* 1865, pt. 1: 103.

18. *OR,* I, 40, pt. 1: 699–702, 704, 707–8.

19. *Ibid.,* 699–702, 704; pt. 3: 676–77; John W. Turner to Edward O. C. Ord, July 30, 1864, Ord Papers, Bancroft Library; Edward K. Wightman to Charles Wightman, August 1, 1864, Wightman Papers.

20. Livermore, *Days and Events,* 385; *OR,* I, 40, pt. 1: 701, 704.

21. *Ibid.,* 246–49, 699–700, 708; pt. 3: 662, 685, 725; Livermore, *Numbers and Losses in the Civil War,* 116; Bartlett, *Twelfth New Hampshire,* 231; Joseph J. Scroggs diary, July 30, 1864, *CWTI* Collection.

22. Edward L. Cook to Laura Cook, August 4, 1864, Cook Papers.

23. *OR,* I, 40, pt. 1: 708–9; pt. 3: 686–87, 722–27; Clark, *Iron Hearted Regiment,* 126–27; Mowris, *One Hundred and Seventeenth N.Y.,* 126–27.

24. BFB to Edward O. C. Ord, August 4, 1864, Ord Papers, Bancroft Library; Ord to BFB, August 5, 1864, Butler Papers, LC; *OR,* I, 42, pt. 1: 737–38, 792–93, 797; pt. 2: 14, 52–53, 63–64; Roe, *Twenty-fourth Massachusetts,* 331; *POCB,* 5: 11; Gideon Welles to his wife, August 7, 1864, Welles Papers.

25. *OR,* I, 42, pt. 2: 94–95; *New York Herald,* August 12, 1864; *New York Tribune,* August 16, 1864; Ella S. Rayburn, "Sabotage at City Point," *CWTI* 22 (April 1983): 31–33.

26. Ulysses S. Grant, "General Grant on the Siege of Petersburg," *BL,* 4: 575; *OR,* I, 40, pt. 1: 691, pt. 3: 570–71; *New York Herald,* July 16, 1864; *POCB,* 4: 552–53; *New York Times,* September 10, 1864.

27. *OR,* I, 42, pt. 1: 657–59; Joseph R. Hawley, *Major General Joseph R. Hawley, Soldier and Editor (1826–1905): Civil War Military Letters,* ed. Albert D. Putnam (Hartford, Conn.: Connecticut Civil War Centennial Commission, 1964), 59; Lyman, *Meade's Headquarters,* 213.

28. *OR,* I, 42, pt. 2: 70; *New York Tribune,* August 16, 1864; Porter, *Campaigning with Grant,* 371; Swift, "Recollections of a Signal Officer," 54; *Army and Navy Journal,* August 20, 1864; *ORN,* I, 10: 345, 366–67; *POCB,* 5: 26.

29. Joseph R. Hawley to his wife, August 11, 1864, Hawley Papers; *OR,* I, 40, pt. 1: 665–66; 42, pt. 2: 158, 160; *ORN,* I, 10: 350; *New York Tribune,* August 16, 1864; *New York Herald,* August 16, 1864, January 5, 1865; James Morris Morgan, *Recollections of a Rebel Reefer* (Boston: Houghton Mifflin Company, 1917), 212; George E. Pickett, *The Heart of a Soldier: As Revealed in the Intimate Letters of Genl. George E. Pickett, C.S.A.* (New York: Seth Moyle, Inc., 1913), 160.

30. *OR,* I, 42, pt. 2: 136; *POCB,* 5: 41–42; Porter, *Campaigning with Grant,* 276–77.

31. Hyde, *One Hundred and Twelfth N.Y.,* 98; Mowris, *One Hundred and Seventeenth N.Y.,* 129; *OR,* I, 42, pt. 2: 150, 163, 186; Francis A. Walker, *History of the Second Army Corps in the Army of the Potomac* (New York: Charles Scribner's Sons, 1886), 571 and n.

32. *OR*, I, 40, pt. 3: 417–18; David Bell Birney to BFB, July 16, 1864, Butler Papers, LC; "Visit to General Butler," 438; Lyman, *Meade's Headquarters*, 266; Arnold A. Rand memoirs, 54, Massachusetts MOLLUS Collection.

33. William Birney, *General William Birney's Answer to Libels Clandestinely Circulated by James Shaw, Jr.* (Washington: Stanley Snodgrass, 1878), 5; *Philadelphia Press*, August 25, 1864; Joseph R. Hawley to William Faxon, January 29, 1865, Hawley Papers; *POCB*, 5: 274–75; Oliver Willcox Norton, *Army Letters, 1861–1865* (Chicago: O. L. Deming, 1903), 219.

34. *OR*, I, 42, pt. 1: 692, 698, 709–10, 718, 724, 727, 738, 744–45, 751, 754, 757, 770, 785, 789; Eldredge, *Third New Hampshire*, 518; Walkley, *Seventh Connecticut*, 152; *Philadelphia Inquirer*, August 17, 1864; *New York Times*, August 29, 1864; Walker, *Second Army Corps*, 569–72.

35. *OR*, I, 42, pt. 1: 677, 687–88, 692–94, 696, 698, 710, 724, 727–28, 738, 744–46, 751, 754, 757–58, 779; *New York Times*, August 29, 1864; Cadwell, *Old Sixth Regiment*, 98–101; Brady, *Story of One Regiment*, 238–40; Beecher, *First Light Battery, Connecticut*, 2: 540–43; James Hadden, *History of the Old Flag of the Eighty-fifth Pennsylvania Volunteers: Civil War, 1861–5* (Uniontown, Pa.: *News-Standard*, 1902), 4; J. C. Haring, comp., *The Sixty-seventh Ohio Veteran Volunteer Infantry* (Massillon, Ohio: Ohio Printing & Publishing Company, 1922), 14.

36. *OR*, I, 42, pt. 1: 677; pt. 2: 183–85; Walker, *Second Army Corps*, 572–75.

37. *OR*, I, 42, pt. 1: 677, 688, 692, 694, 696, 698–99, 710, 718, 724, 728, 738, 746, 751, 754, 788; pt. 2: 186; Beecher, *First Light Battery, Connecticut*, 2: 542; Stowits, *One Hundredth New York*, 287; Walker, *Second Army Corps*, 575; *New York Times*, August 29, 1864.

38. *OR*, I, 42, pt. 1: 688, 692, 694, 696, 699, 710, 724, 728, 746, 751, 754–55, 785, 789–90; pt. 2: 207.

39. *OR*, I, 42, pt. 1: 678, 728, 739, 746, 752, 755, 758, 765–66, 770–71; Brady, *Story of One Regiment*, 244–45; Stowits, *One Hundredth New York*, 287–89; Price, *Ninety-seventh Pennsylvania*, 316–17.

40. *OR*, I, 42, pt. 1: 678, 689, 692, 694, 696, 699–701, 710–11, 718, 724–25, 728, 739–40, 746–48, 752–53, 755, 758, 785–86, 790; Copp, *Reminiscences of the War of the Rebellion*, 442–53; Ransom Bedell to "Dear Cousin," August 24, 1864, Bedell Papers, Illinois State Historical Library; Samuel H. Brink to his father, August 23, 1864, Brink Papers; John J. Miller to his brother, August 21, 1864, George Miller Collection, U.S. Army Military History Institute; Ferdinand Davis memoirs, 113–23; Little, *Seventh New Hampshire*, 292–93.

41. *POCB*, 5: 61, 63; *OR*, I, 42, pt. 1: 110; pt. 2: 231–33, 238, 249; *New York Herald*, August 20, 1864; *ORN*, I, 10: 366–67; Christian A. Fleetwood diary, August 17, 1864, Fleetwood Papers.

42. *POCB*, 5: 62; *OR*, I, 42, pt. 1: 780; pt. 2: 232–33, 238–40; Walker, *Second Army Corps*, 576–77; Brady, *Story of One Regiment*, 250.

43. *OR*, I, 42, pt. 1: 678, 686–87, 695, 701, 712, 725, 728, 748, 753, 755, 790, 851; pt. 2: 350, 352, 381; Cadwell, *Old Sixth Regiment*, 101–2; Joseph R. Hawley to his wife, August 19, 1864, Hawley Papers; Dickey, *Eighty-fifth Pennsylvania*, 358.

44. *OR*, I, 42, pt. 2: 376–81, 402, 413; Hyde, *One Hundred and Twelfth N.Y.*, 99; Palmer, *Forty-eighth New York*, 167.

45. Walker, *Second Army Corps*, 575–76; *OR*, I, 42, pt. 1: 119–21; Livermore, *Numbers and Losses in the Civil War*, 117.

CHAPTER 11

1. *OR*, I, 42, pt. 2: 242–43, 260, 290–91, 376; *POCB*, 5: 69, 85; Orlando B. Willcox, "Actions on the Weldon Railroad: I. Globe Tavern," *BL*, 4: 568–71.

2. *OR*, I, 40, pt. 3: 727; 42, pt. 1: 131, 835, 845–46; pt. 2: 12, 64–65, 242, 389–90, 441, 465; *POCB*, 4: 563–66; August V. Kautz diary, July 30–31 and August 1, 1864, Kautz Papers, LC; August V. Kautz memoirs, 84–85; GRSWR, 10: 204, RG-94, E-160, NA; Merrill, *First Maine and First District of Columbia Cavalry*, 278; *Eleventh Pennsylvania Cavalry*, 138–39; Bolton, *Personal Reminiscences*, 97–100.

3. *OR*, I, 42, pt. 2: 290, 375, 618; *POCB*, 5: 91, 103, 106.

4. David Bell Birney to Alfred H. Terry, August 24, 1864; Joseph R. Hawley to his wife, August 28, 1864; both, Hawley Papers; BFB to Edward O. C. Ord, August 24, 1864, Ord Papers, Bancroft Library; Adelbert Ames to his parents, August 27, 1864, Sophia Smith Collection, Smith College Archives, Northampton, Mass.; *Twenty-first Connecticut*, 288.

5. Warner, *Generals in Blue*, 354–55; Joseph J. Scroggs diary, August 4, 1864, *CWTI* Collection; Charles Henry Pope, ed., *Paine Ancestry: The Family of Robert Treat Paine, Signer of the Declaration of Independence* (Boston: David Clapp & Son, 1912), 254, 256.

6. *POCB*, 5: 94.

7. *Ibid.*, 4: 424; *OR*, I, 40, pt. 2: 287; Earl Schenck Miers, ed., *Lincoln Day by Day: A Chronology, 1809–1865*, 3 vols. (Washington: Lincoln Sesquicentennial Commission, 1960), 3: 267; *New York Herald*, June 25, 1864; Merrill, "Butler in the Campaign of 1864," 558.

8. *Ibid.*, 556; *POCB*, 4: 464, 512–13, 518.

9. *Ibid.*, 5: 119; *OR*, I, 40, pt. 3: 247.

10. James W. Shaffer to BFB, July 23, 1864, Butler Papers, LC; *POCB*, 4: 513–14, 534, 546–47; 5: 120–21; Merrill, "Butler in the Campaign of 1864," 556, 558.

11. *POCB*, 4: 534–36; 5: 67–69; J. K. Herbert to BFB, August 27, 1864, Butler Papers, LC; Merrill, "Butler in the Campaign of 1864," 556.

12. Lincoln, *Collected Works*, 7: 514; *POCB*, 5: 116–18.

13. *Ibid.*, 74–75, 111–12; *OR*, I, 42, pt. 2: 499, 511.

14. Joseph R. Hawley to his wife, September 2 and 7, 1864, Hawley Papers.

15. *POCB*, 5: 124–25; Merrill, "Butler in the Campaign of 1864," 562–63; *OR*, I, 42, pt. 2: 680; *Philadelphia Press*, September 7, 1864.

16. J. K. Herbert to BFB, September 13, 1864, Butler Papers, LC; *POCB*, 5: 136.

17. *Ibid.*, 171–83; *OR*, I, 42, pt. 2: 1058–59, 1082–88.

18. August V. Kautz memoirs, 88–89; August Kautz diary, September 27, 1864, Kautz Papers.

19. *OR*, I, 42, pt. 1: 793, 798, 805, 811; BFB to Abraham Lincoln, October 14, 1864, DVNC, RG-393, E-5046, vol. 4, NA; Edward H. Ripley, "Memories: The Battle of Fort Harrison or Chapin's Farm," 2–3, Douglas Southall Freeman Collection, Alderman Library, University of Virginia, Charlottesville, Va.

20. *OR*, I, 42, pt. 1: 702, 708, 712, 715, 719, 760, 764, 767, 769, 780, 817–20; pt. 2: 817–19; Sommers, *Richmond Redeemed*, 26–38; Clarke, *Back Home in Oneida*, 64–65; Richard White diary, September 29, 1864, White Family Collection, Alderman Library, University of Virginia; Ferdinand David memoirs, 133; Charles Mead to his sister, October 5, 1864, Nina Ness Collection; McMurray, *Recollections of a Colored Troop*, 51–55, 58; Christian Fleetwood, *The Negro as*

a Soldier (Washington: Howard University Printing Company, 1895), 17; Christian Fleetwood diary, September 29, 1864, Fleetwood Papers; Solon A. Carter to Edward W. Hinks, October 3, 1864, Hinks Papers; James H. Wickes to his father, October 2, 4, and 16, 1864, Wickes Papers, Boston Public Library, Boston.

21. *OR,* I, 42, pt. 1: 793, 798; Sommers, *Richmond Redeemed,* 38–43; Henry Snow to his mother, October 3, 1864, Snow Papers; Cecil Clay, *A Personal Narrative of the Capture of Fort Harrison* (Washington, 1891), 6; A. C. Taylor to Cecil Clay, July 8, 1887, C. L. Clay Collection, Historical Society of Pennsylvania.

22. *OR,* I, 42, pt. 1: 798–99; N. A. McKown to Cecil Clay, January 7, 1889; R. C. Taylor to Cecil Clay, July 8, 1887; H. H. Hoye to Cecil Clay, March 26, 1888; J. E. Johnson to Cecil Clay, January 16 and 31, 1884; William S. Hubbell to Cecil Clay, March 29, 1884; Silas B. O'Mohundro to Cecil Clay, February 14, July 29, 1887; all, C. L. Clay Collection; Ripley, "Battle of Fort Harrison," 3–4.

23. *OR,* I, 42, pt. 1: 794; pt. 2: 1114–15; Cyrus B. Comstock diary, September 29, 1864; *BB,* 734; Bruce, "Petersburg—Fort Harrison," 95.

24. *New York Herald,* August 9–10, 1864; GRSWR, 9: 611, RG-94, E-160, NA; *OR,* I, 42, pt. 1: 793–94, 811–12; pt. 2: 1115; Ripley, "Battle of Fort Harrison," 5–9.

25. *Ibid.,* 6–7; Sommers, *Richmond Redeemed,* 66–81; Ward, *Second Pennsylvania Heavy Artillery,* 107–11; *OR,* I, 42, pt. 1: 702–3, 708, 713, 716, 719, 726, 760, 764–65; pt. 2: 1109; Eldredge, *Third New Hampshire,* 537–38; Beecher, *First Light Battery, Connecticut,* 2: 579–80; Ferdinand Davis memoirs, 133; Price, *Ninty-seventh Pennsylvania,* 323; Stowits, *One Hundredth New York,* 306; *New York Times,* October 3, 1864.

26. Edward K. Wightman to Frederick B. Wightman, October 4, 1864, Wightman Papers.

27. *OR,* I, 42, pt. 1: 760–61, 765, 767, 769, 772–74, 780–81; pt. 2: 1110; pt. 3: 253; Sommers, *Richmond Redeemed,* 80–92; John Bell Bouton, *A Memoir of General Louis Bell, Late Col. of the Fourth N.H. Regiment* (New York, 1865), 24–25; Ripley, "Battle of Fort Harrison," 7–8; Silas B. O'Mohundro to Cecil Clay, July 29, 1887, C. L. Clay Collection; Theodore Skinner to "Dear Friends at Home," October 3, 1864, Skinner Papers, U.S. Army Military History Institute; McMurray, *Recollections of a Colored Troop,* 58–61; George R. Sherman, *Assault on Fort Gilmer and Reminiscences of Prison Life* (Providence: Snow & Farnham Co. 1897), 5–14, 61–63; George R. Sherman, *The Negro as a Soldier* (Providence: Snow & Farnham Company, 1913), 21–22; J. M. Califf, *To the Ex-Members and Friends of the 7th U.S.C.T.* (Fort Hamilton, N.Y., c. 1878), 4–7.

28. Richard White diary, September 29, 1864, White Family Collection; Samuel P. Bates, *History of Pennsylvania Volunteers, 1861–5,* 5 vols. (Harrisburg, Pa.: B. Singerly, 1869–71), 2: 290–91.

29. *OR,* I, 42, pt. 1: 848; pt. 2: 1111, 1142, 1149; *New York Times,* October 3, 1864; Sommers, *Richmond Redeemed,* 93–94, 100–106; *New York Herald,* October 2, 1864; Haskin, *First Regiment of Artillery,* 209–10; "Visit to General Butler," 440; August V. Kautz diary, September 29–30, 1864, Kautz Papers, LC; August V. Kautz to "My Dear Mrs. Savage," October 5, 1864, Kautz Papers, Illinois State Historical Library.

30. *OR,* I, 42, pt. 1: 662, 674–76, 708, 761, 781, 818; pt. 2: 1115, 1143–44; *POCB,* 5: 195–96; Ripley, "Battle of Fort Harrison," 10–11; Sommers, *Richmond Redeemed,* 119–25, 128–30.

31. Robert E. Lee, *The Wartime Papers of R. E. Lee,* ed. Clifford Dowdey and Louis H. Manarin (Boston: Little, Brown & Company, 1961), 859–60; *OR,* I, 42, pt. 1: 800–801, 805–6, 818; pt. 2: 1117, 1142–43; Sommers, *Richmond Redeemed,* 136–46; Ripley, "Battle of Fort Harrison," 11–13.

32. Christian Fleetwood diary, September 30, 1864, Fleetwood Papers; Henry Snow to his
    mother, October 3, 1864, Snow Papers; Sommers, *Richmond Redeemed*, 146–49,
    156–57.
33. Dickey, *Eighty-fifth Pennsylvania*, 377; *Seventh U.S. Colored Troops*, 40; Brady, *Story
    of One Regiment*, 273; *OR*, I, 42, pt. 1: 679, 703, 713, 716, 720, 726–27, 730;
    pt. 3: 31, 33–34; Sommers, *Richmond Redeemed*, 158–84.
34. *OR*, I, 42, pt. 1: 133–37; *POCB*, 5: 195, 200.
35. *OR*, I, 42, pt. 1: 662–64, 676; Andrew Byrne diary, October 2–6, 1864; Eldredge,
    Third New Hampshire, 543.
36. *OR*, I, 42, pt. 1: 826; pt. 3: 99; *Army and Navy Journal*, November 5, 1864; August V.
    Kautz diary, October 4, 1864, Kautz Papers, LC; Kautz, "How I Won My First
    Brevet," 375–76.
37. *OR*, I, 42, pt. 1: 823–28, 830–33, 844–48, 852; pt. 3: 107, 109, 114; Ferdinand Davis
    memoirs, 147; "Hermit," *Recollections in the Army of Virginia and North Carolina*
    (Wilkes-Barre, Pa.: *Record of the Times* Press, 1865), 7.
38. *Philadelphia Press*, October 11, 1864; August V. Kautz memoirs, 92; *Philadelphia
    Inquirer*, October 20, 1864; *Life of David Bell Birney, Major-General United
    States Volunteers* (Philadelphia: King & Baird, 1867), 275.
39. *OR*, I, 42, pt. 1: 703–4, 709, 713, 716–17, 720–21, 727, 730–32, 759, 783–89,
    791–92, 853; pt. 3: 108, 110, 112; *POCB*, 5: 237; Ferdinand Davis memoirs,
    148–49; Andrew Byrne diary, October 7, 1864; *Philadelphia Inquirer*, October 10
    and 20, 1864; *New York Times*, October 10–11,1864; *Life of David Bell Birney*,
    266–69; Joseph S. Bowler to James M. Bowler, October 17, 1864, Bowler Family
    Collection, Minnesota Historical Society, Saint Paul, Minn.
40. *OR*, I, 42, pt. 1: 145–46, 825; *New York Herald*, October 10 and 16, 1864; *Philadelphia
    Press*, October 22, 1864; *Life of David Bell Birney*, 275–78.
41. *OR*, I, 42, pt. 3: 182–83, 186–87; *POCB*, 5: 259; *New York Herald*, October 17, 1864.
42. *OR*, I, 42, pt. 3: 183–84, 186–90, 193, 218, 224; *POCB*, 5: 250–51, 254–56; August
    V. Kautz diary, October 13, 1864, Kautz Papers, LC.
43. August V. Kautz memoirs, 92–93; *Eleventh Pennsylvania Cavalry*, 145–46.
44. *OR*, I, 42, pt. 3: 215, 219; *Philadelphia Press*, October 17, 1864.
45. *OR*, I, 42, pt. 3: 686, 690; Dickey, *Eighty-fifth Pennsylvania*, 403.
46. *OR*, I, 42, pt. 1: 146–48, 681–82, 685–86, 690–91, 706–7, 714, 717, 722, 725–26,
    732–34, 740–41, 749–50, 756–57; pt. 3: 213, 215, 218–19, 231; *POCB*, 5:
    259–61; Joseph R. Hawley to his wife, October 13 and 18, 1864, Hawley Papers;
    Dickey, *Eighty-fifth Pennsylvania*, 398–403; *New York Herald*, October 23, 1864;
    John M. Spear diary, October 13 and 18, 1864, Spear Papers; Walkley, *Seventh
    Connecticut*, 171–72; Brady, *Story of One Regiment*, 278–79.

CHAPTER 12

1. *Army and Navy Journal*, October 15, 1864.
2. *OR*, I, 42, pt. 3: 233, 267, 314; August V. Kautz memoirs, 93; *POCB*, 5: 267; *New York
    Tribune*, October 15, 1864; Surgeon's Certificate, October 13, 1864, Charles J.
    Paine's General's GP, RG-94, E-159, NA.
3. *OR*, I, 40, pt. 1: 657; 42, pt. 3: 214, 243, 260–62, 511–12; Bartlett, *Twelfth New
    Hampshire*, 243; *POCB*, 5: 261; Eldredge, *Third New Hampshire*, 549.
4. *OR*, I, 42, pt. 3: 288, 331–32, 366–68; 51, pt. 1: 1187; *POCB*, 5: 273, 282–87, 290–92;
    Walkley, *Seventh Connecticut*, 172; Moore, *Rebellion Record*, 11: 339; Hyde, *One*

Hundred and Twelfth N.Y., 108; Thompson, *Thirteenth New Hampshire*, 549; Joseph R. Hawley to his wife, October 26, 1864, Hawley Papers.

5. *OR*, I, 42, pt. 1: 691–93, 695, 697, 704–6, 714–15, 717–18, 722–23, 734–37, 741–43, 750–51, 762–64, 767–77; pt. 3: 366–68, 390, 393–97; *New York Herald*, October 31, 1864; Brady, *Story of One Regiment*, 280–81; Hyde, *One Hundred and Twelfth N.Y.*, 108–9; Clarke, *Back Home in Oneida*, 174–75; Eldredge, *Third New Hampshire*, 549–51; Clark, *Iron Hearted Regiment*, 161–62; George H. Woodruff, *Fifteen Years Ago; or the Patriotism of Will County* (Joliet, Ill., 1876), 24; *Seventh U.S. Colored Troops*, 47–48; Mowris, *One Hundred and Seventeenth N.Y.*, 140–42; Price, *Ninety-seventh Pennsylvania*, 330–31; Stowits, *One Hundredth New York*, 315–16; James Christman to his wife, October 29, 1864, Miscellaneous Military Papers, Washington's Headquarters and Museum, Newburgh, N.Y.; Edward K. Wightman to Frederick B. Wightman, October 29, 1864, Wightman Papers.

6. *OR*, I, 42, pt. 1: 795–96; pt. 3: 397–98; *POCB*, 5: 289–90; *Philadelphia Press*, November 1, 1864; *New York Herald*, October 31, 1864.

7. *OR*, I, 42, pt. 3: 30, 68.

8. *Ibid.*, pt. 1: 795–97, 802–4, 806–8, 810–19, 821; pt. 3: 366–68, 391, 398–400; Cunningham, *Adirondack Regiment*, 167–69; Charles A. Currier memoirs, 133–35, Massachusetts MOLLUS Collection.

9. *OR*, I, 42, pt. 1: 814–19; pt. 3: 442–43, 762–64; Joseph J. Scroggs diary, October 27–28, 1864, *CWTI* Collection; Joseph T. Wilson, *The Black Phalanx: A History of the Negro Soldiers of the United States* (Hartford, Conn.: American Publishing Company, 1890), 442–43; Carter, "Fourteen Months' Service with Colored Troops," 173–74; *Philadelphia Press*, November 1–2, 1864.

10. *OR*, I, 42, pt. 1: 796.

11. *Ibid.*, 148–52; pt. 3: 399–400; *POCB*, 5: 289–90; Thompson, *Thirteenth New Hampshire*, 507; Currier memoirs, 134, Massachusetts MOLLUS Collection.

12. George F. Hoar, *Autobiography of Seventy Years*, 2 vols. (New York: Charles Scribner's Sons, 1903), 1: 341; Arthur D. Osborne, *The Capture of Fort Fisher by Major General Alfred H. Terry* (New Haven, Conn.: Tuttle, Morehouse & Taylor, 1911), 4–5.

13. Edson J. Harkness, "The Expedition against Fort Fisher and Wilmington," *Military Essays and Recollections* (Illinois MOLLUS), 2: 146–47; *ORN*, I, 11: 358–59; George Dewey, "The Autobiography of Admiral Dewey," *Hearst's Magazine* 22 (October 1912): 48.

14. *JCCW*, 1865, pt. 2: i–ii, 88, 119; Gideon Welles, "Lincoln's Triumph in 1864," *Atlantic Monthly* 41 (April 1878): 459–61; David Dixon Porter, *The Naval History of the Civil War* (New York: Sherman Publishing Company, 1886), 683; James Russell Soley, *Admiral Porter* (New York: D. Appleton & Company, 1903), 407; Richard S. West, Jr., *The Second Admiral: A Life of David Dixon Porter* (New York: Coward-McCann, Inc., 1937), 269; Henry Munroe Rogers, *Memories of Ninety Years* (Norwood, Mass.: Plimpton Press, 1932), 107.

15. *JCCW*, 1865, pt. 2: 120–21; William Lamb, *Colonel William Lamb's Story of Fort Fisher: The Battles Fought Here in 1864 and 1865* (Carolina Beach, N.C.: Blockade Runner Museum, 1966), 1–2; N. Martin Curtis, "Fort Fisher, North Carolina," 1, Curtis Papers, Chicago Historical Society, Chicago.

16. William Lamb, "The Defense of Fort Fisher," *BL*, 4: 642–43.

17. *Ibid.*, 643.

18. *OR*, I, 46, pt. 1: 406–8; pt. 2: 90–91, 215–16; *ORN*, I, 11: 591–92; Porter, *Naval History of the Civil War*, 694; Lamb, *Colonel Lamb's Story*, 3–5; Harkness, "Expeditions

against Fort Fisher," 148–50; Leonard R. Thomas, *The Story of Fort Fisher, N.C., January 15, 1865* (Ocean City, N.J., 1915), 4; William Lamb, "Defence of Fort Fisher, North Carolina," *PMHSM*, 9: 351–53; Charles E. Pearce, "The Expeditions against Fort Fisher," *War Papers and Personal Reminiscences* (Missouri MOLLUS), 358–59; 622–23; George F. Towle, "Terry's Fort Fisher Expedition," *Our Living and Our Dead* 3 (1875): 593.

19. J. C. Bell to BFB, December 7, 1863, Butler Papers, LC; *OR*, I, 36, pt. 3: 425; William H. Steiner to Frederic Hudson, May 22, 1864, James Gordon Bennett Papers.
20. Soley, *Admiral Porter*, 407; Virgil Carrington Jones, *The Civil War at Sea*, 3 vols. (New York: Holt, Rinehart & Winston, 1960–62), 3: 311; *POCB*, 5: 2–3; Benson J. Lossing, "The First Attack on Fort Fisher," *Annals of the War, Written by Leading Participants, North and South* (Philadelphia, 1879), 228–30.
21. *JCCW*, 1865, pt. 2: ii, 3, 67–68, 73, 119–20; Soley, *Admiral Porter*, 407; *BB*, 774; Eldredge, *Third New Hampshire*, 583; Sommers, *Richmond Redeemed*, 3, 122–23.
22. *BB*, 775, 823; Porter, *Naval History of the Civil War*, 684; *JCCW*, 1865, pt. 2: ii, 88–89, 109, 119–20; *ORN*, I, 10: 554–57; 11: 3, 213–14; *OR*, I, 42, pt. 3: 639–44; "Story of the Powder-Boat," *Galaxy* 9 (January 1870): 78–79.
23. *JCCW*, 1865, pt. 2: 109; *BB*, 775–76.
24. *New York Tribune*, October 5, 1864; *Philadelphia Press*, October 12, 1864; *POCB*, 5: 154, 300–301.
25. Edward G. Longacre, "The Union Army Occupation of New York City, November 1864," *New York History* 65 (1984): 133–43.
26. Philip Van Doren Stern, comp., *Secret Missions of the Civil War* (Chicago: Rand-McNally Company, 1959), 201–5; Josiah H. Benton, *Voting in the Field* (Boston: Houghton, Mifflin Company, 1915), 161–68; George T. Strong, *The Diary of George Templeton Strong*, ed. Allan Nevins and Milton Halsey Thomas, 4 vols. (New York: Macmillan Company, 1952), 3: 508; BFB to Edwin M. Stanton, November 7, 1864, Stanton Papers, LC.
27. William B. Hesseltine, *Lincoln and the War Governors* (New York: Alfred A. Knopf, 1948), 297–300; *POCB*, 5: 306–9, 319; E. D. Townsend to BFB, November 2, 1864; BFB to Ulysses S. Grant, November 3, 1864; both, Butler Papers, LC; *OR*, I, 42, pt. 3: 470, 488–89; 43, pt. 2: 531–32, 535.
28. *POCB*, 5: 303, 307–11; *OR*, I, 42, pt. 3: 441, 466, 489–91, 503–4; 43, pt. 2: 535–36, 544, 559–61; *New York Herald*, November 4, 1864; Joseph R. Hawley to his wife, November 11, 1864, Hawley Papers; *New York Times*, November 8, 1864; *New Regime*, November 19, 1864; BFB to Edwin M. Stanton, November 3, 1864, Butler Papers, LC; BFB to Edwin M. Stanton, November 7, 1864, Stanton Papers; Copy of General Order #86, Headquarters, Department of the East, November 4, 1864, BFB's GP, RG-94, E-159, NA; *New York Herald*, November 10, 1864.
29. *POCB*, 5: 315; *OR*, I, 43, pt. 2: 543, 551–52, 558, 569, 580–81, 598, 610; BFB to Edwin M. Stanton, November 7, 1864, Stanton Papers; Kreutzer, *Notes and Observations*, 236.
30. Copy of General Order #1, Headquarters, City of New York, November 5, 1864, Butler Papers, LC; *OR*, I, 43, pt. 2: 551.
31. BFB to Edwin M. Stanton, November 7, 1864, Stanton Papers; *OR*, I, 43, pt. 2: 551, 558, 568; *New York Herald*, November 10, 1864; *POCB*, 5: 315–16, 329; Lincoln, *Collected Works*, 8: 91–92 and n.
32. BFB to Hiram Paulding, November 7, 1864, Butler Papers, LC; *OR*, I, 43, pt. 2: 560–61, 570; Eldredge, *Third New Hampshire*, 557; Haskin, *First Regiment of Artillery*, 445–46; Little, *Seventh New Hampshire*, 332–33; Ferdinand Davis memoirs, 168.

33. *POCB*, 5: 331; *OR*, I, 43, pt. 2: 599.

34. *OR*, I, 43, pt. 2: 576, 601–2; John G. Nicolay and John Hay, *Abraham Lincoln: A History*, 10 vols. (New York: Century Company, 1917), 9: 375.

35. *OR*, I, 42, pt. 3: 567–69; *Philadelphia Press*, November 11, 1864; *New York Herald*, November 12, 1864; Hesseltine, *Lincoln and the War Governors*, 379–84; Eldredge, *Third New Hampshire*, 557; Little, *Seventh New Hampshire*, 334.

36. *POCB*, 5: 309n., 332–34, 337–38, 347–48; *New York Times*, November 8, 1864; *New York Herald*, November 21, 1864; Marcus P. Norton to BFB, November 19, 1864, Butler Papers, LC; Joseph R. Hawley to his wife, November 27, 1864, Hawley Papers; Merrill, "Butler in the Campaign of 1864," 566–67.

37. *New York Times*, November 26–27, 1864; *New York Herald*, November 27, 1864; *New York Tribune*, November 28, 1864; Stern, *Secret Missions of the Civil War*, 257–67; James D. Horan, *Confederate Agent: A Discovery in History* (New York: Crown Publishers, 1954), 213–23.

38. *New York Times*, November 16 and 22, 1864; *New York Herald*, November 21, 1864; *OR*, I, 42, pt. 1: 854; pt. 2: 637–38, 646–47, 652–53, 655, pt. 3: 653–55, 685–86, 691, 701–2; Bartlett, *Twelfth New Hampshire*, 248–52; Musgrove, *Autobiography*, 149; Joseph J. Scroggs diary, November 18, 1864, *CWTI* Collection; Thompson, *Thirteenth New Hampshire*, 511–12; *Vignettes of Military History*, 2 vols. (Carlisle Barracks, Pa.: U.S. Army Military History Institute, 1976–78), 1: 15.

39. Bartlett, *Twelfth New Hampshire*, 253; *OR*, I, 42, pt. 3: 619, 652, 669–71, 685, 702, 709, 716–18; Godfrey Weitzel to BFB, October 29, 1864, Butler Papers, LC.

40. Theodore Skinner to "Dear Friends at Home," December 1, 1864, Skinner Papers; *Philadelphia Inquirer*, November 29, 1864; *OR*, I, 42, pt. 3: 692; Edward K. Wightman to Frederick B. Wightman, November 28, 1864, Wightman Papers; Little, *Seventh New Hampshire*, 339.

41. *New York Times*, December 7, 1864.

CHAPTER 13

1. *ORN*, I, 11: 208–16; *OR*, I, 42, pt. 3: 639–44, 863–64.

2. Richard S. West, Jr., *Gideon Welles: Lincoln's Navy Department* (Indianapolis: Bobbs-Merrill Company, 1943), 298, 300; *BB*, 775–76; John Hay, *Lincoln and the Civil War in the Diaries and Letters of John Hay*, comp. Tyler Dennett (New York: Dodd, Mead & Company, 1939), 243.

3. David Dixon Porter memoirs, 842, Porter Papers, LC; Porter, *Naval History of the Civil War*, 692; H. C. Lockwood, "The Capture of Fort Fisher," *Atlantic Monthly* 27 (May 1871): 625–26; James Parker, "The Navy in the Battles and Capture of Fort Fisher," *Personal Recollections of the War of the Rebellion* (New York MOLLUS), 2: 107; BFB, *Speech of Maj.-Gen. Benj. F. Butler, upon the Campaign before Richmond, 1864* (Boston: Wright & Potter, 1865), 17–18; *OR*, I, 42, pt. 1: 988–90; *Philadelphia Inquirer*, December 30, 1864; *BB*, 787n.; "Story of the Powder-Boat," 79–83; *New York Herald*, November 11, 1864.

4. David Dixon Porter, *Incidents and Anecdotes of the Civil War* (New York: D. Appleton & Company, 1885), 271; David Dixon Porter memoirs, 829–30, Porter Papers; *JCCW*, 1865, pt. 2: 6.

5. *Ibid.*, memoirs, 841, 846–49, 851, Porter Papers; Porter, *Incidents and Anecdotes*, 262, 267; Grant, *Memoirs*, 2: 371.

6. *OR*, I, 42, pt. 1: 971–72; pt. 3: 835; *ORN*, I, 11: 149–50; *BB*, 783; *JCCW*, 1865, pt. 2: 1, 10–11, 35, 69; BFB, *Campaign before Richmond*, 21; Porter, *Campaigning with Grant*, 338–39.

7. *OR*, I, 42, pt. 1: 970; pt. 3: 760, 799; 46, pt. 2: 9–10; *JCCW*, 1865, pt. 2: 6–7, 52; *BB*, 780; appendix, 63; *POCB*, 5: 379.

8. *OR*, I, 42, pt. 1: 966, 974, 980–81, 985; *JCCW*, 1865, pt. 2: 12–14, 17, 20, 28–29, 69, 73, 82, 89–90, 94–95, 222; *POCB*, 5: 388, 398, 460–61; Cyrus B. Comstock diary, December 7–8, 1864; Edwin S. Redkey, ed., "'Rocked in the Cradle of Consternation': A Black Chaplain in the Union Army Reports on the Struggle to Take Fort Fisher," *American Heritage* 31 (October–November 1980): 72–74; Edward K. Wightman to Frederick B. Wightman, December 11–12, 1864, Wightman Papers; Pearce, "Expeditions against Fort Fisher," 365.

9. *OR*, I, 42, pt. 1: 964, 966; pt. 3: 992; *ORN*, I, 11: 268; *JCCW*, 1865, pt. 2: 17, 83, 90, 94, 96.

10. *OR*, I, 42, pt. 1: 964, 966–67, 974, 981, 985; *JCCW*, 1865, pt. 2: 15, 69, 95; *POCB*, 5: 428, 431, 460–61; BFB to Ulysses S. Grant, December 14, 1864, Butler Papers, LC; Hyde, *One Hundred and twelfth N.Y.*, 114; Mowris, *One Hundred and Seventeenth N.Y.*, 145; Solon A. Carter to Emily Carter, December 17, 1864, Carter Papers, U.S. Army Military History Institute.

11. *OR*, I, 42, pt. 1: 967, 981, 985; *POCB*, 5: 461; *BB*, 786; Cyrus B. Comstock diary, December 15, 1864; Cyrus B. Comstock to Theodore S. Bowers, January 1, 1865, Edwin M. Stanton Papers; *JCCW*, 1865, pt. 2: 17.

12. *BB*, 786–87; Lossing, "First Attack on Fort Fisher," 234; BFB, *Campaign before Richmond*, 16; *JCCW*, 1865, pt. 2: 17; Edward K. Wightman to Frederick B. Wightman, December 16 and 22, 1864, Wightman Papers.

13. Christian Fleetwood diary, December 16–17, 1864, Fleetwood Papers; Joseph J. Scroggs diary, December 17, 1864, *CWTI* Collection.

14. Pope, *Paine Ancestry*, 260; *New York Times*, December 16, 1864; *New York Herald*, December 17 and 19, 1864; *OR*, I, 42, pt. 1: 979; pt. 3: 1225, 1233, 1254–55, 1271, 1278–83, 1287; 46, pt. 2: 35; J. Cutler Andrews, *The North Reports the Civil War* (Pittsburgh: University of Pittsburgh Press, 1955), 614–15, 619; *ORN*, I, 11: 205, 359, 409; Gideon Welles to Edwin M. Stanton, December 21, 1864, Welles Papers; *Philadelphia Press*, January 24, 1865.

15. *OR*, I, 42, pt. 1: 964–65; 51, pt. 1: 1290; *POCB*, 5: 430–32; *ORN*, I, 11: 196, 223–24, 227–29; *BB*, 787; appendix, 67–68, 74; "Story of the Powder-Boat," 84–85; David Dixon Porter memoirs, 854–55, Porter Papers; *JCCW*, 1865, pt. 2: 18–19, 70, 83.

16. *BB*, 789; *OR*, I, 42, pt. 1: 965, 967, 981, 985; pt. 3: 1048–49; *JCCW*, 1865, pt. 2: ii, 19, 70–71, 83–84; David Dixon Porter memoirs, 853–54, Porter Papers; *POCB*, 5: 431–32; Redkey, "'Rocked in the Cradle of Consternation,'" 74–75.

17. Porter, *Naval History of the Civil War*, 695; *ORN*, I, 11: 254, 273; Robley D. Evans, *A Sailor's Log: Recollections of Forty Years of Naval Life* (New York: D. Appleton & Company, 1901), 76; Christian Fleetwood diary, December 19 and 21, 1864, Fleetwood Papers; Redkey, "'Rocked in the Cradle of Consternation,'" 75; "Hermit," *Recollections in the Army*, 9; John Ames, "The Failure at Fort Fisher," *Overland Monthly* 4 (June 1870): 492; Mowris, *One Hundred and Seventeenth N.Y.*, 150–51.

18. *JCCW*, 1865, pt. 2: 71; Edward K. Wightman to Frederick B. Wightman, December 22, 1864, Wightman Papers.

19. *BB*, 790; *ORN*, I, 11: 226–27, 238–40, 255; *OR*, I, 42, pt. 1: 967, 978–79; 46, pt. 2: 571–72; *JCCW*, 1865, pt. 2: ii, 18, 21, 30–31, 64, 71, 83, 96–97, 112, 127–31;

Rogers, *Memories of Ninety Years*, 90–91; Thomas O. Selfridge, Jr., "The Navy at Fort Fisher," *BL*, 4: 655.

20. David Dixon Porter memoirs, 842, Porter Papers; *ORN*, I, 11: 269–70; Parker, "Navy in Capture of Fort Fisher," 107.

21. *BB*, 800–808; *JCCW*, 1865, pt. 2: 30–31, 226–27, 250–51; Harkness, "Expeditions against Fort Fisher," 170; Walkley, *Seventh Connecticut*, 178n.; Lockwood, "Capture of Fort Fisher," 627–28; "Story of the Powder-Boat," 88.

22. William Lamb, "Fort Fisher: The Battles Fought There in 1864 and 1865," *Southern Historical Society Papers* 21 (1893): 269; *BB*, 795; "Story of the Powder-Boat," 88; *OR*, I, 42, pt. 1: 979; Scharf, *History of the Confederate States Navy*, 422; *ORN*, I, 11: 263; Porter, *Incidents and Anecdotes*, 272; David Dixon Porter memoirs, 877, Porter Papers.

23. Cyrus B. Comstock to Theodore S. Bowers, January 1, 1865, Edwin M. Stanton Papers; *JCCW*, 1865, pt. 2: 81, 99; "Hermit," *Recollections in the Army*, 10; David Dixon Porter memoirs, 856–58, Porter Papers; Francis P. B. Sands, *The Last of the Blockade and the Fall of Fort Fisher* (Washington, 1902), 15; Edward K. Wightman to Frederick B. Wightman, December 27, 1864, Wightman Papers.

24. *BB*, 792, 791, 815–18; Lamb, *Colonel Lamb's Story*, 16–19; *ORN*, I, 11: 250–51, 256, 366–69, 593; *OR*, I, 42, pt. 1: 967–69, 978–80, 994–97, 1000–1007; 46, pt. 1: 441; *JCCW*, 1865, pt. 2: 21–25, 58, 71–72, 79, 90–91, 113.

25. *POCB*, 5: 435–36; *BB*, 791–92; *JCCW*, 1865, pt. 2: 22, 27, 52, 66–68, 72, 77, 82, 95–96, 99, 101–2, 119; *ORN*, I, 11: 250, 258, 269–70, 356, 366; *OR*, I, 42, pt. 1: 985–86; pt. 3: 1072; *Army and Navy Journal*, February 4, 1865; Harkness, "Expeditions against Fort Fisher," 160; Lamb, *Colonel Lamb's Story*, 17; Lamb, "Fort Fisher: Battles Fought There," 271.

26. *ORN*, I, 11: 251, 257, 270–71; *OR*, I, 42, pt. 1: 967–68, 982, 986; pt. 3: 1075–76; "Hermit," *Recollections in the Army*, 10–11; Lamb, *Colonel Lamb's Story*, 17–18; *BB*, 792; *POCB*, 5: 462; N. Martin Curtis, "The Capture of Fort Fisher," *Personal Recollections of the War of the Rebellion* (New York MOLLUS), 3: 29–30.

27. *BB*, 795, 797; Mowris, *One Hundred and Seventeenth N.Y.*, 153–56; Price, *Ninety-seventh Pennsylvania*, 341; *OR*, I, 42, pt. 1: 968, 981, 983–84, 986; *JCCW*, 1865, pt. 2: 23–24, 75–76, 91, 129; *ORN*, I, 11: 257.

28. Cyrus B. Comstock diary, December 25, 1864; *OR*, I, 42, pt. 1: 981–83; *BB*, 792, 794, 821–22; *POCB*, 5: 463; Pearce, "Expeditions against Fort Fisher," 369–70; Partridge, "With the Signal Corps from Fortress Monroe to Richmond," 95; *JCCW*, 1865, pt. 2: 23, 73, 79–80, 84–85.

29. *POCB*, 5: 437–41, 462–64; *BB*, 792, 795–96; Cyrus B. Comstock diary, December 25, 1864; Barrett, *Civil War in North Carolina*, 269–70; Lockwood, "Capture of Fort Fisher," 630–31, 634; *ORN*, I, 11: 251, 357; *OR*, I, 42, pt. 1: 968–69, 979–81, 983–84, 986–87; pt. 3: 1075, 1098; *JCCW*, 1865, pt. 2: 22–27, 72–73, 75; Solon A. Carter to Emily Carter, December 29, 1864, Carter Papers.

30. Porter, *Naval History of the Civil War*, 705, 710; *ORN*, I, 11: 437, 441n.; Daniel A. Ammen, *The Old Navy and the New* (Philadelphia: J. B. Lippincott Company, 1891), 406; David Dixon Porter memoirs, 858, Porter Papers; *JCCW*, 1865, pt. 2: 25, 57–58, 100, 111, 130; *OR*, I, 42, pt. 3: 1075–76; 51, pt. 1: 1291.

31. *BB*, 798–99; appendix, 78–79; *OR*, I, 42, pt. 1: 965–66; pt. 3: 1076, 1085–86; Cyrus B. Comstock diary, December 26, 1864; *JCCW*, 1865, pt. 2: 26, 32, 35; *POCB*, 5: 442–43.

32. *JCCW*, 1865, pt. 2: 32; Ulysses S. Grant to Edwin M. Stanton, January 1, 1865, Stanton Papers; *POCB*, 5: 452–53; *ORN*, I, 11: 356–58; *OR*, I, 42, pt. 3: 1087; 46, pt. 2:

3–5; John A. Rawlins to his wife, December 26, 1864, James Harrison Wilson Papers.

33. *BB*, appendix, 88–89; Welles, "Lincoln's Triumph in 1864," 461; *ORN*, I, 11: 254–65, 405–6; Adam Badeau, *Military History of Ulysses S. Grant, from April, 1861, to April, 1865*, 3 vols. (New York: D. Appleton & Company, 1881), 3: 324–25; *OR*, I, 46, pt. 2: 20; *JCCW*, 1865, pt. 2: 122–27; *POCB*, 5: 440–50, 458.

34. *JCCW*, 1865, pt. 2: 53; Mowris, *One Hundred and Seventeenth N.Y.*, 150; Curtis, "Capture of Fort Fisher," 32; Beecher, *First Light Battery, Connecticut*, 2: 640; *New York Herald*, January 2, 1865; *New York Times*, January 5, 1865; Christian Fleetwood diary, December 26, 1864, Fleetwood Papers; Edward K. Wightman to Frederick B. Wightman, December 28, 1864, Wightman Papers.

35. Hoar, *Autobiography of Seventy Years*, 1: 336; Welles, *Diary*, 2: 216; Alexander Neil to his parents, January 4, 1865, Neil Papers, Alderman Library, University of Virginia.

36. *OR*, I, 42, pt. 1: 977–90, 995–96, 1000, 1003, 1005; *JCCW*, 1865, pt. 2: 106–8.

37. Rowena Reed, *Combined Operations in the Civil War* (Annapolis, Md.: Naval Institute Press, 1978), 345–46; Edwin H. Simmons, "The Federals and Fort Fisher," *Marine Corps Gazette* 35 (January 1951): 56–58.

38. Ulysses S. Grant to Edwin M. Stanton, January 4, 1865; to Abraham Lincoln, January 6, 1865; both, Butler Papers, LC.

39. Copy of General Order #1, Adjutant General's Office, January 7, 1865, BFB's GP, RG-94, E-159, NA; Copy of Special Order #5, Headquarters, Armies of the United States, January 7, 1865, Butler Papers, LC; *POCB*, 5: 472–73.

40. *New York Tribune*, January 12, 1865; *New York Herald*, January 11, 15, and 18, 1865; *Philadelphia Press*, January 12, 1865; Hilon A. Parker to his sister, January 14, 1865, Parker Papers; Adams et al., *Cycle of Adams Letters*, 2: 248; Marsena R. Patrick, *Inside Lincoln's Army: The Diary of Marsena Rudolph Patrick, Provost Marshal General, Army of the Potomac*, ed. David S. Sparks (New York: Thomas Yoseloff, 1964), 457; Joseph J. Scroggs diary, January 13, 1865, *CWTI* Collection; James H. Wickes to "My Dear Lottie," January 11, 1865, Wickes Papers.

41. *OR*, I, 42, pt. 1: 659; pt. 3: 216–17, 858; 46, pt. 2: 70–71; *POCB*, 5: 247, 2163–64, 268, 388, 475–76; *New York Herald*, January 5 and 17, 1865; Gordon, *War Diary*, 372; *Philadelphia Inquirer*, January 4, 1865; *Philadelphia Press*, September 11, 1864; *New York Tribune*, October 18, December 10, 1864; *Richmond Examiner*, October 20 and 28, 1864, January 12, 1865; *Harper's Weekly*, January 21, 1865.

42. Gideon Welles to Ulysses S. Grant, December 19, 1864, Welles Papers; *OR*, I, 42, pt. 3: 1091, 1098–99, 1100–1101; 46, pt. 2: 5; *ORN*, I, 11: 391–92, 394, 401–2; Lockwood, "Capture of Fort Fisher," 684–85.

43. *POCB*, 5: 455–57, 459–60; August V. Kautz diary, January 1, 1865, Kautz Papers, LC; Ulysses S. Grant to Alfred H. Terry, January 3–4, 1865, Terry Papers, Connecticut Historical Society; *OR*, I, 42, pt. 3: 1101; 46, pt. 1: 394; pt. 2: 15, 19–20, 46; Adrian Terry to his wife, January 24, 1865, Terry Family Collection, Beinecke Rare Book and Manuscripts Library, Yale University, New Haven, Conn.; Solon A. Carter to Emily Carter, January 3, 1865, Carter Papers.

44. *OR*, I, 46, pt. 1: 166–67, 394–95, 403–4; pt. 2: 44–45; Walkley, *Seventh Connecticut*, 181; Towle, "Terry's Fort Fisher Expedition," 464–66; Henry L. Abbot, *Siege Artillery in the Campaigns against Richmond* (New York: D. Van Nostrand, 1868), 174; John Ames,"The Victory at Fort Fisher," *Overland Monthly* 9 (October 1872): 324; James H. Wickes to his father, January 5, 1865, Wickes Papers; Edward K. Wightman to Frederick B. Wightman, January 12, 1865, Wightman Papers.

45. *OR,* I, 46, pt. 2: 35; *POCB,* 5: 466.
46. *OR,* I, 46, pt. 1: 395; pt. 2: 47, 69, 89; *POCB,* 5: 473–74; David Dixon Porter memoirs, 868–69, Porter Papers; Lockwood, "Capture of Fort Fisher," 685; Alfred H. Terry to John A. Rawlins, January 10, 1865, Terry Papers, Beinecke Rare Book and Manuscripts Library; Adrian Terry to his wife, January 24, 1865, Terry Family Collection.
47. *JCCW,* 1865, pt. 2: 102–3; Alfred H. Terry to David Dixon Porter, January 15, 1865, Terry Papers, Beinecke Rare Book and Manuscripts Library; *OR,* I, 46, pt. 2: 90; *ORN,* I, 11: 431.
48. *OR,* I, 46, pt. 1: 396, 415, 418, 423; Adrian Terry to his wife, January 24, 1865, Terry Family Collection; *ORN,* I, 11: 437, 587–88; *JCCW,* 1865, pt. 2: 103, 114–15; *New York Times,* January 18, 1865; Zera L. Tanner, *The Capture of Fort Fisher* (Washington, 1897), 7.
49. *ORN,* I, 11: 432–33, 438, 587–88; Soley, *Admiral Porter,* 427; *OR,* I, 46, pt. 1: 396–97, 418, 423–24, 435, 437; Eldredge, *Third New Hampshire,* 612; Mowris, *One Hundred and Seventeenth N.Y.,* 162–65; Daniel Ammen, *Our Second Bombardment of Fort Fisher* (Washington, 1887), 4; Adrian Terry to his wife, January 24, 1865, Terry Family Collection.
50. Abbot, *Siege Artillery,* 175–76; John C. Taylor and Samuel P. Hatfield, comps., *History of the First Connecticut Artillery and of the Siege Trains of the Armies Operating against Richmond, 1862–1865* (Hartford, Conn.: Case, Lockwood & Brainard Company, 1893), 130–31; *OR,* I, 46, pt. 1: 167, 397, 407; pt. 2: 123.
51. *ORN,* I, 11: 434, 439; *New York Times,* January 17, 1865; *OR,* I, 42, pt. 1: 980; 46, pt. 1: 397, 436–37, 441; Lamb, *Colonel Lamb's Story,* 23; Ames, "Victory at Fort Fisher," 327.
52. *OR,* I, 46, pt. 1: 398, 400; *ORN,* I, 11: 429–30, 434, 439–47, 527–29, 576–86; Selfridge, "Navy at Fort Fisher," 659–60; *Army and Navy Journal,* January 28, 1865; Evans, *Sailor's Log,* 87–90, 93; *New York Times,* January 19, 1865; *JCCW,* 1865, pt. 2: 103, 115, 117–18; Richard A. Collum, *History of the United States Marine Corps* (Philadelphia: L. R. Hamersly & Company, 1890), 172–73.
53. Selfridge, "Navy at Fort Fisher," 660n.; Lamb, *Colonel Lamb's Story,* 27; *JCCW,* 1865, pt. 2: 75, 117; Adrian Terry to his wife, January 24, 1865, Terry Family Collection; Thomas, *Story of Fort Fisher,* 9; *OR,* I, 46, pt. 1: 398, 417, 439–40; pt. 2: 216; *ORN,* I, 11: 592; Towle, "Terry's Fort Fisher Expedition," 593.
54. *OR,* I, 46, pt. 1: 398–99, 415–16, 418–21, 431; Alfred H. Terry to Ulysses S. Grant, January 16, 1865, Stanton Papers; Adelbert Ames to his parents, February 9, 1865, Ames Papers; D. A. Neire to N. Martin Curtis, February 4, 1865; N. Martin Curtis, "Fort Fisher, North Carolina," 3–4; both, Curtis Papers; Surgeon's Certificate, February 8, 1865, Curtis's GP, RG-94, E-159, NA; Alfred H. Terry to John W. Turner, January 17, 1865, Turner Papers; *Medal of Honor,* 184; Adrian Terry to his wife, January 24, 1865, Terry Family Collection; "Hermit," *Recollections in the Army,* 20–21; Hyde, *One Hundred and Twelfth N.Y.,* 118–21; Price, *Ninety-seventh Pennsylvania,* 351.
55. *OR,* I, 46, pt. 1: 399, 416, 421–22; Cyrus B. Comstock diary, January 15, 1865; Bouton, *Memoir of General Louis Bell,* 27–29; MacFarlane, *Reminiscences of an Army Surgeon,* 69.
56. Lockwood, "Capture of Fort Fisher," 687; Lamb, *Colonel Lamb's Story,* 26–27, 32–33; Lamb, "Defense of Fort Fisher," 649; *OR,* I, 46, pt. 1: 435–39; *ORN,* I, 11: 440.
57. *OR,* I, 46, pt. 1: 399, 410–15, 424, 432–34; pt. 2: 1056, 1059–60; *ORN,* I, 11: 577; Adrian Terry to his wife, January 24, 1865, Terry Family Collection; *JCCW,*

1865, pt. 2: 103; Joseph C. Abbott to Joseph R. Hawley, January 23, 1865, Hawley Papers; Alfred H. Terry to Ulysses S. Grant, January 16, 1865, Stanton Papers; Cyrus B. Comstock diary, January 15, 1865.

58. Little, *Seventh New Hampshire,* 374–75; Mowris, *One Hundred and Seventeenth N.Y.,* 173–74; *OR,* I, 46, pt. 1: 399, 438, 440–47; pt. 2: 140; Adrian Terry to his wife, January 15 and 24, 1865, Terry Family Collection; A. G. Jones to Alfred H. Terry, June 4, 1888, Terry Papers, Beinecke Rare Book and Manuscripts Library.

59. *OR,* I, 46, pt. 1: 399, 401, 442; pt. 2: 166–67, 176; Alfred H. Terry to John A. Rawlins, January 27, 1865, Terry Papers, Beinecke Rare Book and Manuscripts Library; *ORN,* I, 11: 436, 441; Adelbert Ames to his parents, February 9 and 23, 1865, Ames Papers.

60. *OR,* I, 46, pt. 1: 402, 406 and n.; pt. 2: 158; Walkley, *Seventh Connecticut,* 196; Alfred H. Terry to Joseph R. Hawley, January 20, 1865, Hawley Papers; David Dixon Porter memoirs, 876, Porter Papers; *New York Herald,* January 18, 1865.

CHAPTER 14

1. *OR,* I, 42, pt. 3: 782, 791, 945, 949, 1113; *New Regime,* January 23, 1865.

2. *POCB,* 5: 116; James W. Shaffer to Robert S. Davis, August 29, 1864, John W. Turner Papers; *New York Tribune,* September 16, 1864; *New York Herald,* September 4, December 25, 1864, March 27, 1865; *OR,* I, 42, pt. 3: 801–2, 836–37; 46, pt. 2: 681.

3. Edward W. Hinks to anon., May 13, 1864; BFB to Judge Advocate General, DVNC, n.d.; Edward A. Wild to Robert S. Davis, May 12, 1864; to Henry Wilson, May 10, 1865; all, Wild's GP, RG-94, E-159, NA; Birney, *General William Birney's Answer,* 5, 8.

4. Warner, *Generals in Blue,* 150–51, 209–10, 212–13; Joseph R. Hawley to Gideon Welles, December 16, 1864, Welles Papers; *OR,* I, 42, pt. 3: 800; 46, pt. 3: 44; George E. Craig, *In Memoriam: Maj. Gen. George L. Hartsuff* (Norwood, Mass.: Charles G. Wheelock, 1875), 4–5, 8; H. E. Matheny, *Major General Thomas Maley Harris* (Parsons, W.Va.: McClain Printing Company, 1963), 176, 178, 188; Thomas M. Harris to Edward O. C. Ord, February 7, 1865, Harris Papers, West Virginia University Library, Morgantown; *OR,* I, 46, pt. 2: 663–64.

5. August V. Kautz diary, December 10, 1864, January 30, February 2, 1865, Kautz Papers, LC; August V. Kautz memoirs, 96–100; August V. Kautz to John W. Turner, January 29, 1865; Alfred H. Terry to Edward O. C. Ord, December 10, 1864; John W. Turner to Edward O. C. Ord, December 10, 1864 (three letters); all, Ord Papers, Bancroft Library; *OR,* I, 42, pt. 1: 825–26, 828–29, 838–39, 844; pt. 2: 282, 306, 363–64, 1161–63; pt. 3: 939–44, 949–50, 1013–14, 1276; 51, pt. 1: 1289; GRSWR, 10: 206, RG-94, E-160, NA.

6. August V. Kautz memoirs, 97–104; August V. Kautz diary, January 9, 1865, Kautz Papers, LC.

7. *OR,* I, 46, pt. 2: 282, 306, 363–64, 1161–63; August V. Kautz to John W. Turner, January 29, February 11, 1865, Ord Papers, Bancroft Library; Ulysses S. Grant to Edward O. C. Ord, February 2, 1865, Turner Papers; August V. Kautz diary, January 30, February 2, 13, 28, March 6, 11–24, 26, 28, 1865, Kautz Papers, LC; Gordon, *War Diary,* 371; *OR,* I, 46, pt. 2: 977; pt. 3: 55, 212–13.

8. *Ibid.,* pt. 2: 947, 950, 977; pt. 3: 55, 66; *Eleventh Pennsylvania Cavalry,* 147; Grant, *Memoirs,* 2: 541; Warner, *Generals in Blue,* 301–2.

9. *Ibid.*, 171–72; John Gibbon, *Personal Recollections of the Civil War* (New York: G. P. Putnam's Sons, 1928); Lyman, *Meade's Headquarters*, 103, 107; *POCB*, 5: 159; John Gibbon to Andrew A. Humphreys, November 28, 1864, Gibbon's GP; John Gibbon to Robert S. Davis, September 18, 1864, Adelbert Ames's GP; both, RG-94, E-159, NA.

10. *OR*, I, 46, pt. 2: 152; Alexander Neil to his parents, January 8, February 21, 1865, Neil Papers; Beecher, *First Light Battery, Connecticut*, 2: 643; Thompson, *Thirteenth New Hampshire*, 532, 534, 536; William H. Newcomb to Lemuel E. Newcomb, December 19, 1864, Lemuel E. Newcomb Papers.

11. *Army and Navy Journal*, February 18, 1865; Kreutzer, *Notes and Observations*, 269–70; Bartlett, *Twelfth New Hampshire*, 258–61; William S. Lincoln, *Life with the Thirty-fourth Mass. Infantry in the War of the Rebellion* (Worcester, Mass.: Press of Noyes, Snow & Co. 1879), 385.

12. Edward O. C. Ord to Charles Wheaton, Jr., January 19, 1865; to John Coughlin, February 2, 1865; both, DVNC, RG-393, E-5046, vol. 5, NA; Charles Hadsall diary, January 31, 1865.

13. *New York Herald*, February 10, 1865; Edward F. Williams to Edward O. C. Ord, n.d. [February 1865]; Edward F. Williams diary, February 11, 1865; both, Williams Papers; Swint, *"Dear Ones at Home,"* 145–46; John Coughlin to Edward O. C. Ord, February 13, 1865, Ord Papers, Bancroft Library.

14. *Army and Navy Journal*, February 18, 1865; *Philadelphia Press*, February 13 and 23, 1865.

15. Ulysses S. Grant to Edward O. C. Ord, January 18, 1865; Charles A. Dana to Ulysses S. Grant, January 16, 1865; both, DVNC, RG-393, E-5063, box 5, NA; *OR*, I, 46, pt. 2: 144–45.

16. *Ibid.*, 173, 181; Gordon, *War Diary*, 376–80, 387–90.

17. Edward O. C. Ord to George F. Shepley, January 23, 1865, DVNC, RG-393, E-5046, vol. 5, NA; George F. Shepley to Edward O. C. Ord, January 22 and 31, 1865, Ord Papers, Bancroft Library; *OR*, I, 46, pt. 2: 504; Gordon, *War Diary*, 377–78, 380; *OR*, I, 46, pt. 2: pp. 929, 939; *New York Herald*, March 16, 1865; Gordon, *War Diary*, 381–82.

18. *OR*, I, 46, pt. 1: 542–44; pt. 2: 782, 790, 812–17, 830, 832, 891, 900, 907–8; Ulysses S. Grant to John W. Turner, March 2, 1865, Turner Papers; *New York Herald*, March 11, 1865; *New York Tribune*, March 11, 1865; *Philadelphia Press*, March 11 and 14, 1865; *Twenty-first Connecticut*, 328–35.

19. James Christman to his wife, December 3, 1864, Miscellaneous Military Papers; Henry S. Graves to his wife, January 8, 1865, Betty Beeby Collection; Alexander Neil to his parents, December 28, 1864, Neil Papers.

20. Joseph R. Hawley to his wife, November 27, 1864, Hawley Papers.

21. Hilon A. Parker to his sister, January 14, 1865, Parker Papers; *Twenty-first Connecticut*, 316.

22. Bartlett, *Twelfth New Hampshire*, 254; George A. Bruce, *The Capture and Occupation of Richmond* (Boston, 1918), 3.

23. James H. Wickes to his father, January 11, 1865, Wickes Papers.

24. *OR*, I, 42, pt. 3: 1037–38; 46, pt. 2: 1143–50; Albert Rogall diary, January 18, 1865; Charles Hadsall diary, January 17, February 21, March 8, 1865; Joseph R. Hawley to his wife, December 22, 1864, Hawley Papers; William H. Newcomb to Lemuel E. Newcomb, December 19, 1864, Lemuel E. Newcomb Papers; Norton, *Army Letters*, 255; Thompson, *Thirteenth New Hampshire*, 534; Beecher, *First Light Battery, Connecticut*, 2: 639; Clark, *Thirty-ninth Illinois*, 247; Kreutzer, *Notes and Observations*, 277, 280, 285, 287.

25. Thomas F. Wildes, *Record of the One Hundred and Sixteenth Regiment Ohio Infantry Volunteers, in the War of the Rebellion* (Sandusky, Ohio: I. F. Mack & Brothers, 1884), 231–32.

26. *OR,* I, 46, pt. 2: 29, 302, 317; *New York Times,* January 2, 17, and 28, 1865; A. D. Brown to Mrs. Albert Phillips, February 12, 1865, Illinois State Historical Library; John A. Rawlins to his wife, December 30, 1864, James Harrison Wilson Papers; *Philadelphia Inquirer,* February 11, 1865; Edward Chase Kirkland, *The Peacemakers of 1864* (New York: AMS Press, 1969), 222–50; August V. Kautz diary, February 6, 1865, Kautz Papers, LC.

27. Edward O. C. Ord to his wife, n.d. [July 31, 1864], n.d. [c. December 15, 1864], Ord Papers, C. H. Green Library; August V. Kautz diary, February 4, 1865, Kautz Papers, LC.

28. *OR,* I, 46, pt. 2: 1259, 1275–76; II, 8: 315; James Longstreet, *From Manassas to Appomattox: Memoirs of the Civil War in America* (Philadelphia: J. B. Lippincott Company, 1896), 583–84; Bernarr Cresap, *Appomattox Commander: The Story of General E. O. C. Ord* (San Diego: A. S. Barnes & Company, 1981), 163–65.

29. *Ibid.,* 165–67; *OR,* I, 46, pt. 2: 801–2, 823–25, 1264; *New York Tribune,* March 23, 1865; Lee, *Wartime Papers,* 911–12; Lincoln, *Collected Works,* 8: 330–31.

30. Hawley, *Major General Joseph R. Hawley,* 69; Herman D. Hamner to his brother, February 11, 1865, Hamner Papers, in possession of Mr. Reginald Pettus, Keysville, Va.; Edward O. C. Ord to his wife, n.d. [c. December 15, 1864], Ord Papers, C. H. Green Library.

31. Charles Hadsall diary, December 17, 1864, February 2 and 17, 1865; *OR,* I, 42, pt. 3: 1089–90; 46, pt. 2: 582–83; Hilon A. Parker to "Folks at Home," January 28, February 17, 1865, Parker Papers; *New York Times,* February 20–21, 1865; *New York Herald,* February 20 and 27, 1865; Kreutzer, *Notes and Observations,* 270–71.

32. *Philadelphia Press,* October 11, 1864; *New York Tribune,* October 11, November 10, 1864; *Richmond Examiner,* January 25–27, 1865; Morgan, *Recollections of a Rebel Reefer,* 218–19; *OR,* I, 46, pt. 1: 165–70, 176–79, 181–82, 186; pt. 2: 210–13, 218–20, 223–27, 236, 239, 241, 237–48, 1211–12; Scharf, *History of the Confederate States Navy,* 739–43; Norton, *Army Letters,* 253–54; Thompson, *Thirteenth New Hampshire,* 527; Cunningham, *Adirondack Regiment,* 166; Beecher, *First Light Battery, Connecticut,* 2: 645–46.

33. Wildes, *One Hundred and Sixteenth Ohio,* 229–30; Hawley, *Major General Joseph R. Hawley,* 69; Bartlett, *Twelfth New Hampshire,* 260.

34. *New York Tribune,* February 6, 1865; Kreutzer, *Notes and Observations,* 294; *Philadelphia Press,* March 24 and 28, 1865; *OR,* I, 46, pt. 2: 939–40, 954, 1309–15; pt. 3: 103, 105, 163; Charles A. Currier memoirs, 144–45, Massachusetts MOLLUS Collection; Theodore Read to Theodore S. Bowers, March 16, 1865; to Edward O. C. Ord, March 25, 1865; John W. Turner to Edward O. C. Ord, March 25, 1865; all, Ord Papers, Bancroft Library; Headquarters, Army of the James, to Robert M. West, March 17, 1865, DVNC, RG-393, E-5046, vol. 5, NA; Alexander Neil to "Dear Brother & All the Rest," March 26, 1865, Neil Papers; Edmund N. Hatcher, *The Last Four Weeks of the War* (Columbus, Ohio: Cooperative Publishing Company, 1892), 17, 34; *Twenty-first Connecticut,* 341.

35. *Philadelphia Press,* March 30, 1865; August V. Kautz memoirs, 103; *Philadelphia Press,* March 29, 1865; *New York Herald,* March 29, 1865; John S. Barnes, "With Lincoln from Washington to Richmond in 1865," *Appleton's Magazine* 9 (1907): 523–24; Grant, "Grant on the Siege of Petersburg," 578.

36. *OR*, I, 46, pt. 3: 207; Godfrey Weitzel, "Entry of United States Forces into Richmond, Virginia, April 3, 1865," 1–2, Cincinnati Historical Society, Cincinnati.

37. *OR*, I, 46, pt. 3: 188, 1160; August V. Kautz memoirs, 104; Weitzel, "Entry of United States Forces," 1.

38. *OR*, I, 46, pt. 3: 105, 189, 210–11, 238–39; *Seventh U.S. Colored Troops*, 66; Wilson, *Black Phalanx*, 455.

39. *OR*, I, 46, pt. 1: 209; Ripley, *Vermont General*, 293; Cornish, *Sable Arm*, 281–82.

40. *OR*, I, 46, pt. 1: 1160; Thompson, *Thirteenth New Hampshire*, 548.

41. *OR*, I, 46, pt. 3: 208, 211, 236; Albert Maxfield, *Roster and Statistical Record of Company D, of the Eleventh Maine Infantry* (New York: Press of Thos. Humphrey, 1890), 309–10.

42. Joel C. Baker, *The Fall of Richmond* (Burlington, Vt., 1892), 5.

43. *OR*, I, 46, pt. 1: 1160, 1173, 1179, 1185, 1192, 1234–35, 1242; pt. 3: 236; *New York Tribune*, March 31, 1865; *New York Herald*, April 3, 1865; Robert Larimer diary, March 27–28, 1865, Alderman Library, University of Virginia; Alexander Neil to "My Dear Friends," April 1, 1865, Neil Papers; William H. Wharff, "From Chapin's Farm to Appomattox," *Maine Bugle* 3 (July 1896): 232.

CHAPTER 15

1. *OR*, I, 46, pt. 1: 1160, 1173, 1179, 1192–93, 1214, 1236; pt. 3: 268–69, 320; *New York Herald*, April 3, 1865.

2. *OR*, I, 46, pt. 1: 1173, 1179, 1185, 1193–94, 1202–3, 1214, 1242; Wildes, *One Hundred and Sixteenth Ohio*, 237; Stowits, *One Hundredth New York*, 333–36; Wilson, *Black Phalanx*, 449–50; *Seventh U.S. Colored Troops*, 67; Shaw, *Our Last Campaign*, 14.

3. *OR*, I, 46, pt. 1: 1174, 1179, 1193; pt. 3: 429–30; Hatcher, *Last Four Weeks of the War*, 97; Humphreys, *Virginia Campaign of '64 and '65*, 365; Alexander Neil to "My Dear Friends," April 1, 1865, Neil Papers; Lincoln, *Thirty-fourth Mass.*, 390.

4. Porter, *Campaigning with Grant*, 444.

5. August V. Kautz memoirs; Thompson, *Thirteenth New Hampshire*, 547.

6. Bruce, *Capture and Occupation of Richmond*, 7.

7. *OR*, I, 46, pt. 3: 212, 237, 271; Thompson, *Thirteenth New Hampshire*, 551; Weitzel, "Entry of United States Forces," 3.

8. *Ibid.*, 4; *OR*, I, 46, pt. 3: 384; Thompson, *Thirteenth New Hampshire*, 550; Abbot, *Siege Artillery*, 176–77; Frederic Denison, *Shot and Shell: The Third Rhode Island Heavy Artillery Regiment in the Rebellion, 1861–1865* (Providence: J. A. & R. A. Reid, 1879), 314; Henry Hall and James Hall, *Cayuga in the Field: A Record of the 19th N.Y. Volunteers, All the Batteries of the 2d New York Artillery, and 75th New York Volunteers* (Auburn, N.Y.: Truair, Smith & Company, 1873), 262; William B. Arnold, *The Fourth Massachusetts Cavalry . . . from Richmond to Appomattox* (Boston, n.d.), 27.

9. George F. Shepley, "Incidents of the Capture of Richmond," *Atlantic Monthly* 46 (July 1880): 19–20.

10. *OR*, I, 46, pt. 1: 1227; pt. 3: 495–96; August V. Kautz memoirs, 104; Frank Allaben, *John Watts dePeyster*, 2 vols. (New York, 1908), 2: 34.

11. *OR*, I, 46, pt. 1: 1170–72; pt. 3: 190, 439–41, 1373–74; August V. Kautz diary, April 1–2, 1865, Kautz Papers, LC.

12. *OR*, I, 46, pt. 1: 1244, 1248; pt. 3: 238–39, 378.

13. Horace Porter, "Five Forks and the Pursuit of Lee," *BL*, 4: 709–11; Starr, *Union Cavalry in the Civil War*, 2: 430–32.

14. *OR*, I, 46, pt. 1: 1160, 1244.

15. Porter, "Five Forks," 711–13; Joshua L. Chamberlain, "Five Forks," *War Papers* (Maine MOLLUS), 2: 227.

16. *OR*, I, 46, pt. 1: 1244–45; Porter, "Five Forks," 713; *Eleventh Pennsylvania Cavalry*, 148–49.

17. *OR*, I, 46, pt. 1: 1244, 1248; Chamberlain, "Five Forks," 244–46; *New York Tribune*, April 4, 1865.

18. *OR*, I, 46, pt. 1: 1160–61, 1174; Michael Egan, *The Flying, Gray-Haired Yank; or, the Adventures of a Volunteer* (Philadelphia: Hubbard Brothers, 1888), 386; Grant, *Memoirs*, 2: 448; Charles W. Smith, *Life and Military Services of Brevet Major-General Robert S. Foster* (Indianapolis: Edward J. Hecker, 1915), 529; Robert Larimer diary, March 2, 1865.

19. *OR*, I, 46, pt. 1: 1161, 1174, 1179, 1214, 1221, 1235; Gibbon, *Personal Recollections*, 299–300; Haring, *Sixty-seventh Ohio*, 19.

20. Humphreys, *Virginia Campaign of '64 and '65*, 369; Morris Schaff, *The Sunset of the Confederacy* (Boston: John W. Luce & Company, 1912), 27–28; Clark, *Thirty-ninth Illinois*, 253; *OR*, I, 46, pt. 1: 1179; Wilson, *Black Phalanx*, 455–56; W. H. Withington, "The West in the War of the Rebellion, as Told in the Sketches of Some of Its Generals," *Magazine of Western History* 4 (August 1886): 510.

21. Maxfield, *Company D, Eleventh Maine*, 315.

22. Livermore, *Days and Events*, 440; Clark, *Thirty-ninth Illinois*, 253.

23. Lincoln, *Thirty-fourth Mass.*, 390–91; Wildes, *One Hundred and Sixteenth Ohio*, 241; Alexander Neil to "My Dear People," April 10, 1865, Neil Papers; Egan, *Flying, Gray-Haired Yank*, 393; Stowits, *One Hundredth New York*, 340.

24. Thomas M. Harris to C. H. Hurd, April 5, 1865, Harris Papers; Matheny, *Thomas Maley Harris*, 182–83; *OR*, I, 46, pt. 1: 1174, 1221–22; Theodore Read to Edward O. C. Ord, April 2, 1865, Ord Papers, Bancroft Library.

25. Grant, *Memoirs*, 2: 453.

26. *OR*, I, 46, pt. 1: 1170–73; pt. 3: 495–96, 500; Ward, *Second Pennsylvania Heavy Artillery*, 136.

27. Edward H. Ripley, "Final Scenes at the Capture and Occupation of Richmond, April 3, 1865," *Personal Recollections of the War of the Rebellion* (New York MOLLUS), 3: 473; *OR*, I, 46, pt. 1: 1227; pt. 3: 501–2; August V. Kautz diary, April 2, 1865, Kautz Papers, LC; August V. Kautz memoirs, 104; Abel E. Leavenworth, "Vermont at Richmond," *Proceedings of the Rutland County Historical Society* 2 (1890): 27; Shepley, "Incidents of the Capture of Richmond," 20–21.

28. Bartlett, *Twelfth New Hampshire*, 267.

29. Bruce, *Capture and Occupation of Richmond*, 5–6; "Evacuation of Richmond: Reports of Gens. Ewell and Kershaw," *Transactions of the Southern Historical Society* 1 (1874): 102–3; Dallas D. Irvine, "The Fall of Richmond," *Journal of the American Military Institute* 3 (Summer 1939): 78–79; *New York Herald*, April 12, 1865; Rembert W. Patrick, *The Fall of Richmond* (Baton Rouge, La.: Louisiana State University Press, 1960), 101–2; John H. Burrill to "Dear Ell," April 4, 1865, Burrill Papers.

30. Baker, *Fall of Richmond*, 9–12; Leavenworth, "Vermont at Richmond," 27; Bruce, *Capture and Occupation of Richmond*, 6, 16.

31. Thompson, *Thirteenth New Hampshire*, 578; S. Millett Thompson to John Hay, February 16, 1890, John Nicolay Papers, LC.

32. Thompson, *Thirteenth New Hampshire*, 554; Bartlett, *Twelfth New Hampshire*, 281–83; Cunningham, *Adirondack Regiment*, 167; Currier memoirs, 157, Massachusetts MOLLUS Collection; *New York Herald*, April 6, 1865; Arnold, *Fourth Massachusetts Cavalry*, 28–29; Thomas T. Graves, "The Fall of Richmond: II. The Occupation," *BL*, 4: 726; *OR*, I, 46, pt. 1: 1227.

33. August V. Kautz memoirs, 104–5; Weitzel, "Entry of United States Forces into Richmond," 6–7; Leavenworth, "Vermont at Richmond," 27–28; *Philadelphia Press*, April 6, 1865; Arnold, *Fourth Massachusetts Cavalry*, 27–28; Edward A. Wild, "Draperisms," Massachusetts MOLLUS Collection.

34. Ripley, "Final Scenes at Richmond," 477, 479.

35. Ripley, *Vermont General*, 295; *OR*, I, 51, pt. 1: 1210.

36. Royal B. Prescott, "The Capture of Richmond," *Civil War Papers* (Massachusetts MOLLUS), 1: 67, 70; Bartlett, *Twelfth New Hampshire*, 273; Cunningham, *Adirondack Regiment*, 167.

37. Weitzel, "Entry of United States Forces into Richmond," 7.

38. Edward F. Williams diary, April 3, 1865, Williams Papers.

39. Cornish, *Sable Arm*, 282-83; Bruce, *Capture and Occupation of Richmond*, 17.

40. Adams et al., *Cycle of Adams Letters*, 2: 264–65.

41. Weitzel, "Entry of United States Forces," 8–9; *New York Tribune*, April 5, 1865; E. D. Townsend, *Anecdotes of the Civil War in the United States* (New York: D. Appleton & Company, 1884), 122–23.

42. *OR*, I, 46, pt. 1: 170–71; pt. 3: 501, 537, 569, 613–14, 637, 680; Ward, *Second Pennsylvania Heavy Artillery*, 136–37; George Alfred Townsend, *Rustics in Rebellion: A Yankee Reporter on the Road to Richmond, 1861–65* (Chapel Hill, N.C.: University of North Carolina Press, 1950), 264; Charles Hadsall diary, April 4–5, 1865.

43. *OR*, I, 46, pt. 1: 1217; *Seventh U.S. Colored Troops*, 68; Shaw, *Our Last Campaign*, 16–17; Wilson, *Black Phalanx*, 456.

44. Grant, *Memoirs*, 2: 457–58; *OR*, I, 46, pt. 1: 1180; pt. 3: 532; John Gibbon to John W. Turner, April 3, 1865, Turner Papers.

45. *OR*, I, 46, pt. 1: 1180, 1186, 1243; John Gibbon to John W. Turner, April 4, 1865, Turner Papers; E. E. Billings, ed., "A Union Officer's Diary of [the] Appomattox Campaign," *CWTI* 1 (June 1962): 22; Porter, "Five Forks," 720.

46. Humphreys, *Virginia Campaign of '64 and '65*, 378; *OR*, I, 46, pt. 1: 1174, 1235; "Order of March, April 5th [1865]," Turner Papers; *New York Herald*, April 10, 1865; Haring, *Sixty-seventh Ohio*, 20; Billings, "Union Officer's Diary," 23; Shaw, *Our Last Campaign*, 19; William Birney to Theodore Read, April 4, 1865, Ord Papers, Bancroft Library.

47. *OR*, I, 46, pt. 1: 1161–62, 1215; Longstreet, *From Manassas to Appomattox*, 612; Lincoln, *Thirty-fourth Mass.*, 393; Henry Bruce Scott, *The Surrender of General Lee and the Army of Northern Virginia at Appomattox, Virginia, April 9, 1865* (Boston, c. 1916), [1].

48. Edward T. Bouve, "The Battle of High Bridge," *Civil War Papers* (Massachusetts MOLLUS), 2: 407–12; C. M. Keyes, ed., *The Military History of the 123d Regiment Ohio Volunteer Infantry* (Sandusky: *Register* Steam Press, 1874), 110–11; P. C. Garvin to "My Dear Sir," June 11, 1865, Massachusetts MOLLUS Collection; *OR*, I, 46, pt. 1: 1162; Joseph W. Keifer, *Slavery and Four Years of War*, 2 vols. (New York: G. P. Putnam's Sons, 1900), 2: 219.

49. Burleigh Cushing Rodick, *Appomattox: The Last Campaign* (New York: Philosophical Library, 1965), 72; Bouve, "Battle of High Bridge," 411; Lincoln, *Thirty-fourth Mass.*, 393.

50. *OR*, I, 46, pt. 1: 1109, 1245, 1248–50; pt. 3: 561–62, 635; Humphreys, *Virginia Campaign of '64 and '65*, 374; *Eleventh Pennsylvania Cavalry*, 152–54; Henry E. Tremain, *Last Hours of Sheridan's Cavalry* (New York: Bonnell, Silver & Bowers, 1904), 171.

51. *OR*, I, 46, pt. 1: 1174, 1180, 1186–87, 1203, 1218; pt. 3: 611, 1389; Grant, *Memoirs*, 2: 481.

52. Porter, *Campaigning with Grant*, 459; Gibbon, *Personal Recollections*, 306; *OR*, I, 46, pt. 1: 1162, 1181, 1187, 1215, 1235, 1243; Lincoln, *Thirty-fourth Mass.*, 395; Clark, *Thirty-ninth Illinois*, 263–64.

53. *OR*, I, 46, pt. 1: 1109, 1162, 1181, 1215; *New York Herald*, April 14, 1865; Scott, *Surrender of General Lee*, [1]; Lincoln, *Thirty-fourth Mass.*, 394; Egan, *Flying, Gray-Haired Yank*, 397.

54. *OR*, I, 46, pt. 1: 1142–43, 1245–46.

55. Stephen Tripp, "The Cavalry at Appomattox, April 9, 1865," *Maine Bugle* 5 (July 1898): 214–16; *Eleventh Pennsylvania Cavalry*, 155–59; Wesley Merritt, "The Appomattox Campaign," *War Papers and Personal Reminiscences, 1861–1865* (Missouri MOLLUS), 125–27.

56. W. G. Cummings, "Six Months in the Third Cavalry Division under Custer," *War Sketches and Incidents* (Iowa MOLLUS), 1: 311.

57. *Seventh U.S. Colored Troops*, 69; John Gibbon to John W. Turner, April 8, 1865, Turner Papers; Shaw, *Our Last Campaign*, 19–22; *New York Herald*, April 14, 1865.

58. George Washington Williams, *A History of the Negro Troops in the War of the Rebellion, 1861–65* (New York: Harper & Brothers, 1888), 302; *OR*, I, 46, pt. 1: 1236; Alexander Neil to "My Dear People," April 10, 1865, Neil Papers; *New York Herald*, April 14, 1865; Joshua L. Chamberlain, "Appomattox," *Personal Recollections of the War of the Rebellion* (New York MOLLUS), 3: 269.

59. Wildes, *One Hundred and Sixteenth Ohio*, 253.

CHAPTER 16

1. Porter, *Campaigning with Grant*, 470–87; Billings, "Union Officer's Diary," 23; Cadwallader, *Three Years with Grant*, 329.

2. Cresap, *Appomattox Commander*, 207–15, 217–18; August V. Kautz memoirs, 107; Shaw, *Our Last Campaign*, 29; Stuart H. Buck, ed., "With Lee after Appomattox," *CWTI* 17 (November 1978): 41.

3. *OR*, I, 46, pt. 3: 696, 736–37; *New York Herald*, April 21, 1865.

4. Joseph Becker, "Richmond," *Frank Leslie's Popular Monthly* 38 (September 1894): 366; Buck, "With Lee after Appomattox," 42.

5. *OR*, I, 46, pt. 3: 685–86, 709–10; *New York Herald*, May 1, 1865.

6. *OR*, I, 46, pt. 1: 1228, 1235–36, 1243; pt. 3: 694–95, 725, 1088–89; *Seventh U.S. Colored Troops*, 27; *Eleventh Pennsylvania Cavalry*, 162.

7. Wildes, *One Hundred and Sixteenth Ohio*, 260.

8. *OR*, I, 46, pt. 3: 745, 762; *Eleventh Pennsylvania Cavalry*, 161; William H. Newcomb to his mother, May 8, 1865, Lemuel E. Newcomb Papers.

9. Washington Vosburgh to "Own Dear Ella," April 25, 1865, Nina Ness Collection; Charles Hadsall diary, April 16, 1865; Charles A. Currier memoirs, 160–61, Massachusetts MOLLUS Collection.

10. *OR*, I, 46, pt. 1: 1175, 1216, 1218, 1220, 1246–47, 1249–50, pt. 3: 796, 813, 826, 837–38, 881; *Eleventh Pennsylvania Cavalry*, 162.

11. *OR,* I, 46, pt. 3: 1175, 1216, 1247; Edward A. Wild to Henry Wilson, May 10, 1865, Massachusetts MOLLUS Collection.

12. *OR,* I, 46, pt. 1: 1228, 1235–36, 1243; pt. 3: 827–28, 1005–8, 1148; Copy of Special Order #99, Headquarters, Army of the James, April 12, 1865, Atherton H. Stevens Papers, Massachusetts Historical Society; James E. Sefton, *The United States Army and Reconstruction, 1865–1877* (Baton Rouge, La.: Louisiana State University Press, 1967), 51–52; August V. Kautz memoirs, 107.

13. *OR,* I, 46, pt. 3: 815, 847, 884, 1055; *New York Herald,* May 22, 1865; *New York Herald,* May 6, 1865; GRSWR, 10: 207, RG-94, E-160, NA.

14. *Ibid.,* 10: 395–96, RG-94, E-160, NA; August V. Kautz memoirs, 107; *OR,* I, 46, pt. 3: 797–98, 816, 867; *Seventh U.S. Colored Troops,* 71.

15. Weitzel, "Entry of United States Forces," 14; *OR,* I, 46, pt. 3: 954, 1169, 1172, 1262; *New York Times,* April 28 and 30, 1865; *New York Herald,* May 2, 1865; Wilson, *Black Phalanx,* 461–62.

16. William Birney to BFB, April 19, 1865; Burnham Wardwell to BFB, July 26, 1865; both, Butler Papers, LC; Edward A. Wild to Henry Wilson, May 10, 1865, Massachusetts MOLLUS Collection; *OR,* I, 46, pt. 3: 835–36, 865, 896–97.

17. *OR,* I, 46, pt. 3: 788, 833, 891, 985–86, 1151, 1197–98, 1213; *New York Herald,* April 25, 1865; Stephen E. Ambrose, *Halleck, Lincoln's Chief of Staff* (Baton Rouge, La.: Louisiana State University Press, 1962), 199; Withington, "West in the War of the Rebellion," 510–11.

18. Charles Hadsall diary, May 15, 16, and 21, 1865; *OR,* I, 46, pt. 3: 888–89, 948, 1005–6, 1084–95, 1159–60; Charles A. Currier memoirs, 166, Massachusetts MOLLUS Collection; *New York Herald,* April 26, May 2, 1865; Alvin C. Voris to N. Martin Curtis, May 8 and 29, 1865, Ord Papers, Bancroft Library; Withington, "West in the War of the Rebellion," 511.

19. *Ibid.,* 511–12.

20. *New York Times,* June 22, 1865; *New York Herald,* May 1, June 24, July 1, 1865; *OR,* I, 46, pt. 3: 688–89; Ambrose, *Halleck,* 203–4.

21. Gordon, *War Diary,* 419; Withington, "West in the War of the Rebellion," 511; *New York Herald,* May 24, June 27, July 4 and 9, 1865; *New York Times,* July 9, 1865; Ambrose, *Halleck,* 203–04.

22. *OR,* I, 46, pt. 3: 1293.

23. *New York Times,* July 16 and 31, August 3–5, 1865; *New York Herald,* July 14 and 20, 1865; *New York Times,* July 13, August 1, 1865; *New York Herald,* July 14, August 1, 1865; Kreutzer, *Notes and Observations,* 357; Sefton, *United States Army and Reconstruction,* 9–10; *Army and Navy Journal,* August 4–5, October 28, 1865.

24. *OR,* I, 46, pt. 3: 1088, 1114, 1169, 1202–3, 1209, 1232, 1315; Kreutzer, *Notes and Observations,* 345; *New York Herald,* May 10, 12–14, and 27, June 4, 1865; Charles Hadsall diary, May 6, 9, and 27, 1865; Robert Larimer diary, May 10–13, 1865; Thomas M. Vincent to Henry W. Halleck, May 29, 1865, DVNC, RG-393, E-5063, box 5, NA; *New York Times,* June 22, 1865.

25. Roe, *Twenty-fourth Massachusetts,* 395–96.

26. Joseph S. Bowler to James M. Bowler, October 23, 1865, Bowler Family Collection.

27. Frederick Pfisterer, comp., *New York in the War of the Rebellion, 1861 to 1865* (Albany, N.Y.: J. B. Lyon Company, 1912), 3,110–11.

28. *OR,* I, 46, pt. 3: 1169, 1172, 1198–99, 1201–2, 1206–7, 1262, 1295; Wilson, *Black Phalanx,* 461; *New York Times,* May 20, June 3, 11, and 16, 1865; *Army and Navy Journal,* June 10 and 24, July 22, 1865; Browne, *My Service in the U.S. Colored Cavalry,* 13; Norton, *Army Letters,* 261, 263–64.

29. *OR,* I, 46, pt. 3: 1165; Grant, *Memoirs,* 2: 545–46; Philip H. Sheridan, *Personal Memoirs of P. H. Sheridan,* 2 vols. (New York: Charles L. Webster & Company, 1888), 2: 208.

30. *Ibid.,* 211–17; Haskin, *First Regiment of Artillery,* 447; Browne, *My Service in the U.S. Colored Cavalry,* 13; Sheridan, *Memoirs,* 2: 213; Norton, *Army Letters,* 265, 269; Horrocks, *"My Dear Parents,"* 145.

31. Shaw, *Our Last Campaign,* 37; Wilson, *Black Phalanx,* 462; Weitzel, "Entry of United States Forces," 15.

32. *New York Herald,* May 22, 1868; Carleton, *Society of the Army of the James,* 1: 15; *New York Times,* July 20, 1871, October 22, 1874.

33. Clarence S. Peterson, *Last Civil War Veteran in Fifty States* (Baltimore, 1961), 27–28.

ESSAY ON SOURCES

THE LIFE AND TIMES OF THE ARMY OF THE JAMES CAN BE RE-CREATED through a wealth of published and unpublished sources. The National Archives houses dozens of boxes of records on its major components. Perhaps the most valuable collection contains the correspondence of the army's geographical command, the Department of Virginia and North Carolina (Record Group 393, numerous entries). An indispensable supplement is the 128-volume *War of the Rebellion: A Compilation of the Official Records of the Union and Confederate Armies* (Washington, 1880–1901), which includes campaign reports and correspondence by Ben Butler and Edward Ord and their subordinates at all levels. Given the many amphibious operations in which the army took part, the interested reader should also consult the *Official Records of the Union and Confederate Navies in the War of the Rebellion* (30 vols. Washington, 1894–1922).

Other primary sources include the unpublished letters, diaries, and memoirs of army members. The largest collection of Butler's papers is in the Library of Congress; others are held by the Chicago Historical Society, Harvard University's Houghton Library, and the Rutherford B. Hayes Library in Fremont, Ohio. Most of the material at those places as well as many nonextant letters are collected in the *Private and Official Correspondence of Gen. Benjamin F. Butler during the Period of the Civil War* (6 vols., Norwood, Mass., 1917), compiled by the general's granddaughter, Jessie Ames Marshall.

Many of Ord's papers are held by the Bancroft Library, the University of California at Berkeley, and the C. H. Green Library at Stanford University in Palo Alto, California. Other valuable collections on the army's hierarchy include the William Farrar Smith Papers at the Vermont Historical Society; the Alfred Howe Terry Papers at the Connecticut Historical Society and in the Sterling and Beinecke Libraries at Yale University; the Adelbert Ames Papers in the Smith College Archives in Northampton, Massachusetts; the John W. Turner Papers at the U.S. Army Military History Institute (USAMHI), Carlisle Barracks, Pennsylvania; the Joseph R. Hawley Papers in the Library of Congress; and the August V. Kautz papers in the Library of Congress, at Carlisle Barracks, and in the Illinois State Historical Library. Additional unpublished material on these and other generals is in two files in Record Group 94 at the National Archives: Generals' Papers (Entry 159) and Generals' Reports of Service, War of the Rebellion (Entry 160), the latter a collection of autobiographies compiled by the War Department during and after the conflict.

More than 150 collections of soldiers' letters, diaries, and postwar writings were consulted in the preparation of this book. One of the most valuable regimental sources was the insightful and articulate correspondence of Edward King Wightman of the 3rd New York Infantry, in the Robert W. Woodruff Library at Emory University in Atlanta. Also rewarding are the journals of Andrew Byrne of the 8th Connecticut Infantry (Connecticut Historical Society); the letters of Edward L. Cook, 100th New York (University of California at Santa Barbara); the memoirs of Charles A. Currier, 40th Massachusetts (USAMHI); the reminiscences of Ferdinand Davis, 7th New Hampshire (Bentley Library, University of Michigan); the letters of Henry S. Graves, 118th New York (Western Michigan University); the correspondence of Hilon A. Parker, 10th New York Heavy Artillery (William L. Clements Library, University of Michigan); the letters of Henry Snow, 21st Connecticut (Connecticut Historical Society); the letters and memoirs of John M. Spear, 24th Massachusetts (Massachusetts Historical Society); the letters of Washington Vosburgh, 115th New York (Bentley Library); and the diary and letters of William A. Walker, 27th Massachusetts (Firestone Library, Princeton University).

The writings of officers of the U.S. Colored Troops help define the socio-military orientation of the army. Sources include the papers of two generals—Edward W. Hinks (Mugar Memorial Library, Boston University) and Edward A. Wild (USAMHI)—and those of four subalterns: Albert Rogall, 27th USCT (Ohio Historical Society); Joseph J. Scroggs, 5th USCT (USAMHI); James H. Wickes, 4th USCT (Boston Public Library); and Austin Wiswall, 9th USCT (Texas Tech University). While there are few writings by African-American enlisted men, among the most valuable are the diaries and letters of Sergeant Major Christian Fleetwood of the 4th USCT, held by the Library of Congress.

The papers of civilians who influenced the Army of the James are readily accessible. The writings of Secretary of War Edwin McMasters Stanton and Navy Secretary Gideon Welles, both in the Library of Congress, include extensive correspondence to and from Butler, Ord, and many of their subordinates. The wartime missives of Clara Barton, matron of nurses of the X Corps, are in the Library of Congress and the Smith College Archives as well as at the American Antiquarian Society in Worcester, Massachusetts. The letters and diaries of Edward F. Williams, Christian Commission field agent with the Army of the James, are at Dillard University in New Orleans; they are critical to an understanding of the army's relations with civilian relief agencies.

Printed sources on the Army of the James are numerous and varied. The major newspapers of New York, Philadelphia, Boston, and other Eastern cities provided almost daily coverage of command affairs. The army's official organ, *The New Regime*, published at Norfolk, Virginia, offers a wealth of information not available elsewhere. A full run of this departmental journal is on file at Princeton University's Firestone Library.

Heading the list of pertinent published diaries, reminiscences, and correspondence is *Butler's Book* (Boston, 1892), a witty, acerbic, and sometimes perjurious memoir. Although it should be consulted in conjunction with other contemporary sources of known veracity, the volume offers a fascinating glimpse into the sometimes brilliant, often devious mind of America's pre-eminent political general. Likewise in need of careful handling is Baldy Smith's *From Chattanooga to Petersburg under Generals Grant and Butler* (Boston, 1893), an exculpatory account of a career steeped in controversy and failure.

Important first-person accounts by regimental officers and enlisted men include Elbridge J. Copp, *Reminiscences of the War of the Rebellion, 1861–1865* (Nashua, N.H., 1911); John L. Cunningham, *Three Years with the Adirondack Regiment, 118th New York Volunteer Infantry* (Norwood, Mass., 1920); B. S. DeForest, *Random Sketches and Wandering Thoughts* (Albany, N.Y., 1866); "Hermit," *Recollections in the Army of Virginia and North Carolina* (Wilkes-Barre, Pa., 1865); William Kreutzer, *Notes and Observations Made during Four Years of Service with the Ninety-eighth N.Y. Volunteers* (Philadelphia, 1878); Thomas L. Livermore, *Days and Events, 1860–1866* (Boston, 1920); and John McMurray, *Recollections of a Colored Troop* (n.p., 1916).

Unit histories exist for more than half of the 100 or so regiments, batteries, and independent battalions and companies that composed the Army of the James. These constitute a major (in some cases, the only) source of information on certain aspects of campaigning and soldier life. Among the more worthy representatives of this genre are A. W. Bartlett, *History of the Twelfth Regiment New Hampshire Volunteers in the War of the Rebellion* (Concord, N.H., 1897); Charles M. Clark, *The History of the Thirty-ninth Regiment Illinois Volunteer Veteran Infantry* (Chicago, 1889); W. P. Derby, *Bearing Arms in the Twenty-seventh Massachusetts Regiment of Volunteer Infantry during the Civil War, 1861–1865* (Boston, 1883); Luther S. Dickey, *History of the Eighty-fifth Regiment Pennsylvania Volunteer Infantry, 1861–1865* (New York, 1915); Daniel Eldredge, *The Third New Hampshire and All about It* (Boston, 1893); *History of the Eleventh Pennsylvania Volunteer Cavalry* (Philadelphia, 1902); J. A. Mowris, *A History of the One Hundred and Seventeenth Regiment N.Y. Volunteers* (Hartford, Conn., 1866); Isaiah Price, *History of the Ninety-Seventh Regiment, Pennsylvania Volunteer Infantry* (Philadelphia, 1875); Alfred S. Roe, *The Twenty-Fourth Regiment Massachusetts Volunteers, 1861–1866* (Worcester, Mass., 1907); and George H. Stowits, *History of the One Hundredth Regiment of New York State Volunteers* (Buffalo, 1870).

Though Butler has received more extensive book-length treatment than many more successful Civil War generals, he continues to lack a thorough, balanced, scholarly biography. The best is Hans L. Trefousse, *Ben Butler: The South Called Him BEAST!* (New York, 1957); other competent efforts include Robert S. Holzman, *Stormy Ben Butler* (New York, 1954), and Richard S. West, Jr., *Lincoln's Scapegoat General* (Boston, 1965). Ord is the subject of a single biography, Bernarr Cresap's *Appomattox Commander* (San Diego, 1981), and Ranald Mackenzie is profiled in Michael D. Pierce, *The Most Promising Young Officer* (Norman, Okla., 1993). None of the army's other commanders have received a biographer's tribute in this century.

Recently published monographs treat episodes in the army's life. Although it focuses on the relationship between the officers and men of black regiments, Joseph T. Glatthaar's *Forged in Battle* (New York, 1990) devotes scant attention to the army that contained the greatest number of African-American units. Some campaigns in which the army played a prominent part, however, have inspired recent operational studies of merit: Bermuda Hundred (William Glenn Robertson, *Back Door to Richmond*, Newark, Del., 1987, and Herbert M. Schiller, *The Bermuda Hundred Campaign*, Dayton, Ohio, 1988); Forts Harrison and Gilmer/New Market Heights (Richard J. Sommers, *Richmond Redeemed*, New York, 1981); the Petersburg Siege (Noah Andre Trudeau, *The Last Citadel*, Boston, 1991); and Fort Fisher (Rod Gragg, *Confederate Goliath*, New York, 1991).

INDEX